where to live in
AUCKLAND

BARBICAN
PUBLISHING

Glendowie Sophistication

Worth getting excited about. This fantastic family home is on the market for the first time in 25 years. Beautifully finished, good flow for decks and views. 3 bdrms, 2 with double gge. Popular Glendowie school zone.

Open Sat/Sun 12-1.

Contact Jacob James on 021 667 6438

Deck-a-
Be quick for this
of room to
great indoor/outdoor. Easy bright and
primary school. Auction on site this Friday at

Open Wed 12-1pm, 5-5 12-1pm.

Phone Michael Sales 021 646 9024

Beautiful rural setting

Karaka - Designed with entertaining and family in mind. Three bedrooms plus office - double garage, and room for the boat. this beautiful property set on over 2,600m2 offers the astute buyer luxury at an affordable price but be quick! It won't last.

Open Sat/Sun 2-3. Auction on site 21st at 3pm.

Contact Vicky Hughes for details on 09 534 7242.

Freemans Bay awaits.

Don't miss the opportunity to purchase this 3 bedroom home with double gge and loads of room to spare 5 mins from city. Warm and sunny aspect with great outdoor living space. Easy walk or sought after schools.

Open Wed 12-1pm, 5-5 12-1pm.

Solid first starter on full site

Brilliant opportunity for first home buyers 3 bedroom home with loads of room to spare city. Beautiful polished flooring, warm and with great indoor living space.

Open Wed 12-1pm, 5-5 12-1pm.

Phone Benjamin Jones 024 835 9345

OWIE   Just   Listed.
sive classic 1970's modernised secured family home. 870m2 section with views to Rangitoto and beyond. 4 generous bedrooms, 4 bathrooms, 2 bedrooms guest suite, 6 car garaging. Glendowie College School Zone. Tender Open Sat 2 - 2.45pm. 260 West Tamaki Rd. Ph Julia 522-3392, 021-281-6899 Ray White (Real Estate) Ltd MREINZ 520-9100.

GLENDOWIE Just listed pretty 2-brm garden unit Ideal business couple or single. Buyers in the late $200,000's. Open Sat 2.45pm, 1/30 Colchester Ave. James, ah 521-9512, foot & Thomp-

back fence an tion this is a dre brm + home office dining, new kitchen. #27209 a. Ph Diana Buc 520-6221 a/h 624-0477 021/408-303 Barfoot & Tho son - MREINZ.

GREENLANE 902m² sectio zoning) all consents issu build 1/hses. Agent on build your dream h Sat/Sun 1-1.45. 3 Woodbine A' Ph Joy Zhao, 360-027-405-0028. 309-9512 Barfoot & Thompson MREINZ. 273207.

GREENLANE Fab trad Tudor home, 4 brms, 2 Goldwater 022 6323 6032 3 living rooms plus d Lovely beams, outdoor c/vin Park

Attention Investors

Grey Lynn - Invest, develop or reside. Absorbing options with this property set on a 816 easy access section on (Sal An ideal investment for the future capital growth or to realise as an excellent family home.

Open Wed 12-1pm, 5-5 12-1pm. $419,000

Phone Katrina Barber 021 846 9324

5 bedrooms! 3 Bathrooms!

Mission Bay - Sun, location, style and class are part of the mix in this attractive home. An entertainers delight with lots of indoor/outdoor flow.

Auction. Open Sat/Sun 12-1pm.

Phone Oscar Sims 021 578 3489

Lush Lockwood Luxury

St Johns - Substantial 3 bedroom home - well appointed near new kitchen with generous open-plan dining and large lounge with easy lawn flat yard and fully fenced. Great family living.

$325,000 neg.

Open Fri 12-1pm, 5-5 12-1pm.

Phone Pete Barber 027 683 2264

Million plus buyers must inspect

Kohimarama - Open the door to prestige and elegance. This substantial home with commanding views must be seen. 5 bdrms, 3 wcs, internal access and top schools. Definitely worth the weekend drive.

Open Sat/Sun 2-3. Auction on site 21st at 3pm.

Contact Vicky Hughes for details on 09 575 7242.

Views and sun

Remuera - Satisfying the demands of a growing family this charming home speaks of pride and ownership. Located on a corner sight in a private and peaceful setting. 3 brms, 2 bthrms, dbl int gge.

Open 5-5 16-11am. $495,000

Phone Michael Barber 021 646 9024

Glendowie dream home

Riddell Road - Wonderful home with views over Tamaki Estuary. 3 dbl bdrms plus office and bathrooms. A must see!

$575,000

Open Fri 12-1pm, Sun 2-3pm.

Phone Oscar Sims 021 846 9324

City living at it's best

Don't wait for the open home. Has 2 bdrm, 2 bath apartment won't last for long. 360° city and harbour views and all the mod cons.

Open Sun 2-3.

Contact Debbie Sims on 09-624 4791 or mob 027 514 9147

Tropical Oasis

Titirangi - Sitting high and proud this delightful contemporary family home is styled to please. Main areas flow to extensive decking overlooking stunning bush and capturing all day sun. Close to schools and shops.

Open 5-5 12-1pm.

Price By Negotiation

Phone Belinda Dreaver 022 856 12687

Rough Diamond

Avondale - Dont drive past this little beauty! There is work to be done but with a bit of hard work and imagination this 3 bedroom original villa will really shine. Popular street and large 636m² section. Get the recipe for success!

$500,900+ Buyers must inspect

Open Wed 12-1pm, 5-5 12-1pm.

Phone Michael Barber 021 846 9324

Tower-o-power!

CBD - Brilliant opportunity for first home investors to grab this lovely 2 bedroom, 2 bath city gem. Parking available close to parks and

Tender

Open Man 3-4pm, 5-5 2-3pm.

Phone Katrina Barber 022 248 8496

Looking for a new house?

The New Zealand Herald
THERE'S A LOT MORE TO IT
nzherald.co.nz

where to live in
AUCKLAND

Where To Live In Auckland

Published in New Zealand by Barbican Publishing Limited.

Barbican Publishing Limited
PO Box 91572
Auckland

Phone: 64 9 336 1183
Fax: 64 9 375 8471
Email: info@wheretoliveinauckland.co.nz
Website: www.wheretoliveinauckland.co.nz

ISBN 0-476-00031-9

Cover: Simon Devitt

where to live in
AUCKLAND
CREDITS

Sources:
Recorded property sales (years ending July 2002, 2003)
- Quotable Value New Zealand

Population statistics and rental information
(1996, 2001 Census data) – Statistics New Zealand

Mosaic neigbourhood classification system 2002 - Supplied by
Pinpoint Target Marketing

Publisher	Stephen Hart
Assistant publisher	James Hodgson
Editors	Sharon Newey
	Jane Binsley
Contributing writers	Alice Bulmer
	Charlotte Cossar
	Sarah Heeringa
	Liesl Johnstone
	Steven Shaw
	Robyn Welsh
Photographers	Simon Young
	Marcel Tromp
Additional images	Manukau City Council
	Waitakere City Council
Proofreading	Alice Bulmer
Design	Leanne Flemming
	Bryce Colley
Imaging	Image Centre
Printing	PMP Print

Acknowledgments: Our sincere thanks and gratitude to the many
industry sources, local authorities and individuals interviewed for this
book. Special thanks to Quotable Value New Zealand, PMP Distribution
Limited and Statistics New Zealand for their invaluable contributions.
Thanks also to The National Bank of New Zealand for their support.

CONTENTS

where to live in
AUCKLAND

CONTENTS

where to live in AUCKLAND

Map of New Zealand

Cape Maria van Diemen   North Cape

Whangarei

Gt. Barrier Island

Hauraki
Gulf

Auckland

Bay of Plenty

Hamilton   Tauranga   East Cape

Rotorua

RAUKUMARA
RANGE

T A S M A N   S E A

Waikato

L. Taupo   L. Waikaremoana   Gisborne

New Plymouth   NORTH ISLAND   Poverty Bay

Cape Egmont   ▲ Ruapehu   Hawke   Mahia Peninsula
                              Bay
                              Napier

Wanganui   Hastings

Farewell Spit

Golden Bay   Palmerston North

Tasman
Bay

Motueka   Nelson   Wellington

Karamea
Bight   Blenheim   Cape Palliser

C. Foulwind   Westport   ▲ Tapuaenuku

Greymouth

SOUTH ISLAND

Pegasus Bay

Mt. Cook ▲   Christchurch

Jackson Head   Banks Peninsula

Canterbury
Bight

▲   Timaru   S O U T H   P A C I F I C

Mt. Aspiring   O C E A N

L. Wakatipu   Oamaru

L. Te Anau

C. Providence   Dunedin

Invercargill

Stewart Island

Cook Strait

Wanganui

Canterbury Plains

Rakaia

SOUTHERN ALPS

Waitaki

Clutha

Foveaux Strait

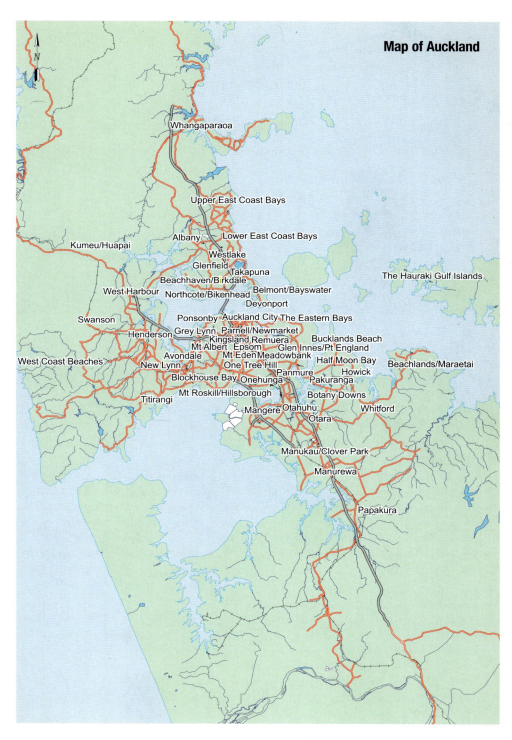

Map of Auckland

Whangaparaoa

Upper East Coast Bays

Albany   Lower East Coast Bays

Kumeu/Huapai   Westlake
                    Glenfield
                            Takapuna   The Hauraki Gulf Islands
                Beachhaven/Birkdale
West Harbour   Northcote/Bikenhead   Belmont/Bayswater
                                Devonport
Swanson   Ponsonby Auckland City The Eastern Bays
            Grey Lynn Parnell/Newmarket
        Henderson   Kingsland Remuera   Bucklands Beach
                Mt Albert Epsom   Glen Innes/Pt England
West Coast Beaches Avondale   Mt Eden Meadowbank Half Moon Bay
            New Lynn   One Tree Hill   Howick   Beachlands/Maraetai
            Blockhouse Bay Onehunga   Panmure Pakuranga
        Titirangi   Mt Roskill/Hillsborough   Botany Downs
                    Mangere Otahuhu Whitford
                            Otara

                Manukau/Clover Park

                    Manurewa

                    Papakura

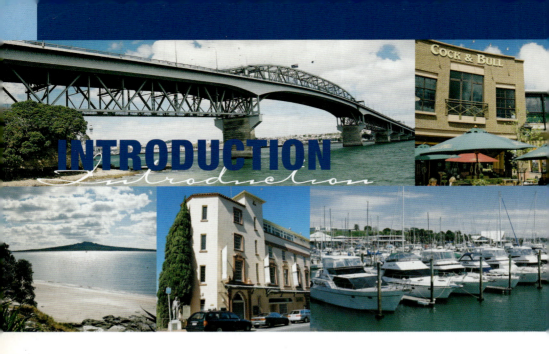

INTRODUCTION

New Zealanders and their houses are a special partnership. In other countries, renting is the norm, or your house is merely a place to lay your head. For New Zealanders, buying a house is an emotive issue.

The Kiwi attachment to his or her quarter-acre paradise is well documented. It's where we spend a lot of our time, it's where we raise our children. Pride in our homes is a particularly Kiwi characteristic - but then we are often blessed with large houses, set within generous gardens and close to all sorts of outdoor spaces and amenities.

The do-it-yourself phenomenon is also rooted deep in our psyche. Part of it stems from the Number 8 wire, make-do mentality and part of it from the fact that we can - our timber houses are easy to chop and change. In generations gone by, if you were a male confessing to not being able to hammer in a nail, you would be hounded from the neighbourhood.

These days, Kiwis are still keen on renovating, but for different reasons. And it's all about location, location, location.

Concentrating much more on the location and what the area has to offer, we are not as concerned about the particulars of the actual house - because you can change it, but you can't change where it is. Buyers are not fazed about throwing renovation funds at a house to make it suit their needs, as long as the location is right and the section has the potential - like the right aspect for sun and enough space to fit a garage or extension. They know that if they stay put for a few years, they will recoup their investment.

Perhaps it's a particularly Auckland thing, too. The story goes that if you live in Christchurch, the question is which school you went to. If you live in Wellington, it's what movies you have seen lately. But if you live in Auckland, it's where do you live?

How to use this book

| CENTRAL | NORTH | WEST | EAST | SOUTH |

Where to Live in Auckland is split into five geographical areas - Central, the North Shore, West, East and South. Each area is, in turn, divided into neighbourhoods - a collection of suburbs and areas close to each other and similar in nature. To find the neighbourhood you are interested in, either refer to the contents page or use the index at the back of the book.

Within each neighbourhood, we look at the character of the area, the people who live there, types of houses typical to the area, real estate trends and prices, as well as the amenities you can find there - the schools, shops, leisure facilities, open spaces, eateries and transport.

At the back of the book, you'll find even more interesting facts - the school zoning maps for secondary schools and the schools' academic results, information about private schools, statistics giving a profile of Auckland's population, useful contact details and a glossary of real estate and housing terms.

Our star ratings: We've given the amenities a rating from one to five and we've also rated each neighbourhood from one to five, based on its desirability, house price level and general access to amenities.

Maps: Each neighbourhood has a map, coloured according to the types of people that live in the area. It's an intriguing insight into the habits, likes and dislikes of your potential neighbours - do they like drinking wine or beer, like sport, use the internet?

Each colour relates to a particular population sector based on demographics, lifestyle and preferences. For an explanation of those see page 208.

Prices: Property values and prices quoted within our Trends and Prices sections are based on interviews with real estate agents and are anecdotal only. Those listed under Average Sale Prices are collated by Quotable Value New Zealand and reflect actual "average" sales for the years ending July 2002 and July 2003. Like any average data, the figures may be skewed upwards or downward as a result of a small number of particularly high or low value property sales. Generally speaking, the higher the number of sales, the more representative the average sales price will be.

ALL ABOUT AUCKLAND
All About Auckland

Auckland is easily New Zealand's biggest city - and it's growing all the time. Its population of just under 1.18 million in the greater Auckland area is about one-third of the population of the whole country. The city sprawls over 60km^2 - an area larger than that of greater London.

Despite being the nation's economic powerhouse, Auckland and its inhabitants seem to inspire extremes of emotion in other New Zealanders, being either admired or reviled. Aucklanders can also be heard complaining about the city's failings - it's a rat-race, it rains too much and the traffic is appalling.

We're also woefully ignorant of our own city. Ask a North Shore-ite where Glendene is and they'll confuse it with Glen Innes on the opposite side of town. Get a Mt Eden dweller to locate Clover Park and they might suggest Australia. But in such a sprawling city in which each area is so well serviced with amenities, venturing out of your own neighbourhood just isn't necessary.

So how is it that Auckland continues to grow faster than ever? The truth is that Auckland's sub-tropical climate, its attractive clean harbours, the number and variety of its beaches and native bush areas, its ethnic diversity, nightlife, cafes, universities, sporting facilities and large job market all make it a great place to live. Love it or not, the city is big, brassy and the closest New Zealand gets to an international cosmopolitan centre.

Auckland is located on the narrow isthmus of the Tamaki Peninsula, between the Waitemata and Manukau Harbours. In this city you're never far from the water - there's a mere 9km of land separating the Pacific Ocean from the Tasman Sea. Huge surf may be pounding the sparkly black sand of Auckland's west coast - while on the same morning gentle waves are lapping the golden sand of the east coast beaches.

Another name for Auckland is the "city of sails". It is said that Aucklanders own more boats per head of population than in any other city in the world. It's certainly true that lots of recreational activity centres around boating and beaches.

The dramatic remodelling of the Viaduct Harbour, and the subsequent creation of a harbourside community of apartments and cafes has made the area a popular drawcard for tourists and locals alike. The viaduct's apartments have helped add glamour to the city's apartment living.

Buying and selling property is another popular Auckland activity; on average Aucklanders sell

We've got everything from the ridiculously expensive

their home once every seven years. The importance of Auckland's coastline is also reflected in real estate. In some North Shore suburbs, for instance, proximity to the beach is the deciding value factor.

The importance of water, boating and property converges in particular on the Hauraki Gulf islands. Property prices on islands where you can buy permanent or weekend homes, like Waiheke Island and Great Barrier Island, have skyrocketed along with their popularity.

It's thought that Maori first settled in the richly fertile Auckland region about 650 years ago. Today, one in seven Aucklanders identify themselves as Maori. Auckland is also a Polynesian centre; one-third of all Polynesian people over the entire Pacific region choose to live in Auckland.

The Ngati Whatua tribe are considered to be Auckland's first tribe. During the 1820s Maori were involved in fierce inter-tribal conflict, and by 1840 the colonising British had either beaten or bought them out. Captain William Hobson, New Zealand's first governor, chose Auckland as a name to honour his patron and former commander, Lord Auckland (at that time, the Viceroy of India). Many Auckland place names carry the influence of Hobson's

patron - Lord Auckland's family name was Eden, for example.

On May 30, 1959, the four-lane Harbour Bridge was opened, connecting Auckland's downtown business centre with the city's northern shore - and true North Shore suburbia was born. Ten years later the bridge was expanded to eight lanes, using Japanese engineering commonly referred to as the "Nippon clip-on". The motorway system has been growing ever since. Auckland's sprawl and relatively limited public transport system means that it's hard to get by without a car. The city's car-culture has been likened to a small-scale Los Angeles.

In 1997 the Sky Tower, New Zealand's tallest building, was completed. Its top viewing platform is 300m above sea level, making it the highest outdoor public viewing platform in the southern hemisphere. In 2001 the city's skyline was dramatically altered again when the lone pine tree on the summit of One Tree Hill was removed following a chainsaw attack by a Maori activist.

Auckland has abundant parks, and during weekends many Aucklanders use them for sport or recreation. The Domain is home to the Auckland War Memorial Museum, opened

in 1929 to commemorate World War I casualties from the Auckland area.

"A better lifestyle", "a great place to bring up a family", are reasons offered by expats or immigrants arriving to live in Auckland. It's therefore no surprise that proximity to the coast, to the West Coast bush, to work, or to urban attractions like Newmarket's shops, or Ponsonby's cafes, are major considerations when choosing where to live in Auckland.

A potted history of housing

Auckland is ever-changing and varied, architecturally speaking. In its 160-year history, it has collected a range of house styles from early worker's cottages, villas, bungalows, state houses, brick-and-tile homes and units to today's terrace and freestanding townhouses, apartments, and plaster and masonry homes.

By 1881, the highest population densities in the whole of New Zealand were on the upper slopes of Freemans Bay and Grafton Gully and the neighbouring areas of Ponsonby and Newton. By 1896, Auckland's population of 50,000 mostly lived in an area 6.5km long and 2.5km wide, made up of the boroughs of Auckland, Parnell, Newmarket, Newton and Grafton. There were also settlements at Avondale, Mt Eden, Epsom and Ellerslie and the maritime suburbs of Northcote, Birkenhead and Devonport.

Access to plentiful timber made it easy to build worker's cottages, which changed rapidly to accommodate family needs. Cottages, however, with their bad sanitation and crowding into urban pockets, affronted Victorian sensibilities enough to spur the creation of the villa.

Today, villas may be sought-after and trendy, but back then they were never viewed very favourably. Villas were seen as architecturally inept and built like packing cases. The classic villa hallway was condemned as a conduit of cold air in the winter and dust in the summer. Burnley Tce in Mt Eden is a landmark example of mass-produced villas in New Zealand.

The housing styles of Auckland continued to evolve from international influences, including the Californian bungalow and various Spanish Mission-style stucco and Art Deco houses. These latter two types were not wholly accepted in a colony that hankered for more classic British styles of housing.

Today, Auckland suburbs are an eclectic mix of styles, from traditional to ultra-modern. Whatever your preference, there's likely to be something to suit.

Real estate trends

The Auckland real estate market is rocketing, especially the sought-after inner-city suburbs. Tales abound of houses selling for $100,000 more than they fetched the year before, without having a thing done to them. This is in some way backed up by Quotable Value New Zealand figures that show Auckland city house prices rising 19.9% in residential value for the year ending June 2003. In that same period, North Shore city rose 15.5%, Waitakere city 10.3%, Manukau city 12% and Papakura 10.7%.

Industry watchdogs put the rise down to a number of influences. One is the return of ex-pat New Zealanders. This trend has been around for a number of years, fuelled by the favourable exchange rate. Some expats have bought investment properties or holiday homes here as a way of entering the market before they return permanently.

Certainly the unrest in the Middle East and terrorist attacks have added impetus to those wanting to escape the mad, bad world.

These expats have added another pool of buyers to the market - and they have also come home with English pounds and US dollars which, when converted with current exchange rates, leaves them with a wad of Kiwi money to spend. This allows them to look in the more

expensive suburbs where a grand seaside house surrounded by gardens and lawns is a far cry from the smaller apartments and houses left behind overseas.

Immigration has also had a net rise (although this is starting to slow), adding yet more people to the buying market.

Another factor is the optimism brought about by the stability of the economy in the past few years. A spin-off of this has been the steadiness and relatively low level of mortgage interest rates, encouraging people to make that move into a bigger house or better area.

The inner city is where most of the frenzy has been concentrated, but this has expanded to surrounding suburbs as supply has decreased. As always, the inner-city suburbs attract people who want to be close to the action.

Our heavily congested motorways spur frustrated commuters to seek alternatives - but there aren't many. We don't have a comprehensive public transport network like London or other international cities. Aucklanders don't tend to express much confidence in the existing public transport system - and there is a certain status in being able to drive to work and not take the bus.

So, the commuter solution is to live closer to work. If you work in the CBD, that's the inner-city suburbs. Some of these are quite small, so demand for houses is always going to outstrip supply.

The next ring out has been heating up as well, especially if these are family-friendly suburbs. Mt Albert and Meadowbank, with their fairly good access to the city, good parks and good schools are places where family homes are in hot demand. Even suburbs like Panmure and Glen Innes are becoming popular.

The big question is - where to now? How long will the frenzy last? Will the market drop back, or simply plateau? Some commentators say the current upsurge in prices is just a catch-up for the deflated prices of the past decade - if houses had increased at a rate akin to inflation during the 1990s, we would be paying the same high prices anyway.

But the Auckland market is anything but predictable. It has always been characterised by peaks and troughs.

As *Where to Live in Auckland* went to press, predictions were that the market would continue to be strong during the 2004 summer and possibly for the rest of next year.

The furore over leaking and rotten buildings may have dampened (excuse the pun) the terrace housing sector of the market, but has only put more pressure on the rest of the housing pool. People do, after all, want to buy, and now there is more demand for houses that are perceived to be solid and long-lasting.

Houses built by the government 40 or 50 years ago, but now in private ownership, are in demand. These ex-state houses tend to be compact, like many terrace houses (typically 90-100m²), but have a strong reputation as being built with extremely good materials (heart rimu stud work, tough matai floors, good joinery and properly applied stucco cladding) and being very sturdy.

The new Zone 8 regulations

People are talking about the new Zone 8 and what it may mean for them. Auckland City councillors may have been tired that night in 2003 but, whatever, they voted unanimously for the controversial Zone 8.

It's a planning scheme allowing for "city intensification". In other words, because Auckland's population is projected to grow substantially over the next 18 years, catering for these new Aucklanders residentially is the job of Zone 8. Basically, new rules now apply within a radius of 2km from the CBD, as well as anywhere near suburban town centres.

Areas immune from Zone 8 allowances and restrictions are those already zoned Residential 1, 2 or 3. Otherwise, anyone, anywhere in the city can apply for a site to be re-zoned.

What it means is that after fulfilling certain requirements relating to looks, size, noise and privacy, developers will be able to erect multi-storey apartment blocks within cooey of suburban centres. Within 2km of the CBD, these blocks could have five storeys. Within a five to 10-minute walk of suburban centres, they could have either three or four storeys.

Likely suburban contenders for re-zoning are the CBD, Newmarket, Glen Innes, Otahuhu, Panmure, Mt Wellington Quarry, Remuera, Ellerslie, Sylvia Park, Grey Lynn, Pt Chevalier,

Mt Albert, Avondale, Onehunga, Mt Roskill, Sandringham, Morningside, Balmoral and Royal Oak. These are suburbs the council is keen for more people to inhabit.

However, before a real-estate-induced panic sets in, rest assured there's a snag for developers. They can't do this unless the zoning has been approved for sites one hectare or bigger, which will require community consultation.

Transportation

Auckland's transport problems continue to be at the forefront of our minds, with no immediate end in sight to the gridlock of the past few years. Planning the perfect route to get to a destination, avoiding peak-hour traffic - which seems constant at all hours of the day - and escaping the constant threat of road rage (yours and other drivers') all adds to the pressure of living in this dynamic city.

Road and transportation issues are the subject of hot debates and strong emotions, and any number of political footballs. Advocates of road, rail and public transport and their various permutations appear constantly in local media. However, Auckland's local politicians are currently putting a lot of effort into solving the city's transport problems, and solutions are emerging, with a number of major projects and proposals currently underway. It's believed that these initiatives will alleviate greater Auckland's gridlock troubles, but with an ever-growing number of drivers and vehicles using the limited roading system, it's debatable whether the problem will ever completely go away.

The biggest, and one of the most controversial proposals, is the eastern corridor. This new motorway will link Auckland's CBD to Botany Downs, following the North Island main trunk railway line - from Tamaki Dr, through Orakei, Meadowbank and St Johns, then through

Panmure, Pakuranga and along Ti Rakau Dr to Botany Downs. Recently, it has emerged there are alternative corridor options following potential different routes to the already promoted Ti Rakau Dr corridor through the city. Alternative corridor options include: the "Parnell tunnel corridor", commencing at Stanley St in the city and progressing through a tunnel under Hobson Bay to the Orakei Basin; the "Kepa Road corridor", moving from the waterfront through Orakei and Kohimarama and ending at St Johns Rd; the "Quarry corridor" running from Meadowbank over Remuera golf course and through to the east of Mt Wellington; the "SH1 corridor" link through Mt Wellington and Panmure; and the "Tamaki River corridor", commencing south of the Panmure Basin and linking to Ti Rakau Dr.

Two further options involve crossing the Tamaki River; firstly, linking Dunkirk Reserve in Panmure and Farm Cove in Pakuranga, and secondly crossing the river from Mt Wellington directly to East Tamaki. The downside of the project is the potential loss of hundreds of houses along the corridor route and the fact that the route(s) cut through the picturesque and mangrove-edged Orakei Basin. Although eastern residents are eager for the quicker drive to town and the potential property value increases, those who live along the proposed corridor routes worry that their properties will lose value. For more details, see page 184.

Other improvements to the city motorway system include the Grafton Gully upgrade, which is now providing direct access between the northern motorway and Auckland's port. A new bridge connecting Wellesley St in the city and Grafton Rd, and improved motorway access from Stanley St to the southern and northwestern motorways is near completion.

State Highway 20 has extension projects planned for Manukau, Mt Roskill and Avondale. The Manukau project intends to deliver a 4km, four-lane motorway from State Highway 1 at Manukau to the Puhinui interchange, which is also being altered to relieve bottlenecks and other congestion. Airport access will also be improved with the Mt Roskill extension. Subject to Environment Court approval, the extension provides a 4km highway from Queenstown Rd to Richardson Rd, including interchanges at Hillsborough Rd and Dominion Rd, and will allow for foot and bicycle traffic. The more politically contentious Avondale extension is intended to complete the northern motorway's western ring road and potential options include Great North Rd and Rosebank Rd. At the time of writing, the SH20 project - particularly the Mt Roskill extension - has come under government review. While this project has already been substantially reviewed, there is no guarantee - given contentious environmental

downtown public transport centre is intended to be a major interchange between rail and road, giving commuters direct rail access to central Auckland and onto major bus routes. How much impact it will have on regional transport has yet to be seen.

Moving out to the city rim

A new phenomenon in Auckland sees many families and retired couples moving away from Auckland's central suburbs and further out to the city's rim. These suburbs on the outskirts of Auckland generally offer more value for money when buying real estate. More often than not, the section size and house are a lot bigger and neighbours aren't usually butted up to your back fence. A rural or bush outlook often replaces views of clotheslines and rooftops, and the streets are a lot quieter.

Cashing up from good sales of inner-city properties, people seeking a more relaxed way of life can generally move into a freehold property, or to a lesser mortgage, and enjoy a better quality of life with their disposable income. However, one downside is the time spent commuting to work in peak-hour traffic. The motorway systems, full to overflowing, make many journeys long and stressful. Outside of peak times, travelling is easier and sometimes even enjoyable. A plus for commuters on the major train lines is the extension of the lines into the central Britomart station. If you ignore the rundown appearance of the suburban stations and the lack of signage indicating where you are, this can be a great alternative to commuting by car - though currently timetables are not always reliable.

Another reason why so many people are moving further out of town is simple economics. They have been priced out of the central Auckland market and don't have a choice. This is happening more and more with the increases of property values in and around central Auckland.

requirements and the fulfilment of overall transport strategy objectives - that it will be completed, either at all or subject to further review and modification.

Other ongoing traffic projects include the refining of inner-city Auckland's Spaghetti Junction - notorious for its bottlenecks. Work involving the widening of the Newmarket viaduct, enhancing motorway-to-motorway connections between the northern and north-western motorways and access from the northern motorway to Grafton Gully is well underway.

Auckland's North Shore is seeing extensive traffic development through the Upper Harbour motorway and the Orewa to Puhoi State Highway 1 extension. In a recent Environment Court decision, the North Shore Busway, providing parallel two-way bus transport along an 8km stretch between Constellation Dr and Esmonde Rd, has been approved.

Also on the North Shore, along the Upper Harbour corridor, a new four-lane expressway is connecting the shore and Waitakere City. Funding was approved for a second bridge crossing the upper harbour and widening the existing causeway on the western side of the bridge, as well as a 5km four-lane expressway at Greenhithe, eastwards from the bridge to bypass the Upper Harbour Dr.

Another high-profile transport project is the recently completed Britomart centre. This new

The apartment and terrace house market

The number of apartment complexes in Auckland City has grown steadily during the past 10 years. The number of inner city apartments is predicted to nearly double in the near future from 4000 units, with at least 7000 units planned to be built.

Much of this current growth is on the back of rental potential from overseas students, which makes some industry players nervous - what happens if government policy changes and the students disappear?

In 2003 student numbers dropped due to the SARS epidemic and uncertainty over government policy. A few language schools, reflecting the drop in numbers, have had difficult times, with one high-profile school closing suddenly in September 2003.

There are four different types of leasehold in the CBD, two of which are in perpetuity and two of which have terminating terms. Thoroughly check out which you are buying.

Another sector which has attracted investors is the hybrid hotel-cum-apartment. Some were sold offering guaranteed returns but as those expire, the previous returns of around 9% haven't always been sustainable. It is thought that the hotels may pull out of the market, leaving what are essentially lovely apartment buildings.

The terrace housing market is a fairly recent phenomenon, and developers continue to fill the demand for compact, low-maintenance, secure, lower cost dwellings.

That demand is fuelled by not only the rental market, but also the growing number of single person households with no children and a preference for eating out and partying rather that spending hours working in the garden or having to stay at home to service a large mortgage. Terrace houses are a perfect match for this lifestyle, and they're the only way many people can afford desirable inner-city suburbs.

Leaky building syndrome

Leaking and rotting buildings have been big news for the past couple of years. New townhouses and terrace houses seem to have been particularly affected. According to some estimates, there may be problems with up to 10,000 units built during the 1990s and early 2000s.

Some builders and building inspectors are focusing on rotting frames and blaming untreated timbers. Meanwhile, the timber industry is pointing the finger at architects and poor modern design, and building practices and cladding systems that allow water to get in, but not out.

How to protect yourself:

- Deal with agents who are apartment specialists. Real estate agents can be in breach of the law if they sell apartments without revealing known faults. Increasingly, agents are refusing to sell buildings with a poor history.
- Talk to the secretary of the body corporate before you buy. They should be aware

of any problems in the building.
- If you are buying off plans, ask your builder/developer for a specific warranty on weathertightness issues in relation to workmanship.

Rental and investment property

Along with the big increase in demand for houses, there's a similar story for rental accommodation. Auckland's brisk expansion through net immigration is one factor fuelling the property market.

While long-term business migration has been around for some time, short-term migration has also rapidly grown - made up mainly of students at secondary schools, tertiary institutions or language schools. This influx of students has strained the available rental accommodation - especially in the central city.

Hence the apartment and terrace housing boom. The flow-on effect has meant that other renters have moved out to fringe suburbs, increasing demand in these areas. This in turn, pushes renting families further out into greater Auckland.

Other types of people are moving into the city. Retiring couples and older couples whose children have left home are looking for low-maintenance, modern dwellings close to the city's amenities, including the waterfront, cafes and restaurants and boutique shopping areas.

Most of these people become permanent residents and will probably buy their apartment - which means it isn't available for rent any more.

Another trend sees families selling their homes and opting for rental accommodation. The recent increase in house prices makes this an attractive alternative.

With predictions of the "bubble bursting", many people are selling now and renting in the hope that the market will drop or at least plateau. Also, many people are being out-priced in the market and their only available option is renting a home.

The government's State Housing policy, which aims to build and buy more rental houses particularly in Auckland, also has an impact. While the present government's stated aim is to set rents at no more than 25% of income and reverse state house sales, this may negatively impact waiting lists. State houses that were sold into private hands were often snapped up by investors and continued to be rented out.

Another factor influencing the rental market is investors concentrating mainly on rental accommodation. With stock markets worldwide having their ups and downs, this type of "bricks and mortar" investment is considered a safer option.

This has meant that long-term investors have sold their lower-end stock, freeing this up for would-be investors.

If you are thinking of buying an investment property, conventional wisdom should always apply. Don't spend more than the property is worth. Think about how you will screen your potential tenants and deal with any conflicts. Will you manage the property yourself or use professionals? Investment property is currently offering higher than normal returns, but always pay attention to the fundamentals:

- Avoid becoming too close to your tenants or you will find it more difficult if things go wrong.
- Don't place all your eggs in one investment basket - times may be good now, but the property market tends to run in cycles.
- Get the construction thoroughly checked if the development is recent - beware the leaky building syndrome.

Thinking about buying a home in Auckland?

We can help.

HOME BUYERS' SERVICES

Expert, professional advice on buying property in Auckland

Where to Live in Auckland now provides comprehensive buyers' services to enable you to buy the right home or investment property at the right price.

Our affilliated partners' services include:
- *Property search and evaluation*
- *Legal advice*
- *Auction bidding and negotiation*
- *Renovation advice*
- *Immigration services*
- *Rental and property management*

where to live in
AUCKLAND

How close are you
to the home of your dreams?

Find out how much you may be able to borrow with The National Bank's
Home Loan Calculators at **www.nationalbank.co.nz** Your dream
home may be closer than you think.

The National Bank
The thoroughbred among banks

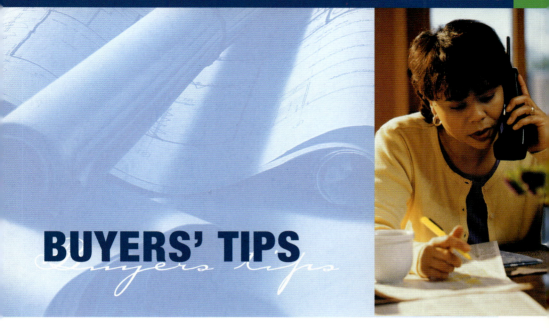

BUYERS' TIPS

Buying and moving house is one of the most stressful times in your life, and buying property is one of the biggest investments you will make. To start you on your way, here is our guide to financing a home, looking for one and how you go about making it your own. The content in this section is not provided by The National Bank. It was independently researched and written by Where to Live in Auckland. We believe that everyone will find something of value in this guide, but inevitably it does not take into account your own individual personal circumstances. We recommend that you take professional advice before acting on the information.

Finance first

Buying a house is all about how much you can afford, or are willing to spend on a property. Most of us calmly and rationally set ourselves a budget - then end up spending more than we thought we would. Knowing how much you can or want to spend underpins all of the decisions you make about buying. It will determine how big the house can be, where it will be and in what condition. However in inner-city suburbs, unrenovated houses can sell for as much as their spruced-up neighbours, bought by people happy to have a blank canvas on which to create their own masterpiece of renovation.

Your pot of money will normally consist of a deposit - money you have saved up - and a mortgage. Under certain conditions, most banks will lend up to 90% of a house's registered value. If you are borrowing a high proportion of the purchase price, the bank may insist on mortgage protection insurance in the event of you losing your income for some reason - injury, death or redundancy.

Your bank will ask you to complete a budget summary showing income and expenses, to determine how much money they think you can comfortably afford to repay.

Banks can also provide you with a pre-purchase finance approval that will enable you to make offers on houses that are free of any finance condition clause, or let you bid comfortably at auction knowing how much you have to play with. Your ability to meet repayments is only one factor. The bank needs to be happy that the property being offered for security is satisfactory, so depending on the proportion of your loan, they may need a pre-purchase valuation. Pre-approval will speed up the processing of the actual mortgage once you have bought.

So, once you know how much you can spend, you can go house-hunting. Check our neighbourhood information for house prices, to find out what areas or types of houses are best suited to your budget.

Visiting the bank

In years gone by, there wasn't much choice about which lending institution to ask for a mortgage - it was the one where you did your day-to-day banking. That's no longer the case. You can shop around, and banks are always advertising special rates or conditions in the hope of netting new mortgage customers. Chances are, if you have your mortgage with one bank, you will take your day-to-day banking with you. Some banks insist on it anyway.

So as well as checking out the home loans your own bank has to offer, research the rest too. Compare not only interest rates and types of loans available but also charges for processing a home loan and other conditions. For example, can you make lump sum payments on a fixed interest loan without incurring penalties? To top it off, consider which bank you feel best about - which one has given you good service and good advice.

Types of loans

Consider which type of loan suits your ability to pay and your lifestyle.

Table: this is the more common type of loan which spreads regular payments over the term of the loan, which only change when the prevailing interest rate changes. Initially, a bigger portion is made up of interest and a smaller portion of the principal, but that reverses over time. The benefit of this type of loan is that it lets you budget well with a set amount each fortnight or month.

Reducing: this type of loan starts off high but reduces with each payment. Each repayment includes the same amount of principal. If you can cope with the higher initial payments, it's rewarding to see your principal steadily reducing. The benefit is that over the term of

One-off costs

When doing your budget, don't forget the one-off costs of buying a house. These might include:

- legal fees
- a valuation
- a builder's, engineer's or architect's report
- moving costs (not just the truck, but also reconnections for phone, Sky TV etc)
- insurance (house and possibly mortgage protection)
- bank administration fees
- urgent maintenance

Does the house need any urgent renovations or repairs before you move in? Talk to the bank about extra finance for these.

the loan, you will have paid less in interest than with a table mortgage.

Interest only: some lending institutions will allow you to pay just the interest and none of the principal, but usually only for a short time and under certain circumstances.

Mixed: many banks offer essentially tailor-made loans that suit your particular circumstances, made up of a mix of different types of loan and interest. Check with your bank about this option.

The types of interest rates

Floating interest: this is the more commonly used, and allows you to benefit from any reductions in the floating interest rate. Conversely, your payments will increase if the rate goes up. Floating interest rates have been relatively low and steady recently.

Fixed: this is when the interest rate is fixed for a certain term (anything from six months to several years) and is not affected by fluctuations in the floating rate. Depending on the economy, these may be offered at slightly below or slightly above the floating rate. You gain the benefit if the floating rate stays above the fixed rate or, better still, rises. In more volatile times, however, you risk the floating rate dropping below your once-attractive fixed rate. Lump sum payments usually can't be made on fixed interest loans without incurring penalties.

Mixed: a combination may be best so that you can benefit from the advantages of both floating and fixed. Any lump sum payments can be made on your floating mortgage. Once the term of the fixed-interest loan is up, you can either negotiate another fixed term or put it in with the floating interest loan.

The term of the loan will affect the payments. The longer the term, the lower the payments will be but at the end of the term you would have ended up paying more interest.

You can also choose the frequency of payments, the options usually being fortnightly or monthly, whichever suits your income and payment structure.

Going shopping - the area

Once you have done your mortgage homework, you can start looking for your perfect house. Read about the areas you have identified as having potential in the following chapters. Are they likely to include the type of house you prefer? Will you have like-minded people as your neighbours? Does the area have the amenities you need - shops, schools, parks? Does it match your budget? Check the commuting distance to work or public transport routes. What sort of setting would you like - quiet cul-de-sac, busy urban, established, new?

Drive around the areas, maybe refining your choices into certain streets.

The house

What type of house do you want or need? The style (villa, bungalow, 1970s family home, ex-state, contemporary etc) will determine not only the general characteristics but also maintenance levels and costs. Are you prepared to renovate, or do you just want to arrive and unpack?

If you're buying the house with someone else, discuss everything in detail. Is storage for the windsurfer more important than a dishwasher? Work it out. Buying a house is stressful enough, without having it threaten your relationship.

You may like to make up a score card and use one for each house, so you don't have to rely on memory when you have been to numerous open homes.

Split your list of requirements into two - the must-haves and the would-likes. Think about the following variables and rate them according to your preferences:

- How many bedrooms? Do you also need a study or home office, or will a desk in the corner of the family room do?
- Do you need a guest room?
- How many bathrooms? Would an extra toilet be handy?

- A separate laundry? Or will a cupboard or back of the garage do?
- How many living areas? Formal and casual, or will the one do?
- Formal dining?
- Do you prefer open-plan living?
- Off-street parking? A garage? Double? Internal access?
- Aspect: do you want living areas to be north-facing for the sun?
- Is outdoor living important? Should it flow well from internal living areas?
- How big a garden do you need, if any? Big enough for a kids' cricket game, or is a small courtyard fine? Does it need to be fully fenced for the dog or toddlers?
- What sort of mod-cons do you want? Dishwasher? Filtered water tap? Gas fireplace? Gas heating? Underfloor bathroom heating?
- What level of security? Alarm? Video intercom?
- How much storage do you need, or are you going to be brave and have a big clean-out between moves?

The hidden things

Many faults can't be seen with a cruise through the open home. If you are not going to use a builder to inspect the property, watch for:

- level floors and sound piling
- rot in the weatherboards and timber joinery
- insulation
- water pressure - turn on the taps and flush the toilet
- noisy neighbours
- dampness (smell and/or mildew)
- leaks

In light of the leaking building syndrome, a building inspection on any plaster-clad house would be extremely sensible.

Armed with your wish list, start looking at the houses advertised - check the *New Zealand Herald's* Weekend Real Estate section, *Property Extra* and *Property Press*. Peruse

How much can you afford?

NBJ 9515

local real estate agency windows. Check out websites - most real estate agencies put all listings on the internet. Also see our Useful Contacts section at the back of the book. Ring agents and visit open homes to see what type of houses are available. Start to consolidate your ideas. Be prepared for any eventuality - you may fall in love with the first house you see, or it may take months to find the perfect home. Make sure you visit the property at least twice before you buy it, preferably at different times of the day.

Buying methods

Selling by negotiation used to be the favoured way of marketing a house, with only very special properties or rural land being put up for auction. Now, especially in a competitive market where demand is outstripping supply, auctions and tenders are much more common. In a volatile market, it may be difficult to assess a house's worth so an auction or tender allows the upper limit to be left wide open.

Some houses are marketed by negotiation but without an asking price. After one or two open homes, the agent may give an indication of value - this may be a price range or it may just be the bottom limit.

For a buyer, these methods of selling make it harder to know if you can afford a particular house. You have to do more homework, look at comparative recent sales in the area (ask the agent for a list of these) and visit lots of open homes. A house's CV (capital valuation) may be of some help. Even if it is out of date, you may be able to compare the CVs of recent sales with the actual sale price or ask real estate agents how much houses in the area are selling for in comparison to CV. Then you can apply that formula to the CVs of houses you are interested in.

If you are interested in a house being sold privately, make sure your lawyer thoroughly checks any contracts before you sign. If you don't feel comfortable negotiating directly with the homeowner, ask a friend to help.

Sale by negotiation

Agents have standard contracts for making offers on a house. You may want your lawyer to check it over and help you with the wording of any conditional clauses you might add. Remember that the real estate agent is working for the vendor, so it is best to get independent advice.

A conditional contract is one which gives you a set time, say one or two weeks, to sort out various things. Common conditions may be:

- finance (so you can organise a mortgage) - make sure you stipulate that the finance is satisfactory to you, not just the bank
- a valuation (which will probably be part of the mortgage requirement anyway)
- a title search, checking for easements, covenants or restrictions
- a Land Information Memorandum (LIM) from council. The LIM is used to highlight anything that exists on the property that may not be permitted. If there's a garage or a deck that's higher than one metre from the ground on the property but no permits showing for these on the LIM, alarm bells should ring. Once you have bought the property, the onus shifts

on to you to remedy these problems

- a satisfactory builder's or engineer's report
- sale of the buyer's own house - not an attractive offer to the vendor, although on today's market, this may not worry them too much

The vendor may add a "cash-out" clause to any conditional offer, which means that if they receive an attractive back-up offer, they give the first buyer a set time (usually about three days) to satisfy the conditions.

If not all of the conditions are satisfied, it doesn't mean you should walk away from the deal. If you are still keen on the house but, say, the deck has no permit, you may renegotiate a drop in the sale price in compensation or add a clause that the vendor has to remedy the situation before settlement.

In today's heated market the fewer conditions, the more attractive your offer is going to be. For example, if you need all of the above conditions fulfilled and maybe another that relies on you selling your existing house, and someone else is making a cash, unconditional offer even for $5000 less, they

are likely to be the successful buyers.

The offer will specify the chattels to be left in the house (curtains, dishwasher, etc) and a settlement or completion date, which is when you pay over all the money in exchange for the key. A common time frame is six weeks, although it can be shorter or much, much longer (called a delayed settlement). In today's market when houses are selling quite readily, if you are needing to sell your existing house, a delayed settlement may be more attractive to the vendor than an offer conditional on you selling, but will still give you the time to take action.

Once your offer is drawn up, it is presented to the seller (or vendor in real estate speak) and they will usually counter-offer. More counter-offers may follow and the negotiations will either be successful or fail.

Auctions

Many houses are taken to auction these days to take advantage of the heated and competitive market. Some agents and homeowners also find it difficult to judge the value of a particular property, so will let the market decide, as such.

Auctions normally follow a fairly high-profile advertising campaign that lasts three or four weeks. You may not have all of this time, however, to make up your mind, as some houses sell before auction. A buyer wants to guarantee they are going to get the house of their dreams, so will offer an amount that's too good to refuse.

On the other hand, beware of the agent who tells you something is going to sell before auction in order to prise an offer out of you - this may mean that they have identified you as the only real bidder in the running, but still want you to believe you are in a competitive situation. Or agents may use pre-auction offers to assess the sort of money people are prepared to pay to help guide the vendors on a reserve price, but then still take the property to auction.

If you are serious about a house that is being

Investing in residential property?

NBJ 9515

sold by auction (or tender), make sure you let the agent know. Don't be coy, or you may find out the property has already been sold and you've missed out on the chance.

To buy at auction you need to be sure of your finance. An auction sale is cash and unconditional and you must front up a cheque for 10% of the sale price straight after the bidding. This means doing any homework on the property beforehand, which can involve some costs - for example, if you want a LIM or a valuer's report. Real estate agents selling auction properties will often prepare a pack of information for you, including such things as a copy of the title and maybe even a LIM. They'll provide a copy of the sale contract with the usual details such as the settlement date, etc, for you and/or your lawyer to peruse.

The actual auction is an emotion-charged and fast-paced affair. You might want to go to another auction beforehand, just to watch what happens. Try to be calm. Go along with your top bid in mind and be prepared to stick to it. Be confident and firm - it will help psyche out the other bidders. If you don't feel confident at all, an agent can bid on your behalf.

The vendors would have set a reserve, which is the minimum price they want for the property. A property cannot be sold "under the hammer" until the bidding has reached that reserve. Once the bidding has reached the reserve, the auctioneer will say something like "this property is now on the market", which lets you know that from now on, the top bid wins and that the buyer is committed.

If the bidding doesn't reach the reserve, the property is "passed in" and normally negotiations will ensue between the vendor and the top bidder.

Tenders

A tender is like an auction but without the public bidding. Essentially, you fill out an offer document that states a price. On the day the tender closes, all of the tender offers are opened and the most acceptable (if any) chosen.

For a vendor, a tender gives the benefit of privacy - the sale price isn't shouted out in an auction room. They also don't have to accept any of the tenders. If they are not happy with the price or conditions, they will ask the agent to negotiate with one or more of the potential buyers to see if an agreement can be reached. They normally have five days to do this.

One buyer may be so keen, they will offer a good deal more than the others, so the vendor gets a premium price. This is a common characteristic of tenders.

It's trickier for a buyer, because you have no idea what level your competitors are at. The idea is to do your homework, study the market, get advice from a valuer and give it your best shot if you are serious about buying. Unlike other methods of selling, you probably won't get a chance to make another offer and you need to ask yourself how you would feel if you missed out by a thousand dollars.

One advantage is that you are able to ask that certain conditions be added to the tender offer, much like a negotiated sale - but remember that a cleaner offer is always more attractive to the vendor. Most tenders are "closed" or "blind", where buyers cannot be told what the other bids are.

Buying land

Usable land is scarce in the more established parts of Auckland. A good percentage of subdividable sections have already been

cut up and infill housing is now a feature of many suburbs.

When buying land, there are certain things to check. Make sure there is a clear title to the property. If it has only just been subdivided, the paperwork may still be going through council, so any offer should be conditional to clear title.

Check that there are no covenants or caveats on the land, or if there are, that you are happy with them. If it's someone's back yard you are buying, they may have lodged a caveat on the title stipulating that you can't build within so many metres of their boundary, or that your new house must be designed in such a way as to not encroach on their privacy. In a new subdivision, there may be covenants restricting the types of building materials or the style of house you may use, in order to keep the neighbourhood up to a certain standard.

Many developers will offer land and design packages, where you have a choice of sections and a choice of house designs. They then build for you and will often offer their own finance packages. Although these sorts of deals are standard, always have your own lawyer check the contract. You might want to add a penalty clause for completion, for example, if the developer doesn't build the house in the time they say they will, they incur financial penalties.

Your lawyer

Whenever property is bought or sold, the ownership has to be legally transferred - known as conveyancing. This is normally carried out by a solicitor, either your regular one or there are specialist property and conveyancing groups set up, often offering set fees.

Conveyancing includes things like searching and approving the title, checking the sale agreement, making sure the mortgage documents are in order and properly signed, explaining the documents to you and registering them.

The cost of conveyancing will vary depending on the complexity of each deal, and may range from $600 to $1200.

Settlement day

Before settlement day, you are entitled to a pre-settlement inspection of the property. This is to check that the property is in the condition agreed upon and that nothing has happened to it between signing the contract and moving in - like any sort of damage, or removal of stated chattels.

It's best to do this as close to settlement as possible, preferable once the previous owners have moved out, although this may be tricky. This allows you to see the condition of the property much more clearly.

If you do notice a problem, inform your lawyer, who will inform the vendor's lawyer. Your lawyer may decide to withhold some of the money until the problem is remedied.

Once the funds have gone through to the vendor (often electronically these days rather than by bank cheque), you get the key and move in. Break open the champagne and congratulate yourself on your new home.

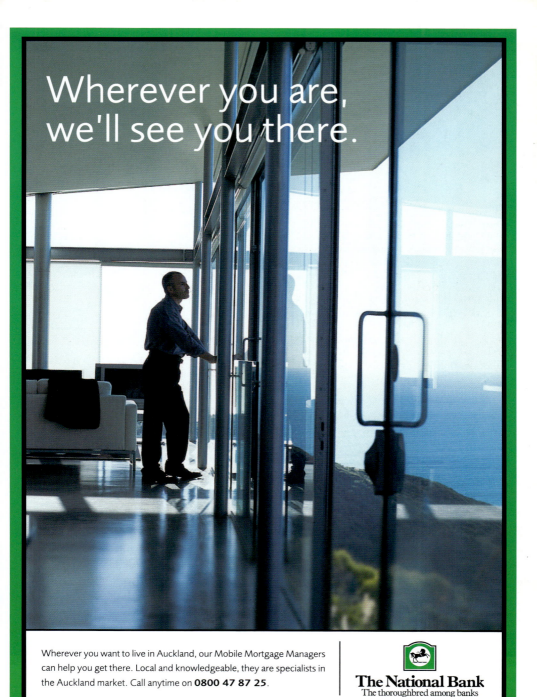

Wherever you are, we'll see you there.

Wherever you want to live in Auckland, our Mobile Mortgage Managers can help you get there. Local and knowledgeable, they are specialists in the Auckland market. Call anytime on **0800 47 87 25**.

The National Bank
The thoroughbred among banks

CENTRAL
Central

CHANCERY

LITTLE HIGH S

AUCKLAND

CENTRAL

CENTRAL

The central suburbs of Auckland are where it all began. It's from here that Auckland has sprawled, around its two harbours and edging ever further north and south, to become the largest city in New Zealand. This is where most of Auckland's history lies and where its heart should be. In the past, Auckland has been called a donut city - nothing in the middle but everything happening on the outer rim. This is no longer the case. Auckland's central business district is a happening place to live. And along with the new apartment dwellers came more restaurants and other amenities, all helping to lift the energy of a once empty-after-hours city. The other growth area is the gulf islands, as locals and offshore purchasers alike make places like Waiheke Island their permanent home rather than just a holiday destination.

Auckland central encompasses a large area, from the southern edge of the Waitemata Harbour, west to Avondale, east to Panmure and south to Onehunga. The central suburbs are where any new real estate trends are first felt, and the price increases are at the higher end here. The trend towards auctioning houses, combined with low interest rates, has seen many houses sell for well in excess of their valuations. As areas like Ponsonby, Parnell, Remuera and Mt Eden become too expensive, attention turns to the next suburban ring. Suburbs that used to be called "outer" are now "fringe", and the list of suburbs referred to as "inner" gets longer.

The rest of Auckland's homeowners wonder why inner-city residents continue to pay huge sums for houses with no garaging that sit so close together you can hear your neighbour sneeze. Conversely, people who have prised themselves away from the inner areas marvel at the space they can buy for half the price out west or on the shore. And you can still get a decent cup of coffee! The truly desirable suburbs, of course, don't suffer from inconveniences. Herne Bay, Remuera and Epsom boast some gracious properties with large houses and plenty of room for the cars - and tennis court, and swimming pool.

With Auckland's ongoing road congestion woes, the central city is an attraction for CBD workers keen on spending as little time commuting as they can. The abundance of new apartments and townhouses on in-filled sections mean that living near the city is still affordable. Rental prices have not kept increasing at the same rate as housing prices.

The amenities for central dwellers are plenty and long-established. Great shopping, plenty of big parks, the sparkling Waitemata Harbour, top restaurants and cafés, plenty of sporting facilities and clubs. Central Auckland does have it all.

The housing architecture is hugely varied. Much of it is older - villas, bungalows, state cottages - while many new and snazzy homes now share the land with their older neighbours. Whatever type or age of house you are seeking, you can find it somewhere in central Auckland.

the sparkling Waitemata

coffee and **cafés**

high energy nights

high-ticket **houses**

AUCKLAND CITY ★★★★★

including the Central Business District, Newton and Grafton

Ten or so years ago, who would have thought of living in central Auckland, addicted as we all were to our quarter-acre suburban paradise? Now that's all changed, and inner-city apartment living is becoming increasingly accepted by Aucklanders. According to census figures there were just 1728 private apartments in the CBD in 1996. By 2001 there were 3500, with a market projection of 4100 by 2004, plus over 2000 serviced apartments. In 1996 the residential population was 2880, and has risen steadily ever since.

Factors such as the strong New Zealand dollar, bad press in Asia over safety worries and the SARS crisis have all impacted negatively on the numbers of Asians coming to the inner city market as either tenants or investors. Despite this, Auckland's inner city market is still seeing growth.

Some factors behind this trend include changing perceptions about the CBD being a safer environment (partly because there are now many more people in town), the importance of careers over children for young couples, the convenience of inner-city living for running a business from home, and the status of a city address.

Who lives there?

The city-based population is increasingly young. In the rest of New Zealand, the proportion of the population over 65 years is growing - but the older age group is declining in numbers in the inner city. Instead there are higher numbers of people of working age, and a higher proportion of Asian people.

A recent Auckland City survey found that the majority (68%) of residents are aged between 14 and 40 and that 52% of the survey respondents walked to work, school or university. Most residents are working or studying in the CBD, and a large percentage of people moved to the CBD from elsewhere in Auckland for employment. The majority of those who responded to the survey eat in restaurants or cafes at least one or two nights a week. Many residents are students. Of those who work, most are employed in management or financial, property and legal fields.

From 1997 to 1999, 1936 building consents were issued for new residential units in the CBD. This represents almost 24% of all the residential unit consents in Auckland city during that period. This rate of development levelled off to 11.6% in the two years to September 2001, but judging by the cranes on the skyline,

developers are still busy. According to Auckland City Council sources the quality owner-occupier market in the CBD has become stronger in the past few years, and there is also a growing trend of New Zealanders from outside of Auckland buying apartments in the CBD.

Asian immigration has slowed a little, but real estate agents report good interest from ex-pats and other overseas buyers. New Zealand's image as a secure country, our policy of no capital gains tax or stamp duty, plus low interest rates and the favourable exchange rate are all incentives for overseas buyers.

Typical dwellings

Most dwellings in the CBD are apartments, including high rises, such as the New York-style Metropolis looming over High St, and mixed-use developments like those on Princes Wharf. There are a few houses in nearby Grafton, and Newton has some terrace houses.

Quality of construction throughout the CBD and surrounds is variable, so it's a case of buyer beware. Not all apartments are freehold, for example, all viaduct and Princes Wharf apartments are leasehold, as is the development near the old railway station.

REAL ESTATE

Trends

One factor causing prices to plateau is the on-going arrival of new apartments onto the market. These tend to be priced lower than existing apartments and tend to push prices down. Countering that is the tendency for the new apartments to be ever smaller - see *Look Out!* overleaf.

The leaky building syndrome continues to have a serious effect on buyer demand for affected buildings. As well as affecting the saleability of apartments, if problems emerge this can have a big impact on body corporate fees if costs cannot be recovered from builders or developers. One $150,000 inner city studio apartment that would normally have had annual body corporate fees around $2000 to $2500 ended up with fees over $4000 a year. These days, buyers are cautious and it has become routine to request a building inspection.

The current building boom also means that possible loss of view is also of concern to buyers. If you are buying with capital gain in mind make sure you check the district plan for future developments - if a neighbouring high-rise steals your view, it could also steal any potential for your apartment to increase in value.

Car parks are often highly sought after in the central city. They can cost anything from $35,000 to $50,000 and may be on a separate title from the apartment. According to the Auckland City Council, approximately 22% of CBD households don't have a car, and 33% don't have a car park space in their building.

Asian buyers are still a major force in the apartment market. Agents report that the majority of CBD buyers tend to be investors or Asian residents, with New Zealand residents tending to buy more in the CBD fringes. As with houses, very few single people buy.

Prices

A one-bedroom entry level apartment costs between $100,000 and $160,000, depending on size and view or lack of it, plus another $20,000 for a car park. A one-bedroom apartment of decent size (50m² plus) with a carpark now sells in the early to mid $200,000s. By comparison a reasonably sized two-bedroom apartment with a pleasant outlook might cost from $260,000 up to the mid $300,000s, depending on position and parking.

On the fringe of the city, a Newton two or three-bedroom house costs $300,000 plus. Over the past 12 months Newton has lost its "tatty" image and become more of an established area. Demand is growing, helped by the arrival of commercial developments and cafes, such as those along New North Rd. Newton and the marginally cheaper Eden Terrace both offer proximity with slightly lower prices than the CBD. One-bedroom apartments in Eden Terrace range from $160,000 upwards, and two-bedroom apartments are $185,000 up.

Older converted buildings are a particular niche market. Solidly constructed and often with a loft style high stud, they are very sought after. Most apartments in the George Courts building in K'Rd, for instance, are around the $335,000 to $390,000 range, with two-bedroom dwellings on the lower level still selling in the high $200,000s, and penthouses in the mid to high $500,000s.

The loss of the America's Cup has affected top rental returns, but it's argued that its impact on the buyers' market has been overstated. In The Point, a premium viaduct development and one of the market leaders, one-bedroom dwellings that sold for $395,000 to $465,000 three years ago now sell from $550,000 to the early $600,000s. Two-bedroom apartments which sold in the early to mid $600,000s now sell around $850,000 and three-bedroom places that sold from $850,000 to $950,000 now sell between $1.4 million and $1.6 million. A premium three-bedroom dwelling (700m²) sold three years ago from $1.245 million to $1.425 - and one sold recently for $2.7 million.

Average sale prices

	House	Flat	No. sales
2002	$278,798	$253,122	653
2003	$271,723	$239,739	442

Rental and investment

According to the Auckland City Council, approximately half of the CBD apartments are owner occupied and the other half rented. Because of this the apartment market is more driven by investors than your average suburb. By and large apartments don't enjoy the same

capital gain as houses, but produce a higher rental return on investment. The rule of thumb is that smaller apartments generate the greatest return. When the market takes a downturn it is also a lot easier for a $1 million apartment to loose 25% of its value than for a $150,000 dwelling to lose as much.

Many inner city properties are on leasehold land. Buying leasehold is attractive from an investor's point of view because of the potential for good returns. It's a way of buying into a desirable area without the capital outlay in land. Leasehold properties become less attractive as interest rates drop. Another factor to consider is the ground lease, as some leasehold properties are due for rent reviews on their ground leases in the next few years.

As with other properties in the suburbs, appreciation comes down to location - and it's important to remember that with new apartment blocks springing up all the time the quality of the view can change. Positioning on the building also has a huge bearing on how light and warm an apartment is. There might be $10,000 difference in value between similar apartments on different floors.

Rents have stabilised since the loss of the America's Cup and some in the viaduct have gone down. Where some dwellings were being rented for outrageous sums, they now fetch $700. While top rates have come down, people are still prepared to pay a premium to live on the waterfront, and occupancy rates are still very high - reports suggest they are between 95% and 100%. Rental returns in the city are generally around the 8% to 10% plus mark, which is better than the suburbs, but there aren't the same capital gains as with houses.

Best buildings

The best building in the viaduct is The Point, the top freehold buildings in the city are the Metropolis, Highgate, the Connaught (but some apartments in this building are about to lose their views) and Quay West, plus character buildings like George Courts or Westminster Courts.

AMENITIES

Schools ★★

Only a few children live in the CBD. Many go to private schools such as the central Jewish school Kadimah while others attend Freemans Bay Primary. An area west of Queen St is in the Auckland Grammar School zone, and Auckland Girls Grammar School is on the edge of the city in Howe St. Senior College is also in the CBD.

Shops ★★★★

Auckland's Queen St shopping is gradually improving. There is now a good cross-section of chain stores rubbing shoulders with the tourist traps and stately old institutions like Smith & Caughey. Anyway, Newmarket's not far away for serious retail therapy. The recently built Victoria Park New World supermarket has gone some way to meeting inner-city food shopping needs.

Leisure ★★★★

The waterfront, in particular Princes Wharf and Viaduct Harbour, offer several kilometres of pleasant strolling. Despite the passing of the Cup, the viaduct still offers the occasional visiting superyacht to drool over and a plethora of wonderful cafés with promenade-side tables for hours of people watching. Further up, Albert Park spills down between the university and the city. Myers Park is off Queen St and Victoria Park has popular sports grounds. A $1.01 million development of Newton's Basque Park is due to begin in November, involving an amphitheatre, sculptures and extensive plantings.

LOOK OUT!

New to Auckland is the growth in mini-apartments. This sector of the apartment market is dominated by investors largely targeting Asian students. Small apartments can provide good returns but represent a higher risk due to their dependence on a specific tenant population. Some recently built apartments are less than 20m² in size. Cramped apartments with poor ventilation, no soundproofing, little natural light and windowless, cupboard-like bedrooms do not make for happy tenants, and concern is growing that current trends towards building tiny apartments may lead to a glut in unwanted, poor quality flats. Construction of such dwellings in the future could be banned under a proposed Building Industry Authority review.

Travel times

North-western, northern and southern motorways	5 min
Airport	30 min
Newmarket shops	10 min

The transport facilities are great - everything starts and ends here. The Intercity Bus terminal is under the Sky City casino. The ferry terminal services the gulf islands, the North Shore and Half Moon Bay. And the controversial $204 million Britomart Transport Centre is finally here. As well as providing a central connection point for bus, ferry and rail services, it has brought the first public trains back to downtown in over 70 years. Most trains leave from Britomart, with a couple still leaving from the old train station - now called The Strand. The buses that used to use the old bus terminal are returning to Britomart. Other buses, such as those going to the North Shore and the Hibiscus Coast, depart from other points in the city, including Victoria St, Queen St, Wyndam St and Wellesley St, and will continue to do so. Queen Elizabeth Square and surrounding streets have been redeveloped, along with what the council envisages as "exciting new public spaces that will bristle with energy and people 24 hours a day". While enthusiasts say the centre makes public transport easier and more attractive, critics moan about late trains. Time will tell if Britomart helps solve Auckland's public transport woes.

SMART BUY

Yes - as long as the building is soundly constructed. Investors do well to buy well-located, central city apartments such as those close to the university and Queen St. By 2020 it's predicted that 80% of all home occupiers will be singles with high disposable incomes; DINKS (double incomes, no kids), empty nesters (parents of older children who have left home) or single parents with one or two children. Three out of these four categories will find the central city apartment lifestyle attractive. The growing student population will further strengthen the city rental market. Even if the influx of Asian students loses its phenomenal momentum over the next few years, market commentators predict other demographic groups will come along to fill their shoebox-size CBD studios. As suburb prices and commuting times rise, one upcoming trend to look out for is that of Crash Pads - basically weeknight domiciles for the out-of-town-based city worker. Newton in particular looks like a good place for first home buyers and singles to get their toe in the market.

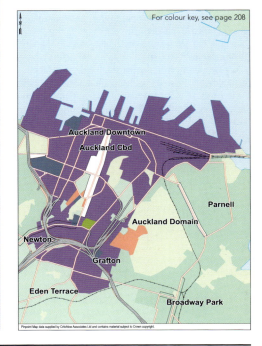

For colour key, see page 208

Auckland Downtown
Auckland Cbd
Parnell
Auckland Domain
Newton
Grafton
Eden Terrace
Broadway Park

Pinpoint Map data supplied by Critchlow Associates Ltd and contains material subject to Crown copyright.

AVONDALE ★★★★★

including Rosebank and Waterview

Avondale has had its 15 minutes of fame; first when its large hairy spider namesakes had star billing in the movie Arachnophobia, then in the acclaimed short film Avondale Dogs. More than 10 years ago, the suburb had lots of dodgy rental properties and dilapidated houses, but now estate agents insist Avondale's going upmarket. This can, in part, be credited to the late Phil Raffills, the controversial former head of Avondale College, who turned the college around - and the suburb.

Waterview is a betwixt and between suburb. It has no village and is flanked by two centres with distinct identities - the more expensive Pt Chevalier and the cheaper Avondale. One Waterview boundary is Great North Rd, and it is backed by water. Waterview's proximity to the north-western motorway makes it a good commuting suburb. It is also near Unitec so it has lots of rental properties to cater for the student market.

Who lives there?

Avondale is richly multicultural. Traditionally, it has been a blue-collar and Polynesian area, with numerous rental properties, mixed in with the now-older generation who moved to the suburb in the 1960s.

Many of today's buyers are Asian, mostly Chinese, and the area is popular with young couples who are attracted to the do-up bungalows and villas. There is still a large Polynesian community. There are many families with teenage children, some of whom have bought to be near the reputable Avondale College.

Typical dwellings

Avondale has a few villas, but the majority of its houses are bungalows that are around 45 years old.

Infill housing has brought some modern plaster-finish houses. There are also new subdivisions including Axel Pl, Nacton Lane, Saintly Lane and Hollyfield Park.

Waterview was created in 1861, but was slow to develop. It has many stucco bungalows and worker's cottages of 1930-40s vintage, mixed with 10 and 20-year-old places. The area has brick-and-tile 1970s houses and state houses from the 1940s and 1950s.

REAL ESTATE

Trends

Growth started in this area about five to 10 years ago. Prices have gone up "amazingly", and developers, according to agents, are screaming out for land.

Traffic flow was helped considerably by the opening of the Rosebank Rd motorway interchange around five years ago. Since then a number of commercial tenants have relocated to Avondale.

Prices

Entry level is $160,000 up. A three-bedroom property on a half site might fetch $190,000, whereas a new townhouse might be closer to $400,000. A three-bedroom bungalow in reasonable condition on a full site is upwards of $280,000.

The premium quarter of Avondale is called Avondale Heights, on the slopes behind the shops - villas here are much sought after. If they are renovated and within the Avondale College zone, they can fetch up to $400,000. Top houses on Blockhouse Bay Rd sell between $300,000 and $400,000.

In July 2003, a 1960s weatherboard house complete with studio went for $424,000, which was $30,000 more than real estate agents anticipated. A Waterview bungalow, bought for $266,000 three years ago, recently sold for $405,000. The empty cross-leased section in front of it garnered a further $215,000 for the happy vendor.

Average sale prices

	House	Flat	No. sales
2002	$231,204	$186,099	891
2003	$258,232	$208,212	568

Rental and investment

With many ex-rentals now being done up by owner-occupiers there is less available to rent and prices have increased. Rental rates in Avondale are roughly $120 a bedroom. Greatest rental demand is near the Unitec and within the Avondale College zone.

State housing is sprinkled about, generally only one or two in a street, with a pocket at the end of Riversdale Rd.

Best streets

Blockhouse Bay Rd (a main road but with good views) and Holly St.

AMENITIES

Schools ★★★

There is a public primary school at each of Avondale, Rosebank and Waterview plus at least three private church schools. Avondale Intermediate and the popular Avondale College are next door to each other.

Shops ★★★

Big malls like Lynmall and St Lukes have badly affected the high streets of surrounding suburbs, and in past years the Avondale shops had become quite dumpy.

Last year, however, Avondale centre got a shot in the arm with a newly paved town square, a stage, modern toilets and a 3m-high spider sculpture.

A major new mixed-use development is planned for the middle of the strip, involving new shops, cafés, offices and residential space above. It will help fill the hole created when the supermarket left town.

Leisure ★★★

West Coast beaches such as Bethells and Piha are easy to reach, and Pt Chevalier beach is just down the road. Closer to home there are a number of reserves.

Waterview has nearby mangrove wetlands accessible via Waterview Park and Howlett St Reserve. Backing Waterview is the Motu Manawa / Pollen Island Marine Reserve. Heron Park is in limbo pending further motorway development. Local facilities include the Avondale Racecourse and Avondale Jockey Club, an ice-skating rink, a number of gyms and sports clubs including bowls and soccer. There are a number of other sports facilities at the college.

The area offers a mixture of different ethnic foods, including the Thai Pot, and many dairies selling Samoan food like taro and green bananas.

Avondale has a library and community centre. Avondale College runs an extensive community education programme.

Why I live there

Artist Darlene Te Young

"Affordability and proximity to town were major reasons behind our decision to buy here about five years ago," says Avondale artist Darlene Te Young.

"The area is diverse - on any street you get young professionals sitting side-by-side with people of a much lower socio-economic group, mixed in with RSA types who've been in the area for donkey's years. The older locals tell some fascinating stories like when the buildings that are now Avondale College were an R-and-R base for the American troops, for medical treatment and homemade cooking."

Living in Avondale means Darlene can work from her own studio at home, while husband Mike takes half an hour to cycle to work in downtown Auckland

According to Te Young the town centre has improved a lot. "The area is not by any means fully evolved, but it's definitely happening."

Local hero - the Hollywood Cinema

To many, the classic cult movie *The Rocky Horror Picture Show* is forever associated with Avondale's Hollywood Cinema. The film flopped in 1976 but was re-released two years later. Hollywood's then manager, the late Jan Grefstad, decided to release the movie with extras - balloons, water pistols, banners and song sheets. It was a hit, with regulars arriving in fishnet stockings and suspenders. Ten years on, *Rocky Horror* became our longest running movie. In 1999, the Hollywood celebrated its 75th birthday as the country's oldest cinema still being used as it was originally.

LOOK OUT!

It may be happening as you read; the extension of State Highway 20 through Avondale. If you live here you may curse it today, but love it tomorrow. The new roading will link to the North-Western motorway (SH16) and the Upper Harbour Motorway (SH18), which will mean a huge stride forward for commuters. Traffic will be able to bypass existing clog-ups through the central city and the Auckland Harbour Bridge. In spring of 2003, Transit NZ's preferred route for the SH20 extension was from Richardson Rd in Mt Albert, cutting through New North Rd and following a section of Great North Rd (beside Unitec), and up to the Waterview interchange. Check out any recent developments on: www.transit.govt.nz/sh20

SMART BUY

Avondale is a colourful and relatively affordable city fringe option. Edged with water and close to good shopping, it's been changing for a while. Forget the real estate hype; it's not Ponsonby and may never be - but for those for whom Ponsonby prices are not an option, it's a viable alternative.

Waterview is small and isolated, and that has its own charm - complete with water views from many properties. You probably still get more dwelling and land for your dollar in Waterview than in any other inner-city fringe suburb. But the motorway is close, it's hemmed in by the frantically busy Great North Rd and concerns about the proposed motorway extension hover over the district.

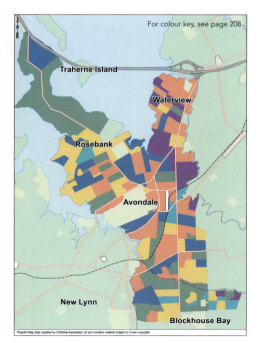

For colour key, see page 208

Traherne Island
Waterview
Rosebank
Avondale
New Lynn
Blockhouse Bay

Pinpoint Map data supplied by Critchlow Associates Ltd and contains material subject to Crown copyright.

Travel times
From Avondale shops

CBD	off-peak 10 min peak 30 min
Britomart CBD by train	25 min
North-western motorway	off-peak 5-7min peak 15 min
Airport	30 min
Lynnmall shopping centre	3-4 min
St Lukes shopping centre	10 min
West City, Henderson	7-8 min

The train currently goes up Rosebank Rd and along the top of Blockhouse Bay Rd. One idea is to have it come into the centre of town along Crayford St. Avondale and Waterview are well served by buses, especially along Great North Rd.

including Wesley, New Windsor and Lynfield

It may not be much to look at itself, but Blockhouse Bay and its surrounding suburbs have surprisingly good views. Many of the elevated streets overlook the Manukau Harbour to Puketutu Island, the airport and Waiuku. Container ships, fishing trawlers and jet-ski riders are always to be seen, along with the aeroplanes coming and going from the airport. Another view is the night-lights of the Glenbrook Steel Mill across the southern horizon. On the city side of Blockhouse Bay, some streets can see the lights of surrounding suburbs while others get a view of the Sky Tower. Blockhouse Bay takes its name from the fortifications built across the isthmus in the mid-19th century, when European settlers feared a Maori attack. Lynfield is out on something of a point which means there is no through-traffic. It's quiet and high resident satisfaction means properties don't come up for sale very often.

Who lives there?

Traditionally the kinds of people living in this area have been average, middle-of-the-road Kiwis. As with all of Auckland, the suburb has become more cosmopolitan. There's a large Fijian Indian community here, and about 60% of recent buyers have been new immigrants. People currently buying into the area are most commonly of Indian and Chinese-Asian ethnicity, plus Aucklanders buying investment properties. Rapidly rising prices mean the area is largely out of range for first home buyers.

Lynfield College has a great reputation so it attracts education-conscious immigrants who also see the district as a good starting point in the Auckland market. Blockhouse Bay, Wesley and New Windsor are a mix of rental and owner-occupied properties. Blockhouse Bay is particularly family oriented, which is reflected by its number of schools. It's popular with rental investors, too, but buyers tend to be owner-occupiers in the 30- to 55-year-old age bracket. There is a state housing area at the bottom of Blockhouse Bay.

Typical dwellings

The most common type of houses in these suburbs are weatherboard bungalows built around 25 to 30 years ago, usually with a brick or concrete base, with timber floors and iron roofs. There is some terrace housing at the bottom of Blockhouse Bay. Infill housing is far more common, typically with an older bungalow on the front section, and a 10 or 20-year-old house at the back.

REAL ESTATE

Trends

In 2002 the area saw price rises of up to 10%, and since then prices have continued to go up. One agent estimated an 18% to 20% increase over the past six months, with nine out of 10 properties selling above vendor's expectations. A lot of movement in the area is due to developers making speculative sales. For example one three-bedroom ex-state house in Blockhouse Bay was bought recently for $292,000, and after surveyor plans were drawn up establishing it could be cross-leased, the property was sold again a few weeks later for $421,500. The area has many long term Kiwi owners who tend to be very stable. By contrast, immigrant families often sell and buy again within two or three years to consolidate their equity. Other properties coming onto the market are through elderly couples selling to go into retirement villages.

Land size makes a huge difference to prices, with anything of subdividable size (generally over 750m²) in huge demand.

Properties at the bottom of New Windsor don't sell as fast at the moment due to uncertainty over the proposed motorway extension. Many properties in the path of the motorway have already been bought, and some dwellings have been removed (for more information see Mt Roskill section).

Prices

House prices in the area can range from $180,000 to $600,000 plus for a waterfront or cliff-top property.

Entry level for New Windsor and Wesley starts above $180,000 for a two-bedroom dwelling, with some units selling for as much as $220,000. Average properties sell for around $250,000 for a two-bedroom house, and $290,000 for a house with three bedrooms.

Average three-bedroom homes on a half site in Blockhouse Bay are from the high $200,000s to the low $300,000s, while two and three-bedroom bungalows closer to Avondale and New Windsor range between $220,000 and the low $300,000s with a larger, but not necessarily subdividable, section. Two-bedroom terrace houses sell for $190,000. Two-bedroom units in a block can still be bought for less than $200,000. Four-bedroom townhouses around Blockhouse Bay Rd sell in the high $400,000s to the low $500,000s, and up to the high $500,000s for something renovated with a large section and a good view.

Average prices in Lynfield range from $350,000 to $450,000. Given the area's quiet character there are quite a few retired people in the area. A two-bedroom unit might sell for $200,000 to $225,000. Some properties along the waterfront in Lynfield sell between $400,000 and $600,000.

For $1 million plus you can buy a five-plus bedroom, multiple bathroom home in Lynfield on a full 800m² section on a private, elevated ridge top location, with large garaging, maybe also a pool, and dream views across the harbour. But such properties are hard to come by.

Average sale prices

	House	Flat	No. sales
2002	$258,331	$182,522	327
2003	$296,080	$204,283	538

Rental and investment

Demand for rentals is still very high but prices have stabilised of late. Typical tidy three-bedroom townhouses with internal garaging rent for around $350 a week in Blockhouse Bay. A four-bedroom, two-bathroom Hillsborough property in zone for Lynfield College costs around $400 a week. The more modern properties are scarce so there is greater demand for them.

Best streets

Gilfillan St, Mitchell St, Endeavour St and the water end of Blockhouse Bay Rd.

AMENITIES

Schools ★★★

There are six primary schools in the area. Many people buy here because of Halsey Drive Primary in Lynfield. The two intermediates are Blockhouse Bay and Wesley Intermediate. Secondary schools include Lynfield College, Green Bay High School and Avondale College.

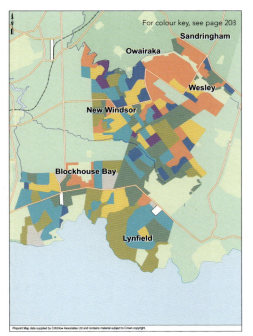

For colour key, see page 203

Sandringham

Owairaka

Wesley

New Windsor

Blockhouse Bay

Lynfield

Pinpoint Map data supplied by Critchlow Associates Ltd and contains material subject to Crown copyright.

Shops ★★★

The Blockhouse Bay shopping centre has a village atmosphere, with approximately 20 shops including cafes, butcher, florist, medical centres and a supermarket.

Plus, at Lynfield there is a brand new complex of shops, including several new convenience food outlets and a Countdown supermarket.

Leisure ★★★

The beach inlets are accessible to residents via many of the streets. It's possible to swim at Blockhouse or Wattle Bays but the beaches are tidal. There are, however, beautiful parks with play areas for children near the beaches.

Open spaces in the area include Craigavon Park, Avondale South Domain, Manukau Domain, Wattle Bay Reserve and Waikowhai Park. Waitakere's Centennial Memorial Park is also handy.

The area has a number of sports clubs including tennis, bowling, rugby league, soccer and others. Within close proximity are also three golf courses (Titirangi, Maungakiekie and Akarana) the Scout Camp Motu Moana, and a number of health and fitness gyms in the vicinity.

There are a few cafés now, plus a restaurant in Blockhouse Bay village. More refined dining needs are catered for in nearby Titirangi.

SMART BUY

Yes - this is still a clever place to buy. While not strictly in the inner city, the area is no longer considered far away from the central business district. The district has sea views in places, little crime, hardly any graffiti and caters for the elderly with easy access to facilities and good supermarkets. Factors pushing prices upwards include the demand for good schools, immigration, the fact that few houses come onto the market, low interest rates and more people looking to buy investment properties. Yet despite all this homes can still be found in the area for less than $300,000.

Travel times

From Blockhouse Bay shops

CBD	off-peak 20 min peak 30 min
North-western motorway	10 min
Airport	20 min
St Lukes mall	10 min
Lynnmall shopping centre	5 min

Stagecoach Auckland provides a regular bus service to Blockhouse Bay and Lynfield.

Why I live there
Manager Shane Rogers

Shane Rogers' first house purchase was in New Windsor, and he and his wife Tracey later used this as a stepping stone to buy their current home in Blockhouse Bay. According to Shane, Blockhouse Bay is far enough from town to get a reasonable amount of space and feel away from the city, but central to everything he and Tracey are involved in. "From here it is only 20 minutes into town, 15 minutes to my work in Mt Eden, and close to both the football fields where I play and the Maungakiekie golf course. Plus it's also near the Lynfield recreation centre where Tracey and I sometimes play squash." Shane and Tracey's house is only five minutes' walk to the beach, a place they will no doubt visit often as their baby daughter Alex grows. "There's a coastal walk which we haven't done yet, but plan to do one day," says Shane. "I definitely feel we'll be here for a while."

EASTERN BAYS ★★★★★

including Mission Bay, Kohimarama, St Heliers, Orakei and Glendowie

With their sunny northern slopes, stunning harbour views, white sand beaches and closeness to the CBD, the leafy bay suburbs represent some of the best real estate Auckland has to offer. Each suburb has its own qualities; Mission Bay is the liveliest, and St Heliers is still quite sleepy. Glendowie is the least desired because it's close to the working-class Glen Innes, but is increasingly becoming gentrified. Locals maintain they are just a 15-minute drive to town, and besides, sitting in Tamaki Dr traffic is a lot more scenic than spaghetti junction. Not so pleasant are the major bottlenecks like Kepa Rd and Kohimarama Rd, where large trucks rumble past - as many as 1300 a day use Kepa Rd, according to council figures. Many locals are, therefore, keen to see progress made with the proposed eastern corridor. Exactly where the highway goes, and how its impact is mitigated is still a topic of hot public debate. Auckland City has begun work on a project to improve sand levels on Kohimarama beach. Up to 60,000m³ of sand will be pumped ashore to provide beach goers with recreation space at all tides.

Who lives there?

Most residents are middle-class Europeans. There is an overall economic comparability across these suburbs which includes the very wealthy, but with still a number of fairly average-income people in family homes. There are many retirees.

Newcomers are increasingly well-off. The bay-lifestyle is hugely popular with any young and families who can afford it. As older people move into apartments or rest homes, a new generation of affluent 30-something professionals have been encouraged to buy by capital gain possibilities and lower interest rates. Approximately half of current buyers are New Zealanders, if you include returning expats, and others who have moved to Auckland from further south. The remaining mix is roughly 30% new immigrant Asians, 15% Americans, and the rest English, Indian, Iraqi and others. A few South African immigrants buy in the area but most prefer the North Shore.

The site of one of New Zealand's most significant Maori land protests, Bastion Point's fabulous Takaparawha Reserve remains the seat of the Ngati Whatua iwi and the tribe have a number of dwellings on the point.

Typical dwellings

The bays have everything from spectacular mansions, particularly along Orakei's Paritai Dr, to state houses. There are many ex-state houses that have been extensively renovated, often beyond recognition. Most of the houses are younger than 60 years old, with pockets of 1970s subdivision-style housing at the back of the bays. And there are some monuments to dubious 1980s style along the waterfront. State houses along Kitemoana St, Orakei, have the best sea views of the entire city.

REAL ESTATE

Trends

Prices and sales started moving upwards in November and December of 2001 and then shot up during 2002 and 2003. Many people moved from renting to buying. One estimate suggests that the value of selected properties has gone up more than 14% in the past six months. Do-ups or subdividable properties are particularly sought after.

The New Zealand exchange rate has favoured returning expats, new immigrants and overseas buyers - they make up roughly 10% of the buyers. As with all the central areas, the bay market is characterised by huge demand and poor supply. Consequently, even the classic squat brick-and-tile sausage block units are now being bought by first-home buyers as well as investors. Glendowie, traditionally the least desirable of the suburbs, is coming into its own as a popular, well-priced area. Riddell Rd is in demand for its views, and Glendowie College is a drawcard.

Prices

At entry level two-bedroom units sell for between $230,000 and $345,000. Anything freestanding is over $350,000. A tidy three-bedroom, ex-state house on a half site in Orakei sells for around $400,000. Glendowie prices are lower due to the suppressing effect of state rentals and the fact that it's next to Glen Innes. But even a three-bedroom do-up on a half site here sells for between $370,000 and $405,000.

New townhouses or older large properties that need refurbishing can sell from $600,000 to $800,000. Prices shoot to the $3 million-plus range for anything cliff-top with sea views. A three-bedroom designer home with tropical gardens and sea and park views in Kohimarama recently went for a modest $1.2 million. One top property recently sold for $5.5 million. For that kind of money buyers can expect a north-facing waterfront property with a large section, sea views, four to five bedrooms, modern decor, three-car garaging and a swimming pool and possibly a tennis court. Ten million and then some is the current top of the market.

Average sale prices

	House	Flat	No. sales
2002	$481,537	$318,752	1355
2003	$668,493	$417,397	731

Rental and investment

The rental market is strong. Two-bedroom units cost $300-350 a week. Upscale properties with four bedrooms, a pool and landscaped gardens might rent for $1000-1500 a week.

Best streets

Paritai Drive, Cliff Rd, Springcombe Rd and The Rise. Riddell Rd in Glendowie.

AMENITIES

Schools ★★★★

The bays have eight primary schools, some of which are private. Kohimarama School is particularly popular. Some local students attend Remuera and Meadowbank Intermediate, otherwise the local secondary schools are Selwyn and Glendowie Colleges, and the private Sacred Heart College. Many students also attend private schools in Epsom and elsewhere.

Shops ★★★

Aside from a small supermarket at Kohimarama, the bays were a bit of a wilderness for grocery shopping, forcing

Why I live there

Financial journalist Rod Oram

"The choice of Mission Bay was a simple one," says Rod. "After moving from central London in 1997, we were looking for somewhere within an 8-9km cycle commute to the city - and this is arguably the best cycle commute in the world.

"The neighbourhood is wonderfully mixed with everything from gorgeous beachfront houses, famous locals like Lucy Lawless, to more humble blocks of flats. It's centrally located for the family's various activities."

locals to do the loop to Meadowbank mall. But with the development of Kepa Rd's Eastridge Mall, there's a New World and more than 20 speciality stores. Shops are otherwise sprinkled thoughout the bays. Those at St Heliers have a village atmosphere whereas Mission Bay doesn't really have shops anymore - it's all eateries.

Leisure ★★★★
The beaches and the grass areas that edge them are a real plus, facing north and with Rangitoto Island right in front of you. All of the bays are suitable for swimming, and the reserve bordering Mission Bay beach is well-frequented by picnickers, walkers and sunbathers. There are also numerous green

Wards of the state
Most Kiwis have a state house lurking in their psyche. If we didn't live in one ourselves, we had friends or relatives who did. We're talking the state houses built by Micky Savage's new Labour Government between 1935 and 1949, the squat cottages with Monopoly house rooflines and devoid of any ornamentation.

State housing epitomised the Savage Government's promise of a good family suburban home for everyone. During its 14 years in power, the government built 32,000 of these homes. The idea was that if you couldn't afford to buy your own, you could access a decent solid home through the state. Vintage state housing of this sort can be found in Orakei, the first state housing suburb for Auckland. It was called a garden suburb; a suburb of family homes lining curved streets, cul-de-sacs and open spaces. The original "garden" concept was of stand-alone cottages, but duplexes and low-rise flats were also built because they could be offered at cheaper rentals and used less land. To avoid social discrimination these multiple dwellings were deliberately designed along similar lines to the stand-alone homes and distributed amongst them. Most properties were initially unfenced so

that each unit would be at one with the wider community.

The houses had tiled hip roofs and were clad with either lapped weatherboards, bricks, or bricks and stucco. Joinery was always timber - a material New Zealand had in plentiful supply.

Once you knew the layout of one house, you tended to know the layout of them all and there was something comforting about such familiarity. The living room was the largest room in the house, but this didn't mean it was going to be a big room! To save space, the kitchen and dining areas were combined, a fairly new concept in the home. Yet there were separate rooms for the bathroom, toilet and laundry!

This era of state housing ended when the National Government came into power in 1949. In 1950 the new Government started selling off the older houses to tenants. Since then state houses have periodically been sold, either to tenants or on the open market, depending on government policy. The most sought after properties were those on quarter-acre sections and those in areas where the land value far exceeded the house value, such as Orakei.

These days it isn't unusual to see substantially renovated state houses in many areas of New Zealand. They were well constructed and well centred on large sections, providing plenty of space for additions. Although poky dwellings by today's standards, opening them up to the sun and indoor/outdoor flow is easily accomplished.

The leaky building syndrome has inspired a revival of interest in state houses, because of their reputation for solidity. Their size and style is an attractive alternative to those who might have bought a terrace house.

Local hero - Tamaki Dr

The fabulous Tamaki Dr links all of the bays, starting right back at Mechanics Bay near the city, running past Hobson Bay, Okahu Bay, Biddicks Bay, Mission Bay, Kohimarama, ending at St Heliers. It winds around the foreshore, past beaches and beneath pohutukawa trees, and is ideal for cycling, walking, roller-blading and fine weather cruising in an open-topped sports car.

The pavement is split down the middle with a cycling track nearest the road, so keep a look out when you're walking. Tamaki Dr is also a high-density zone for three-wheeler buggies being pushed by upwardly mobile parents.

areas including Orakei Domain, the small but lovely Dingle Dell, Glover Park, Madill's Farm, Kepa Bush Park, the large Churchill Park, Glendowie Park and numerous smaller reserves. Auckland is the city of sails and many locals are boat owners. The bays also have the usual range of sports clubs. There is the Tamaki Yacht Club, cinemas at Mission Bay, sea life at Kelly Tarlton's Underwater World, and Ian Ferguson Marine Sports on Tamaki Dr for kayak hire - late-night paddles to Rangitoto Island are an alternative harbour cruise for romantic sporty types. Down at the water, many older locals religiously take their "constitutionals".

For eating out, Mission Bay has a busy strip of restaurants and cafes - in fact, there is little else. Defontaine, which recently replaced McDonald's on the corner of Patteson Ave, offers the closest thing to nightlife in this quarter. At Orakei there is Hammerheads. St Heliers' restaurants include the top Saints Waterfront Brasserie.

LOOK OUT!

If the proposed eastern corridor goes ahead, it will not only wreck the views of many Orakei homeowers across the Orakei basin to the city skyline but will cut across Auckland's biggest area of mangroves. The mangroves are on one side of the railway line edging Purewa Creek and are widely considered an ecological treasure especially as they are situated only 5km away from central Auckland. Some of the mangroves have a coastal protection order prohibiting their removal.

For colour key, see page 208

Travel times

From Mission Bay (add 5 min for St Heliers)	
CBD	off-peak 15-20 min peak 30 min
Britomart CBD by train	8 min
Greenlane interchange	15 min
Airport	25 min
Newmarket	15 min

Stagecoach Auckland and Howick & Eastern Buses provide regular services to St Heliers. There is also a train that runs between Glen Innes and Meadowbank and along the bottom of Orakei Rd.

Epsom is a gentrified, gentle, flat, tree-lined suburb of established gardens and top schools. Some would say that all adds up to boring but for the people who live here behind their decorous fences and tree-studded front gardens, that's exactly what they've paid the high prices for, thank you very much. In terms of price and desirability Epsom has always been strong, and sits alongside other blue-chip areas like Remuera and Herne Bay. Its highly sought after schools, both public and private, are a key reason.

Marring the image of leafy traditional Epsom is the spectre of infill housing and the large pastel townhouses that have appeared during the past 10 years. Townhouses on smaller sections are particularly popular with Asian families, who mostly prefer new houses. They are not so popular with European New Zealanders, and some consider the area has lost a certain consistency of style.

Who lives there?

Epsom is middle to upper-middle class. Many of Epsom's residents have lived there for 20 to 30 years. Most buyers coming into the area today are families with teenage children who hope to attend either of the well-reputed public schools, Auckland Grammar School (boys only) or Epsom Girls Grammar School.

The impact of school zone legislation has been felt in the market for the past three years. The premium gained for in-zone houses has prompted some older residents to cash up and move to South Epsom or southern Mt Eden. Blurring the zoning effect is the fact that many Epsom residents send their children to local private schools such as Diocesan School for Girls, St Cuthbert's College, or St Peter's College, or over to Saint Kentigern in Pakuranga.

Epsom is still a suburb for young professionals - provided they are earning big money. Some are expat professionals, mostly from Britain. There is also a trend for young but well-off families from inner city suburbs such as Herne Bay to move here seeking room to grow.

The neighbourhood is extremely popular with education-conscious Asian families. One agent estimated that 30% to 40% of recent sales at their office had been to Chinese families, with the remainder to a mix of New Zealanders, English and some Indian immigrants. Another reported that most buyers recently seeking to build new houses in the area were of Pakistani and Indian ethnicity, along with some Asian.

Typical dwellings

Epsom was settled mainly around the turn of the century so there are many villas of 1900-1920s vintage as well as 1930s bungalows. Infill housing during the past decade means there are now also many large modern townhouses, mostly of brick-and-tile or plaster construction. Small units, sometimes in blocks, complete the spectrum of properties.

REAL ESTATE

Trends

Auckland Grammar School and Epsom Girls Grammar School are key to Epsom's demand from buyers. Under current public school zoning legislation only those students living strictly within each school's zone can attend.

This has created two tiers of value - houses in and out of zone.

It costs around $100,000 more for the same level of property situated inside the zone as one outside, say local real estate agents.

Values in the Epsom area have tended to keep up with those on the southern side of Remuera. Some northern streets once considered to be in Royal Oak are now referred to as Epsom South.

Demand for property outstrips supply and Epsom has been impacted by the buying power that expat and British immigrant pounds bring to the market.

Between October and Christmas 2002, properties at the top end of the market went up on average by $200,000, says one local real estate sales consultant. Immigration was a major factor fuelling this rise. It's not uncommon at an auction for the local market to be bidding at $800,000, and for outsiders to offer $1 million. Properties in the second price tier started moving upwards from March 2002 onwards.

Prices

For an entry level three-bedroom bungalow or villa do-up on a full site in Mt Eden/Epsom non-grammar zone, buyers can expect to pay $500,000 plus. A large but old-fashioned four-bedroom house goes for around $750,000, and a renovated villa on a full section in Bracken Ave recently went for $1.13 million at auction.

A small two-bedroom unit, apartment or terrace townhouse might sell from $280,000. At the other end of the scale are million-dollar plus properties, such as Florence Court, the "$8 million house" on Omana Ave.

Average sale prices

	House	Flat	No. sales
2002	$612,692	$283,911	309
2003	$771,439	$291,874	259

Rental and investment

The area is very much in demand for its rental properties. The average rent for a two-bedroom unit ranges from $300 to $400 depending on location.

Rental properties within the desired school zones can create a bit of a frenzy with prospective tenants vying for the right address, even if they have to rent it. Recent reports have described letting agents holding Dutch auctions in the front yard of such properties and settling on higher rents than those initially asked as a result. For landlords, that's good news although, of course, you pay a premium for the property in the first place.

Best streets

Mountain Rd, Shipherds Ave, Brightside Rd, Almorah Rd, Omana Ave.

AMENITIES

Schools ★★★★★

Epsom is fantastically well served for schools, both public and private, especially for girls. There are two private and three public primaries and an intermediate (most private schools include intermediate years). At secondary level there is one public girls, two private girls, one public boys and two private boys (one of which is the charitable school Dilworth Boys School). There are no co-ed secondary schools.

Why I live there
Surgeon Philip Allen and Joanne Allen

Closeness to work was one reason colorectal surgeon Philip Allen and his wife Joanne bought their half-acre Epsom property a few years ago. More space and access to good secondary schools for their five children (pictured, Mary Rose) were other deciding factors. "We looked for two years before buying," says Joanne. "Unlike many in the area, ours is not a character home. Instead, it's a rather boring 1940s brick and weatherboard house but we couldn't go past the garden, sleep-out, three-car garage and boat shed." According to Joanne, the neighbourhood doesn't have quite the community feel of the more ethnically diverse Mt Roskill where the family used to live. But there's no doubt that this gracious suburb is a great place to grow up.

Shops ★★★

Apart from the collection of antique and other small shops at Greenwoods Corner, Epsom itself is not big on shops. It is next door to Newmarket and Royal Oak, however, as well as the Dominion Rd strip and Mt Eden Village.

Leisure ★★★★

Parks include Melville Park, Alexandra Park and Mt St John Domain but Epsom is also bordered by two of Auckland's largest parks, One Tree Hill Domain/Cornwall Park and Mt Eden Domain. It's also very close to the Auckland Domain.

Epsom has a number of sports clubs covering hockey, football, bowling, croquet, tennis and netball as well as the Auckland Trotting Club. There is also the recently refurbished Lido Cinema, the Epsom Library and Epsom Community Centre. There are a lot of hospitals in or near Epsom and while hospitals are not a destination stop as such, it might be a comfort to some to know they're right next door!

Epsom has numerous restaurants offering international cuisine including Haveli India, One Italy, Phoenix Garden Chinese and the Sake Bar Nippon.

LOOK OUT!

So what's to stop the neighbours from taking away the character bungalow next door and building a huge new plaster townhouse? There was a big re-zoning of the area about six years ago when the council established areas that could not be further developed below a certain section size. As a rule, restrictions cover the streets where traditional homes are still in the majority. If new developments are in the majority, it's fair to assume there will be more development in the future.

SMART BUY

Epsom is a trend leader - it's one of the first suburbs to go up and the last to go down. High-quality central suburbs always appreciate over time, and tend to maintain value in low periods. You do have to be able to afford it, however. Should school zoning legislation be changed or the zones themselves redefined, you may suddenly find yourself out of zone and your house dropping in value.

Travel times

From central Epsom

CBD	off-peak 10 min peak 25 min
North-western motorway	10 min
Southern motorway	1-5 mins
Airport	15 min
Royal Oak shopping centre	5 min
Newmarket	5 min

Stagecoach Auckland provides a regular bus service to Epsom. The area is well served for buses, with many travelling along the major roads of Gillies Ave and Manukau Rd on their way to and from perimeter suburbs.

The major artery of Gillies Ave, which runs through Epsom, is both a blessing and curse for local commuting residents; getting onto this busy road at peak time is a tedious exercise but once they're in the flow of traffic, commuters are well connected.

On the dotted line

Owning a property used to be straightforward in the days when the Kiwi quarter-acre section came complete with one simple wooden house, three back steps, a lemon tree and a rotary clothes-line in the back yard. To own one of the above, you simply paid your money, collected your certificate of title and that was that. After all, freehold land ownership wasn't also called "fee simple" for nothing.

With increasing urbanisation and the need for higher density housing, different forms of legal land ownership became necessary.

The 1950s "sausage blocks" of several units within one dwelling led to the crosslease method of ownership, which gives each owner a freehold proportional share of the land and improvements and a 999-year lease on the building they occupy in return for a peppercorn rental of a few cents.

Crosslease also means shared obligations, including the maintenance of common areas such as the driveway and the consent of all leasees for any structural changes to any building. Crosslease offered developers a cheaper way of subdividing property than the alternative of freehold subdivision, largely because they avoided having to pay a reserves contribution towards new parks and reserves in the community.

As a result, huge areas of crossleased infill changed the flavour of established suburbs with new, often brick-and-tile, homes sprouting out of what was once the back lawn of the original house. Infill housing had mixed public support. It improved the range of affordable housing stock close to the city, but in the eyes of the architectural purists, it compromised the heritage appeal of suburbs such as Pt Chevalier, which was one of Auckland's first bungalow suburbs.

Many of the practical and financial anomalies between crosslease and freehold sub-division disappeared under the Resource Management Act of 1991. As a result, there have been virtually no new crossleases created in Auckland City during the past six years, says Ross Miller, the Auckland City Council's subdivisions' team leader.

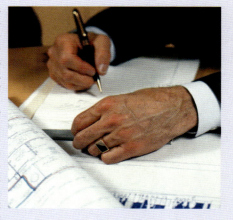

The Law Commission has publicly documented flaws in the crosslease system and it has recommended that the Government abolish crosslease ownership and require all existing crossleases to be converted to another form of ownership. This could be either freehold subdivision or a simpler form of unit title, which is the most common form of ownership for apartment buildings and terraced housing developments.

A unit title (also known by the Aussie term strata title) gives freehold ownership of the airspace that contains the building, and requires common land to be administered by a body corporate made up of all the owners.

Another form of ownership that's evident throughout Auckland's eastern suburbs is that of leasehold land as administered by such boards as the Melanesian Trust, the Dilworth Trust and the St Johns Anglican Trust. Such leasehold land has been subdivided into freehold lots with the actual land leased, rather than sold, to the owner of the dwelling and any improvements on the land. The value of the lease, which is payable by a ground rental, depends on the length of the rent reviews, so with this, as with any form of land ownership, it's vital to seek the advice of a property law specialist.

GLEN INNES/PT ENGLAND ★★★★★

Up until World War II most of this area was paddocks; today Glen Innes and Pt England are the kind of rough-and-ready working class neighbourhoods where locals look out for each other. Houses in elevated locations look over the estuary and some have great views across to Bucklands Beach but despite this, the many state houses and low-grade rentals make it among the least desirable parts of the city. Many Glen Innes buyers are first-timers and investors. Around 60% of the dwellings are rented.

Pt England is a little more upmarket, though Housing New Zealand is still a big property owner. About half of the properties are rented. The district has had more than its share of crime. A new community development plan involves tree plantings, and improved paving and lighting to make the area safer. Also, there are strong social networks, many churches and no obvious gang presence or ethnic violence. Just as in any neighbourhood, there are desirable and less desirable streets; and houses in sunny spots with sea views, as in Glen Innes Heights, are the best. Residents living on the fringes of these suburbs tend to want to dissociate from the area, so some boundary fudging goes on - for example around the Tamaki and St Johns borders of Pt England. Coastal areas like Wai o Taiki Bay have lovely water views and attractive residential pockets.

Who lives there?

The area has great ethnic diversity. There are many immigrants including Arabs and Albanians. Many Asian immigrants have moved here attracted by low rents and house prices. Proximity to the University of Auckland's Tamaki campus makes it attractive to students.

The low house prices attract first-time buyers, who like the renovation potential of solid ex-state houses. Some subsequently upgrade closer to the sea, or to neighbouring St Johns or Glendowie.

Typical dwellings

Archetypal houses are current and former state houses and bungalows of 1940s vintage onwards, including typical 1950s two-storey duplexes. Some ex-state houses have been nicely renovated. Wai o Taiki Bay is pepper-potted with state houses and new houses put up by developers.

When the state sold a lot of properties in Orakei, it spent the proceeds in Glen Innes, building a lot of duplexes and terrace houses to maximise land use. Examples are in Maybury St and Rowena Cres. Since the late 1980s, some parts, such as Ropata Ave, have seen a fair amount of infill housing, typically single-level variety. There are still many two-bedroom houses on large plots.

REAL ESTATE

Trends
One factor positively affecting prices and bringing about change is the construction of the eastern corridor expressway. When built, this will dramatically shorten commuting times to the central city. This should transform the image and desirability of Glen Innes.

Another positive is the expansion of Auckland University's Tamaki Campus. A huge development due to be finished in the next few years is the university's sports medicine division. Some students have already started to use the area for course-related community experience.

Six to eight years ago many state houses were sold in Glen Innes, going "like hotcakes" as investment properties. Ex-state houses are very sought after and don't stay on the market very long.

The Government had a huge impact on the local market when it stopped the sale of state houses in 1999, and the market dropped away again. After a while there was a shortfall in available properties and prices picked up. Approximately a year ago the market in Pt England and Glen Innes started moving and properties started selling faster.

At the beginning of 2003 prices started to rise, and the year saw some top prices, especially in Pt England, where investors have been buying rental properties for incoming Asian migrants. There is a current shortage of stock and while these trends are positive, only time will tell if they have a long-term impact.

The kind of change possible was demonstrated a few years ago by the transformation of the neighbourhood's most derelict and crime ridden street, the infamous Madeleine Ave on the Glendowie / Glen Innes border. Once dubbed Auckland's "street of shame", the 169 ghetto-like state houses on this and neighbouring Esperance Ave were bought by a developer for around $13 million. The street was totally overhauled, renamed Mt Taylor Dr, and its

new designer houses subsequently sold for around the high $400,000s.

Prices
At entry level in central Glen Innes, one bedroom dwellings sell for around $100,000. A standard three-bedroom home that's in reasonable condition will cost you around $190,000 upwards.

Properties at Pt England sell for between $250,000 and $280,000 and a three-bedroom brick-and-tile home in Glen Innes can fetch around $330,000.

On the area's borders the difference in prices from one street to another can be dramatic. Patterns are hard to pick because of the mixed nature of most streets.

Houses in elevated locations look over the estuary, so are in demand and fetch prices from $220,000 upwards. Many houses in Wai o Taiki Bay have unobstructed water views and values are around $100,000 more than elsewhere nearby - top price for a three-bedroom house on a full site by the sea is upwards of $350,000.

Average sale prices

	House	Flat	No.sales
2002	$201,560	$157,000	137
2003	$319,397	$247,905	222

Rental and investment
The area's rental market is very strong, with generally more demand than supply. In

addition Housing New Zealand uses privately owned rentals to cater for their overflow. Standard prices are $150 per week for a one-bedroom dwelling and $220 upwards for a three-bedroom family home, though it's becoming more common to see rentals with a harbour view going for around $400 a week.

Best streets

In Glen Innes, the top end off West Tamaki Rd, Weybridge Cres, and Paddington St.
In Pt England, Dunkirk Rd and Riki Rd. In Wai o Taiki Bay, Silverton Ave and Inglewood St.

AMENITIES

Schools ★★

The area has five primary schools, and Glen Innes Intermediate. The local secondary school is Tamaki College with top Catholic boys' college Sacred Heart nearby. There is a local total immersion Maori school and the Auckland Japanese Supplementary School.
Glen Innes Intermediate was recently ranked decile 1, putting its community in the lowest ranking possible. Some have recommended that it needs as a total upgrade if the school is to continue.

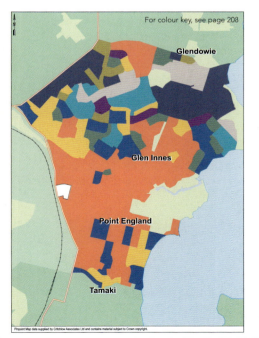

For colour key, see page 208

Glendowie

Glen Innes

Point England

Tamaki

Pinpoint Map data supplied by Critchlow Associates Ltd and contains material subject to Crown copyright.

Shops ★★

Glen Innes has a supermarket and individual shops. The closest otherwise are at Panmure.

Leisure ★★★

Along the waterfront there are fabulous adventure walks, and at low tide it looks as though you could almost walk across to Half Moon Bay. The area has a number of sports clubs including the University Rugby Club, YMCA Aquatics & Fitness Centre and a skating rink. The nearby Merton Rd sports grounds cater for rugby, cricket, soccer and tennis.
The area is not especially known for its culinary specialities but has a number of ethnic food eateries including the local Indian, Tasty Bite.

LOOK OUT!

The Talbot Park renewal area, bounded by Pt England Rd to the north, Apirana Ave to the west and Pilkington Rd to the east, is under development by Housing New Zealand. The $27 million, three-year plan is to provide better housing by refurbishing 108 units and providing 97 new homes; and to develop two new parks to replace the existing reserve. The idea is that the area will be safer, more open and usable, but pessimists predict it might deteriorate quickly and become a new ghetto instead.

SMART BUY

In real estate desirability terms this area still has a long way to go, but it may be the last chance to get reasonably priced waterfront property within Auckland City. While the area will never be a new Ponsonby, it might be a new Onehunga.

Travel times

From Glen Innes shops

CBD	off-peak 20 min peak 40 min
Britomart CBD by train	10 min
Southern motorway	15 min
Airport	30 min

The area is well serviced by Stagecoach Auckland buses and the Tranz Metro train.

including Westmere, Pt Chevalier and Arch Hill

A little bit of money has to rub off when you stand shoulder-to-shoulder with your expensive neighbours. That's exactly what's happened to Grey Lynn, Westmere and Pt Chevalier - the expensive neighbours being Ponsonby and Herne Bay. When prices go loopy and we all wring our hands at not being able to afford the posher neighbourhoods, what do we do? Take one step out.

So the idiosyncratic inner-city suburbs of Grey Lynn and Arch Hill, and pleasant waterfront areas of Westmere and Pt Chevalier are blue-collar quarters made good. In the past, renters were the norm and owner-occupiers in the minority. These days the numbers are reversed and the sounds of renovations often heard. The area's best locations are near or within sight of the water at Westmere or Pt Chevalier. In Grey Lynn, it's any elevated bits - those that look across the park or cityscape, or to the water at Cox's Bay.

Who lives there?

There are more wealthy people in Ponsonby, but that difference aside, Grey Lynn broadly attracts the same types - bourgeois bohemians, many media types, arty professionals and grown-up hippies. These suburbs attract young hipster renters who want to be close to the city centre, the clubs and cafes along Ponsonby, Kingsland and Karangahape Rds. Add to the mix old ladies who moved to the area as young brides, and a significant number of Maori and Polynesian families living in long-held family homes.

Westmere and Pt Chevalier are less obviously arty, but are just as multicultural, with quite a community of new immigrants, and second and third-generation Indians, Pakistanis and Asians living alongside the professional Pakeha 30 and 40-somethings. Westmere is just that bit closer to the city; its centrality and waterfront reserve are attractions.

The flat Pt Chevalier has always been popular with older people. Before Meola Rd linked it to Westmere in the late 1970s, the peninsula suburb was a backwater. Today it's in demand from young professionals and families as a commuter suburb, appealing in particular to upwardly mobile single women.

Typical dwellings

Grey Lynn and Arch Hill are older suburbs dominated by villas and bungalows, with the occasional block of flats. New houses exist but are very much in the minority. Arch Hill has narrower streets, smaller villas and more miners' cottages, compared with Grey Lynn. Most properties don't have off-street parking. Westmere and Pt Chevalier were originally developed as bungalow suburbs in the 1920s, when trams were in their heyday. Westmere has mostly wooden bungalows, some brick or stucco state houses, and a few brick and tile units and modern townhouses on half sites. The larger sections of Pt Chevalier have also made crossleasing a popular option.

REAL ESTATE

Trends

The past three to four years has seen an urban movement from the east to the west as more people have discovered these central suburbs. Westmere and Grey Lynn especially have experienced dramatic price gains lately. Grey Lynn because it's that bit closer to the city, and is on Ponsonby's doorstep, Westmere because of its coastal views and nearness to top suburb Herne Bay. Prices continue to rise in the area, exacerbated by a lack of properties on the market. Some movement in the area is due to young expats returning to buy houses, or simply buying to rent out with the plan of returning home eventually.

For ages Grey Lynn has been an area that is "going to go", and in the last year prices have rocketed. Previously down-at-heel rental properties are being totally renovated by their owner-occupiers or upgraded to appeal to young-professional renters. A renovated three-bedroom property that sold in 2001 for $440,000 was resold recently for $646,000. A "shack" on Williamson Ave that was bought for $490,000 at Christmas 2002 sold in August 2003 for $550,000. In 2003 several Grey Lynn properties have sold for $900,000 and more - record prices for the area. One had been bought three years before for $475,000.

Prices

Grey Lynn do-ups now sell for around $550,000. Fully renovated houses in Westmere or Grey Lynn sell from $650,000 to the mid $800,000s in the better parts. One Crummer

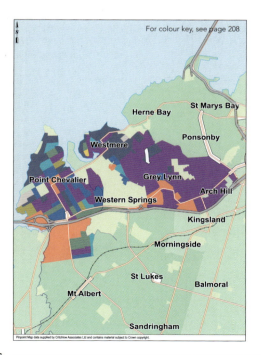

Rd renovated villa divided into four flats sold for $564,000 in January 2002, and again in May 2003 for $901,000.

In comparison, three-bedroom bungalows in Arch Hill sell for around $380,000 upwards depending on condition and parking. One house in Cooper St recently fetched more than $500,000.

Modernised four to five-bedroom Westmere homes sell for $2 million plus. Westmere used to be a bit cheaper than neighboring Ponsonby because people preferred villas to Westmere's more typical bungalows. Now buyers cannot be so choosy - besides, unlike Ponsonby, here you can almost always get off-street parking. Unrenovated ex-state houses have sold in the area for more than $500,000, and one well renovated and extended three-bedroom ex-state house sold for $850,000. Really nicely renovated Westmere houses with no views sell these days for $600,000 to $700,000 plus.

Pt Chevalier prices are divided by Meola Rd with properties to the north having significantly higher land values. South of Meola Rd, average three-bedroom bungalows in reasonable condition on half sites sell for $350,000 upwards. In Pt Chevalier a big house on a corner section, but with no view, sold for $850,000 a year and a half ago. Now it is worth $1 million.

Average sale prices

	House	Flat	No. sales
2002	$380,599	$264,873	567
2003	$460,397	$253,339	514

Rental and investment

There are still lots of investors looking to buy in the area. The prices of some of the area's apartments have been held back by the leaky building crisis, but others are strong. For example, one two-bedroom apartment with a view sold recently for $450,000; others in the high $200,000s in 2001 now fetch over $300,000. Demand for rental properties is high, due to proximity to the CBD. Prices range from $220 to $300 plus per week for a one-bedroom flat or studio, to $800 to $900 for a three or four-bedroom executive home. Three-bedroom Grey Lynn and Westmere houses are around $480 to $500 per week. Pt Chevalier rentals can be 5% to 10% less, unless the property has sea views or is close to the beach.

Best streets

In Westmere, Rawene St and lower Garnet Rd. In Pt Chevalier, Harbour View Rd and Lynch St. In Grey Lynn, the upper reaches of Ariki St and Beaconsfield St.

AMENITIES

Schools ★★★

There are six local primary schools, including some private. While this area wasn't previously known for its schools, these days a number are well-regarded, including Westmere and Pt Chevalier. There is Pasadena Intermediate, and the local secondary school is Western Springs College. Grey Lynn Primary faced closure a few years ago, but enrolments and standards have been turned around by principal Bill Barker and community fundraising, including an event featuring local artists including Dave Dobbyn. A number of additional programmes run alongside the school, including the George Parkyn Centre for Gifted Education and an Italian language school.

Shops ★★★

In Grey Lynn, some shops and cafes are clustered at the junction of Williamson Ave and Great North Rd along with one of the areas two 24-hour supermarkets. More shops at West Lynn include cafes, a boutique wine shop Weta, clothing store Moa and Harvest Wholefoods.

Travel times	
From Grey Lynn shops	
CBD	off-peak 10 min peak 15 min
From Westmere shops	
CBD	off-peak 10 min peak 20 min
North-western motorway	5 min
Airport	30 min
St Lukes mall	10 min

Pt Chevalier's shape creates a bit of a traffic bottle-neck. Beach-end properties are more expensive partly because of the alternative route to and from the city via Meola Rd. The whole area has excellent public transport with Stagecoach providing a regular service to the entire area, especially along major routes like Williamson Ave and Great North Rd.

Westmere has a dozen shops along Garnet Rd including a specialty wine shop, a butcher, and antique and retro stores such as Ritzy Bits. Pt Chevalier has a shopping strip along Great North Rd, and other shops on the peninsula.

Leisure ★★★

There are plenty of open spaces with a few small reserves by the sea. Grey Lynn Park includes sports grounds and a free toddler pool. Coyle Park and the restful Pt Chevalier beach is at the end of Pt Chevalier peninsula. The Cox's Bay area in Westmere was a landfill site in the 1950s. After locals began picking the stones out, the council levelled it and created the Seddon fields. Nearby Meola reef is still an untouched green space that is home to cows, birds and mangroves.

Western Springs Park is a tranquil lakeside reserve and wildlife sanctuary off Great North Rd - except on Speedway nights in the summer. The spring-fed lakes are home for many species of wildfowl. Paths wind through the landscaped grounds - great for walking or for small children learning to ride a bike. The huge Pasifika festival held annually in the park gives the 100,000 or more people who attend it a dynamic experience of Polynesian culture and arts. Auckland Zoo is over the fence. Depending on the wind, you can hear the lions roar in the surrounding neighbourhoods. This area has sports clubs catering for soccer, tennis, bowling, squash, cricket and rugby league.

For eating out, Grey Lynn has cafes such as Occam, while Pt Chevalier has four or five restaurants including Point 5 Nine. Westmere has a popular cafe Garnet Rd Foodstore.

LOOK OUT!

So you're moving to Grey Lynn because of its arty, villagey feel, and all those historic villas and bungalows. Under a new 'zone 8' rule adopted by the Auckland City Council in late 2003, the character could change. It's now possible for a developer to erect multi-storey apartments in the 'burbs, and the closer in to the CBD, the higher the potential 'intensity housing.' The good thing is the developer needs zoning approval on a large plot of land first. But to be absolutely safe, you'll have to buy at least ten minutes' walk from your suburban village centre, and preferably outside a 2km radius of the CBD. Good luck!

including Waiheke Island, Great Barrier Island and Rakino Island

Over the past decade Waiheke Island has made a name for its friendly community atmosphere, unspoilt beaches, protected bush and regular ferry transport to the CBD. About 26km long by 19km at its widest point, it is the Hauraki Gulf's second largest island. In the early 1950s and 60s most of Waiheke's few residents were retired, and cars were scarce. These days the population is close to 7000, and it is an attractive but busy suburb of Auckland, with major communities at Oneroa, Palm Beach, Onetangi on the north side and Rocky Bay, Ostend, Surfdale, Kennedy's Bay and Blackpool on the south.

Lying 90km northeast of Auckland, Great Barrier Island covers an area that is more than half the size of the Auckland metropolitan area. The terrain is rugged and about 75 percent of it is conservation land. The island's residents must still generate their own power.

The small and beautiful Rakino Island is only 19km from Auckland but is still very primitive. There is one small shop. There are about 200 pieces of land on the island, 25 in 4-5ha lifestyle and coastal blocks, the balance in 800-1200m² sections. Rakino has no power or phone services.

Who lives there?

During the 1960s and 70s Waiheke's laid-back style and cheap houses made it attractive to hippies and alternative lifestylers. Crucial to growth was a fast daily ferry service. By the early 1980s Waiheke had started to attract commuters. Today the island has 7000 permanent residents with numbers swelling to 40,000 or so during holidays.

In the past Waiheke's population was very eclectic, and included beneficiaries, young families, single women, empty nesters, first home buyers, as well as rich weekenders; everyone from average Kiwis to millionaire holidaymakers. As the island has become more popular, busy and expensive, some of the beneficiary renting population has moved on to quieter areas like Great Barrier Island and the Far North. These days the population is more homogenous, white and wealthy, and the island is increasingly the domain of people with established money - typically elite professionals and urban establishment types, with only around 10 to 20% of the population being beneficiaries.

Waiheke has long been popular with artists and craftspeople. Now it's also a trendy haven for media personalities, plus it's sought after by overseas buyers - most often English, German, American, French and South African. Overseas buyers tend to buy properties in the $500,000 plus bracket. They can't buy over 0.2ha unless they are buying to live here. Today's typical buyers also include expats; some coming to live, others investing in property then returning overseas. There are a large number of people who commute to work in the city. A few older locals nowadays combine island living with a CBD apartment and car.

Great Barrier Island's population is mainly farming based. Its 1100 or so residents live clustered in scattered coastal settlements, namely Port FitzRoy and Okiwi in the north, Okupu and Tryphena in the southwest and Claris and Oruawharo (Medlands) in the east. Residents have to provide their own power with generators. The island's population swells to about 5000 during summer.

Rakino Island's permanent population is 20 to 25, and is a bizarre mix of very rich and others who are scratching out a living. Not all islanders have a phone, and sitting in the center of the island is possibly the last free red phone box in New Zealand. Rakino is for the hardy and the adventurous; the only power is from solar power, wind generators, and batteries, but rich island dwellers don't go without, arriving with cell phones, laptops and so forth.

Typical dwellings

During the past 10 years Waiheke's classic, often fibrolite, basic kiwi baches have been tarted up or demolished and replaced with luxury homes. Some do-ups remain, but they sell fast, especially those close to water or with a view.

New house styles vary. There are a few mud brick, a lot of board and batten cladding, barn-style architecture and lots of Mediterranean style stucco. Relocated houses, usually bungalows that have been brought over from the mainland, are popular provided they have been well renovated. Coloured steel, Zincalume and black-stained marine plywood are currently hot. There are also a few houses of an ultra-modern concrete style.

REAL ESTATE

Trends

In the 1970s young couples could buy a good Waiheke house for $15,000 to $20,000. When the quick cat ferry service was introduced in 1987 property prices jumped around $30,000. Sales have gained steadily ever since. Prices have risen a lot during the past five years, and especially since last October.

The northern end of the island is the premium area, followed by the southern, then around Oneroa Village and Blackpool closest to the ferry. The most desirable beaches are the northern facing sand beaches such as Oneroa, Palm Beach, and Onetangi. At the eastern end are beautiful private beaches accessible by boat. Properties in Blackpool were once very hard to sell due to flooding, but since the council fixed the roads, values have risen by more than 30%.

Waiheke Island's property market continues to be buoyant, following the usual seasonal fluctuations over the past 12 months. Most sales are either between existing Waiheke residents or Aucklanders buying weekend homes, investment properties or permanent homes as they move to the island to live. Most are professional couples or middle income earners. Given the island's continued popularity, it is not uncommon for sales to be made via the internet, sometimes site-unseen, and for properties to sell at the asking price.

Commuter numbers have risen hugely in recent

years. There is still a lot of interest in the island from expats who usually buy at the upper end of the market. Some are young people looking to buy a first home after their OE, or even buying while remaining overseas.

Of all Auckland's suburbs Waiheke has seen the most capital gain. The ultimate buy in Waiheke is waterfront with a white sandy beach, which can still be bought for $1 to $1.5 million plus, compared with $3 million plus in Takapuna. Averaged out over the past seven years, white sand beachfront properties have gone up by approximately $100,000 a year, regardless of what is happening in the Auckland-wide market. Even when the Auckland market slumps, Waiheke Island sales volumes keep going up and prices hold their own.

There are a few crossleases available but only on bigger sites. An 800m² section is considered a small site on the island. There is no infill housing allowed because of septic tank requirements, and this puts the squeeze on land. Currently 83% of all sections have been built on. Sections and lifestyle blocks are extremely hard to get hold of.

Rakino Island is subdivided into four distinct residential areas surrounded by rural blocks of roughly 4ha (10 acres). The council is currently considering whether to allow subdivision or some form of additional development of these rural properties. Due to New Zealanders' insatiable desire for coastal property, prices on Rakino have seen some dramatic rises, with certain coastal lifestyle blocks doubling in value in as many years, to now be worth more than $850,000. In February 2000 a peninsula with very small jetty and boatshed, but no house, was sold for $600,000; 18 months later it sold again for $900,000.

Prices

A humble Waiheke do-up with one to two bedrooms and no view now sells for $250,000 plus. Apartments range in price from around $220,000 for a one-bedroom residence to well over $1 million for the best three-bedroom dwelling. Apartments tend to be cheaper, but turnover is kept down by the fact that due to council effluent requirements, they cannot be used as permanent dwellings but only by weekend or part time visitors. Council effluent requirements also prevent the construction of townhouses on Waiheke.

An average three-bedroom home in good condition costs around $320,000 upwards, and

Travel times
From Waiheke Island

Onetangi to ferry wharf	15 min
Ferry wharf to CBD	35 min
CBD to airport	1 hour bus trip from downtown Auckland or 15-20 min by chartered plane

The first ferry leaves Matiatia Bay on Waiheke for Auckland at 6.10am Monday to Friday and ferries run hourly from 8am to 4pm. The last ferry off the island during the week is 12.30am, and 11.45pm is the last ferry from Auckland. More ferry runs have been added in the past year, and a new terminal opens at Matiatia Bay in November 2003.

Car ferries depart regularly from Western Viaduct near Wynyard Wharf in downtown Auckland, and Half Moon Bay marina, to land at either Matiatia Bay or Kennedy's Pt. A new $6 million car and passenger ferry from Half Moon Bay is planned to start in the 2003/04 summer with an hourly service capable of carrying 500 passengers. This will significantly open up Waiheke to south and eastern Aucklanders.

Getting to Great Barrier involves a 30-minute flight from Auckland City, the North Shore or Mangere. The car ferry takes four hours or in high season, two hours on the fast ferry.

A mail run stops at Rakino Island three times a week, and the prospect of a daily service remains unlikely.

something with a peep of a view is now $360,000 plus on the south side, and $450,00 to $500,000 plus on the north side. Prices range from $350,000 upwards for do-ups in good areas without sea views, that are close to the beach. At the lower end of the market a little one-bedroom bach in Blackpool with no view might have sold 18 months ago for $169,000; now it will go between $285,000 and $290,000. One top recent sale was $4 million for a big beachfront house with land, but Waiheke has large pieces of land that are worth even more. A waterfront section with no house on it sold recently for $930,000. Another cliff-top property with a new house on it went for $1.8 million. One property is currently listed at $5 million plus. Two adjacent cliff-top coastal sections sold in the same week for $875,000 and $1.05 million. Another property with a little two-bedroom bach situated at the end of a road, right in front of Onetangi's white sand beach, sold this year for $1.9 million. Over the past few years many substantial mansions have been built on equally valuable properties, but they have not yet come back on the market for re-sale.

Entry level on Great Barrier is $180,000 to $260,000 for a cottage do-up, and three-bedroom places in good condition are around the mid $260,000 plus. Top of the market prices are around $400,000 to $500,000. $550,000 buys something close to water. The Auckland City Council has changed the septic requirements in the past 12 months and this can mean expensive upgrading work for those wishing to build. Island rentals are around $7000 to $8000 a year, obtained either by charging a weekly rent or higher rates during the peak summer season. There are relatively more sales on Great Barrier than on Rakino, but both islands continue to be held back by access issues.

About $120,000 might buy a basic bach in the middle of Rakino, and $70,000 a piece of land. Properties on the coast go from $350,000 upwards. Some properties have been bought as investments to be on-sold later. $1.2 million has been paid for a 4ha waterfront block, but not many similar properties are available.

Average sale prices

	House	Flat	No.sales
2002	$262,984	$251,929	392
2003	$344,975	n/a	190

Rental and investment

Typical buyers in the Waiheke investment market are 40-plus investors with multiple properties. With prices moving higher all the time, and rental returns lower than on the mainland, if buyers need a 95% mortgage to buy a rental property the numbers don't always stack up. That said, demand for rental is strong, and average rent for a three-bedroom family home is about $285 to $400 a week, with most priced around $320. A two-bedroom house typically rents for $220 to $250 a week, while a one-bedroom cottage is around $180 to $250 weekly. Top properties with sea views, elevated positions or close to the beach with executive homes rent for $750 upwards. The potential for capital gains is higher on average than many other Auckland suburbs.

Best streets

Any beachfront Waiheke roads like The Strand, Beach Pde, Palm Rd or Waikare Rd.

REAL ESTATE

Schools ★★★

Waiheke Island has two primary schools including the Fossil Bay Steiner School, and another is at the planning stage. The island has the secondary school Waiheke High, and some students commute to colleges in Auckland city. Great Barrier's primary school is Mulberry Grove School.

Shops ★★★

On Waiheke the main shopping area is Oneroa with a supermarket at Ostend and village centres elsewhere. There's also an arts and crafts market. Great Barrier Island has some nice cafes, an Irish pub and several stores.

Leisure ★★★★★

"Waiheke" means cascading waters - referring to the waterfalls now within the Whakanewha Regional Park. In addition to its gorgeous white sand and pebble swimming beaches, it is a great place for sea kayaking, horse riding, golf, fishing and diving, walks in the Forest and Bird reserve at Onetangi, or the Whakanewha Park near Rocky Bay. The island has explorable concrete gun emplacements and mazes of tunnels, built by the army during World War II. In addition to great beaches, much of Great Barrier Island is covered with second generation native trees with pockets of regenerating native forest and remnants of kauri forest in the north. There are the remains of New Zealand's last whaling station, plus the Kaiarara Kauri Dam.

Waiheke has 22 established vineyards, New Zealand arts and crafts display at Artworks, Oneroa, and a museum. The island's annual jazz festival is a hugely popular event. Waiheke has everything from cheap and cheerful eating establishments through to top dining, including The Mud Brick Cafe, Vino Vino and Nourish.

SMART BUY

Yes - if you can afford it. Waiheke beachfront property has been a leading area for capital growth for the past 10 years. The entry price is rapidly becoming less affordable but the island's popularity shows no sign of abating. The new ferry will further increase demand. The island is attractive both to permanent residents because of its proximity to Auckland's CBD and to holidaymakers because of its easy access, great beaches and other recreational features. Sadly, buyers looking for cheap properties in a great location are about seven years too late and will probably come away disappointed.

For colour key, see page 208

Great Barrier Island

Otata Island

Rakino Island

Enclosure Bay
Blackpool
Onetangi   Man O'war Bay
Motuihe Island   Waiheke Island
Omiha   Cowes

Orapiu

Ponui Island

Beachlands
Cockle Bay

Wade Island   Pakihi Island
                        Karamuramu Island
Whitford

Ruakawakawa

Pinpoint Map data supplied by Critchlow Associates Ltd and contains material subject to Crown copyright.

including Eden Tce, Western Springs and Morningside

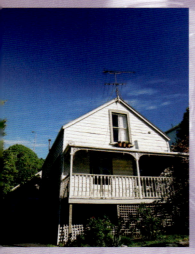

A few years back this inner-city area was quite grungy and dominated by rentals - these days it's the stomping ground of many young urban groovers and professional couples. In the past few years Kingsland's identity as a bohemian, arty neighbourhood has become more defined - as you can see in its funky strip of shops, cafes and galleries. The area's roll call includes many artisans - and unconventional Green MP Nandor Tanczos. Kingsland and Eden Tce's narrow streets and close houses are of a vintage and style similar to nearby Ponsonby. Like Ponsonby this was once a solidly working class area with established Maori and Polynesian communities. Western Springs was considerably more well-to-do with its larger homes and wider streets. Long before the arrival of the north-western motorway and its relentless flow of traffic, the area was a peaceful valley. How times change!

Who lives there?

From its blue collar and predominantly rental origins, the area started to change as keen young buyers bought the grotty do-ups. This process has been going on for more than 10 years now and Kingsland, in particular, has been earmarked as one to watch. During the past few years, the area has become a much more fashionable place to be, which has accelerating the changes already taking place. Nowadays the typical buyers are 30-something city workers, and second- and third-home buyers. Or in the words of one agent, "more high-earning young professionals and legal-beagle types, and less riff-raff."

Western Springs, meanwhile, has developed from a rental into a family area. Part of this has been a natural progression as young couples who bought do-ups have stayed on and had families.

Kingsland, along with the rest of the inner city, is sought-after by returning expats, and this has helped push the process of gentrification along. According to one agent, a third of those attending open homes lately have been expats "desperate to buy". The area's closeness to the city, the club scene and the cafes along Ponsonby, Kingsland and Karangahape Rd also makes it popular with gays. Some of the many Polynesian families remain, many living in homes owned for several generations.

Typical dwellings

These suburbs were established over time so there's a range of house styles from Victorian villas and cottages through to transitional villas and Californian bungalows. Most houses in Kingsland are villas. Because of small section sizes and housing often built on steep streets there are only a handful of subdivided sections with newer townhouses. There is also a growing number of apartment complexes, such as those near the railway line in Morningside or further up New North Rd in Eden Tce.

REAL ESTATE

Trends

Of Kingsland's 600 dwellings, around 10 years ago roughly 500 would have been rented and 100 owner-occupied. These days the numbers are reversed, and with every second house or garden being done up or modified, lots of money is being spent on improvements.

A good example of the direction of the area is the housing development near the motorway originally owned by a Pacific Island trust. Once painted in garish, lollipop colours, the properties degenerated to a very poor state. After being bought and fixed up by developers, with a sophisticated colour scheme, lockable gates and stainless steel appliances they were sold off individually as sought-after dwellings.

Prices are largely dictated by how close you are to the motorway. On the one hand, traffic noise can dampen the value of a property, but quick access to an on-ramp also adds value.

With Eden Tce's nearness to the motorway and mix of residential and commercial properties, parts of it can be noisy and parking can be a problem in its narrow streets. But it is extremely central to the CBD, feeding directly into Upper Queen St and other major routes. Much of Eden Tce has a sunny aspect with views across the valley to Newton and Arch Hill and the area has an idiosyncratic, bohemian character.

Prices

In the mid 1990s an average bungalow on a half site might have gone for $230,000 to $250,000. From 1998 to 1999 the market plateaued, and while properties generally held their value, the rate of sales slowed. Now the same property, without having had any major work done to it, would fetch around $400,000.

Prices in Kingsland have increased dramatically during the past two years, with do-ups going for $400,000. Well-appointed three-bedroom homes, like the big houses along New North Rd or the tidy villas high up on the ridge in Western Springs, are fetching up to $600,000.

Well-built terrace houses and apartment complexes, not affected by leaky building problems, are sought after and hold their value. They are particularly popular among single working women keen on low-maintenance and personal security.

The area has long been scoured for do-ups and while there are still many houses yet to be renovated, very few outright bargains remain.

For total doggy do-ops on a steep street or close to the motorway, buyers have recently paid around $180,000. It's worth remembering that properties with poor locations have an upper-value threshold, even if they are well renovated. The current threshold for such properties is $250,000 to $260,000.

For an entry-level two- to three-bedroom Western Springs bungalow in reasonable condition on a half site, buyers can expect to pay $300,000 to $380,000. A new record price for the area was set in May 2002 when the Western Springs Rd's historic Hastings Hall sold for $1.3 million.

Average sale prices

	House	Flat	No. sales
2002	$312,092	$193,232	256
2003	$399,714	$290,255	123

Rental and investment

Overall, the rental market is high, with properties less affected by motorway noise commanding higher rents. Average rent for a three-bedroom bungalow on a half-site ranges from $380 to $420 a week, and a four-bedroom house fetches $450 to $520.

Best streets

First Ave and Second Ave in Kingsland, and Springfield Rd in Western Springs.

AMENITIES

Schools ★★

Mt Albert Primary is in Morningside and Newton Primary is in Eden Tce. Kowhai Intermediate is off the top of Sandringham Rd. The nearest secondary schools are Auckland Girls Grammar and Western Springs College.

Shops ★★★★

Kingsland's neighbourly main strip of high-fronted Victorian shops includes an assortment of cafes, bakeries, service stores, artist workshops, designer clothing stores, galleries and antique shops. There are commercial outlets like a builder's merchant and plumber's supplies as well as a Briscoes in Morningside. For grocery shopping, locals can choose between the supermarkets at Grey Lynn, in the Eden Quarter along Dominion Rd or St Lukes mall.

Leisure ★★★

Green areas include Western Springs Park, the Auckland Zoo, Fowlds Park, Nixon Park and several smaller reserves.

The area has a number of sports clubs including rugby soccer and cricket. Both the Eden Park and Western Springs Stadiums are within walking distance and the public club of Chamberlain Park Golf Course is next to Western Springs.

Kingsland's strip includes groovy cafés such as Roasted Addiction and well-regarded ethnic restaurants including Canton Café and the Mekong Neua for Thai food. Kingsland has a growing reputation for its night life and the place really pumps in the evenings after there has been something big on at Eden Park.

Local cultural features include the Black Grace Dance company, Workshop 6 arts studio, community organic gardens and several large Pacific Island churches.

Detractors say Kingsland is too hemmed in with the north-western motorway at its base, busy Bond St and New North Rd to the side and top, and the flat-filled Don Croot St on the fourth side.

Motorway noise and visibility holds back value in some streets. Road engineering is a lot more advanced now, than the days when the north-western motorway was built. Impact-reduction measures are well-developed. Now that the inner-city stretch of motorway is no longer lined by cheap rentals, it's time for some retrospective improvements like high fences and strategic tree plantings. Watch this space!

SMART BUY

The area's central location and distinctive character are becoming more appreciated, but prices are still below those of other inner-city areas, and there are plenty of houses waiting to be renovated. These suburbs still, however, follow in the wake of the trends affecting more expensive neighbouring suburbs, so capital gain is highly likely. Another plus is the recent expansion of the nearby St Lukes shopping mall. Kingsland is a protected heritage area under the council's district scheme.

Travel times

From Kingsland shops	
CBD	off-peak 5-7 min peak 15 min
CBD by train	15 min
North-western motorway	5 min
Airport	30 min
St Lukes mall	5 min

Stagecoach Auckland provides a regular service to the area especially along New North Rd, and the Tranz Metro commuter train's Waitakere route includes a stop at Kingsland station, by the Kingsland shops, and Morningside.

For colour key, see page 208

Newton
Arch Hill
Eden Terrace
Kingsland
Morningside
Balmoral

Pinpoint Map data supplied by Critchlow Associates Ltd and contains material subject to Crown copyright.

(For Western Springs, see page 70)

including St Johns and Ellerslie

A lot of Meadowbank is ex-farmland. Many state houses were built here after World War II and many are still owned by Housing New Zealand. By comparison, the suburb of St Johns Park is less than 25 years old and clusters around the Remuera Golf Club. Quite a bit of boundary fudging goes on between Meadowbank and the more upmarket Remuera, and between Meadowbank and St Johns Park. Basically, St Johns Park is everything south of St Johns Rd, west of College Rd, north of Abbott's Way and east of Grand Dr. Meadowbank is to the north of St Johns Rd, and at the end of St Johns Rd is an area sometimes referred to as Old St Johns, which these days is closer in character to Glenn Innes. Neighbouring Ellerslie has a strong sense of local identity among residents. The more desirable part of the suburb, Ellerslie Heights, has views across the racecourse to One Tree Hill.

Who lives there?

There are many middle-income families in Meadowbank, with richer pockets in St John's Park around the golf course. Significant numbers of Asian buyers have moved into the area in recent years. St Johns and Meadowbank have never been first-home buyer territory and are popular with high-earning, dual-income couples who can support relatively high levels of debt.

Ellerslie is considered more desirable than neighbouring Mt Wellington (the border between the two runs up the middle of Ballarat St) and some believe it is better value than Remuera. It has many family homes and more second-home buyers.

Typical dwellings

Meadowbank has lots of 1940s bungalows, many of which are solid ex-state houses. The late 1950s and early 1960s saw a further building boom. Most properties are on full sites, with relatively little infill. There are no empty sections but some houses are ripe for removal. Consequently, there are many developers hovering.

Over in St Johns Park, houses are typically much newer and there are still some sections available. The area has more infill housing.

Infill housing is also common in Ellerslie. Land is expensive and there is high demand for large houses. The bigger, older bungalows that might have once only sold to developers are now increasingly being sought out by families. Around the Ladies Mile/Pukerangi Cres intersection, some grand old merchants' houses can still be seen, mostly hiding behind ivy-clad walls or stands of trees.

There are some old villas and bungalows but generally fewer than across the southern motorway in One Tree Hill. New terrace housing complexes have been built near the village during recent years, and there are a few older units.

At the Ellerslie/Mt Wellington border there are two and three-level housing developments such as Ellerslie Piazza Terraces and Ellerslie Court.

REAL ESTATE

Trends

According to real estate agents, Meadowbank has recently experienced a significant increase in market confidence and volume of sales. But they maintain that Meadowbank has not experienced the 14% growth that other suburbs have over the past year.

Ellerslie has been in demand for the past five years, especially the past three. These days, families are buying sections to build on rather than developers.

St Johns Park has a lot of leasehold land owned by the St Johns Trust. Depending on the terms of the lease and ground rents, leaseholds make properties cheaper and therefore an attractive entry point.

Prices

Entry level in Meadowbank is in the mid $300,000s, which will buy a "fairly tired" two- to three-bedroom ex-state house, on a generous piece of dirt (say 650-700m²). Meadowbank property tops out at $650,000 to $750,000.

Entry level in St Johns for a leasehold property is around $130,000 for a two-bedroom unit. In St Johns Park, entry level buyers can get three-bedroom townhouses in the early $300,000s. At the upper end a new, top quality townhouse will cost around the mid $500,000s and up. Top

prices achieved are just under $900,000.

The top price bracket for Ellerslie is $500,000 plus. For that buyers can expect a new solid plaster townhouse with four or five bedrooms, double garage, several living rooms and possibly a pool. At the other end of the scale a new two-bedroom terrace house on the border of Ellerslie and Mt Wellington is around $240,000. A renovated villa will easily command over $350,000.

Average sale prices

	House	Flat	No. sales
2002	$545,996	$348,460	1252
2003	$433,513	$243,202	733

Rental and investment

St Johns has more rentals than Meadowbank; an average 20-year-old home or ex-state with three bedrooms rents for around $300 to $350 a week, whereas the equivalent in Meadowbank is closer to $380. St John's Park is more pricey and its houses larger. Typical rent for a near-new townhouse is $600-650 a week. For a decent house in Ellerslie, you're looking at between $420 and $500 a week.

Best streets

Any by the golf course in St Johns Park such as Panapa Dr, Coldham Cres and Charles Fox Pl. There's no stand-out in Ellerslie because of the mixed nature of most streets. Meadowbank's Temple St is well considered.

AMENITIES

Schools ★★★

Throughout the three suburbs there are as many as six primary schools including several private primaries, the Michael Park and Rudolf Steiner School and the sought-after

Local hero - Michael Park and Rudolf Steiner School

There are only two Steiner schools in Auckland - in Titirangi and in Ellerslie. The Michael Park and Rudolf Steiner School was founded in 1978 as a result of parent initiative. It is a state integrated co-ed area school applying the educational principles of the early 20th century philosopher Rudolf Steiner, who developed the concept of anthroposophy, or wisdom, of the human being. The school's teaching methods are based on a close observation of the phases in a child's development and work with each one's unfolding needs. Today, it has around 430 pupils from kindergarten to high school levels.

Meadowbank Primary. Remuera Intermediate borders Ellerslie. Glendowie College is a popular nearby secondary.

Shops ★★★

The Meadowbank shopping complex was revamped five years ago and includes a new-look Foodtown supermarket. Ellerslie's shopping is village style, with small shops, eateries and coffee bars.

Leisure ★★★

The large Waiatarua Reserve has excellent walkways, and is popular with joggers. It is still used for grazing cows, an unusual sight in the middle of suburbia. This and Michaels Ave Reserve have small bird sanctuaries - so keep the dog on the lead. There is also the Remuera Golf Club, racecourse, numerous smaller reserves and the lovely grounds of St John's Theological College.

The Auckland Racing Club's Ellerslie Racecourse hosts some of the country's biggest horse racing events and incorporates a golf driving range and nine-hole course, convention facilities, and a plant nursery. A car fair is held there every Sunday morning. A Lollipop's Playland and a Montessori School are also on the grounds. There are a number of sports clubs catering for squash, bowling, cricket, rugby and rugby league. There is the YMCA, New Zealand Grand Prix Club, Auckland Motorcycle Club, and the Ellerslie Theatrical Society-Stables Theatre.

Ellerslie has restaurants including The Cock & Bull pub, a bawdy English-style tavern popular with the locals.

Meadowbank has a community centre, and St John's College. St John's Ambulance training school is also in the area.

LOOK OUT!

The planned eastern corridor highway through Auckland's eastern suburbs may have a large impact on Meadowbank. Though unconfirmed, the "Quarry corridor" option would run from Meadowbank over Remuera Golf Course and through to the east of Mt Wellington. Parts of Meadowbank that may be affected include: Tahapa West Reserve, Tahapa Cres, Mamaku St, Koa St, Meadowbank Rd, Mara St, Harapaki Rd, Temple St, Lucia Glade, Blackett Cres, Kinder Pl, St Johns Rd, Meadowbank Shopping Centre and Norman Lesser Dr.

Travel times

From Meadowbank

CBD	off-peak 15 min peak 20-25 min
Britomart CBD by train	8 min
Southern motorway	5 min
Airport	30 min
Remuera shops	5 min
Newmarket shops	10 min
From Ellerslie	
Britomart CBD by train	14 min

Stagecoach Auckland and Howick & Eastern Buses provide regular services especially along major arteries like the Ellerslie-Panmure Highway and St Johns Road. The Tranz Metro train stops at Ellerslie and Meadowbank.

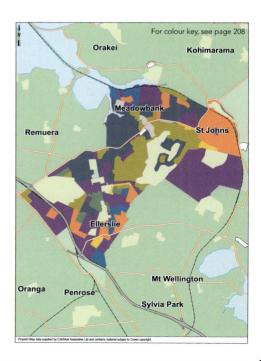

For colour key, see page 208

Orakei | Kohimarama
Meadowbank
Remuera | St Johns
Ellerslie
Oranga | Penrose | Mt Wellington
Sylvia Park

Pinpoint Map data supplied by Critchlow Associates Ltd and contains material subject to Crown copyright.

including Sandringham, St Lukes and Owairaka

If you're looking for a typical cross-section of Aucklanders, look no further than Mt Albert. This large suburb has everyone from rich residents living in genteel tree-lined streets to relatively poor immigrants renting in blocks of flats. Mt Albert suburb sprawls around its namesake extinct volcano. From the hill's summit there are spectacular views over the Waitemata and Manukau Harbours, and the houses on Mt Albert's northern slopes have striking views back towards the city centre. Mt Albert is part of the Bible-belt strip that runs from Avondale through to Mt Roskill, so there are lots of churches, and as a consequence of the district's time as a dry area it has no unsightly taverns. On the other side of Mt Albert, the flat suburb of Sandringham is often used as a spill-over suburb for people who can't afford Mt Eden.

Who lives there?

Traditionally Mt Albert was a solid Kiwi middle to working-class suburb. Now, it's much more cosmopolitan, and younger. Mt Albert's residents include a number of Polynesian families plus Indians, Sri Lankans and other ethnic groups. There's a Somali community in Owairaka.

A major change to the area's ethnic composition has been the recent influx of Asian students, attracted to the area's tertiary institutions, namely Unitec on Carrington Rd and the privately owned AIS St Helens on Asquith Ave. AIS specialises in language and commercial studies, and most of its students are Asian. There is a wider ethnic mix at Unitec, with about 50% being Asian. As well as the growing student numbers, the working-age sector of Mt Albert's population has got bigger compared to retirees. This is because young families are attracted to the area's solid homes, large sections, and good schools.

Typical dwellings

Much of Mt Albert was established 70 or so years ago from farmland. Typical houses include bungalows, state houses, and large family homes. It also has a few villas as well

as modern houses on half sites. Sandringham has bungalows and villas which are generally not as grand as those found in neighbouring Mt Eden. There is also a lot of state housing, much of it now passed to private ownership. There is not a lot of infill housing here because of its generally smaller sections. Sandringham also suffers from a smattering of ugly 1960s and 1970s blocks of flats.

REAL ESTATE

Trends

The further development of St Lukes mall and the surrounding commercial zone has increased the desirability of this area. New apartment complexes continue to appear over the area, especially on major arterial routes. A block of apartments on the corner of Western Springs Rd and New North Rd that sat uncompleted for a number of months is now finished and tenanted. Futher development in this area includes the conversion of factory space to apartments along Morningside Dr, plus a block of around 250 apartments next to St Lukes where construction was delayed but will now begin.

Rising prices can lead to rapid property turnover as speculative buyers enter the market. One example is an average Sandringham house that was bought this year for $219,000 and sold again six weeks later for $278,000.

Trends pushing prices in the area continue to be low interest rates and steady immigration numbers. Houses in average condition are tending to sell about 25% to 30% above the current CV that came out in September 2002.

Prices

At entry level in Mt Albert around $300,000 gets a reasonable condition ex-state house on a half site. Two-bedroom units on the edge of Sandringham and Mt Roskill can sell around $195,000. Character bungalows that need doing up sell in the high $300,000s, and anything renovated usually sells over $400,000. The asking price for new townhouses, featuring four bedrooms and three bathrooms, is now up to $650,000.

The best homes in Mt Albert are priced between $600,000 and $900,000 with the top end of the market going over a million. One four-bedroom Mt Albert Rd property with a granny flat sold for $1.5 million. But most properties range within the $500,000 to $700,000 price bracket.

The neighbouring suburb of Sandringham is generally cheaper, but anything in the area that is subdividable can fetching from the mid $300,000s up. Sandringham prices are being driven up by developers who are competing with families; one recent Sandringham do-up sold for $410,000 after there were nine serious bidders. An ordinary three-bedroom Sandringham villa in need of work and with no garage sold for $420,000 a year or so ago and again in mid 2003 for $565,000.

Average sale prices

	House	Flat	No. sales
2002	$311,743	$202,464	902
2003	$386,444	$196,006	739

Rental and investment

Last year Mt Albert's rental market was very strong, largely due to students who studied in the area and wanted to rent locally. Over the past few months rental demand has dropped away somewhat. As a popular area for investment it is possible that too many people investing in rental properties and a slow down in the number of Asian students coming to the area has caused an oversupply. The current surplus properties on the market means a property that would have rented at $450 per week six months ago, now rents at $360. Others that rented at $460, nine months ago, now rent at $420. Typical three-bedroom average condition bungalows rent at around $350 or more depending on the state of the property. For an executive home with features such as a swimming pool and a large landscaped garden, rents are closer to $880 per week.

Best streets

In Mt Albert, it's Stilwell Rd, Summit Dr and the surrounding streets. In Sandringham, it's the roads nearest Mt Eden, essentially those north of Balmoral Rd, and those with more villas or bungalows than state houses.

AMENITIES

Schools ★★★★

Mt Albert is well served for schools including four primary schools (two private, two public). Gladstone School is very popular and is Auckland's largest primary school. There are at

Why I live there

Deputy vice chancellor of AUT, Derek McCormack

Says Derek: "I like Mt Albert because it's very central without being right in town. I like the sense of separation between the city and here, where we can have a big section and lots of established trees. It's not as expensive as suburbs like Mt Eden and has none of its snob value. But you can still get a good coffee and breakfast at the shops as well as lots of Asian food. As a community it is very diverse. There are still some Polynesian families around plus lots of other nationalities, especially Asian students who've made a big impact on the local shops. There are plenty of old RSA types who are of the generation who whistle when they work in the garden."

least another three schools in the suburbs of Sandringham and Owairaka.

Many children from Mt Albert go to Kowhai Intermediate in Kingsland. Secondary schools include Mt Albert Grammar and Hebron Christian College. There is also the total immersion Maori school Te Kura Kaupapa Maori O Nga Maungarongo.

At tertiary level, Unitec Institute of Technology and Auckland Institute of Studies St Helen's are in the area.

Shops ★★★★

The impact of the Asian student population is obvious at Mt Albert's once standard strip of shops which has become noticeably younger and cyber-orientated, and now features more late model cars, numerous noodle bars, and at least three internet cafes. Older locals complain that the shops have been "taken over" and that there is now nowhere to park.

Westfield St Lukes shopping centre is one of the largest in New Zealand.

Sandringham shopping strip is having a bit of a makeover with the first stage, the burying of overhead power and phone lines, nearing completion. Stage two will see the installation of new footpaths, paving, lighting, trees and street furniture.

Leisure ★★★

Green areas include Owairaka Park around the Mt Albert summit, Alan Wood Reserve, Unitec's landscaped grounds, the popular Rocket Park and others.

Mt Albert has many sporting facilities and clubs, including the Philips Aquatic Centre with its wave pool, the Mt Albert Recreation Centre (YMCA), and clubs for tennis, karate, rugby, croquet and bowling. There is also the Chamberlain Park Golf Course (public), the Crystal Palace Theatre and the Mt Albert Aquatic Centre. Unitec has a gymnasium, squash and other sports facilities.

Alberton, a colonial home museum built in 1862 at the foot of Mt Albert, is open for functions.

Mt Albert's range of eateries has benefited from the arrival of new nationalities to the area. They include the Sing Court, Hong Thai, the Mt Albert BBQ Noodle House and Balti House. There is also a Croatian-run Baker Boy pizza café, and for coffee there is the Trinity of Silver cafe.

SMART BUY

House prices in areas with good schools and a reputation for being solid community suburbs, with good amenities, may ease off in lean times but will never plummet.

Travel times
From Mt Albert shops

CBD by car	off-peak 8 min peak 12 min
CBD by bus	peak 25 min
North-western motorway	5 min
Airport	30 min
St Lukes mall	5 min

Mt Albert has excellent public transport with Stagecoach Auckland providing regular services, and the Tranz Metro commuter train running through Mt Albert on the Waitakere route. Buses travel regularly through Sandringham and especially around St Lukes shopping mall.

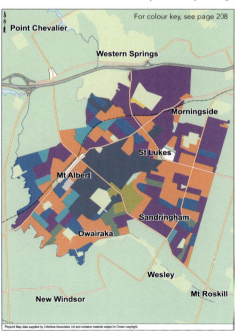

For colour key, see page 208

Point Chevalier
Western Springs
Morningside
St Lukes
Mt Albert
Sandringham
Owairaka
Wesley
New Windsor
Mt Roskill

Pinpoint Map data supplied by Critchlow Associates Ltd and contains material subject to Crown copyright.

including Three Kings and Balmoral

Mt Eden may be regarded as more ethnically and socio-economically diverse, and therefore more interesting, than its staid neighbour Epsom, but it's still pretty much the domain of good middle- to upper-class families wanting the quiet life. A key factor is that a third of the suburb is in the Auckland Grammar School and Epsom Girls' Grammar School zones. One fabulous feature of Mt Eden is, of course, the extinct volcano Mt Eden; another is its lovely tree-lined streets and established gardens.

Nearby Balmoral is not so much a distinct suburb from Mt Eden as a quarter of it. Balmoral has benefited from the flow-on effect of its neighbour's popularity; the trend of doing-up dumpy old renters and turning them into family homes is well underway here. The small area of Three Kings still has a lot of state rentals but is being discovered by those who can't afford Mt Eden or Balmoral.

Who lives there?

Locals tend to be loyal Edenites, and like its trendy reputation as "home of the arts". Given the area's gentrification, though, the suburb is probably not quite the arty or bohemian enclave that many residents fondly imagine, but is rather more bourgeois these days.

The area is very much a solidly middle-class family suburb of predominantly European and Asian ethnicity, and significant numbers of Indians and Polynesians. All the local primary schools appear to be bursting at the seams due to the district's numerous young families. Anywhere in the grammar zone is highly sought after by families with teenagers, or some families move east to Epsom or Remuera when their children reach secondary school age.

Typical dwellings

Mt Eden has lots of big old villas of a chunky style, with a mix of Californian bungalows and transitional villas. Mt Eden and Epsom used to be quite similar, but there was a lot less development in Mt Eden than Epsom during the 1980s due to legislative differences between the two areas. Simply put, it was easier for developers to operate in Epsom so Mt Eden doesn't have as many of the flasher townhouses as Epsom. Subdivided sections, infill and modern townhouses are still in the minority. These days, most of Mt Eden is zoned 6A residential.

There are also a fair number of low-level sausage block one- and two-bedroom brick-and-tile units in the area, plus a couple of recently built terrace apartment blocks. There are still some fairly horrible 1960s and 1970s single and double-storey blocks of flats spoiling otherwise attractive streets of character villas - the upper end of Grange Rd is a classic example.

The large Eden One and Eden Two terraced housing development is at the northern end of Mt Eden, a bit hidden amongst the surrounding commercial buildings.

Balmoral has some large bungalows. From Mt Eden village towards the city, the sections are on average smaller, while larger sections are generally found between the village and Balmoral Rd. Three Kings has a lot of ex-state housing of the brick and weatherboard or brick-and-tile variety typical of the 1940s and 1950s.

REAL ESTATE

Trends

The Mt Eden market continues to be strong, with demand on houses in the grammar zone continuing to push up prices in those parts of

Mt Eden. According to one agent the market really lifted in February 2003, with prices taking off after that time. The positive flow on effect of high Mt Eden prices also continues throughout the wider suburb to Three Kings and Balmoral and on to neighbouring areas such as Sandringham and Mt Roskill. Typical buyers in the area, according to local agents, are people who are trading up on the basis of the capital gain on existing properties - in other words they are buying big because they are selling big. Other buyers are frequently wealthy immigrants or young couples with big double incomes, confidence in the market and high debt tolerance. There are lots of cash buyers and prices are being driven up by a shortage of properties on the market.

Construction of apartment blocks and terrace house complexes are continuing at both the city end and Three Kings end of Mt Eden road. Some apartment dwellers convert their garages into offices and operate businesses from home. There is also huge demand for duplexes and the smaller brick and tile properties as a way for young professional couples to get into the area.

Between Mt Eden and Dominion Rds are lots of classic ex-state houses that are now really coming into their own due to the upward pressure of other properties in the area.

Prices

Even $500,000 doesn't buy much anywhere within close radius of Mt Eden village or in the grammar zone. According to statistics from June 2003, 22% of sales were at $250,000 and below, 29% of sales fell in the $250,000 and $500,000 range, 38% between $500,000 and $750,000, and 9% were from $750,000 to $1 million and more.

At entry level one-bedroom units in a block of four to eight flats cost around $160,000 to $170,000. For a house, entry level prices are in the high $300,000s to mid $400,000s. For that you might get an unrenovated bungalow on a half site at the Three Kings end of the suburb. Properties in the heart of Mt Eden or anything with "a bit extra" regularly sell over $700,000. A renovated property on a reasonable site (say 500 to 600m^2) can sell for $1 million plus depending on the quality of the refurbishment.

Two-bedroom duplexes can sell for $350,000 and above. One tiny little old villa with no garage on an equally tiny section at the city end of Mt Eden was bought in early 2003 for $407,000, and sold again recently for close to $700,000 after it was extended and renovated. Another totally renovated out-of-zone three-bedroom house was sold lately for $710,000. A few properties sell for over $1 million, but there are not a lot of them.

A two-bedroom unit in a large block in the Auckland Grammar zone currently costs in the low to mid $200,000s. One property - an absolute do-up on a 480m^2 site in zone for Grammar - was recently valued in the high $400,000s. Another example is an in-zone, large Valley Rd villa, needing major work done, that sold in February 2003 for $435,000, and again in April for $485,000, with no improvements having been made.

Another Valley Rd property that sold in October 2002 for $435,000 was resold in August 2003 for $840,000 after being extensively renovated and extended.

Reasonable bungalows on a half site in zone for the popular Maungawhau Primary school are at least $450,000, and $600,000 for anything on a full section. Entry level in Balmoral is generally over $400,000 for two to three-bedroom bungalows on a half site. Fully renovated Balmoral villas sell from the

Why I live there
Photographer Gil Hanly

Gil Hanly and artist husband Pat bought their Mt Eden "quarter-acre five minutes from Queen St" in the early 1990s. As one of New Zealand's best-known garden photographers, Gil was attracted by the area's rich free-draining volcanic soil as well as its central position. A pick-axe is an essential gardening tool in these parts and Gil is building a series of low walls with the rocks she digs up. On the property, Gil has managed to fit a tropical garden, a number of fruit trees plus a kitchen garden. "It's good for the grandchildren to learn where vegetables come from. I can send them out to pick parsley, gather cape-gooseberries, or help shell the peas."

$450,000s to the $500,000s. An unrenovated three-bedroom bungalow on a half site at the southern (Three Kings) end of Mt Eden costs around $400,000. A good quality four-bedroom townhouse on a subdivided site costs $600,000 to $800,000 depending on where it is, and small two or possibly three-bedroom terrace houses sell in the late $200,000s and upwards.

There is still some subdividing going on, but most that can be done has been done, and this is adding to a shortage of central city land. One steep but subdividable Three Kings property with a good view was bought for $485,000 in mid 2003, and sold again a few months later for $480,000, after the owners had moved the dwelling over a bit and subdivided the remaining half of the section.

Average sale prices

	House	Flat	No. sales
2002	$344,151	$226,141	1029
2003	$489,257	$216,680	535

Best streets

Anything in grammar zones and those streets close to the Mt Eden village. Fairview Rd, and Woodside Rd have some big gracious houses as do Horoeka Ave and Bellevue Rd at the northern end of Mt Eden.

Rental and investment

The rental market has softened a little at the top end of the market in the past three or four months. A 350m² property that would have fetched over $1500 a week during the America's Cup, now might only get $1200 to $1300, and finding a tenant could be difficult. The top of the market also typically goes quieter in winter. It is a small market and doesn't have a huge impact on the middle and lower rental market. Reasonable condition three-bedroom homes that might have rented a while ago at $550 to $600 a week are now closer to $500. One-bedroom flats range in price between $200 and $275 a week, with reasonable condition one-bedroom units renting for around $250 a week. Two-bedroom flats are from $280 to $380 a week, and three-bedroom houses are anything from $340 a week upwards.

AMENITIES

Schools ★★★★

There are eight primary schools in these suburbs including the popular Maungawhau School, and the area has two intermediates. Mt Eden has no secondary schools, but about a third of the suburb is zoned for Auckland and Epsom Girls grammar schools. Other parts of Mt Eden are zoned for Mt Roskill and Mt Albert grammar schools which also have good reputations. At the tertiary level there is the Auckland College of Education and the Auckland City Art School.

Shops ★★★★

Despite the busyness of Mt Eden Rd, the Mt Eden shops from Valley Rd down have a pleasant village atmosphere much valued by locals. They include delicatessens, bakeries, butchers, and a fish shop as well as bookshops and unique toy shops. There are more shops near the Mt Eden Prison, including specialist foodie store Sabato, and now the area is no longer "dry" there are a number of pubs including De Post (a Belgian beer cafe) in the old Mt Eden Post Office. New specialty shops include a take-home gourmet food store and a cookbook shop.

The shops known as the Eden Quarter, at the city end of Dominion Rd, have a 24-hour Foodtown supermarket and boutique shops. Along Dominion Rd are a range of service stores and fabulous shops for bargain hunters such as Antique Alley, and Geoff's Emporium. The Three Kings shopping centre isn't much to speak of, with a supermarket and a sad mall.

Leisure ★★★★

As well as the obvious Mt Eden Domain, the area has numerous smaller parks and reserves including Edenvale Reserve, Nicholson Park, Potters Park, Taylor Reserve and Centennial Park. At Three Kings there is the Big King Reserve and Three Kings Park. Mt Eden has numerous sports clubs for tennis and squash, soccer, bowling, and more.

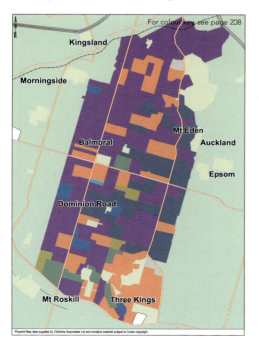

For colour key see page 208

Pinpoint Map data supplied by Critchlow Associates Ltd and contains material subject to Crown copyright.

There is also the Mt Eden Swimming Pool, and, of course, Eden Park which is the site of many historic rugby encounters.

For residents around Eden Park the stadium is both a blessing and curse; when games are on the parking is terrible, surrounding streets become very congested, and there is the inconvenience of noise and light pollution from evening games. On the other hand, it's pretty convenient for local fans.

During the past 10 years Mt Eden has gained a good selection of restaurants, like Bowmans. Dominion Rd also offers a diverse range of national cuisines and cafes. Among Balmoral's best are Tusk Thai Restaurant and Bombay Duck. At the northern end of Mt Eden you'll find a cluster of quirky cafes and an Irish pub.

SMART BUY

Yes. Demand for distinctive central suburbs like Mt Eden and Balmoral with excellent schools and well proportioned villas and bungalows can only continue. Three Kings has seen price rises, but is still good buying with its more humble dwellings and lesser profile, fairly conveniently situated for the city, the airport, and major shopping centres from Westfield St Lukes to Onehunga.

Travel times
From Mt Eden village

CBD	off-peak 10 min
	peak 30 min
North-western motorway	10 min
Southern motorway	5 min
Airport	30 min
St Lukes mall	5 min

Balmoral is clustered around Dominion Rd, which runs directly out from the heart of the city in a straight line. Another major arterial, Balmoral/St Lukes Rd, runs at right angles, making Balmoral very conveniently located. Dominion Rd is, however, quite congested so travelling times are hard to predict. Stagecoach Auckland provides a regular service to all suburbs in this area. Dominion Rd, Mt Eden Rd and Balmoral Rd are all major bus corridors.

Pimples on the landscape

Mt Eden, Mt Albert, Mt Wellington, Three Kings, One Tree Hill… we proudly call them mountains, but on the worldwide scale of great volcanoes, they're really only hills or "little pimples", as Auckland University geologist Dr Ian Smith likes to call them.

They may be small in stature, but they're a big part of Auckland's tourist marketing, as the most visible features of Auckland's active volcanic field. Regional authorities have even created "viewing protection planes" so that no large buildings obscure the views from key vantage points, which is why the Sky Tower wasn't allowed to be built in Symonds St, where it would have stolen Mt Eden's limelight.

These days, the mountains have been protected as parks and domains for our enjoyment. They're regarded by the experts as extinct, although the Auckland volcanic field could reawaken at any time. Any future eruptions will occur somewhere else in the field where new cones will be formed, says Dr Smith. The Wellington-based Institute of Geological and Nuclear Sciences and the Auckland Regional Council work together to monitor the field round the clock for any signs of earth movement that would give us - based on overseas experience - several days' to several weeks' warning of a pending eruption. Some comfort, maybe!

The mountains we see today are just a few of the volcanic features from several past

eruptions, the earliest of which created Lake Pupuke on the North Shore. Uncertainty has surrounded the real age of the lake but new data puts its age at about 250,000 years old, not the 149,000 years as previously thought, says Dr Smith.

This lake, along with the Panmure Basin, the Onepoto Basin, Pigeon Mountain, Mangere Mountain, Mt Victoria and North Head are some of the 50 or so volcanic features that make up the landscape - and the walls you see on Mt Eden properties that have been built of volcanic scoria rocks.

Before the mountains were protected, they were quarried for scoria to the extent that Three Kings, which was originally five peaks, is now just one.

Most of our visible mountains are less than 30,000 years old. Mt Eden dates back 23,000 years and Mt Wellington was formed about 10,000 years ago. Rangitoto Island is Auckland's most recent volcano, formed some 700 years ago.

including Hillsborough and Waikowhai

If you move to Mt Roskill, you'd better bring your Bible. That's been the traditional view of this suburb with its wealth of churches and reputation for fundamentalist Christian thinking. That's changing a little as the area attracts a growing range of races and religions. With the incoming immigrant families, it now also has many more children than it once had. To the south, Hillsborough has great views of the Manukau Harbour. Many Aucklanders know Hillsborough only as a "through suburb" en route to the airport and Manukau City. But some parts are quite private and leafy with the most sought-after spots being those on the seaward side of Hillsborough Rd.

Nearby Waikowhai lost its identity when it lost its post office, and has quietly merged into Hillsborough. It is also overshadowed by Lynfield, which is newer and a bit more expensive. Like Hillsborough, Waikowhai's coastal properties look across the Manukau.

Who lives there?

The area doesn't tend to attract many first home buyers. These days it is very multicultural - according to government statistics there are 169 different ethnicities represented in the Mt Roskill borough. Many of the people buying into Mt Roskill and Sandringham continue to be Indian, Korean, Chinese and Somalian plus a minority of Middle Eastern peoples. One agent estimated that 80% of recent buyers have been immigrants, with the remaining 20% consisting of New Zealanders buying investment properties. As one agent put it: "the area used to be Auckland's Bible belt - now it's more like downtown Bombay."

Typical dwellings

Mt Roskill was mostly developed in the 1950s and Hillsborough in the 1950s and 1960s. There's a mix of brick base, tile roof weatherboard bungalows, and brick-and-tile bungalows of 1950s vintage - good modest suburban homes. Solid ex-state houses are also common. Extensive subdividing and infill housing means there are now also many newer townhouses and single-level modular houses. About 70% of subdividable properties have already been chopped up. Mt Roskill South is a subdivision developed

from the 1980s onwards with executive-style homes. Due to recent zone changes, the area is now zoned for Lynfield College and not Mt Roskill Grammar School.

There has been a new apartment block built in Mt Roskill called Key Stone Ridge Apartments - a first for Mt Roskill.

REAL ESTATE

Trends

The transfer of some of the Mt Roskill school zone to Lynfield College has affected prices in the area. Mt Roskill South, which tends to have the better houses, and the sea-view side of Hillsborough, are now part of the less-sought-after Lynfield zone, which has intensified demand for properties that remain in the Mt Roskill zone.

The arrival of new immigrants and expats in the area, and lack of properties has had a spill-over effect into the rental market. Recent demand for rentals "overwhelmed" supply in the area, but this has dropped off somewhat. A lot of the people who came into the area over the past two years and took up rental properties are now buying in the area - where possible they buy in zone. Land is still available - but only in the form of crossleased sections. Subdivision continues as a trend, with the larger, four-bedroom townhouses on half sites proving very popular with immigrant families.

Prices
Entry level at the fringe of Mt Roskill is around $195,000 upwards for a two-bedroom unit in a block. Elsewhere in the area, units have been selling for around $220,000. Three-bedroom bungalows in Mt Roskill South typically sell in the low $300,000s. Two-bedroom houses sell for $250,000 to $265,000 upwards, with the cheapest three-bedroom properties going for $280,000 upwards. One tidy but original condition three-bedroom fibrolite and tile ex-state house with a half site on a busy in-zone street recently sold for $272,000.

At the top end of the market in Mt Roskill new townhouses sell in the mid $400,000s - even for properties on a half site with an ex-state house in the front. For $350,000 to $450,000, buyers might still get a subdividable site - but there are very few available.

Average house prices in Hillsborough are from $300,000 upwards, and basic homes with a sea view along roads such as Hillsborough Rd and Donovan St now cost $400,000 upwards. Below this, more humble houses such as older two-bedroom cottages start at around $260,000. If you want to buy a unit in a block of two or three, you can expect to pay between $200,000 and $300,000. Forty-year-old, three-bedroom homes typically cost around $400,000 and modern townhouses around $500,000. The top of the market in Hillsborough is around the $1 million mark, and premium properties have sold for $1 million plus in nearby Lynfield.

Average sale prices
	House	Flat	No.sales
2002	$272,233	$190,525	523
2003	$329,771	$226,119	457

Rental and investment
At the height of recent "silly prices" some two-bedroom dwellings in this area were being rented out for more than $300 per week, but rates have dropped back since then. Rental demand slows over winter, but picks up a bit from August on, when families typically start thinking about enrolling their children in schools. One two-bedroom brick and tile unit in a block of three, returning a rent of around $240 a week, sold in 2002 for $195,000 and again in 2003 for $225,000. Two-bedroom dwellings in average condition can return rents of $290 to $315 a week, with rents from $380 to $400 plus for average three and four-bedroom houses.

Investors buy both units as well as family homes to rent. The area's renters are typically families rather than flatters (unlike the inner city suburbs). Two-bedroom homes are most in demand because they are cheaper for families to rent. One- and two-bedroom units in the Mt Roskill Grammar zone rent for up to $300 per week, and around $260 to $280 if not in zone. Three-bedroom homes in zone rent between $350 and $390, with $400 to $450 per week for something with four bedrooms.

Best streets
In Hillsborough, any street near the sea. In Mt Roskill, Stamford Park Rd and Oakdale Rd.

AMENITIES

Schools ★★★★
There are at least four public primary schools in the area, one private plus Sunnydene Special School. There is huge demand to get in the Mt Roskill Primary zone. At the intermediate level there is Mt Roskill and Waikowhai Intermediates. Mt Roskill Grammar is a very popular school with a roll of 2300. The school zone has been decreased recently. Lynfield College caters for many Asian and overseas students. The private and co-ed Marcellin College on Mt Albert Rd is also a popular choice with Hillsborough residents.

Shops ★★
Mt Roskill has a modest strip of shops, otherwise there is the Three Kings shopping centre and St Lukes mall not far away. There is also a new 24-hour Countdown and shopping complex in nearby Lynfield.

Leisure ★★★
Mount Roskill has about 12ha of parks and reserves including the major sports facility Keith Hay Park, Winstone Park and the War Memorial Park. The area has two beaches - they're tidal so not the greatest for swimming but are popular with boaties and windsurfers.

The area is well served for sports with the two

nearby golf clubs Akarana and Maungakiekie, the Lynfield Recreation Centre (YMCA) and Cameron Pool (Roskill Aquasport). Sports clubs in the area include the New Zealand Hockey Federation, the Eden Roskill District Cricket Club, as well as clubs for bowling, rugby, soccer and tennis.

Now that dry areas are a thing of the past and with the area's multinational composition, there is more culinary variety in Mt Roskill than before, including lots of ethnic food outlets.

LOOK OUT!

The long-proposed motorway extension from Hugh Watt Dr will ultimately link Hillsborough with Richardson Rd and may negatively affect demand for nearby properties during construction. When finished, the project will result in a 4km motorway extension from the Queenstown Rd interchange, with further interchanges at Hillsborough Rd and Dominion Rd. There will also be bridges across the motorway at Hayr Rd and May Rd. Dedicated pedestrian and cycle bridges will be provided at Keith Hay Park and Ernie Pinches St. The project also includes a cycleway along the southern side of the motorway extension. The extension will end at a roundabout and a local road will provide a new link between Maioro Rd and Sandringham Rd. Thereafter, the motorway will continue with the proposed SH20 Avondale extension.

Once the project is completed, the motorway extension will significantly relieve the pressure on the major arterial routes Dominion Rd and Hillsborough Rd as well as surrounding smaller roads. The estimated cost of the SH20 Mt Roskill extension is $139 million.

The project has reached the surveying and property buying stage, and the official word is that all resource consents have been obtained and most property purchases concluded. Detailed design is near completion. Subject to the successful outcome of a major projects review, construction is due to begin in 2004. Signs of progress in the area include the purchase of properties, including a number at the back of Mt Roskill Grammar, the moving of the bus depot and relocation of businesses along Carr Rd.

The area around Wesley may experience a lift in prices after the motorway extension is completed - potential buyers should look closely at where the motorway is going and buy accordingly.

SMART BUY

Yes - apart from leafy parts of Hillsborough and places with a sea view, this is not the most sophisticated part of town but it has plenty of pluses - close to Unitec and only 10 minutes from the city outside of rush hour, and with Mt Roskill Grammar rating as one of the top academic and sporting secondary schools nationally. Yet it is still relatively affordable compared to the inner city

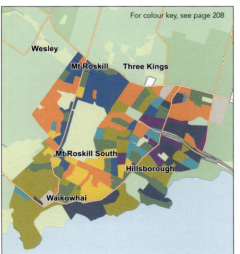

For colour key, see page 208

Wesley

Mt Roskill   Three Kings

Mt Roskill South

Hillsborough

Waikowhai

Travel times
From Mt Roskill shops

CBD	off-peak 15-20 min
	30-40 min
Airport	10-15 min
St Lukes mall	10 min
Royal Oak shops	10 min

Hillsborough is handy for residents wanting to get to the airport, but otherwise it's a bit land-locked. Mt Roskill residents rely on major arterials such as Dominion and Mt Albert Rds.

including Oranga, Te Papapa and Penrose

Onehunga is a suburb that has long been tipped as "one to watch". Only 20 years ago, Ponsonby was very similar to this historic port town. Onehunga's champions compare it to Kingsland and Avondale, a Pacific suburb characterised by turn of the century villas and bungalows. The insurmountable difference is location - one is within minutes of the CBD, near the sparkling yacht-filled Waitemata. Onehunga, instead, has the Manukau Harbour, which is devoted to industrial activity. Then again, the sight of a cargo ship looming in front of you as you top Selwyn St can be awe-inspiring.

There is undoubtedly a lot to recommend Onehunga; large sections, wide streets of character homes, harbour views, with a regenerating main street and the popular Dressmart retail outlet. It's also right beside Cornwall Park and One Tree Hill Domain. Gentrification is well underway and Onehunga's growing trendiness among young buyers is reflected in rising prices. Oranga is a neighbouring suburb, often described as "rugged". Penrose and Te Papapa are industrial and commercial.

Who lives there?

Onehunga is an old settlement with a strong sense of community enterprise. Traditionally the area has been solidly working class and home to many Maori and Polynesian families. A diversity of ethnic groups has taken up residence in recent years. There are currently 52 different nationalities enrolled at Penrose High School - you could say Onehunga today is a snapshot of where cosmopolitan Auckland might be in 20 years' time.

Today's typical buyers include young New Zealand couples looking for a first home do-up, and immigrants from Asia and other nations. Onehunga's location is popular with businesses and families that want access to both the city and South Auckland. It is also handy for airport staff and others who use the airport frequently.

Typical dwellings

Onehunga is one of the older towns of central Auckland, with some houses dating back to the mid-1800s. Most houses are either turn-of-the-century and pre-1915 villas, or bungalows in a variety of styles. There are a number of weatherboard state houses and ex-state houses as well as stucco duplexes. Among a number of historic properties is the one-time residence of Governor Grey, in Symonds St.

Onehunga village grew around a coastal trading port. A number of the more significant homes on the western side of Onehunga were built for sea captains and harbour masters; many of the steets bear their names. Onehunga was once home to a number of Fencible Soldiers (retired British soldiers who lived in the area to help protect early European settlers). Around the 1870s, the Fencibles were provided with land and modest cottages as payment. Many of the tiny cottages remain today and are popular do-ups. Infill housing is plentiful. Large properties are becoming harder to find.

There are also apartments, built mostly on old industrial land during the past five years.

A new development is underway at the northern end of the old Onehunga Mall, involving approximately 100 rental properties.

REAL ESTATE

Trends

Local agents complain of a huge shortage of properties to sell and since the middle of 2001 when immigration numbers increased, there has been an even more dramatic shortage of rental properties.

Prices look set to continue to rise, especially given the crowds that show up on auction days. Many investors keen to enter the Onehunga market are competing with first-home buyers, and this pushes prices up.

Terrace houses are popular with Asian couples and families either to rent or buy. The top area of Onehunga, nearest One Tree Hill, commands higher prices than the lower part with its busy roads and proximity to the industrial area.

Buyers are now having to go further down Church St to find do-ups.

Prices

Fencible cottages are very popular and some can be bought for around $330,000. A typical three-bedroom bungalow on a half site sells for between $320,000 and $400,000. The same dwelling on a full site with crosslease potential is closer to $400,000 or $450,000. At the other end of the scale, a two-bedroom ex-state house off Victoria St went for $306,000 in July 2003.

In Oranga, two-bedroom state houses can still be found for $300,000, while new townhouses are $500,000 to $600,000.

Average sale prices

	House	Flat	No. sales
2002	$290,015	$190,965	731
2003	$359,926	$207,680	634

Rental and investment

To rent a three-bedroom apartment now costs around $330 a week, where two years ago it might have only cost $280. A three-bedroom bungalow, by comparison, costs $360 to $400 a week.

Best streets

Mariri and Huapai Rd, the western end of Grey St and Arthur St, and Quadrant Rd.

AMENITIES

Schools ★★★

The primary schools are Onehunga Primary School and Te Papapa School. The nearest intermediate is Royal Oak Intermediate. The secondary schools are Onehunga High School and Penrose High School.

Shops ★★★★

Onehunga surrounds the Onehunga Mall, which 15 years ago was a dead area. It has gradually picked up ever since the mall was re-opened to cars in the early 1990s. These days the town's shopping strip offers a variety of retail, banks, service stores and eateries. Then there's Dressmart (see below).

Local hero - Dressmart

The driving power behind the rejuvenation of Onehunga's shops is the newly expanded seconds mall Dressmart. With over 60 retail factory outlets including fashionable brands such as Levi's, Sartori, Nike, Keith Matheson, Adidas, and Max, Dressmart is the major shopping attraction, drawing in thousands of bargain-hunting shoppers who would never otherwise visit Onehunga.

Onehunga is also home to some quirky and unusual shops. As well as a school uniform shop and a new and used comic specialty shop, there's the legendary Hard to Find (but Worth the Effort) Secondhand Bookshop, at 171 Onehunga Mall. Built in the 1890s, it was once a fruit, vegetable and Chinese supplies store owned by the Sai Louie family. The family still owns the building and the original sign writing is still on the shop window. Open seven days, its 90,000 or so books make it the North Island's largest secondhand book shop. It has a smaller twin across town in Devonport.

Leisure ★★★

Open spaces include One Tree Hill Domain and Cornwall Park as well as Jellicoe Park, Waikaraka Park, and the motorway-edged Onehunga Wharf. The Waikaraka Park Cemetery where past members of religious orders have been buried is an interesting place for a stroll. There are also a number of heritage walks in the area.

As an old Maori and then European settlement, Onehunga has a rich history. In Jellicoe Park, for instance, is the Blockhouse Museum, housed in a blockhouse built in 1860. It was intended for use in the defence of Auckland during the land wars of the 1860s. There is also a replica of a 1850s double unit Fencible cottage, and Laishley House, originally built as a manse for the Congregational Church in 1859.

Onehunga has a number of sporting facilities including the Onehunga War Memorial Pool (Onehunga Aquasport), and the Manukau Cruising Club, as well as clubs catering for bowling, soccer, rugby, squash and rowing.

The area has many new cafes and restaurants including The Blue Strawberry Cafe in the historic ex-Post Office building. There are a few ethnic eateries including the excellent Flavour Of India.

The community house recently established in the old Onehunga school building is very busy with educational programmes. Onehunga has a fantastic new library, community centre, several medical centres and The Dolphin Theatre.

SMART BUY

Onehunga has long been tipped as "one to watch", meaning it's probably too late for outright bargains, but there are still do-ups waiting low on the slopes. There is no denying the gentrification already going on in the area and the widespread perception of the area as an emerging trendy place can't but help prices. Of new developments in the area, buyers should watch out for those that have been cheaply or poorly constructed.

Travel times

From Onehunga Mall

CBD	off-peak 15-20 min
	peak 1 hour
Airport	10 min
Royal Oak shopping centre	2 min
Southern motorway	5 min

Stagecoach Auckland provides a regular service to Onehunga, with a lot of buses intersecting at this point from different parts of the city.

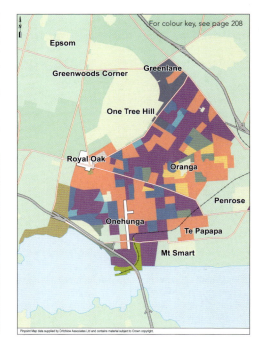

For colour key, see page 208

Pinpoint Map data supplied by Critchlow Associates Ltd and contains material subject to Crown copyright.

ONE TREE HILL ★★★★★

including Royal Oak and Greenlane

If you took a map of greater Auckland and stuck a pin in the middle, One Tree Hill and the surrounding suburbs would be pretty much at the centre. One Tree Hill and Cornwall Park are obviously big drawcards for the area, with many houses within walking distance.

Despite their shared feature, the three suburbs have distinct characters. Royal Oak is one of Auckland's smallest suburbs, grouped around its busy roundabout - it used to have a large oak tree in its centre and was a main tramline stop. Greenlane, between Cornwall Park and the motorway, has suffered from an image problem, due to an abundance of car dealerships. It's close to, but traditionally much cheaper than, both Epsom and Remuera.

Leafy One Tree Hill is popular because it's central, but out of the bustle of the traffic. People pay a premium to be on the slopes or within walking distance of One Tree Hill (which is also known by its Maori name, Maungakiekie), and some will buy here just to be close to the park. Some homes have views to the Bombay Hills in the south, but the suburb's best orientation is north-east. To sample how pleasant the area is, take a gentle drive down Wheturangi Rd from Greenlane - the tree-lined road hugs the eastern side of One Tree Hill. Multi-level tudor-styled housing and huge bungalows are abundant.

Who lives there?

Typical Royal Oak buyers are middle-aged people with families, and some older individuals. They're predominantly Pakeha/European and not many are first-home buyers. Some agents have noticed a recent increase in Asian buyers.

There is a strong community of older people in Royal Oak. Some younger professional couples buy locally, using the area as a stepping stone to Remuera or Epsom. Being en route to the airport, the neighbourhoods surrounding Royal Oak are popular with airport staff and regular travellers.

One Tree Hill attracts young professional couples and people with young families. Mixed in are older residents who moved into its 1940s bungalows when they were new.

Typical dwellings

There is a big variety of dwellings. Established in the 1930s, Royal Oak doesn't have villas, but has a mix of everything else from classic bungalows to new apartments. There are a few brick-and-tile bungalows and some 30-year-old single-level units in blocks of four. The high proportion of infill housing has brought in new plaster and tile townhouses. There are a few townhouses on

Manukau Rd but no high-rises. There are some big bungalows still on large sections nearer Onehunga.

There are many old villas and bungalows in One Tree Hill, and both One Tree Hill and Greenlane have lots of post-war bungalows. There are still many state houses as well as brick-and-tile units, concentrated in streets like Te Rama Rd. Infill housing has also brought townhouses to the area.

REAL ESTATE

Trends

The surge in sales over the past couple of years has had the biggest impact on houses with full sites nearest Epsom, increasing their value by up to 15% each year. Older houses on full sites in Greenlane are being removed and large, modern brick-and-tile or plaster homes built instead.

Greenlane is also divided as a suburb between houses that are in and out of the Auckland Grammar School zone, with an approximately $100,000 price difference. Properties that back on to One Tree Hill are exclusive but not in-zone.

Prices

Two-bedroom Royal Oak units with an

internal access garage sell for between $230,000 and $290,000. On the border of Royal Oak and Onehunga Heights, houses in Trafalgar St, Forbes St, and Normans Hill Rd are selling for $350,000 and up. $400,000 is not uncommon, and some of the big old homes sell for much more. A three-bedroom bungalow in reasonable condition on a half site in Royal Oak will be $400,000 plus.

Upmarket Royal Oak townhouses sell for $460,000 to $580,000. At the top of the scale, a large site close to or bordering the park with a pool and a three to five-bedroom refurbished character home is around $2 million. Top One Tree Hill properties typically sell for $650,000, and these days buyers won't get much of a house on the slopes for under $480,000. Bargain hunters can pay $300,000 plus for a little ex-state house in reasonable condition.

A three-bedroom Greenlane bungalow in average condition on a half section that's not in the grammar zone is between $320,000 and $360,000. For an in-zone house, prices are $450,000 to $500,000.

Average sale prices

	House	Flat	No. sales
2002	$523,905	$275,627	350
2003	$677,251	$325,468	238

Rental and investment

The rental market is strong, with a tidy two-bedroom unit renting out at around $280 per week. Some properties in the area cost as much as $1000 per week to rent.

Best streets

Maungakiekie Ave and Wapiti Ave in Greenlane, Haydn Ave, Raurenga Ave and Lewin Rd in Royal Oak and Kowhatu Rd and Irirangi Rd in One Tree Hill.

AMENITIES

Schools ★★★

There are three state primary schools in the area. The local intermediate is Royal Oak Intermediate. The nearest colleges are Marcellin College, Onehunga High School, Penrose High or those in Epsom.

Shops ★★★

The main shopping centre is the Royal Oak Mall with more than 50 shops, a supermarket and food hall. Nearby Greenwoods Corner has an interesting stretch of shops and cafes, and Newmarket is about seven minutes further north along Manukau Rd.

There are some nice shops on the corner of Rawhiti and Tawa Rds that serve One Tree Hill, and there is a large supermarket at Greenlane.

Leisure ★★★

The area's biggest asset is the fabulous recreation area of Cornwall Park and the One Tree Hill Domain. The lone pine was finally and sadly removed when it failed to recover after a couple of chainsaw protest attacks so the icon is now known as None Tree Hill. Thankfully, the Auckland City Council is taking action to replace the tree.

Local hero

Cornwall Park's Acacia Cottage, Huia Lodge and Garden Café

Clustered together into what seems like Auckland's pretty English quarter, these three Cornwall Park icons breathe a tiny bit of colonial history and beauty into our modern lives. As joggers slug it out uphill from Greenlane Rd towards the One Tree Hill circuit, these buildings signal the start

of flatter, easier running. Consequently, you see more people running the other way!

Built in 1841 in downtown Auckland, Acacia Cottage was moved here in 1920. The lodge and café have been on-site longer. All three are part of Cornwall Park's leafy establishment. Huia Lodge was officially opened in 1903, and is a cute, gingerbread-cottage-like piece of Queen Anne Revival architecture. Having housed successive park caretakers, and latterly kiosk managers, it's an information centre in its current incarnation. It's a great place to call in and collect brochures about this fabulous park, as well as city events.

The kiosk, which began in 1908 as an open-sided pavilion for serving refreshments, is now both an ice-cream pick-up point and a genteel indoor-outdoor dining and café space (the Cornwall Park Garden Café restaurant). Its civilised, traditional feel seems more Christchurch than Auckland, somehow, and its popularity never seems to wane. When both sun and blossom are out, the diners appear contented and mellow.

Cornwall Park has recreational areas, barbecues, a restaurant, information centre, and a working farm the public can walk through. Local facilities include the Alexandra Park racecourse and its neighbouring showgrounds, where many major exhibitions and shows are held. There is also an aquatic and fitness centre, the nearby Ericsson Stadium and speedway, and various sports clubs.

The area has a sprinkling of cafés and restaurants, including the longstanding Ollie's ice-cream parlour near Royal Oak roundabout.

For colour key, see page 208

Mt Eden
Market Road
Epsom
Greenwoods Corner
Greenlane
One Tree Hill
Royal Oak

Pinpoint Map data supplied by Critchlow Associates Ltd and contains material subject to Crown copyright.

Travel times

From Royal Oak

CBD	off-peak 10-20 min
	peak 30 min
North-western motorway	4-5 min
Southern motorway	4 min
Airport	15 min
St Lukes mall	10 min

Stagecoach Auckland provides a regular service to Royal Oak and neighbouring suburbs. The five arterial roads that splay out from the roundabout at Royal Oak make accessing other parts of the city easy by car.

including Mt Wellington and Tamaki

The name Panmure strikes fear into the hearts of drivers. Its namesake roundabout is to Auckland as the Arc de Triomphe roundabout to Paris - a madcap raceway to be negotiated with care - or with your eyes closed! Judging by the rate Panmure is growing, negotiating the roundabout is not going to be getting any easier. Between 1991 and 1999, the number of people living in Panmure increased by 21.5%, and has continued to grow. Panmure's first European settlers were retired Fencible soldiers, who with their wives and children arrived in Auckland between 1847 and 1852 and developed the communities of Onehunga, Howick, Panmure, and Otahuhu. In 1956 Woolworths opened its first New Zealand "Food Fair" store at Panmure, giving New Zealand a first glimpse of the supermarket retailing revolution to come. Panmure's Queen St has the dubious honour of having Auckland's third highest concentration of massage parlours after Karangahape Rd and Fort St. But nestled in its more salubrious parts, Panmure has its very own small golden triangle: Riverview Rd, Queens Rd, Kings Rd and Sunset View, plus the waterfront roads of Dunkirk Rd and Riverside Ave.

Who lives there?

A cross-section of people make these areas home, including many first-home buyers. An increasing number of new immigrants from all nations are settling in the district, attracted by the lower prices and proximity to major working areas like the industry of Mt Wellington and further south.

Overall, it's a working to middle-class area that acts as a gateway to the eastern suburbs. In Panmure and Tamaki, the University of Auckland's Tamaki campus attracts students and lecturing staff.

The new terrace and apartment complexes appeal to young professionals and child-free couples. Tamaki is 50% state housing and is a big rental area for lower socio-economic groups.

Scattered throughout Panmure and Mt Wellington are a few homes of the very rich, including families who have made their mark on industry - such as the Fletchers and the Spencers.

Mt Wellington has been described as "one step down from Ellerslie in the desirability stakes". It's billed as the most affordable Auckland City suburb for young couples who

work in the metropolis. It's the place where bargains may yet be found by discerning buyers and a suburb for people who want big family homes at affordable prices, but who don't want to buy in South Auckland. Many Mt Wellington buyers aim to eventually upgrade to Ellerslie or One Tree Hill.

Typical dwellings

Mt Wellington and Panmure are characterised by housing from the 1960s and 1970s. Development and infill has seen new townhouses and some largish terrace houses and apartment complexes. An average dwelling typically has three bedrooms and separate garage on a half site. Villas and older style bungalows are in the minority.

REAL ESTATE

Trends

As with the rest of Auckland, the market surged during 2002 and 2003. A growing awareness that Panmure is an affordable suburb with access to water (the pretty Panmure Basin and Tamaki River and estuary) has inspired interest. Also fuelling change over the past two years has been the arrival in

Local hero – The Panmure Basin

Although Parnell and Remuera types may turn up their noses at the thought of a picnic at the Panmure Basin, the fact remains; it's an attractive respite from totally urban surroundings; maybe even an underrated recreational resource. The city council probably thinks so; it's recently been holding community meetings in a bid to forge ahead with plans for the area. Ringed by a walking/running track that suffers a surface slightly too uneven for roller-blading, the Panmure Basin is an 'explosion crater', formed

approximately 27,000 years ago. Initially a fresh water lake, the basin has become a tidal lagoon, and is appreciated by local water-sport clubs and water-skiers.

Layers of bedded ash around the basin are now covered in houses and, at one end, the Waipuna Hotel complex. Real-estate-wise, and in spite of recent market surges, this would have to be a relatively reasonably priced location in terms of Auckland's waterfront property. The odd run-down good buy could still be in the bag, but that's not to say there aren't some wildly expensive pads (complete with riparian rights) along the river around here. Anything with its own jetty is in a class of its own.

Accessed from Lagoon Dr, Ireland Rd (where there's a high tide boat ramp), Peterson Rd and Watene Rd, the basin's rim provides the ideal distance for a decent run or 45 minute walk - great for both fitness-conscious locals and indulged hotel guests! It's also a good picnic place for young families, with a couple of playgrounds dotted around the edge.

It's surprising, really, that more Mt Wellington lunchers don't take time out here during the eight-till-five. Maybe what it needs now is a few open-air cafes nearby. Watch this space!

the area of young middle-class couples buying newly built townhouses in the $300,000 to $400,000 price range. The buyers are capitalising on the fact that Panmure lies between the bay suburbs of Meadowbank and St Johns, and the eastern suburbs of Pakuranga and Howick.

Over the years a number of ideas have been mooted for the redevelopment of Mt Wellington's old quarry land. One involved using the site's contours to create a sports amphitheatre and parking, another a golfing range. A few years ago Fletcher Residential had plans for a large development mixing retail, light industrial and residential, but construction did not go ahead.

Prices

An entry-level three-bedroom terrace house with internal access garage and views over the basin costs around $320,000. A brick-and-tile three-bedroom townhouse in a complex of 10

is $300,000. On or near the water, prices jump markedly with $1 million-plus sales not uncommon. Bargain hunters need to move quickly; one "terrible" Dunkirk Rd house with a water view sold last year for $250,000, and a large Bridge St property with a big house, double garage, a boat mooring and riparian rights went for $500,000.

Mt Wellington apartments and two-bedroom units sell between $140,000 and $210,000. Modern three bedroom homes are priced around $300,000 to $350,000. The common factor determining value is proximity to water.

Average sale prices

	House	Flat	No. sales
2002	$209,979	$159,052	668
2003	$234,346	$175,457	565

Best streets

Bridge St in Panmure; Marine Lane in Mt Wellington and Dunkirk Rd in Tamaki.

Rental and investment

Aside from the Housing New Zealand property in Tamaki, the area is popular for rentals with students and staff of the university campus. Rents have been increasing and you now pay $260 plus a week for a two-bedroom dwelling. In Mt Wellington, a three-bedroom stand-alone rental goes for between $330 and $400 a week.

AMENITIES

Schools ★★★

There are eight primary schools as well as Portland House Montessori School and the special needs Somerville School. Tamaki Intermediate shares grounds with Tamaki Primary, and Tamaki College is in nearby Pt England. Carey College covers years one to 15.

Shops ★★★

Panmure has high-street style shopping with just about all needs met, and a recently upgraded New World. The Auckland City Council has earmarked a couple of million dollars for a much needed spruce-up of Panmure's Queens Rd. Near the corner of the Ellerslie Panmure Highway and Mt Wellington Highway is a bulk retail area with all the usual outlets, including an enormous Harvey Norman. Big Fresh supermarket is in Mt Wellington and a large retail complex with supermarket and other shops is planned for the old army barracks land at Sylvia Park by State Highway One. Tamaki has no shopping centre.

Leisure ★★★

The area has multiple green and blue spaces like Mt Wellington Domain, Colin Maiden Park, and waterside reserves like Mt Wellington War Memorial Reserve and Panmure Domain.

Panmure Basin is a recreational playground for swimming, sailing, fishing, rowing regattas and raft races. Mt Wellington's grassy Hamlins Hill (Mutukaroa) near the motorway is not particularly scenic at the moment but more track maintenance and planting is planned.

Massage parlours aside, there are the usual sports clubs. The Lagoon Leisure and Fitness Centre has a hydro-slide and swim school. For the littlies, a miniature railway runs in Peterson Reserve on Sundays.

There are plenty of eateries on Panmure's main drag offering a range of food.

Travel times
From Panmure roundabout

CBD	off-peak 13 min
	peak 20 to 25 min
Britomart CBD by train	15 min
Southern motorway	5-7 min
Airport	25 min

The Tranz Metro services Tamaki and Panmure railway stations. The area is also well served by Stagecoach buses in some parts and Howick and Eastern Buses elsewhere.

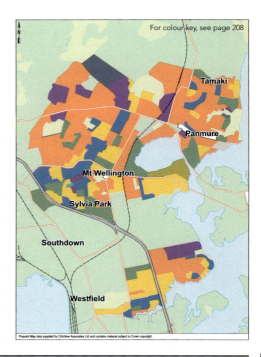

Parnell may be small but, in real estate terms, it packs a huge punch. This is where those exasperating Auckland property trends begin - if Parnell starts to take off, hold on to your hat because the rest of the city is sure to follow, in steady but sweeping concentric bands. With only about 2200 dwellings its established leafy streets contain some of New Zealand's most expensive property.

In days past, trucks used to rumble up and down Gladstone Rd to the port. New Zealand's oldest railway tunnel is in Parnell and what is now the Axis building was a chocolate factory. Workers from local industry lived in humble cottages like those around St Georges Bay Rd that now command big prices and are inhabited by urban sophisticates.

Newmarket is also small with few residents and a large commercial and retail area, much of which is owned by Singaporean Chinese business interests.

Who lives there?

There are many old Auckland families in Parnell, who have lived here for generations. The suburb has been an established centre for the artistic intelligentsia; many Parnell residents are classic bourgeois/bohemians. They are high socio-economic, upwardly mobile go-getters who tend to be employers rather than employees. They pride

themselves in being tolerant and culturally sensitive. There are many writers and artists but not the "starving in a garret" variety.

As with the eastern suburbs, the CBD's waterfront and other desirable inner-city suburbs, Parnell is very popular with expats who have chosen to return to New Zealand post-September 11, and following the "tech-wreck" which brought an end to many computer-related job contracts. In recent years real estate agents have witnessed "floods" of expats looking to buy in Parnell. Parnell buyers are predominantly Pakeha and European plus a few Asians. By comparison, Newmarket attracts more Chinese buyers; it is a cosmopolitan, professional area with lots of business people, older couples whose children have left home and a few families.

Typical dwellings

Parnell dwellings are very diverse - from tiny ex-worker's cottages, stucco villas and stately old mansions with more than eight bedrooms, to state-of-the-art townhouses and apartments. Business four zoning has meant a lot of obsolete older commercial buildings have made way for residential developments, to achieve greater density and mixed-use properties. Roughly 10-15%

of Parnell's dwellings are now terraced housing, which is considerably more than in nearby Remuera.

Newmarket has very few houses, and many more commercial properties and apartments. The residential area of Newmarket blurs into Grafton, Epsom and Remuera. The densest residential block is Broadway Park, a combination of terraced homes, duplexes and mid to high-rise apartments along with tennis courts, a heated pool and gymnasium that was opened in 1994. Newmarket has some 1840s worker's cottages but, unlike Parnell, it has few substantial family homes.

REAL ESTATE

Trends

According to one estimate, Auckland inner city median sales increased by 34.3% for the period July 2002-2003. Such obvious demand has translated into dramatic price rises. In March 2002, for instance, a house with one off-street carpark sold for $625,000, then sold again in August 2002 for $675,000 with nothing having been done to the property.

There is always a bun fight when old family homes come on to market - one almost original 1930s home in St Stephens Ave sold recently for $2 million. By comparison, a new three-bedroom house in Bradford St sold recently at auction for $1.2 million.

Construction on a new luxury apartment complex is underway at the top of Parnell Ridge, on the corner of Parnell Rd and Birdwood Cres. Trinity Apartments are named for their proximity to Parnell's Cathedral of the Holy Trinity. Scheduled for completion by the end of 2004, two-thirds of the 31 luxury units were sold off the plans. At time of print, there was still a good selection left priced from $600,000.

Newmarket has a highly mobile population, and its real estate market is affected by business confidence levels, immigration, interest rates, corporate transfers and trends among off-shore buyers.

That didn't deter the developers of the Joseph Banks Apartments in Broadway Park, who estimate the 40-unit apartment complex will be completed in 2004. Situated in Middleton Rd, bordering Remuera but just around the corner from the Broadway shopping district, Broadway Park attracts buyers in from the eastern suburbs. Prices here range from $345,000 for a one-bedroom, lower level unit, to $1.2 million for a 200m^2 penthouse apartment. Nearby apartment complexes include the six-storey, 21-unit Gifford Apartments and the 10-storey, 50 unit Ascot Apartments.

The area is very popular with Asians new to New Zealand, and prices rose sharply following immigration increases between 1994 and 1996. Changes in immigration policy after 1997 to 2000 saw a 10 to 20% fall in sales and a corresponding drop in prices. In November 2001 business confidence was high and interest rates low so the market took off, almost doubling sales during the March quarter. Sale volumes dropped back for a while, but in the year to June 2003 rose by around 10%.

Prices

There is nothing with sea views under $500,000. Along St Georges Bay Rd cottages with tiny sections, some with only 200m^2 of land, can sell for up to $700,000.

Why I live there
Interior designer Cathy Veninga

"One of the best things about living in Parnell is that it takes me two minutes to drive to work," says Veninga. "Quite a few of my colleagues live in the area as well as most of my client base. An eclectic and aesthetically aware mix of people live here, but they're not at all pretentious.

"Parnell is generally more conservative than, say, Ponsonby but on the up side it feels like a safe place to be, which gives me freedom. And unlike the suburbs, come the weekend you don't have to drive anywhere - there's Judges Bay, the rose gardens, and summer jazz in the Domain."

For an older house on 1400m², buyers have been known to pay $3.2 million. A classic Parnell cottage in Scarborough Tce with two bedrooms, no off-street parking, and a 350m² sloping section with no afternoon sun recently sold for $518,000.

A house on a full site in Gladstone Rd was bought in 1971 for $23,500, and sold in 1981 for $49,000. Today, when properties are selling well in excess of their CVs, the same property has a CV of $1 million.

Parnell has two ridges - one down to the sea and the other away from it. The second, by Brighton Rd, is south-facing so less sunny but it still commands high prices.

At Newmarket's entry level are a few brick and tile "sausage block" units. An average one with a floor area of approximately 60 to 70m² plus a carport costs around $270,000. A really nice three-bedroom terrace home in Newmarket's Broadway Park with a double garage and access to shared leisure facilities costs $550,000 to $650,000.

Average sale prices

	House	Flat	No. sales
2002	$446,584	$268,127	488
2003	$748,196	$427,213	244

Rental and investment

Predictably for a suburb as central as Parnell, there is huge demand for rentals, and very little available. As a rule prospective tenants are looking for quality rentals. The going rate is $250 to $300 a week for most one-bedroom apartments. For a well-appointed studio apartment, expect to pay $360 per week. Terrace housing bordering Auckland's Domain has rented at $450.

Around $850 per week is standard for a fully furnished, three-bedroom home. Weekly rents of $900 per week are nothing for Parnell, and tenants can pay up to $1500 per week for full-site family homes. This high demand in turn puts pressure on investment properties.

Apartments are currently very sought after by investors because of the great returns. At Arena in Heather St, apartments sell for late $400,000s to $500,000 each. The price for a penthouse suite with three bedrooms and three bathrooms is $1.2 million. One apartment in Augustus Tce with sea views sold for $350,000, others in Birdwood Tce overlooking the railway, with a shared pool and tennis court sold for between $320,000 to $340,000 for two bedrooms and a study.

Best streets

The lower end of St Stephens Ave and the streets that run off it, such as Bridewater Rd, Crescent Rd and Judge St.

AMENITIES

Schools ★★★

There is a state primary school in Parnell and another in Newmarket, plus the private Junior College of New Zealand. Parts of the area are in zone for Auckland Grammar School and Epsom Girls Grammar School.

Shops ★★★★★

With 14 galleries from high-end fine art to lesser known talent, Parnell is a hub of New Zealand art. No other precinct has as many

Travel times
From Parnell Rise

CBD	off-peak 5 min
	peak 15 min
	15 min walk
Southern motorway	3 min
Airport	25 min
Remuera	5-6 min
From Newmarket	
Britomart CBD by train	10 min

There is a regular bus service to the city, with Parnell Rd and Broadway as major connecting routes in the public transport grid. Trains also run directly past Parnell and Newmarket.

According to one local, travelling times to elsewhere in Auckland are not a major consideration: "People don't tend to travel much to other parts of Auckland - everyone comes here."

galleries so close together.

Parnell is also known for its cafes, restaurants, upmarket fashion and a range of other boutique stores. With its cobbled paving and low-profile heritage buildings the area mixes chic retail with a village atmosphere.

Parnell has plenty of small service stores including a butcher, deli and fruit shops, but for groceries residents either go to Newmarket's Two Double Seven, or the New Worlds at Remuera or Victoria Park.

By comparison, Newmarket's shopping strip is busier and more commercial, with a mix of boutique retail and chain stores. Newmarket's Two Double Seven complex has recently expanded to 61 specialty shops, and has a foodcourt and Woolworths supermarket.

Leisure ★★★★★

There are plenty of open spaces - the Auckland Domain, The Parnell Rose Gardens and Dove-Myer Robinson Park and a number of smaller reserves.

There is the Parnell Baths (see below) and the Auckland Tennis Centre. At Newmarket, there is the Olympic Pools & Fitness Centre, many gyms and two big cinema complexes.

Upgrades to Newmarket Park, bounded by Parnell Rd, Ayr St and Bassett Rd, have been underway over the past year, and Auckland City Council expects full completion of the project in 2004.

Both the Auckland Museum and the new Auckland Cathedral are major icons and centres of cultural activity. Parnell also has a library.

Well known for its night life, Parnell Rise was the place in the 1980s to be spotted, schmoozing over lunch or quaffing Bolly on Friday night. Its status has since been dealt a blow by the increased prominence of Ponsonby's café scene, and the creation of Viaduct Harbour.

It still has a range of excellent eateries, including the institutions of Antoine's and the Veranda Bar and Grill. Newmarket has numerous eateries including Pearl Garden, Rikka and Tribeca as well as plenty of fast food outlets.

For colour key, see page 208

Mechanics Bay

Parnell

Auckland Domain

Newmarket   Broadway Park

Pinpoint Map data supplied by Critchlow Associates Ltd and contains material subject to Crown copyright.

Local hero - Parnell Baths

The historic Parnell Baths, on Auckland's waterfront, are one of the city's unique features. The 60m salt water pools reopened in January 2003 following a $4.2 million upgrade. The facility is a great place for the whole family, with new features including a partially heated children's pool with water toys and a water playground. Three hot pools designed for toddlers, children and adults keep swimmers of all ages warm on cooler days. There are qualified attendants on duty at all times, lounging chairs and an all-weather café serving up ice-creams and healthy snacks. Originally opened in 1914, the Parnell Baths were redeveloped in the 1950s in the Modernist style. A striking abstract mosaic mural of swimmers adorns the changing room walls. According to architecture lecturer Peter Shaw, the baths are one of the great Modernist icons of New Zealand architecture.

PONSONBY ★★★★★

including Herne Bay, St Marys Bay and Freemans Bay

Ponsonby, Herne Bay and Freemans Bay represent a unique market. People buy into the area because they like the location and the image that the area has; it's like buying a label item from one of the many designer stores along Ponsonby Rd.

Ponsonby is home to the pink dollar and good coffee. Go to any open home here and you'll see interiors as slick as the men's designer shaving balm in the bathroom. Despite its little workers' cottages, narrow streets and dearth of off-street parking, Ponsonby is every real estate agent's favourite rags-to-riches story, and is frequently used as a by-word for gentrification. Next door, Herne Bay has been highbrow for a long time, thanks to its fabulous harbour views, grand old homes, gracious leafy streets, and north-facing slopes. St Marys Bay generally has better views than Herne Bay, but has smaller sections, and the motorway running beneath it is one of the busiest stretches in New Zealand. Freemans Bay has great city views but a reputation for losing the sun early in the day.

Who lives there?

The residents here pride themself on being arty and well informed - they're the original chardonnay socialists. A more recent term, "bobos" or bohemian/bourgeois, sums up this neighbourhood well with its concentration of advertising and media-types, creatives and assorted hippies-made-good. Ponsonby and surrounding suburbs are cosmopolitan and revel in their image of being the "fun side of town". They are hugely fashion-conscious, both in dress and in their houses - you've got to have the right sort of cookware and the latest sofa.

Originally a blue-collar and Polynesian area, Ponsonby became the student flatting mecca of the 1960s and 1970s. The drift back to the

inner city and away from traffic jams has seen prices rise and a steady gentrification of scruffy old flats.

Local agents have observed a drift of people from the eastern to the central suburbs - one explanation is that while the eastern suburbs are classic white middle class professional neighbourhoods, the central suburbs are a touch more cosmopolitan.

All of the western inner-city suburbs appeal to a mix of double income professional couples who can afford to buy into the area (with or without a couple of children), singles, and gays. Very few, if any, Asian immigrants buy in these areas - mostly due to the higher maintenance older houses and lack of a good public high school.

Typical dwellings

The majority of houses are villas. The classic three-bedroom workingman's cottages are very typical of Ponsonby, St Marys Bay and Freemans Bay, though by now many have been extended and renovated beyond recognition. That said, Ponsonby is still fashionable grot; most streets still have homes that are scruffy or just pretty ordinary. Despite the area's buzz, there is still a huge amount of renovating potential.

Herne Bay has larger villas and more stately

Why I live there
Magazine editor Claire McCall

Editor of home magazines, *NZ Home & Entertaining* and *Your Home & Garden*, Claire McCall describes her neighbourhood as the five-minute triangle. "It's five minutes to work, to the CBD, to the gym, to the supermarket, to the motorway and to the cafes of Ponsonby Rd." And for an aficionado of style, Ponsonby is where it all happens, she says. It's the first place to see new design stores and new types of food.

Claire's "non-leaky" ex-council unit in Freemans Bay gave her an affordable entry into an otherwise expensive area. "It has simple lines so you need to do very little to achieve a great look." The diverse mix of neighbours is something she treasures. "Prices have skyrocketed in the area over the past few years, moving beyond the reach of many. I feel very fortunate to have been able to buy here when I did."

homes. Section sizes in St Marys Bay and Freemans Bay are typically 300m², while in Herne Bay the average is 500-600m². Small section sizes mean many Ponsonby, St Marys Bay and Freemans Bay properties do not have off-street parking.

Proportionally there are not as many million dollar sales in Freemans Bay as St Marys Bay, due to the mixed styles and quality of the homes in Freemans Bay. Where St Marys Bay is almost exclusively residential, Freemans Bay is mixed use. There's ongoing construction of new apartment complexes in Freemans Bay. One complex, consisting of seven separate buildings and 83 apartments with road frontage to College Hill, England St, Runnell St and Cascade St, is expected to be completed in August 2004.

REAL ESTATE

Trends

All the inner city suburbs are still in huge demand and the market continues to be strong, but some suggest it isn't "hiking" as much as it was 18 months ago. Buyer demand in these areas is still being fuelled by the return of expats, increased immigration and aversion to rush-hour commuting - plus the leaky building syndrome scare, which reminds buyers of the robustness of old villas and bungalows.

Ongoing discussion about a second harbour crossing creates a little uncertainty about the future of St Marys Bay.

Prices

A high percentage of sales in the St Marys Bay area - possibly 50% or more - are over the

million dollar mark. There are only a few more humble dwellings in the area and even they go for a tidy sum - such as $395,000 for a two-bedroom unit.

Herne Bay is divided down the middle by Jervois Rd. The northern, harbour-facing slopes command the premium prices. On the southern side of Jervois Rd are gracious, tree lined streets such as Kelmarna Ave, Wanganui Ave, and Ardmore Rd. A tidy home with four bedrooms and two bathrooms in one of these streets can sell in the mid $700,000s plus, while a tidy three-bedroom home on a half site can sell for around $620,000 upwards. On the northern slopes but away from the waterfront, a three-bedroom weatherboard house on a regular section would sell from the low $800,000s to the high $900,000s. Larger houses in the better streets sell for $1.3 million and more. Recently a two-storey older style house in need of renovation sold for $3.9 million, with the highest price in the last three months being $4.475 million for a substantial home on a good section in Marine Pde.

Three years ago houses could be bought in neighbouring Ponsonby for $380,000 to $400,000, but these days entry level here is around $500,000 even for a shabby do-up. Once renovated, houses sell for a lot more, even without off-street parking. One nicely renovated two-bedroom property recently sold for $670,000, while several four-bedroom houses went for $820,000 and $840,000. In one high-profile case a former Ponsonby corner dairy that had been bought for in 2001 for $318,000 sold in mid 2003 for $613,000. According to one agent, even a bare section would be $500,000 - if you could find one.

Generally speaking, properties higher up the ridge or close to either Ponsonby and Jervois Rd command the highest prices.

In Freemans Bay two-bedroom terrace houses in reasonable condition and with off-street parking sell for $350,000 plus. Reasonable condition one-bedroom ex-council units sell for up to $250,000, and those with three bedrooms cost up to $300,000. Two to three-bedroom apartments built in the past couple of years sell from $395,000 to over $500,000.

Some houses at the top of the Freemans Bay ridge sell for $700,000 up to $1 million-plus; others that are in not such good positions or condition sell from $500,000 up.

Average sale prices

	House	Flat	No. sales
2002	$517,624	$337,201	633
2003	$685,592	$419,550	316

Rental and investment

The loss of the America's Cup doesn't seem to have affected prices in this area - only at the top of the rental market, where rents have dropped back a bit. But there are still lots of investors looking to buy in the area as well as overseas buyers. Three-bedroom villas in Ponsonby and Herne Bay rent out between $490 and $610 plus per week. One-bedroom dwellings average around $270 per week.

Protecting our housing heritage

Ponsonby, one of the earliest of Auckland's inner-city suburbs, is an area steeped in history with landmarks dating back 100 to 150 years, including Ponsonby and Jervois Rd commercial facades and the jumble of homes that line residential streets off the main thoroughfares.

Wander down a side street off Ponsonby Rd, such as Renall St, and you'll see a neighourhood of houses with exteriors that have been lovingly preserved as historic treasures. Indeed, you'll

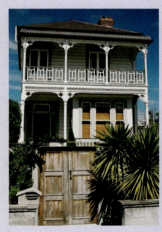

be hard pressed to find a street in the area that doesn't have a good smattering of well-tended cottages and villas.

The first residential growth in Ponsonby occurred in pockets during the 1850s. Cottages for workers were built in areas such as Freeman's Bay while more substantial homeswere built for the wealthier in St Mary's Bay. Ponsonby boomed in the 1870s and 1880s. Many ornate homes were built and during the following years streets continued to expand haphazardly as the fortunes of the Ponsonby area rose and fell.

Dwellings that have survived the wear and tear of time and the modifications of the 1970s and 1980s are now zealously protected by the Auckland City Council's Ponsonby Centre Plan and designated zoning regulations. Since the early 1990s most streets in the Ponsonby area have been zoned residential 1, 2, or conservation, which means homeowners must maintain their home in keeping with the character and history of the area - "to ensure that these small areas of the isthmus retain their unique character and remain as visible evidence of the particular style or era they represent," to quote the council district plan. This includes renovations and additions. No more aluminium windows in old villas!

When applying for renovation building consents you'll be asked to modify or review anything that jars with the character of the house and the neighbourhood. Adding a simple modern necessity such as a garage needs careful consideration because its design mustn't detract from the house or street. Exteriors are the main concern - nobody will be denied a designer kitchen or bathroom. Even paintwork should reflect the age of the house with care required to ensure that the colour scheme highlights rather than overwhelms the fretwork and design of these old houses.

This strict residential zoning, set in place in the early 1990s, is aligned with the Ponsonby Centre Plan, which regulates the look of the commercial centre of Ponsonby area as well.

Best streets

Marine Pde, Sarsfield St and Argyle St in Herne Bay. Vermont St, O'Neill St and Summer St in Ponsonby. Dunedin St, Hackett St and London St in St Marys Bay, and Arthur St, Pagent St and Hepburn St in Freemans Bay.

AMENITIES

Schools ★★★

The area is well served for primary schools, but is not so good at the high school level. Some residents move elsewhere to be closer to high schools, or send their children to private schools. There are five primary schools in the area including the very popular Ponsonby Primary. There is also Ponsonby Intermediate, and at the secondary level, St Pauls College and St Marys College. The closest state secondaries are Auckland Girls Grammar and Western Springs.

Shops ★★★★★

Ponsonby and Jervois Rds are boutique-mile of clothes, home accessories, bakeries and specialty stores. There are more than 40 fashion, gift, homeware and jewellery stores on Ponsonby Rd. Top frock shops include Trelise Cooper, Wallace Rose, Minnie Cooper and Glory. To view Ponsonby Rd's destination website go to www.ponsonbyroad.co.nz. The area has supermarkets at Victoria Park Market or Richmond Rd (both quite new) and a great number of service stores, bakeries, flower and fruit shops. For more choice, the city, Newmarket or St Lukes mall are all close.

Leisure ★★★★

The best open spaces are the area's fabulous views of the harbour and city. Green areas include Victoria Park, Western Park with its buried building sculptures, Grey Lynn Park, Pt Erin Park, Bayfield Park and other smaller reserves. Coxs Bay, Herne Bay and Home Bay are also pleasant spots. The historic outdoor Pt Erin Baths are well frequented. Westhaven Marina is right there for those who don't have a mooring off their Herne Bay property! There are numerous local sports clubs including bowling, yachting, rugby, soccer, snooker, tennis and squash. Major local leisure activities include drinking coffee and people-watching from strategic cafe windows or sidewalk seats.

Having been temporarily abandoned during the last America's Cup as everyone flocked to the Viaduct Harbour eateries, Ponsonby Rd is famed across town as a major dining strip, and is a favourite swilling spot of Auckland's beautiful young things and their wealthy consorts. Between Ponsonby Rd and Jervois Rd are more than 100 cafes, restaurants and bars. Some to try are Box.house Cafe, Delicious, Leonardo's, Estasi, Provence, Red, Shahi Cafe, Rocco and Vinnies.

Travel times

From Three Lamps

CBD	off-peak 5 min
	peak 10 min
CBD on foot	15 min
North-western motorway	3 min
Airport	35 min
St Lukes mall	15 min

The area has excellent public transport with Stagecoach Auckland providing a regular service, and especially with the Link Buses that run in a continuous circuit from Ponsonby Rd to Newmarket via the city.

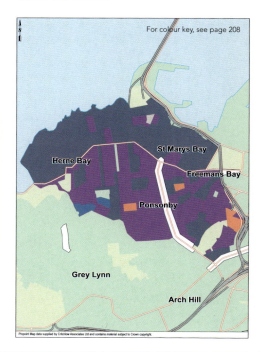

For colour key, see page 208

Herne Bay · St Marys Bay · Freemans Bay · Ponsonby · Grey Lynn · Arch Hill

Pinpoint Map data supplied by Critchlow Associates Ltd and contains material subject to Crown copyright.

Blue blood, cultured accents, Italian-made (but probably sensible) shoes, and a BMW to take the kids to private school. That's Remuera (or Remmers to its detractors). This has always been Auckland's most distinguished suburb and its residents take great pride in their 524, 529 or 520 prefixed phone numbers. The rest of Auckland uses Remuera as an epithet for anything from snobbery to enviable wealth. Nowadays it faces strong competition in the top property price bracket from trendier suburbs like Herne Bay and coastal North Shore. With the current importance of school zones, it's maintaining its edge, however, particularly with returning expats and wealthy new immigrants eager for their sons to attend Auckland Grammar School. Residents love the area's traditional style, mature trees, old churches and stately family homes. This character is partly protected under the zoning legislation of 1999.

Who lives there?

Remuera appeals to the medium to high socio-economic bracket. It is the established stomping ground of captains of business and industry and their families. This is also where you'll find Auckland's old money.

As Remuera is both within the Auckland Grammar School zone and close to a number of private schools, it's also popular with well-heeled, education-conscious families looking for a nice suburban area in which to live. School zoning is also a major drawcard for the significant numbers of wealthy, immigrant families. There are also lots of retired people living in apartments so they can be near grandchildren and the shops.

High property prices and relative distance from town don't deter numerous young professional couples from buying. According to one estimate, at least half of the area's current buyers are aged less than 40. For couples on a high joint income the area's excellent resale prospects make a large mortgage look like a good bet. Remuera also appeals to returning expats, who enjoy decent buying power with their British pounds and US dollars.

Typical dwellings

Remuera has some of the largest old homes in Auckland and a few are still on extensive grounds. Heritage zones protect the character of certain streets - parts of Bassett Rd, Arney Rd, Portland Rd and Seaview Rd are designated special character zones on the district plan.

There is also a lot of new development and infill housing. Often this will mean the complete removal of an old house and the building of two or three similarly styled townhouses, rather than just building a townhouse in the back yard. Around 60% of Remuera properties have been built on multi-unit sites, with an estimated further 25% having the potential to be developed.

Most of Remuera's high rise dwellings are on Remuera Rd. Built in the 1950s and 1960s, subsequent legislation means that more of the same is unlikely. Typical high rise blocks are about 30 years old, with around 14 floors and 30 apartments. They're fairly unattractive but have a great location right next to the shops. They are popular with the established men and women of Remuera - the twin-set and pearls brigade - due to their security and convenient location. They are also in hot demand with Asian immigrants. More recent developments have around six dwellings per block over three levels, selling for around $2 million each. They generally attract younger buyers.

REAL ESTATE

Trends

Remuera Rd is a dividing line; the side of the street known as the "northern slopes" has traditionally been worth a staggering $400,000 more than the other side. On the southern side, Armadale Rd, from the motorway back, has more bungalows. It is the cheaper end of Remuera, but only relatively speaking, with properties from $560,000 upwards.

Any tired bungalows are of little value but the land on which they sit is at a premium. The demand is for full 700m^2 sections and there aren't many, so they're quickly snapped up. Anything with four bedrooms or more does not stick around either. Five years ago $800,000 might get a nice family home in a good street. Today's buyers would need to pay at least $1.2 million to secure the same property.

Prices

At entry level you won't get much for $550,000; perhaps a small section with a three-bedroom bungalow in need of a drastic do-up. The average sales are around $900,000 for family homes of a reasonable standard. A plain-looking brick and tile house on Ascot Ave, originally

Local hero - Jack Lum's fruit and vege store

Billed by the locals as the top fresh fruit and vege store in Auckland, Jack Lum & Co in Clonbern St is the place to get your daily greens. Whether it's out-of-season baby cauli, globe artichokes, pak choi or shiitake mushrooms, this is where many eastern suburb hostesses dash for their essential dinner party ingredients. The store is frequented by a number of top restaurant chefs and other foodie notables such as Jo Seagar. Jack Lum established the business 32 years ago and is credited with introducing Auckland to the concept of buying mixed lettuce around 10 years ago.

million. The new generation apartments range from $900,000 upwards. $1.8 - 3 million gets a really well-appointed single-level apartment of around 350m², with a northern slopes aspect and distant harbour views.

Average sale prices

	House	Flat	No. sales
2002	$600,786	$401,270	1070
2003	$890,778	$429,497	491

Rental and investment

The eastern suburbs rental market can only be described as chaotic, with streams of people every day looking for places to rent. Some of these are merely looking for an address in the grammar zone. The high demand and low supply means rents are $500 to $600 a week for anything half-way decent.

Best streets

All of the streets north of Remuera Rd are desirable. Stand-outs are: Victoria Ave, Arney Cres, Arney Rd, Eastbourne Rd, Waiata Ave, the upper part of Portland Rd, Seaview Rd and Westbourne Rd.

Schools ★★★★★

There are seven primary schools in or near Remuera including St Kentigern and Kings prep schools. Corran School and Remuera Intermediate are in the area, and the suburb is in zone for Epsom Girls Grammar and Auckland Grammar schools, as well as being

bought for $300,000 in 1992, sold for $940,000 in July 2003 after the owners turned down an initial offer of $700,000. Although the high end of the market hasn't been as affected by recent growth, one top Victoria Ave property with grand home, pool and tennis court recently sold for $3.7 million. On the same street the mansion of a well-known businessman and two adjoining properties sold for $10.8 million.

Quality new townhouses are around $1.5

For colour key, see page 208

Parnell

Remuera

Market Road

Greenlane

Pinpoint Map data supplied by Critchlow Associates Ltd and contains material subject to Crown copyright.

Travel times

CBD by car	off-peak 10-15 minutes
	peak 25-45 minutes
CBD by bus	30-40 minutes
Britomart CBD by train	10 min
Southern motorway	1-5 minutes
North-western motorway	10 minutes
Airport	30 minutes
Newmarket	5 minutes

Stagecoach Auckland provides a regular bus service, plus the area is serviced by the Tranz Metro commuter train service on the Papakura route.

within reach of the private Diocesan School for Girls and St Cuthbert's College, both in Epsom. Baradene College of the Sacred Heart is at the bottom of Victoria Ave and Junior College is in Parnell. The charitable trust school of Dilworth is in Remuera.

Shops ★★★

Shopping is of the village-style, high-street kind, but is fairly limited due to the much more extensive shopping in nearby Newmarket, Greenlane and Meadowbank. In the words of one local: "By 9pm, you would think everybody had died." There are a few boutique stores around the intersection of Benson and Upland Rds and the old Remuera village is at the top of Upland Rd.

Leisure ★★★

One of Remuera's best outdoor assets is the view of the Waitemata Harbour and Hauraki Gulf. Sitting about 100m above sea level, on a clear day views can stretch to the islands at the entrance of the gulf, such as Great and Little Barrier, and the Hen and Chickens. Other spaces include Mt Hobson Domain and Waiata Reserve.

There are numerous sports clubs in or near Remuera covering cycling, lawn and court tennis, bowling, squash, badminton, netball, football, plus the Remuera Golf Club which is actually located in Meadowbank. The Ellerslie Racecourse is nearby.

The area is fairly well served with restaurants, including some in the old Remuera village at the top of Upland Rd.

Remuera has a library, at least three medical centres and two hospitals nearby. The beginning of Remuera Rd is New Zealand's medical specialists' mile. Three popular retirement homes are St Vincent's, Remuera Gardens and the Remuera Life Care Retirement Village.

LOOK OUT!

Of some concern is the proposed eastern motorway corridor, which may cut across Remuera's sensitive mangrove swamps and lessen the value of nearby properties. Check with www.aucklandcity.govt.nz for updates on the eastern corridor.

Why I live there
Publisher Stephen Hart and Prue Hart

Having emigrated from England 10 years ago, Stephen and his wife Prue were attracted to Remuera for its central location to lifestyle facilities like shopping, the airport, beaches, the city and schools. Their children, Belinda and Max, started at Remuera Primary and have since gone on to Diocesan School for Girls and Auckland Grammar School respectively.

Even though Prue and Stephen didn't know much about the city, they knew Remuera was an established Auckland suburb. It had similar housing styles to England – spacious, with a mix of classical and contemporary designs. Says Stephen: "Now that we have lived here we continue to appreciate the closeness to the city, the green spaces in the area and the fact that many of our neighbours turned out to be younger than we had expected."

NORTH
North

NORTH   AUCKLAND

SIERRA

The North Shore is synonymous with golden beaches, water sports and big shopping malls. It evokes a sense of lifestyle potential, epitomised by the stunning million-dollar beachfront and cliff-top mansions of Takapuna and Milford's Golden Mile. Even those living in deepest suburbia are within easy reach of the beaches. But this isn't a city of beach bums. The shore has a reputation for being a very white, middle-class city, a safe secure place to bring up children, with great amenities and schooling. Around 70% of schools on the shore are decile eight or above and it was a coup for the area when Massey University established its gracious campus at Albany.

Whatever the attraction, new residents are pouring in, particularly to Albany, which is the fastest growing area of the North Shore. Albany's expanding commercial and retail area has predictably brought extensive new housing into the area. It's also being credited with raising the profile of the upper East Coast Bays, which have traditionally been the poor relation of the suburbs nearer Takapuna. The spin-off is what one long-time estate agent describes as "a significant jump in values" with buyers moving to be close to work in the Albany basin. It's a demographic change that is seeing top income buyers picking up prestigious suburban and fringe lifestyle property in a previously undervalued area.

North Shore's amenities have developed along with the population. Sporting facilities, leisure centres and shopping complexes have all grown rapidly across the city, many touted as the biggest and best in greater Auckland. A lesser known attraction is the shore's green areas. There are 454 reserves covering 1579ha.

Real estate values reflect this diversity. Multi-million dollar waterfront properties aside, there are plenty of suburbs packed with modest first homes. Recently the shore has sprouted an abundance of new subdivisions and terrace housing, as well as more infill housing. Sale prices plus the market blowout mean even real estate agents have trouble assessing a home's worth - so comparable current average values are anyone's guess.

Devonport was the first area of the shore to be populated by Europeans. Settlements grew as paddle steamer ferry services began plying their way across the Waitemata Harbour into areas such as Bayswater, Takapuna, Northcote and Birkenhead. When the Harbour Bridge opened in 1959 the North Shore woke up with a start! Within 10 years housing developments were sprouting up everywhere - note the proliferation of 1970s homes in most suburbs. Families were planned for and industry boomed, offering local employment as well.

Now the latest northern motorway extension is doing to Albany, Silverdale, Orewa and the Whangaparaoa Peninsula what the Harbour Bridge did to the more southern suburbs.

The main thorn in the side of North Shore-ites is the transport situation. Peak hour traffic crawls along most of the main arterial routes, as well as the motorway. Moves are afoot to improve this, however, with schemes such as the council's busway concept. Busway stations are also part of future plans to ease congestion.

sun-kissed sands

rangitoto island's silhouette

family-**friendly**

schools **aplenty**

including Paremoremo, Greenhithe, Brookfield, Rosedale and North Harbour

Albany continues its cracking pace as the expanding commercial, retail and light industrial centre of the North Shore. Its population is mushrooming and demand continues to outpace new housing developments. Most of Albany's residential land is owned by development companies and sections are typically pre-sold. There's a shortage of land for spec builders and of completed homes to meet the demand.

Albany is a picture of contrasts. There's the quaint original Albany village, where roosters crow in the sun. Then there are the sprawling new homes, the Albany Mega Centre, Massey University's European-styled campus and the iconic curves of the North Harbour stadium. Inland there's the commercial area of Rosedale, and there's Greenhithe just across the harbour with its mix of new and established homes. Paremoremo, just five minutes from Albany, has lifestyle appeal for locals who love its rural beauty - but not for the inmates at Her Majesty's prison institution of the same name. Not put off by the proximity to the prison, one local describes Paremoremo as probably the safest place in Auckland should one of the prisoners decide to escape.

Who lives there?

Couples with young families step up to substantial homes here and young professionals, including single women looking for safe, secure homes, go for the townhouses and terrace houses.

Migrants from Britain, South Africa and throughout Asia are just a small part of the picture here, with most buyers coming from throughout the North Shore and wider Auckland area. International buyers are generally settling here rather than buying property for investment only.

Students coming to Massey University tend to rent rather than buy, hence the sustained interest among investors. Real estate agents are eagerly awaiting the next wave of new homes that'll come onto the market throughout next year once siteworks begin in earnest during summer. Greenhithe's village atmosphere and semi-rural location attracts families looking to escape suburbia. English migrants also like the big sections and the characterful houses here.

Typical dwellings

In the past three years hundreds of terrace houses have sprung up, and now the landscaping is catching up to soften the area and help create an established ambience. Oteha Valley Rd's terrace houses are typical of those that have suffered bad press in the wake of the leaky building syndrome, but sales agents report that terrace houses sell and rent well when backed up by building inspections confirming their structural integrity.

Greenhithe's new housing developments are pitched at professional people and they're popular with long-time Greenhithe residents downsizing from bigger homes on the 1200 to 1500m² sections that are the average in the established part of town.

Low maintenance brick or plaster homes feature on the smaller 600 or 800m² sections in the newer areas developed by Universal Homes and the more established St Johns College development at Wainoni Heights.

In the commercial area of Rosedale, studio and warehouse developments have outpaced demand. Some buyers live and work in them or live upstairs and rent out the lower level; others use both levels for living in.

REAL ESTATE

Trends

The most significant change throughout Albany has been the shortage of land for developers. It looks as though there is a lot of development going on here, but most of the land has been pre-sold ahead of construction scheduled for the forthcoming summer. Throughout 2004 there will be many more new homes on the market and many keen buyers on the books of sales agents throughout the area. There's sustained interest among first home buying professionals wanting terrace housing to get onto the home ownership ladder. Albany is also a popular choice for families upsizing from Glenfield and Unsworth Heights, who don't necessarily aspire to living along the East Coast Bays.

In Greenhithe there's new building earmarked for Roland Rd, where a 2.6ha block of land that sold for $3.1 million has been subdivided into 17 sites, each averaging 1500m².

Prices

Typical pricing is hard to pinpoint in Albany, but indications are that townhouses have gone up between $50,000 and $100,000 in the past 12 months, with three-bedroom versions starting in the mid $200,000s. Executive family homes start from $400,000, with top end prices well into the $500,000s. In The Oaks, palatial homes sell for $700,000; quality executive homes in the The Landing, overlooking Lucas Creek, now start from $400,000 compared with last year's entry price of $350,000.

Greenhithe has its million dollar gems hidden in the bush, with buyers from the North Shore and Britain paying prices in the high $800,000s and $900,000s for charm, character, seclusion and land. One established four-bedroom home backing onto the water, with a pool, sold for $1.6 million. First entry into Greenhithe is in the low $300,000s for an older home, with most in the mid to high $400,000s. New homes in Admirals Court, priced in the high $300,000s in late 2002, have jumped to the mid $400,000s.

Average sale prices

	House	Flat	No. sales
2002	$348,823	$294,000	126
2003	$421,723	$212,857	450

Rental and investment

Rents in Albany and Greenhithe are comparable, with a two-bedroom cottage or townhouse costing about $250 a week, and a three-bedroom home about $350. A new three-bedroom home is about $450. Greenhithe isn't typically an investors area. It is locals who tend to buy a second property because of their emotional ties to the area.

Best streets

The Landing and The Oaks in Albany, and Oscar Rd and Kingfisher Grove, Greenhithe.

AMENITIES

Schools ★★

Albany and Greenhithe have good primary schools, but huge population growth has prompted recent announcements of two new schools. In Appleby Rd, Albany Flat, a year seven to 10 state junior high school will open in 2005. It's a new state schooling concept adopted by the Ministry of Education in direct response to the wishes of the local community. In Kyle Rd, Greenhithe, a new primary school is to open in 2005. Greenhithe has an early childhood centre and a playcentre. In the Oteha Valley Rd area a new primary school, under construction, is due to open in 2004.

Secondary pupils travel to state schools

Local hero - North Harbour Sports Stadium

Its sleek curves reflecting the rolling hills of the surrounding countryside have made this stylish events centre in the centre of Albany a North Shore icon. Since its opening in March 1997, it has been the happening place on the North Shore, with sporting and cultural events from rugby and gridiron to opera and rock concerts. It's ideal for more sedate functions too.

outside the area - Long Bay College in Torbay and Glenfield College. Kristin School, a private school catering for children of all ages, has expanded. Pinehurst School in Albany is a co-ed primary and secondary school.

Shops ★★★

Albany's Mega Centre is a huge retail development with every kind of shop imaginable. For those who prefer the mall, there are Westfield malls in Glenfield and Takapuna. Westfield plans to start building its "international shopping centre" in Albany midway through next year, with the first stage scheduled for opening 12 months later. Greenhithe's local shops include a bakery, a takeaway and a garage.

Leisure ★★★★

Despite the boom in subdivisions, there are plenty of reserves offering crowd respite, such as Lucas Creek Reserve, Wainono Park and Albany Scenic Reserve. Lucas Creek is good for canoeing and rafting - you can paddle a canoe down the creek to the harbour. There is also a lot of bush-covered land, native and

pine, in behind Rosedale and Greenhithe. A special spot is Wharf Reserve, a tiny reserve just off the Albany Highway where you can hear native birds by the creek.

Horses are a big part of the scene, as the pony clubs and equine centres indicate. For golfers, the North Shore Golf Club borders Albany Highway. Each community has the usual sports grounds and clubs, like tennis, soccer etc. Albany locals are close to amenities such as Glenfield Leisure Centre and the new Millennium Centre in Mairangi Bay, and there's a cinema complex and fitness facility planned for the mega centre. Hordes of four wheel drives will be heading to Albany if the proposed artificial ski field near the Silverdale turn off to East Coast Rd comes off.

The Wine Box is one of many small, appealing eating places in Albany Village. The Albany Inn is a long-standing watering hole. Predictably, the mega centre has fast food outlets, as well as a couple of cafés. New boutique café Collins House is a first for Greenhithe. There is also the Malthouse and the Purple Rain Brasserie in Greenhithe.

SMART BUY

One of the fastest-growing suburbs in the country in recent times, this area still has plenty of potential for future growth. It's a reasonably quick drive from the city at off-peak times, yet some areas retain a peaceful rural atmosphere. Sensible buying.

For colour key, see page 208

Travel times	
From Albany	
CBD	off-peak 30 min
	peak 60+ min
Harbour Bridge	15 min
Airport	45-60 min
North Shore Hospital	15-20 min

Shopping malls are seconds or minutes away, depending how close you live to the mega centre.

Regular buses service Albany, some stopping at Takapuna. Others are express buses that go straight through to the Harbour Bridge and central city.

including Island Bay and Mariner's Cove

Years ago, city dwellers used to take the ferry to their holiday baches in the bush of Birkdale and Beach Haven. They'd dance at the local hall and dine at the tearooms that used to be on the beach.

Now smart cookies who have been pushed out of the prestigious water's edge market along Takapuna, East Coast Bays and Herne Bay are jostling for prime position along Island Bay, Mariner's Cove and coastal Beach Haven. Collectively these and the little bays that dot the coastline are part of Beach Haven, but locals like to refer to these distinct areas for their lifestyle and status value.

New first home buyers often start off in "inland" Birkdale and most often "do up" and "move up" within the area, supporting excellent local schools and enjoying the beaches, windsurfing spots off Island Bay and indoor and outdoor leisure facilities. With its Titirangi-style bush, elevated harbour views and streets that snake down off main bus routes, this area boasts some of the North Shore's most appealing locations. You're right to feel on top of the world here, with spectacular views across the upper Waitemata to Hobsonville and beyond.

Who lives there?

A cross-section of buyers gives this area its flavour. There are young couples who have settled to raise a family, buyers from elsewhere on the North Shore, expat Kiwis returning from Britain and Europe, overseas holidaymakers who've bought a place to go sailing from every weekend, and migrants from as far afield as Europe and South Africa. It's popular with professional couples working in the CBD or the North Shore.

Typical dwellings

Baches "au naturel" and baches that have steadily morphed into impressive family homes dot the streets that were once surrounded by orchards stretching into neighbouring Birkenhead. There's infill housing made possible by large sections that have been subdivided for stand-alone townhouses.

This area is much newer than neighbouring Birkenhead with its 19th century villas. The impetus for development here came after the Auckland harbour bridge was completed in 1959, and throughout the 1960s and 1970s trendy new products like Hardiplank and aluminium joinery adorned houses proud to announce their new fashionable, low

maintenance status. There are many standard Reidbuilt homes dotted throughout the area that were designed and built for the first home buyer market. Newer homes built within the past 10 years reflect contemporary tastes.

REAL ESTATE

Trends

Coastal streets and elevated locations offer the most affordable seaside living on Auckland's North Shore and the buying public hasn't been slow to appreciate the lifestyle appeal and value for money. Investment in new housing is bringing confidence into the area too. Astute local and Auckland-wide buyers are buying sizeable properties with subdivision potential. In many cases, the value is in the land rather than the tired old dwelling and the growing trend here is to demolish the original house and build two new homes, rather than put a new home behind a renovated one.

Prices

At the top end of the market, premium homes in Mariner's Cove and coastal Beach Haven with spectacular views are now selling in the $700,000s compared with the high $500,000s three years ago, and there's fierce buyer competition too. Homes recently valued in the

Why I live there
"King of the Castle" Ron Reid

One of the founders of Reidbuild Homes, Ron Reid wasn't joking when he decided to build "something that no-one else in the street has" on his Verbena Rd, Birkdale, property. Inspired by a picture of an English castle, he drew up plans for the five-bedroom, three-storey home known as Lymington Castle. Ron hand-cut the Hinuera stone that would arrive in eight-tonne truckloads twice a year. He can't remember how long his DIY project took but he thinks it stretched from the 1950s into the 1970s. All he remembers of the completion date was pulling on his beret to keep the stone dust out of his hair and heading out to cut more stone - until his wife told him he'd finished the previous day!

high $700,000s would be expected to reach the $1 million mark if they were to come onto the market. A three-bedroom home in Island Bay or Mariner's Cove on a full site with good harbour views will generally sell in the mid $300,000 to $400,000s. One property with three bedrooms, double garage and boat parking on 810m² recently sold for $402,000. The days of buying a three-bedroom home "inland" for under $200,000 have now gone. That's what you can expect to pay for a two-bedroom unit. Entry level is now in the mid $200,000s for an older home on a full site. A freestanding townhouse in Beach Haven without views that sold for $164,000 three years ago recently attracted six tenders and sold for $251,000.

Average sale prices

	House	Flat	No. sales
2002	$202,932	$197,572	557
2003	$233,248	$183,164	679

Rental and investments

There's keen competition among investors and first home buyers to buy rental property in Birkdale. Their attention is usually focused in the $240,000 to $260,000 range where properties return a weekly rental of $300 to $340. The mix of rented housing and owner/occupied housing is about 50:50 in Birkdale, where there's steady demand for two-bedroom units in the $230 to $240 range. A two or three-bedroom home or townhouse will cost about $290 a week. Weekly rentals for larger homes range from $375 to $450. Coastal areas have far fewer rental properties - a prime home could cost $500 plus to rent.

Best streets

Valkyria Pl and water's edge Brigantine Pl, Beach Haven; Gatman Pl, Birkdale.

Schools ★★★★

A choice of primary schools and the local Birkenhead Intermediate School supports a growing family area. Birkenhead College won the 1999 Goodman Fielder School of the Year and has added to its academic successes with a strong reputation in sport (orienteering and hockey) as well as music, drama and art.

Shops ★★★

The opening of the Kaipatiki Bridge link from Beach Haven to Glenfield has opened up a direct route to the Glenfield Mall. In the other direction there's mall shopping in Birkenhead with its Countdown supermarket and The Warehouse, as well as a variety of strip shopping along Mokoia Rd. Birkdale and Beach Haven each have their collection of local shops tucked in the neighbourhoods. At Verrans Corner there's an antique shop next door to Toad's Manor café.

Leisure ★★★

Beach Haven's best known eatery is the Au Bon Coin, which means "to the good corner". Located on the corner of Beach Haven Rd and Rangitira Rd, its French influence extends beyond the birthplace of its owner Chris Mainas to include home-made French-inspired food and a boutique wine list. For those needing to eat and rush, there is an Asian bakery, a fish and chips takeaway and a pizza shop.

For leisure, there's Shepherd's Park with its sports ground, tennis and squash facilities. There's also the recently completed coastal walkway and parks and reserves to wander through.

LOOK OUT!

The views are gorgeous, but if you tell too many people everyone will want to live here, then the locals won't be happy.

SMART BUY

There are pockets of real estate treasure still to be found in coastal Beach Haven. A good home on a full site with or without views is likely to be a good investment in one of the most affordable waterside suburbs of the North Shore. If long term proposals for a ferry service from Beach Haven firm up, it'll certainly improve prospects even further in this area.

Travel times
From Birkdale

CBD	peak 45 min
	off-peak 15 min
Birkenhead shops	5 min
Glenfield mall	10 min
North Shore hospital	15 to 20 min
Airport	45 min

Peak hour priority lanes (rapid bus transit in council-speak) for buses and car pooling cut the time to the city by a third. For others, getting out of Birkdale and Beach Haven down Onewa Rd can be slow during peak hours.

Birkenhead Transport is based at Verrans Corner and it does a loop of the area down Birkdale Rd, Beach Haven Rd and Rangitira Rd before heading into the city through Birkenhead. Locals note how quick it is to get into town by bus and tell you they'd rather not bother driving there and trying to find a park.

The new Kaipatiki Bridge between Beach Haven and Glenfield has opened that area up. It takes less than five minutes to get to the mall from Beach Haven.

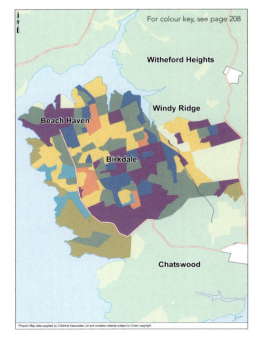

BELMONT/BAYSWATER ★★★★☆

including Narrow Neck

Bayswater and Belmont are seen as a kids' paradise. Picture them biking along wide streets, playing in large trees, swimming at beaches an easy walk from home or squelching in gumboots through Bayswater's mudflats at low tide. Once considered a nothing location between Takapuna and Devonport, the suburbs of Belmont and Bayswater are now coming into their own. And not just because they offer affordable housing within striking distance of Takapuna's beaches, cafes and shops and Devonport's arty, historical ambience. Belmont's eastern shoreline between Cheltenham and Takapuna beaches has the same golden sands and views of Rangitoto Island as its upmarket neighbours. Bayswater Pt has wonderful harbour views and access to the marina and the windsurfing haven of Shoal Bay, which more than compensates for the sou'westerly winds that occasionally hit the point.

Who lives there?

The suburbs of Bayswater and Belmont have well-established communities with a good mix of older and younger families. Many elderly couples downsize but stay, adding to the community feel. Belmont has traditionally been more blue-collar than Bayswater, but that is changing. Belmont homes are either receiving a lot of attention in the way of renovations or are being demolished and replaced with the latest and greatest in modern architecture - all of which adds value to the area.

Many expats come looking for lifestyle and affordability. Japanese, German and Chinese are buying into Bayswater, seeing it as cheaper than Devonport but with similar views. While Bayswater is attracting more of these buyers, Belmont is following in its footsteps.

Typical dwellings

An eclectic mix of 1960s and 1970s architecture, gracious villas, renovated baches and state housing sit side-by-side in these suburbs. There are also a growing number of opulent clifftop homes, although not nearly as many as in Takapuna and Milford. Clusters of state housing remain in both suburbs, particularly Belmont. Some have been sold and done up, many not. Infill housing is common in these areas where many homes traditionally sat

on more than 900m² of land. If you're keen on naval neighbours, check out houses around Philomel Cres, Roberts Ave, Hillary Cres and Lowe St. The navy owns a lot of residential property, much of which is 1940s state housing style. Bayswater is one of the few places left in Auckland where you can still buy a home on a 1000m² section at the water's edge and see change from $2 million.

REAL ESTATE

Trends

As with other water's edge suburbs, Bayswater and Narrow Neck are bringing ex-pat investors back home, often as first home buyers. Interestingly, buyers moving into Narrow Neck are calling the area by its correct name rather than part of Belmont/Bayswater, to identify its special appeal as a beautiful beachside spot that's only a 20 minute walk from Devonport.

This area has traditionally lagged behind Devonport in real estate status but the past 12 months has seen a noticeable catch up in prices with buyers who've found Devonport out of their financial reach. The improved Bayswater Fullers ferry service has lifted the appeal of this area to city-bound commuters preferring to avoid the main arterial road north to hook into the harbour bridge's traffic queues.

This area's wide mix of housing styles now includes many townhouses on subdivided sites and new homes on full sites that once contained an old house that may have been in one family for many years. Belmont and Bayswater lack the charming villas of Devonport which, on the positive side, also means that new homes don't have to comply with restrictive heritage zone design constraints. Schooling is a key drawcard for families and Asian students.

Prices

Prices across the board have increased enormously in the past 12 months - from sausage block units for $250,000 to $2 million premium clifftop homes. Ex-state houses that sold for $200,000 and $240,000 a year ago now sell from $350,000 depending on the section size and the quality of renovations. Astute would-be buyers know that the average three-bedroom home in Belmont is up from the mid to high $300,000s to around $450,000. In Bayswater the same sort of home will sell for around $550,000.

Premium properties in Bayswater have continued their steady rise with several $1 million plus sales. As is typical of waterside suburbs, homes on one side of the street with views are worth double those across the road without a view. Prices are out of reach of traditional first home buyers but achievable for young double-income professionals.

Average sale prices

	House	Flat	No. sales
2002	$400,240	$284,488	233
2003	$438,387	$260,052	224

Rental and investment

Block units built in the 1960s and 1970s for retired people range in rental from $280 per week, even less if they need redecorating. There's a shortage of rental stock for families, who should expect to pay from mid $300 to mid $400 as a typical weekly rental. The past 12 months has seen urgency creep into the rental market here as owners have sold their investment homes to free up their capital gain and tenants have had to move to whatever rental homes they could find. Now, with the shortage of sales stock, tenants are moving by choice or because their personal needs change and they're fussier about what they want in a rental home.

Best streets

Norwood Rd, Beresford St and Marine Tce in Bayswater offer fantastic views because they edge the shoreline around Bayswater Pt. Views win out in Belmont, too, with top streets being Williamson Ave, Seacliff St and Hamana St, Merani St, overlooking Narrow Neck Beach.

Local hero - windsurfing

Like a multitude of butterflies darting about on the water, windsurfers skim across Shoal Bay, zig-zagging in the wind. The bay is a mecca for windsurfers because the prevailing sou'westerlies blow straight into the bay, accelerating between the headlands and the Harbour Bridge. The water conditions vary with the tide, adding to the excitement and unpredictability. The easy accessiblity is a plus and the windsurfing retail outlets of Barry's Pt Rd and Sir Peter Blake Dr are handy.

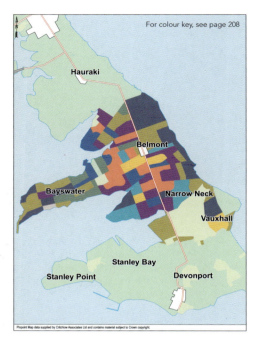

For colour key, see page 208

Hauraki

Belmont

Bayswater

Narrow Neck

Vauxhall

Stanley Bay

Stanley Point

Devonport

Pinpoint Map data supplied by Critchlow Associates Ltd and contains material subject to Crown copyright.

AMENITIES

Schools ★★★★

Unsurprisingly, school options are good in these family-oriented suburbs. Belmont is home to Takapuna Grammar School, one of the biggest high schools in New Zealand. It is on Lake Rd and has panoramic views of the sea. The school's reputation with international Asian students has brought many Asian families into the area. Belmont Intermediate is next door and primary schools include Belmont Primary and Bayswater Primary.

Shops ★★

There's the $10 haircut shop, a $3 shop in Belmont and a liquor wholesaler. The local shops also include various takeaway outlets, a pharmacy and a doctor's surgery.

Leisure ★★★

Bayswater Park hosts rugby league, Aussie rules and touch football. The Waitemata Golf Club is at the Devonport end of Lake Rd. Bayswater Marina adds to the ambience, providing boating and water recreational

activities for everyone. A village proposal for the marina is on the cards, although some locals are wary of how it might affect their current friendly community lifestyle.

Sure proof that plenty of families live around this area - McDonald's is in the shopping centre. Fast food delivery addicts have Pizza Hut to call upon as well.

There are plenty of adventures for children and adults alike with the mangroves and mudflats around Bayswater, golden sands of Narrow Neck Beach and recreational options at Bayswater Marina, where Takapuna Boating Club is based. Narrow Neck is a great beach for children and not just because of its sailing club and safe waters. It also has a reserve with playground equipment and a shop - bonuses when heading to the beach with kids. If wetlands are your thing, check out Kawerau Reserve in Bayswater - easily accessed on boardwalks wide enough for wheelchair users.

SMART BUY

Sitting between the North Shore's prestigious suburbs of Takapuna and Devonport, Belmont and Bayswater can't really miss being on the up-and-up. Belmont's eastern shoreline even has the same views as Takapuna. The style of housing (small and often state dwellings) has held the area back but with the sea on both sides, these are being either replaced or substantially renovated.

Travel times

CBD by car	off-peak 10 min
	peak 40 min
CBD by ferry	15 min
North Shore Hospital	10-15 min
Hauraki Corner New World	5 min
Devonport New World	10 min
Airport	45-60 min

Stagecoach Auckland runs a reasonably regular service to Takapuna and the CBD. At the weekends this service is offered by Urban Express. Locals working in the CBD have the alternative of the Bayswater ferry, which leaves from the marina.

Ferry across the Waitemata

Travelling to work across the Waitemata Harbour by ferry is a simple pleasure. No road rage, traffic snarls or carbon dioxide - just a quiet, relaxing trip across the inner harbour reading the newspaper, catching up on work files or having a coffee and a snack. Before the Harbour Bridge opened in 1959, ferries were the only option for North Shore locals wanting to cross the harbour. Initially the bridge took a lot of custom away from ferry services as people indulged in the novelty of driving to work - and paid a toll to do so! In more recent years ferries have become popular again as commuters from Devonport, Waiheke Island, Stanley Bay, Northcote Pt, Bayswater, Birkenhead, Gulf Harbour and the eastern coastal suburb of Half Moon Bay recognise the merit of travelling by water.

Fullers Group is the main ferry service provider in Auckland. Caro Cats operates the Gulf Harbour ferry and Subritzky Line has a vehicle and passenger ferry option to Waiheke and Great Barrier islands. Subritzky Line recently purchased the Devonport Wharf facilities and, with the local rumour mill working overtime, Subritzky's assure locals that it's "business as usual".

Today's ferry fleets, which include catamarans, usually have catering and bar facilities on board. Pleasure is catered for as well as convenience. They are a far cry from the original paddle steamer ferries that plied the Waitemata Harbour from the mid-1800s. The first custom-built ferry for the Devonport run was launched in 1865 and ferries were doing daily trips to Devonport, Takapuna and Northcote from 1881 onwards.

In those days ferries provided an essential lifeline to the mainland. The service extended to Birkenhead and Chelsea and operated regularly for many years. They weren't just for workers either. Yes, even 120 years ago, day-trippers were enjoying the exhilaration of bracing sea trips across the harbour.

Modern-day tourists have many more options when it comes to enjoying the harbour from the comfort of a ferry. The sandy coastlines of the islands dotting the Hauraki Gulf are popular ferry tourist attractions, including the volcanic grandeur of Rangitoto Island, the beaches and vineyards of Waiheke Island, and the isolation and beauty of Great Barrier Island. There are also harbour cruises that include a guided walk through the bird sanctuary island Tiritiri Matangi and a service to the picturesque Kawau Island with its heritage mansion house.

including Stanley Bay, Stanley Pt, Cheltenham and Vauxhall

Genteel is the enduring image of Devonport, the gracious old lady basking by the sea. This historic seaside resort village has become a haven for people with a keen sense of heritage and the income and interest to preserve its Victorian and Edwardian architecture. The suburb is steeped in history, particularly maritime history. The New Zealand Navy Base is still in Stanley Bay and there are old gun emplacements on North Head and Mt Victoria. Tourists and other Aucklanders swell the numbers during weekends and holidays, giving the surburb a relaxed ambience. There are few streets without a glimpse of the sea. Devonport and Stanley Pt look across the harbour to Auckland City and the harbour bridge, Cheltenham has Rangitoto Island and the Hauraki Gulf. Devonport is the shore's St Marys Bay without the motorway buzz. Cheltenham is Mission Bay without the highrises.

Who lives there?

The seclusion, peace and historical beauty of Devonport traditionally attracted lifestylers, nautical types, artists and writers and North Shore-ites retiring from other areas. These days the area is attracting many young professionals, often with school-age families.

Aside from an appreciation of the area's heritage character, they're looking for large homes, big sections and a laid-back lifestyle close to beaches, parks and good schools.

There's still plenty of interest among international and ex-pat buyers. Devonport people are traditionally a pro-active lot. Concerned about noisy Navy activities on local defence land, they have agitated for

a legal change that now means the Royal New Zealand Navy will keep residents better informed - without releasing state secrets - about what is happening at their Devonport base. Devonport locals also banded together to form a "Save the Cinema" group when it was sold a year ago. Now, in conjunction with Rialto cinemas, the Devonport cinema opens for specific screenings and the new owner is happy for this to continue for the time being.

Typical dwellings

Gracious Victorian and Edwardian villas dominate the architecture, making it the largest collection of villas on the shore. The majority of homes are still on reasonable sites - infill housing is rare.

The heritage character is strongly supported by the North Shore City Council through zoning which requires renovations to enhance the historical nature of individual buildings and the area as a whole. The street facades of buildings erected before 1930 can't generally be altered and back-additions or renovations should be done in sympathetic materials. That doesn't stop the interiors being up-to-the-minute, however. Wandering around streets such as Marine Pde and King Edward Pde, it is easy to envisage life 150 years ago when wealthy

Why I live there
Artist Lyndsay Brock

Eccentricity is treasured in Devonport, says artist Lyndsay Brock, who has lived all her life, bar five homesick years, in the area. "I'm addicted to the place. I love the old homes, the rabbit warren streets and the amazing coastline. Watching a sunset from Mt Victoria is so beautiful it almost makes you weep." The 59-year-old lives in an "ordinary" 1920s cottage near Ngataringa Bay (between Stanley Pt and Bayswater). An environmentalist, Lindsay says the area brings out a protective attitude in people, as the heritage zoning indicates. "There is an interesting conglomeration of people which is very stimulating for artists. People often stereotype Aucklanders, but it is not just a big bland city, rather a whole gamut of small communities like Devonport."

maritime merchants built their homes looking across to the Auckland port. The number of apartment blocks in the area can be counted on one hand. This is considered a major attraction and the reason people buy in the area instead of Mission Bay or Kohimarama.

REAL ESTATE

Trends

Buyers here continue to be a steady mix from further up the North Shore, ex-pats returning home and migrants, especially from the UK. The number of properties for sale has dropped recently, partly because the market has caught up with vendors' previously ambitious price expectations and partly because other vendors have lowered their expectations to meet the market. Not everyone sees Devonport's one road in, one road out status (for those who can't take the ferry) as a commuter's nightmare. According to one real estate agent, others see it as a positive sign that Devonport is a secure area, not just a transit suburb.

The market for terrace-house-style units has changed dramatically over the years, moving between owner/occupier and investor-owned as the market has fluctuated.

Prices

The long-term picture here is one of 10% per annum price increases over the past 10 years. Put it this way, double what you paid for that scruffy cottage ten years ago and you'll know roughly what the highly refined, lovingly renovated version you're now living in is likely to sell for. The properties that enjoy clifftop or waterfront views have increased at an even greater rate.

First entry point here is $500,000-plus, which buys a cottage on a small site, a three-bedroom bungalow or something on a larger site in a lesser street. A three-bedroom home needing renovation sells for $680,000 to $780,000; premium homes throughout the area are nudging the $1.5 million mark. One villa in King Edward Pde sold for $1.29 million - the first time it had been on the market since 1910.

Brick and tile units (of the two-up, two-down block-of-four style) start at $250,000 and they're now sought after for long-term capital gain. One such unit in near derelict condition inside sold as a deceased estate for $235,000. If there's stiff competition for such homes, chances are the successful buyer will be an owner/occupier seeking long-term capital gain, rather than an investor.

Average sale prices

	House	Flat	No. sales
2002	$524,117	$321,932	220
2003	$699,019	$343,190	133

Rental and investment

Locals are keen to buy second and third homes to rent out, having watched the steady capital gain. As a result the rental stock has increased dramatically. Those wanting to rent are generally families moving to be close to the ferry and good schooling and with $500 a week to spend on a three-bedroom renovated home. Top quality homes cost between $500 and $700. Corporates whose $2000 a week rents for the most prestigious properties are paid by their parent companies in the US and UK make up a small corner of the rental picture here.

Best streets

Jubilee Ave in Cheltenham and the end of Stanley Pt Rd, or down First and Second Ave in Stanley Pt. Homes in these areas have stunning harbour views and spacious sections.

AMENITIES

Schools ★★★★

Good schools are one of the attractions in this area, as with other suburbs on the North Shore. No high school is based in Devonport, Cheltenham or Stanley Bay proper, but students are zoned for Takapuna Grammar School on Lake Rd, which is one of the oldest high schools on the shore.
Belmont Intermediate is next door to the grammar school. Primary schools in the area include St Leo's Primary in Devonport, Devonport School, Vauxhall School and Stanley Bay School.

Shops ★★★★

Devonport Village is like a charming old village with traditional facades on most of the shops, including the grand old Esplanade pub, at the bottom of the main street, which has recently been refurbished.
The New World supermarket is discreetly located on a side street. Dotted among the plethora of cafes and bars are a couple of great book stores, three museums, specialist craft shops and reputable art galleries.

Leisure ★★★★★

You can't beat this area for open spaces. On the end of a peninsula, Devonport residents have easy access to beaches from east, south and west.
Cheltenham Beach is arguably one of the most beautiful in Auckland with its panoramic view of Rangitoto Island, golden sands and pohutukawa trees. Non-beach walks include the Old Devonport Walk, which takes about an hour and highlights historical treasures in the area.
North Head and Mt Victoria are both accessible and have great views.
Watersports are popular and five boat ramps dot the Devonport shoreline. Sport lovers have plenty to do - tennis, cricket and bowling clubs and grounds, the Waitemata Golf Course and Devonport Domain. The Navy Museum is another drawcard and the navy has regular open days.
Often dubbed the museum village, there is plenty of history, arts and crafts to view, along with cafes, bars, and the elegantly refurbished Devonport cinema (parents - it has a crying room). The group of locals who are keeping it running regularly advertise in the NZ Herald to build up patronage.
During the past 10 years cafes, brasseries and bars have multiplied in Devonport Village, drawing locals and offering a romantic option for Aucklanders keen on a ferry trip and a meal. Locals reckon Thai Taste 99 is worth a visit. Try

Local Hero - Devonport Domain's trees

Planted some 50 years ago, these beautiful London plane trees have been allowed to grow naturally, unlike some in other suburbs which are pruned annually to little more than a trunk stump, a technique known as pollarding. Devonport's plane trees are "protected" trees under the North Shore City Council's tree and bush protection regulations, which means maintenance work must have council permission. As beautiful as they are, these trees are not on the council's list of "notable" trees. Trees listed on the Schedule of Notable Trees are documented on the district plan for their exceptional historical, cultural, botanical or amenity value.

a beer and pub meal at the Masonic, exclusive dining or Sunday brunch at the Esplanade, or a quick coffee and snack at one of the many cafés. Ice-it in Church St is a current favourite for good cake and coffee. On sunny days or balmy evenings, you can buy takeaways and sit on the beachfront. The annual food and wine festival brings Aucklanders from far and wide.

A number of artists live and work in the area. Depot Artspace, a community-based centre with a recording studio as well as gallery space, is one of many art spaces in Devonport.

LOOK OUT!

If pulling down old homes to put up a space-age apartment is your thing, then this area may not work for you. The olde-worlde charm of Devonport has survived because the community is zealous about protecting it.

Also, living on the peninsula may give you a great sense of solitude, but there is only one main route in and out (Lake Rd) so snail-like traffic is common in peak hours.

Travel times

CBD	off-peak 15-20 min
	peak 1 hour
CBD by ferry	12 min
Northern motorway (Northcote on-ramp)	off-peak 15 min
	peak 45 min
Takapuna shops	10 to 15 min
Airport	45 min

The ferry is a godsend to Devonport residents, providing the opportunity for CBD workers to live a 12-minute ferry ride - and another world - away. The late night weekend ferry timetable means Devonport, Stanley Pt and Cheltenham residents can sample the nightlife until 1am. That's a bit early if you're a teenage clubber but many Devonport residents are parents of young children.

The first passenger ferry started 150 years ago and was the only way to reach Auckland from the shore until 1959 when the Harbour Bridge opened.

There are no trains on the North Shore, but there is a comprehensive Stagecoach Auckland bus system.

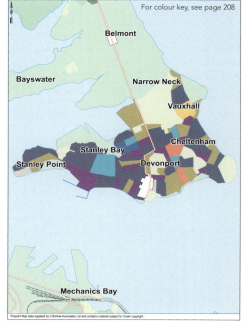

For colour key, see page 208

Belmont

Bayswater

Narrow Neck

Vauxhall

Cheltenham

Stanley Bay

Stanley Point

Devonport

Mechanics Bay

Pinpoint Map data supplied by Critchlow Associates Ltd and contains material subject to Crown copyright.

GLENFIELD ★★☆☆☆

including Wairau Park, The Palms and Unsworth Heights

Glenfield's claim to fame is twofold. Firstly, its population is said to personify average New Zealand. Secondly, "our" Rachel Hunter, model and ex-wife of international rocker Rod Stewart, came from Glenfield. She may now live in Hollywood but she's a Glenfield girl through and through. Glenfield is the heart of North Shore suburbia. The buzz of the lawn mower is alive and well here. The affordable housing makes it attractive to people who are not suburb snobs, many of whom work in the light industrial areas around Link Dr and Wairau Park. Although Glenfield is known as a first-home buyer suburb, there are plenty who have chosen to stay put because of the good schools and access to shore amenities. Glenfielders may not be living within cooee of the beach, but they're still only a few minutes' drive from the eastern or western coasts, Takapuna cafes, the Albany Mega Centre or Massey University at Albany.

Who lives there?

Twenty or thirty years ago Glenfield had the "nappy valley" tag firmly attached, and in some ways it has been a hard label to shake off. In those days it was the focus of affordable housing developments to suit young families. The streetscapes might have been barren then, as all new areas are, but planners had enough foresight to incorporate parks and playgrounds into the neighbourhoods. These days the trees have matured and the children have grown up, but the appeal of the area keeps families moving in.

Glenfield remains one of Auckland's rare affordable suburbs for traditional home owners on a single income. Glenfield has always enjoyed - or endured, depending on your viewpoint - strong investor interest too and this is a continuing feature. Manuka Cove is bringing in a mix of new professionals as both owner/occupiers and investors.

Typical dwellings

There's abundant choice from the group housing rectangular Hardiplank homes of Glenfield's earliest developments to older and new free-standing brick and tile homes.

New developments down Glendhu Rd include eight free-standing homes. Weatherboard terrace townhouses feature in the 39-unit Manuka Cove development along Manuka Rd. For buyers wanting family homes, well presented homes on full, rather than sub-divided sites are popular and competition is stiff.

REAL ESTATE

Trends

Despite community resistance to terrace housing, the Manuka Cove development is seen as adding choice to Glenfield's housing stock. With the first 10 units on the market, the development, which includes a communal pool, spa and gym, is expected to bring a mix of affluent professional owner/occupiers and investors into what has been seen as a backwater of Glenfield.

Glenfield's traditional investor interest remains strong for its good rental yield and comparatively affordable purchase prices. The past three years have seen significant buyer activity here. Multiple offers on properties are common, compared with a year or two ago. Factors include high immigration from China and Korea, Glenfield's status as a genuine

Local hero - Westfield Glenfield

You can't miss it. It's on Glenfield Rd and it's the hub of the retail area that services the western area of the entire North Shore. Westfield Glenfield is the biggest mall on the North Shore, with 114 shops including major department stores like Farmers, The Warehouse, Foodtown and Woolworths. There are numerous specialty shops and a foodcourt to suit all tastes. The mall opened in October 2000 after redevelopment of the old Glenfield Mall and it is close to bus routes, local businesses and other amenities including the Glenfield Leisure Centre.

first home buyer's area despite Auckland-wide price rises, more North Shore employment opportunities and the move of investors into Glenfield from the more expensive East Coast Bays rental properties.

Glenfield's profile suffered when buyers headed for the townhouse developments of neighbouring Albany, but in the wake of the "leaky building syndrome", it is enjoying renewed attention from buyers who have opted for tried and trusted weatherboard over new plasterclad homes.

Don't let anyone tell you that it stinks big time out at Unsworth Heights and The Palms. Big changes at the nearby wastewater treatment plant at Rosedale have virtually eliminated major sewage odours and "minor" odours are being targeted. New technology means open-topped tanks have been covered and large filters have been eliminated. The plant's management regularly consults with community groups.

Prices

For around $250,000 you've got choice in Glenfield - from a simple 1970's do-up to a terrace townhouse with access to a gym and pool at Manuka Cove. Here two-bedroom townhouses sell for $235,000 and the three-bedroom ones "in the high $200,000s".

First entry point has moved from $225,000 or $230,000 for a basic three-bedroom house to between $255,000 and $270,000. Units have increased from $150,000 to $160,000 up to between $180,000 and $200,000. Little pockets of housing sit in the $400,000 plus bracket. New homes in Glendhu Rd include five in the $340,000 to $420,000 price range and three more are about to be built in a bush setting for sale at $289,000. One real estate agent believes they'll be worth "in the $300,000s" on completion. Three-bedroom single level homes, including double garaging,

in the Daldy's Bush development sell for more than $450,000.

Interest in established homes is yielding multiple offers and outstanding prices. One three-bedroom home with two living areas and two bathrooms brought eight offers and a sale price of $361,800. It would have realistically fetched about $280,000 on last year's market. Top dollar was $675,000 paid for a home in the Treetops area, close to Albany.

Homes near the industrial area of Wairau Park sell in the mid to high $300,000s. Meadowwood has some group housing in the $240,000 to $280,000 bracket.

A four-bedroom brick and tile executive home on a full size 500 to 600m² section in The Palms sells for $480,000. Unsworth Heights is popular for first home buyers trading up. It has more subdivided sections and prices reach around $400,000 for a four-bedroom home on a half site.

Average sale prices

	House	Flat	No. sales
2002	$225,040	$186,585	743
2003	$264,054	$196,123	1253

Rental and investment

A three-bedroom home in Glenfield costing $250,000 will return $320 a week. The yields are better than more highly priced areas of the North Shore and investors are acting accordingly. Basic three-bedroom homes with a carport average around $300 a week; a new three-bedroom home about $350 and two-bedroom units about $250 to $280 a week.

Best streets

High Rd and Glendhu Rd in Glenfield; Calypso Way, The Palms, Westminster Gardens, and any streets in Unsworth Heights.

Schools ★★★

True to its name, Glenfield College is the main

high school in the area. The decile seven school was one of the first to bring in paying international students and it has a strong pastoral emphasis.

If you're wanting single-sex education, Westlake girls' and boys' highs are only a short distance from Glenfield. However, only some areas of Glenfield are zoned for the Westlake schools, so you need to check the zones on the schools' websites or at the back of this book. It is important to check individual school zones carefully if you decide to buy a home on the basis that it is in a particular school zone.

There are eight primary schools including a special school (Wairau Valley School) and Westminster Christian School. For middle education, there is Glenfield Intermediate.

Shops ★★★★

Glenfield locals are spoilt for choice when it comes to opportunities to indulge in any kind of retail therapy. Wairau Park, the commercial heart of North Shore, has grown like topsy. It contains everything you might need to refurbish, renovate or furnish your home - and more! Wairau Park also has cinemas, a bowling alley, casual pub-style eating places, Valentines and plenty of fast food outlets.

Retail therapy is also well catered for by Westfield in Glenfield. Revamped in 2000, it is currently the largest on the shore with The

Warehouse and two supermarkets included in the complex.

Leisure ★★★★

The food courts in the mall attract regular punters, as do eateries at Wairau Park such as Mad Dogs & Englishmen.

As seems typical of the North Shore, Glenfield has a number of parks as well as a coastal walkway. People are attracted to Glenfield for its easy access to both coastlines.

Rosedale Park is near the south and west of the waste water treatment plant. It's a lovely place, now that sewage odours have virtually been eliminated. The walkway around the Manuka Reserve has been upgraded. There's a boat ramp for use when the tide is right and a children's playground.

For kids, there's also Chipmunks Adventure Playground including a café, which is next to the Westfield Mall.

The Glenfield Leisure Centre includes gym, conference facilities, indoor heated swimming pools, hydroslides and diving boards, saunas and spas. There are also the usual Kiwi community facilities, such as a local library, citizens' advice bureau (CAB) and community centre. The North Shore Events Centre, where the Silver Ferns have fought many a battle, is in Glenfield.

SMART BUY

Yes. With its mall, proximity to beaches and relatively cheap houses, Glenfield is a smart place to buy. Settled families make great tenants and investment properties here usually offer good yields. For a tried and true step onto the home-ownership ladder, you can't go past a 1970s Hardiplank three-bedroom home. Pick one in a street that has established trees and a little playground, and you can get on with family living while your investment grows.

North Harbour
For colour key, see page 208
Meadowood
Unsworth Heights
Chester Park
The Palms   Totaravale
Cuthill
Wairau Park
Bay View
Wairau Valley
Glenfield
Witheford Heights
Marlborough
Windy Ridge
Hillcrest

Travel times
From central Glenfield

CBD	off-peak 10 min
	peak 1 hour
Airport	10-20 min
Westfield Glenfield	10 min

There are good regular bus services to Takapuna and the city.

including Whangaparaoa, Orewa, Silverdale, Red Beach and Gulf Harbour

It's holiday time! The Hibiscus coastline settlements of Orewa, Whangaparaoa and Red Beach are favourite summer havens for Aucklanders. Orewa's 2.5km beach is considered one of the best swimming beaches in the north, and then there are the Whangaparaoa Peninsula beaches, from Red Beach to Shakespear Park. While it's still a sleepy township until summer holidaymakers arrive, Orewa is starting to develop. The

northern motorway extension and bypass is causing a gradual transformation of the Hibiscus Coast from a holiday and retirement spot to a suburb of greater Auckland. People are moving here to enjoy the small town atmosphere and beaches, with Auckland's city amenities 30 minutes south and recreational spots to the north. Whangaparaoa Peninsula boasts a unique island atmosphere while not far inland Silverdale has a small, close-knit community enjoying a slow rural lifestyle.

Who lives there?

When you're talking permanent dwellers, not holiday hordes, Orewa has traditionally been popular with retired people, who appreciate the flat terrain, beach and shops. It is now also attracting midlife couples and young families who are buying into the new subdivisions.

On the peninsula there's a mix of families and couples, including retirees. We're not talking octogenarians though, but couples in their late 50s and 60s with children off their hands who can afford a reasonable home and boat by moving to the peninsula.

The newish Gulf Harbour School is bringing in families as well. The Gulf Harbour canal complex attracts well-heeled folk with an interest in boating and golfing. Around 70% of the apartments are not permanently occupied. A sprinkling of South Africans, English and Asians are buying in the peninsula and Orewa but not in the same numbers as in other areas of the North Shore. Gulf Harbour's apartment developments have brought an estimated 1000 new residents into the area and more buyers are owner/occupiers than in previous years. Buyer interest from the Asian market has largely disappeared. It is Kiwis buying and moving here, ex-pats returning home and international buyers relocating.

Such is Gulf Harbour's appeal, there are even buyers from the Middle East, including Dubai.

Typical dwellings

Fibrolite and weatherboard baches still have a strong presence in Orewa and Whangaparaoa Peninsula. On the flat in Orewa are houses favoured by retirees, single level brick-and-tile retirement homes, with an occasional newer, larger home adding to the landscape. A large number of subdivisions are occurring between the Orewa shops and the motorway, many located on slopes that offer views of Orewa Beach. The new homes are large, usually four-bedroom, and made of brick and tile, plaster exterior or a mix of brick and weatherboard.

Homes on the Whangaparaoa Peninsula are a mix of baches, modest 1960s and 1970s homes and flash modern dwellings. Many of the homes on ridges get great views of the sea. As well as the Gulf Harbour marina and apartment complex, Gulf Harbour has some subdivisions where large homes and terraced apartment blocks have been developed during the past six or seven years.

REAL ESTATE

Trends

Big developments on the Hibiscus Coast are

Why I live there

Rock Salt chef Justin Thomson

"I always feel I'm on holiday here. I love the bachy feel and the locality of the beaches," enthuses Justin, who dreams of eventually owning a boat. He and wife Alix came to the peninsula to work in the restaurant trade with Justin's parents and siblings. Justin and Alix love the views from their hillside location above Red Beach, looking across the sea to the islands beyond.

changing the flavour of this area and the apartment scene in Gulf Harbour looks like broadening the appeal of this popular "island" community. The opening of the private co-ed school Wentworth College at Gulf Harbour has eased the vexed issue of secondary schooling.

The new motorway that was widely predicted to cause a slump in Orewa's popularity has, in fact, given it wider family appeal than just the place you stop for an ice cream on the way north. Family buyers are coming from wider Auckland and inner-city suburbs - according to one busy real estate agency, 91% of its buyers on the Hibiscus Coast come from greater Auckland. The new housing developments near the motorway exit in Orewa were well under way before the motorway actually opened, in keeping with the area between Orewa and Silverdale's reputation as one of Auckland's future key growth areas.

In Gulf Harbour there is substantial land available for development and for those Auckland-based boaties, the village to be built by the canal development promises to make this the ultimate in desirable destinations. It's still early in the planning stages but there will be marina berths - admittedly with pay and display stations - but you'll be able to moor your yacht and shop, dine and dance 'til you drop.

Albany's commercial development has quickened the pace of residential sales across the whole area. The trend continues for older buyers along the East Coast Bays to downsize to Orewa's affordable brick and tile units, a short flat walk - and a short flat white - from the beach. For the upwardly mobile elderly, there's the 153-unit Nautilus apartment block under construction in Orewa. Such is the investor and owner/occupier interest that several apartments have already been sold.

Prices

There's cottage-style living at Hatfields Beach for $176,000 or palatial clifftop - on top of the world - living along the Whangaparaoa Peninsula for ten times the money. At the top end of the market, there's keen overseas interest, although the bulk of such properties are being bought by Kiwi owners moving from the wider Auckland area. One unique clifftop property north of Gulf Harbour sold for $1.81 million to an ex-pat Kiwi family returning home. Two years ago it would have been worth $1.2 million to $1.3 million.

Whangaparaoa clifftop prices now typically top $1 million for a good home on a 1000 to 1500m² site. One Stanmore Bay clifftop property sold for $1.239 million, another for $1.03 million, the same figure as for a Red Beach property with an outstanding home. At Gulf Harbour one property with a huge 500m² home fetched $1.06 million.

Gulf Harbour's apartments range from the most affordable in Alverna Heights now fetching $380,000 (compared with original sale prices of $345,000 to $350,000) to $1.3 million for a penthouse in the newest Quayside development.

All of the Santa Rosa apartments that were pre-sold for high $200,000s upwards are now fetching $325,000 to $350,0000 on re-sale. New apartments range from $300,000 for a one-bedroom, $320,000 for two-bedroom and $375,000 for a three-bedroom. Studio apartments in the Nautilus average $250,000, one-bedroom apartments about $450,000.

In Orewa, established, well-maintained brick and tile executive homes keep pace with the prices of the new housing developments to the west of the township which range from $400,000 to $700,000. Sections start from about $130,000. About $200,000 will buy a brick and tile unit, but expect to join a queue of a dozen other retirees or investors. The first entry point of the market up to $220,000 offers bach-style cottages or a unit.

Average sale prices

	House	Flat	No. sales
2002	$259,489	$242,704	1119
2003	$298,974	$288,635	1453

Rental and investment

In Orewa a two-bedroom brick and tile unit costs $250 to $280 a week, a stand-alone three-bedroom home with double garaging about $380 a week. On the peninsula, three and four-bedroom homes range from $340 to $380. Expect to pay $600 for a smart house with awesome sea views. A three-bedroom, three-level apartment with one garage in Gulf Harbour costs between $320 to $450 a week.

Best streets

Anything on the beachfront. In Orewa, West Hoe Rd and The Grange. In Red Beach, Chalverton Tce. In Stanmore Bay, Duncansby Bay Rd. In Gulf Harbour, Tiri Rd (an up-and-coming street that looks back over the gulf).

AMENITIES

Schools ★★★★

There's plenty of choice for children of all ages, boosted by the opening of the private co-ed Wentworth College in Gulf Harbour for year seven to 13 children. Primary schools are located in Orewa, Whangaparaoa, Gulf Harbour and Silverdale. There's Kingsway School, a Christian school in Orewa. Hibiscus Coast Intermediate is on the peninsula.

Shops ★★★

Orewa's town centre, which is headquarters for Rodney District Council, has a friendly small-town feel, with its mix of commercial and light industry. It is hard to get lost there; and the local people are happy to point you in the right direction.

Whangaparaoa township has the Pacific Plaza complex which includes some big stores like Farmers. There are also shops at Red Beach, Manly Village and Gulf Harbour.

Heading inland, the popular Silverdale shopping centre offers plenty of options for bargain hunters, with its mix of designer label factory outlets, boutique shops and an industrial park. The weekly Saturday markets attract enthusiastic crowds as well.

Leisure ★★★

Orewa Beach Holiday Park is one of those rare wonderful holiday parks located on the beachfront. Next door is the Orewa Reserve, where there's a skating rink and the Orewa Surf Lifesaving Club. Red Beach on the peninsula also has a surf club and surf life-savers, which means you can enjoy the challenge of the surf while bronzed bodies keep an eye on you - and you on them, no doubt!

The peninsula's numerous sandy beaches offer any number of recreational options, from swimming, surfing and fishing to windsurfing and boating. At the tip there's sprawling Army Bay and Shakespear Regional Park, full of picnic spots, little bays and walking tracks. Kids enjoy the Hibiscus Coast Youth Centre along the

Local hero - Gulf Harbour

To some it is the jewel of the peninsula; to others it's a blot on the landscape. Gulf Harbour is an upmarket waterfront development halfway along the Whangaparaoa Peninsula, modelled on a Mediterranean village. Based around a waterway with canals leading to the marina, there are townhouses and apartments grouped around the waterway, many with exclusive marinas. In fact, exclusive sums it up, from village to canals and golf courses. It is certainly not what you'd expect on this peninsula, which generally clings to a slow Kiwi pace of life. Despite the trappings, there is an air of expectation, as if everyone is waiting for something to happen. The apartments are mainly owned by weekenders and investors, which gives the place a ghostly feel at times.

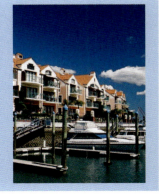

Hibiscus Coast Highway, which offers activities including rock climbing and abseiling. Orewa and most Whangaparaoa beaches have part-tide boat ramps and trailer boat launching facilities. There are also boating clubs. The Whangaparaoa Coastal Walkway starts at Amorino Reserve in Red Beach and continues to Matakatia Beach.

If beachy pleasures aren't your thing, there are plenty of other options. The Hibiscus Coast Leisure Centre at Stanmore Bay, Whangaparaoa, has an indoor heated swimming pool, squash courts and fitness facilities. There are two golf courses at Gulf Harbour, the Whangaparaoa Steam Railway and activities such as rock climbing, 10-pin bowling, mini golf and horse riding.

The Centrestage Theatre and Orewa House Gallery offer more genteel recreation. And Waiwera Thermal Pools are a mere five-minute drive over the hill from Orewa.

The Rock Salt Restaurant and Café Kaizen Coffeehouse, both on the Hibiscus Coast Highway in Orewa, draw locals and visitors alike with their Ponsonby-style food and friendly Orewa-style service. The café scene is just starting to develop, so there are still eateries offering simple fare, such as egg sandwiches, caramel squares and pots of tea.

Fast food junkies have many options, including McDonald's and KFC.

Peninsula locals say Manly Village is a great place to congregate and the many little restaurants are well patronised, particularly from Thursday to Sunday.

SMART BUY

The northern motorway extension has brought two big benefits to Orewa - it is now 10 minutes closer to Auckland City, and has taken away the clogging, smelly traffic from the main street (shop owners along this stretch may not see this as a plus, however). With its magnificent beach and resort atmosphere, more homebuyers will continue to discover its Gold Coast style charms. It will be the best of both worlds - a holiday spot close to work.

For colour key, see page 208

Hatfields Beach

Orewa

Maygrove

Red Beach

Hibiscus Coast

Gulf Harbour

Hobbs Bay

Silverdale

Stanmore Bay

Matakatia Bay

Big Manly

Arkles Bay

Whangaparaoa

Okura

Redvale

Long Bay

Pinpoint Map data supplied by Critchlow Associates Ltd and contains material subject to Crown copyright.

Travel times

From Orewa

CBD	off-peak 30 min
	peak 60 min plus
North Shore Hospital	20 min
Pacific Plaza	10 min
Airport	60 min
Motorway	a few seconds
From along peninsula	
Motorway	up to 20 min
Silverdale to the bridge	15 min

Regular bus services run from Orewa and the peninsula to Takapuna and central Auckland. It takes about an hour to get from the coast to Takapuna by bus. There's also a daily commuter ferry from Gulf Harbour to Auckland's CBD and back. The proposed 7km toll road is expected to cut travel time from the top of the East Coast Bays to Whangaparaoa from 30 minutes to 5 to 10 minutes. Construction is scheduled to start in June 2004, pending tolling legislation being passed by Parliament this year. The road will open mid 2007 and cost the commuter $2 each way or, as the experts put it, save you much more than that in time and petrol.

including Castor Bay, Campbells Bay, Mairangi Bay, Murrays Bay and Rothesay Bay

It's a love affair, we're told - a rather hot, salty, sandy one. Most people who move to the East Coast Bays fall in love (with the area, that is) and never move out! The attraction is the proximity to the water, Rangitoto Island views and peaceful village-like neighbourhoods. Sailing is also a major attraction - it's here that many of New Zealand's top sailors learned to sail.

This string of bays on the North Shore that hug the coastline from Castor Bay up to Long Bay began as sleepy beach retreats. After the Harbour Bridge opened in 1959, more people began living permanently in the bays. As the motorway has extended north, travelling time into the CBD has decreased, and employment opportunities have developed on the shore itself. This area has another huge drawcard - Rangitoto College. "Rangi" zone is the shore equivalent to grammar zone in central Auckland.

Who lives there?

The community feel in the bays is partly due to the good cross-section of people living in the area, from elderly to young families. Dog lovers add to the mix as well. Many older retired people in their late 50s and 60s are looking to move from family homes into smaller places in the neighbourhood.

A large number of South Africans have moved into this area, attracted by the peaceful environment and reputation of Rangitoto College. Koreans and mainland Chinese are also buying here for similar reasons.

People move here and stay here and the population is generally stable. For those who move out to newer homes in the Albany area there are any number of families coming in for the schooling, the village sense of community and the never-ending feel of being on holiday down by the beach.

Typical dwellings

Sea views are the main focus of any house design in these suburbs. Bay after bay, houses have been sited to maximise sea views, often looking down or over other properties. As a result, more than a third of East Coast Bays properties have views of the sea. Many of these fabulous vistas offer a panoramic sweep of the coastline and Rangitoto Island, helped by the ridges and gullies of the terrain leading from East Coast Bays Rd down to the shoreline.

Homes tend to be a more eclectic mix than many other North Shore 1970s-vintage suburbs. You'll see a fair number of architect-designed properties. A few of the old cottages and baches of pre-bridge days are still around, although most have been substantially renovated or demolished.

Apartments are now part of the scene in Mairangi Bay, with one development by the shops and another under construction by the beach. Some larger sections have been crossleased to provide new dwellings but most people wanting new homes tend to head towards Albany.

REAL ESTATE

Trends

Shortages of housing stock arise partly from the lack of choice for older people downsizing from large family homes and demand for the Rangitoto College zone. There's also a trend for families to borrow off the equity in their family home to buy a second home to live in and then rent out the more valuable family home. Families move here from first home buying areas simply for the schooling. Biggest demand is for homes on full sites and they sell quickly.

New housing includes the nine terrace houses in Ramsgate Rd in Mairangi Bay which all sold to North Shore buyers, heading off early overseas interest. The 14 apartments in The Georgian, a development that's under construction in Mairangi Bay, are attracting buyers from within the bays, cityside suburbs such as Kohimarama and overseas for their owner/occupier rather than investment appeal. Top end buyers are a mix of North Shore families, ex-pat Kiwis returning home and international buyers. A strong Japanese presence in the $700,000 to $800,000 bracket is creating stiff competition for local families wanting tidy homes with coastal views.

Prices

Castor Bay and Campbells Bay are regarded as the most expensive bays because homes here are, in some cases, right on the clifftop; Mairangi Bay and Rothesay Bay are the most affordable. Family-sized homes such as the typically large 1970s style houses with open-plan living, downstairs rumpus and double garage sell for close to $500,000. Top quality homes close to the coast sell in the $700,000 to $800,000 bracket. Clifftop properties even several houses back from the water now cost $1 million; exclusive cliff edge properties go for $4 million.

Terrace houses sell in the mid $400,000s. The Ramsgate three and four-bedroom townhouses sold for between $470,000 and $510,000. The Georgian apartments range from $608,000 to $880,000 for a ground-level apartment that includes the land. Elsewhere two-bedroom townhouses range from $350,000 to $420,000, depending on location and quality.

Average sale prices

	House	Flat	No. sales
2002	$414,984	$314,167	568
2003	$468,491	$329,794	564

Rental and investment

Investors selling homes to grab the high prices are creating a shortage of rentals. Demand is fuelled far more by the demand for housing in the Rangitoto College zone than by migration, which is only a small part of the picture. Rents have increased from $350 a week for a four-bedroom home to $450. A three-bedroom home costs about $400 a week; a three-bedroom stand-alone townhouse is up to $400 a week. A two-bedroom brick and tile unit in Murrays Bay is $240 a week.

Best streets

Anything the seaward side of Beach Rd. The Esplanade in Campbells Bay; Whitby Rd, Sidmouth St and Ramsgate Tce in Mairangi Bay; Churchill Rd, Portal Pl and Bournemouth Tce in Murrays Bay.

AMENITIES

Schools ★★★★

The highly desired Rangitoto College, which is the largest high school in New Zealand with 2700 students, is a co-educational college zoned for teens from Rothesay Bay

Local hero - East Coast Bays Coastal Walkway

Yes, East Coast Bayers sometimes break out, leaving their beloved home bay to walk part or all of the East Coast Bays Coastal Walkway. The walkway begins at Long Bay and is designed so people can walk the length of the stunning East Coast Bays coastline. Walkers take in the panoramic views of Rangitoto Island and the Hauraki Gulf on one side, while checking out the lifestyles of each little settlement hugging the shoreline. And it is a healthy pursuit, although less so if you decide to take a break at one of Takapuna's cafés and bars at the far end.

(from Glencoe Rd south), Mairangi Bay, Murrays Bay and Campbells Bay (from Centennial Park).

Murrays Bay Intermediate, which is the only intermediate within these bays, is zoned for students from Rothesay Bay down to the edge of Milford. On an adjoining site is Murrays Bay Primary School. Also check out the sunny-coloured Campbells Bay School with its stunning sea views. Mairangi Bay also has a primary school.

Shops ★★★

Mairangi Bay's pleasant paved village caters for all the basic shopping needs. Unless you're after a tattoo or a movie, you need never leave the bays area. The village is the biggest within these five suburbs, and includes cafes, restaurants and great shops like Seamart - the fish looks almost too fresh to eat.

There is also the larger Browns Bay main street shopping centre, which is a five-minute drive along Beach Rd, the scenic road that threads throughout the East Coast Bays settlements. The newest attraction there is a nightclub.

Campbells Bay has a dairy with postal facilities and a petrol station, and Rothesay Bay has a handful of shops.

Leisure ★★★★

Shall we be obvious and say the golden sand of the east coast beaches? Then there are parks, like Centennial Park in Campbells Bay, which is one of the North Shore City's largest parks, and Kennedy Park in Castor Bay. This park has two claims to fame. At its southern end is Rahopara Reserve, the site of a traditional Maori fortified village.

Pupuke Golf Club in Campbells Bay is a good 18-hole course. There are also sporting facilities, including sports grounds, for young and old, such as bowling, sailing, racquet, soccer, rugby etc.

The latest addition to sport facilities on the shore is the Millennium Institute of Sport and Health, a new state-of-the-art sports centre in Mairangi Bay complete with Olympic-size pool, gym, restaurant and conference facilities. Currently the pool is open to the public only at the weekends. The centre is the base for many Commonwealth athletes.

Prefer a more gentle leisure activity? The Mairangi Arts Centre is a thriving community arts centre that offers a wide range of classes, including pottery, painting, sculpture and print making.

As long as you're not prone to having a wine or two over the limit, a short drive leads to interesting café and restaurant choices throughout the bays, such as Castor Bay's The Edge Restaurant and Campbell Bay's Feathers Olde English Restaurant, or the Fayre and Firkin in Mairangi Bay. Mairangi Bay village also has a number of good lunch places, including the Courtyard Café, Paper Moon and Devito's. A local favourite is fish and chips under the pohutakawa trees framing one of the many beaches.

Travel times

From Mairangi Bay		
CBD	off-peak	15-20 min
	peak	45 min
Northern motorway		5-10 min
Airport		45 min
Albany Mega Centre		10 min

East Coast Rd and Beach Rd have regular Stagecoach services that increase in frequency during peak periods.

For colour key, see page 208

Rothesay Bay

East Coast Bays

Pinehill

Murrays Bay

Mairangi Bay

Windsor Park

Sunset North

Campbells Bay

Sunnynook

Castor Bay

Crown Hill

Pinpoint Map data supplied by Critchlow Associates Ltd and contains material subject to Crown copyright.

NORTHCOTE ★★★★★

including Birkenhead, Chatswood and Hillcrest

What's in a name? Big dollars and status if you're talking the difference between Northcote central and Northcote Pt, and Birkenhead and Birkenhead Pt. In the mid 1990s, citysiders woke up to the appeal of Northcote Pt and Birkenhead Pt, with their wide coastline and 100-year-old villas. But that's not to overlook Birkenhead with its apartments and mix of family housing stock, nor the energy of Northcote's businessmen who are revamping the shopping centre as part of a Mainstreet project that will include regular festivals and cultural activities. This is an area of contrasts, from the characterful homes and affluence of the waterside areas to the rich European and Asian cultural diversity within Northcote

itself. Just stand awhile and watch the old Chinese men who come out in the spring sunshine to play board games in the shopping centre courtyard. Chatswood rates a mention too, as home to the late Sir Robert Muldoon, one of our most colourful and controversial Prime Ministers. Politics is still a theme around here with many streets named after political heavyweights.

Who lives there?

A mix of wary North Shore buyers, delighted cityside buyers, sad missed-out-on-Devonport buyers and overjoyed international buyers love these peninsula suburbs. North Shore buyers tend to quibble over the prices; those conditioned to Herne Bay prices are delighted with the value for money and tend to ask "what's wrong with it?" as a reaction to the favourable price comparisons.

Northcote Pt buyers are locals and others who prefer character homes, coming from Parnell, Kingsland, Grey Lynn, Herne Bay, Devonport and beyond. They're also prepared to wait to buy - years in some cases for the best home with the best views; perhaps a few months if they're happy to settle on a home with a lesser outlook for around $400,000.

Typical dwellings

Historically Birkenhead was isolated from Auckland and known as "the company town" when it was set up for the workers at the Chelsea Sugar Refinery who lived in its cottages. Original worker's cottages dotted throughout the suburb on what was once orchard land are now popular renovation projects for energetic families.

On the road down to the refinery itself, the original brick cottages built for shift managers are still owned by the refinery but are available for lease.

Character homes typify Northcote Pt and Birkenhead Pt, which were established about the same time in the late 1880s. Near the centre of Birkenhead a number of near-new apartment buildings offer easy living to professional people as a complement to the wide mix of homes suitable for family living.

The Chatswood estate was developed as an executive subdivision in the early 1970s, offering the sort of modern housing stock on big sections with wide streets that appeal to Asian buyers.

Northcote central and Hillcrest have a catchment of 6000 houses with styles ranging from renovated ex-state houses, townhouses built during the in-fill boom days and quality weatherboard homes in Hillcrest - and the creme de la creme of more modern homes in the Onepoto Basin area of Northcote.

REAL ESTATE

Trends

Water's edge character homes are bringing buyers over the bridge from the expensive north-facing harbourside suburbs. Cityside buyers see fantastic value in $1.5 million of water's edge character that's half the price of a similar place in Herne Bay. North Shore buyers will "um" and "ah" to haggle the price down. Six years ago buyers from right across cityside Auckland from Grey Lynn to Parnell took themselves off to Northcote Pt.

Within Northcote central, buyers tend to move up to Hillcrest with its elevated views. Both are key family suburbs for the choice of local schooling and the central location close to both the CBD and the Albany industrial area. Three or four years ago Chatswood went through the doldrums but renewed interest in big homes ripe for renovation has seen a revival in demand, with a corresponding steadying of prices.

Prices

Northcote Pt and Birkenhead Pt score the big sales dollars despite the fact that few properties come onto the market. Clifftop villa do-ups with views sell for $800,000; a premium, renovated character home for well over $1 million.

One Northcote Pt cottage that sold for $265,000 in 1993 and for $362,000 in 1997 recently went for $555,000. Another property, worth $333,000 in 1992, fetched $1.1 million this year. Similarly one worth $280,000 in 1991 fetched $650,000 in 2002.

In Birkenhead, a unique 5560m^2 farmlet in the heart of the suburb, complete with tennis court and a few sheep in the fields, recently sold for $770,000.

In Chatswood, family homes range from $400,000 to $600,000 depending on how well

they've been updated. There are million dollar homes on the big 2000m^2 sites on the seaward side of Onetaunga Rd, in Chatswood. In central Birkenhead a basic three-bedroom home worth $280,000 last year would now fetch $320,000. Two-bedroom apartments sell for about $270,000, which is up from the $180,000 that one sold for during a market low point a few years ago. A two-bedroom unit in Hillcrest sells in the mid $200,000s. In both Northcote and Hillcrest the average three-bedroom home is priced from the high $200,000s into the low $300,000s. In Hillcrest, a five-bedroom home with elevated views of Birkenhead and the city recently sold for $650,000. The Onepoto Basin subdivision developed in the 1970s has $600,000 and $700,000 homes with properties near the basin itself having near $1 million sales prospects.

Average sale prices

	House	Flat	No. sales
2002	$276,124	$209,512	1447
2003	$315,413	$223,199	948

Rental and investments

Apartments are very popular in central Birkenhead, bringing the significant number of investor owners a good return. Rents for a two-bedroom apartment are about $350 a week, compared with $250 last year. One high-end two-bedroom apartment currently returns $385 a week. In Chatswood, an executive three-bedroom home with double garaging costs about $450 a week. Birkenhead's first entry homes cost about $330 to $350 a week to rent.

Why I live there
Former All Black captain Gary Whetton

Gary has lived in both Northcote Pt and Birkenhead Pt and says he wouldn't live anywhere else. His was one of the first young families to move into a street that's now predominantly family orientated. "It's a fantastic place," he says. "It's out of the so-called big city but the city is visually right there in front of you. The ferry is right there, there are beaches, plenty of green parks and great people, lovely people." He'd rather not let slip any more secrets though. "It's an undiscovered part of Auckland and we don't really want to tell too many people about it," he quips.

Best streets

Clarence St and Queen St in Northcote Pt; Bridgeview Rd and Wanganella St in Birkenhead Pt; Puawai St in Northcote; Onetaunga St in Chatswood; Mountbatten Ave in Hillcrest.

AMENITIES

Schools ★★★★

Both local co-ed secondary schools Birkenhead College and Northcote College are thriving on a proven record of national and/or local academic, cultural, musical and sporting achievements. Northcote College's acclaimed jazz band has won collective and individual awards at recent regional competitions. The top rugby and netball teams at each school compete annually.

Local primary and intermediate schools feed into both schools. Northcote College's new home zone has restricted entry to North Shore pupils only, which now means that Herne Bay and Ponsonby families in an area previously served by the school, must now apply for out-of-zone places. Auckland University of Technology's Akoranga campus is in Northcote.

Shops ★★★★

Birkenhead is well catered for with its strip shopping that includes everything from fresh fish, fruit and vegetables to boutique clothing and stationery shops. It adjoins the Birkenhead Shopping Centre (ex Highpoint Mall) that includes a food hall, The Warehouse and a Countdown supermarket. There's plenty of undercover parking. The Northcote Shopping Centre has lots of Asian shops as well as general mall shops and a Woolworths supermarket. Northcote Pt's group of local shops includes a boutique wine shop and a fish and chip shop quaintly named Point Taken.

Leisure ★★★

There's fabulous Asian food to be had at the Northcote Shopping Centre, especially at the food hall known as Food City.

The café scene has strengthened, especially in Queen St, Northcote Pt, with the opening of Pearl opposite Sausalito and the adjoining refurbished Bridgeway Theatre. Along the road the Northcote Tavern is the oldest licensed tavern on the North Shore. In Birkenhead there's Café 98 and the new café Grace that is bringing the Ponsonby set across the bridge.

Want to walk round the coastline? Take the tunnel under the Harbour Bridge at the bottom of Tennyson Ave to where Sulphur Beach used to be before the bridge was built in 1959.

Local hero - Chelsea Sugar Works

The appropriately candyfloss-pink Chelsea Sugar Refinery is an icon on the North Shore coastline. Named Chelsea after the refinery's first customs officer's home town, it opened in 1885, and still has cute historic brick cottages on site. The privately owned park-like grounds are open to the public and are a popular spot for wedding photos, walks and picnics.

The annual 2.36km Chelsea Swim takes place late November or early December depending on the tide. About 500 proven ocean swimmers take part, leaving Herne Bay about noon and stepping out of the water anywhere from 30 minutes to two hours later to a barbecue and prizegiving in the grounds of the Chelsea Sugar Refinery.

If you don't mind the lack of toilets and having to take your rubbish with you, you're allowed to picnic in the beautiful grounds of the refinery and book the tennis court for your own use.

For lovers of nature, there are plenty of bush reserves throughout Birkenhead to enjoy. For youngsters there's rock climbing at the Birkenhead Leisure Centre, a skate park next door and Lollipop Land in Onewa Road. In Akoranga Rd, there's the Takapuna Athletics Club and the YMCA.

Arts are strong with the Northart Community Arts Centre and many local artists and craftspeople producing works out of their own local studios.

The peak hour traffic can test your patience along Onewa Rd, so skip the jams and take the ferry to the city.

Travel times

From Northcote	
CBD	peak 7-10 min
From Birkenhead	
CBD	off-peak 15-20 min
	peak 1 hour
Northern motorway	10 min
North Shore Hospital	15 to 20 min
Airport	40 to 45 min
Glenfield shopping centre	10 min

For buses and car poolers, peak-hour priority lanes (or rapid bus transit lanees in council-speak) cut the driving time to the city by a third. For others, getting out of these suburbs can be a slow process during peak hours, despite the fact that there's only one traffic light between Northcote Point and the central business district. Birkenhead Transport runs a bus service through Birkenhead, Beach Haven and beyond, scooping up commuters en route from its base in Birkdale Rd. The new Kaipatiki Bridge between Beach Haven and Glenfield has opened up access to Glenfield Mall and the light industrial area of Glenfield. Fuller's Birkenhead ferry service collects commuters from Fisherman's Wharf.

TAKAPUNA ★★★★★

including Milford and Hauraki

Location, location, location - a Takapuna or Milford address denotes prestige and money, especially if it has a sea view or is on the beachfront. These two suburbs are the most stylish, affluent and sought-after areas on the shore - and the residents are damn proud of it. To live in the best streets here requires a couple of million and plenty of the latest toys, like a Mercedes or even a helicopter (guess it makes crossing the harbour quick and painless).

It's a big change from 100 years ago, when Takapuna was a quiet seaside settlement of baches, plus some grand holiday homes on the beach and around Lake Pupuke. So what's the attraction now? A stunning beachfront framed by pohutukawa with unbroken views of slumbering Rangitoto Island, just a stroll from shops, restaurants and bars, and not far from Auckland City. It's a mini Gold Coast without the Australians - and with a community heart.

Who lives there?

There are a lot of tanned bods and a big emphasis on outdoor and leisure activities - swimming, walking, jogging, jet-skiing, sailing, windsurfing. If you're looking for an ethnic melting pot, you're in the wrong part of town. These suburbs attract a Pakeha middle to upper-class community with plenty of cash for home upgrades. More recently, the South Africans and Asian communities have grown significantly. Returning Kiwis are another group buying into the area, particularly those with English pounds.

Milford has a large elderly community that loves the closeness to North Shore Hospital and short walk to the shops and beach. Older affluent people are also buying into apartments for a secure and comfortable lifestyle.

Hauraki, down at the far end of Takapuna, is a more affordable area near the water and right in the heart of Takapuna Grammar School zone. The bulk of the most expensive homes are being bought by affluent New Zealanders from throughout the North Shore and Auckland. Contrary to what a lot of punters think, it's not all being handed over to anonymous overseas buyers and savvy ex-pats. Only about 20 to 30% are overseas buyers; the rest are Kiwis from within Takapuna, Milford and from areas north and west on the North Shore, making what one agent calls "a migratory drift" towards the water.

Typical dwellings

Palatial high-tech mansions sit next to gracious old homes along the seafront. On streets further back from the beaches you'll still find some modest homes, although they'll still be relatively expensive. Many of the original cottages have been renovated beyond recognition, or demolished. People are sacrificing space for location. Crossleasing or subdividing is on the increase, with a number of large two-storey houses going up on pocket-sized sections, often one behind the other. Sections on the seaward side are zoned to to be a minimum of 600m². The rest of the area is 450m² which can reduce to 350m² with resource consent.

Low-rise luxury apartments are on the increase, particularly near the waterfront, but are not yet dominating the landscape. Needless to say, they're not cheap buys!

Rock solid brick and tile units built in the 1960s and 1970s are in big demand by first home buyers and for investors. Developers Franchi & Ion built lots of two-bedroom homes throughout Takapuna, Milford and surrounding suburbs which were popular with older people moving out of large homes. They're the best bet for traditional first home buyers wanting a foot in the door.

REAL ESTATE

Trends

The pace and yield of real estate here has hotted up right across the board from the water's edge to inland Takapuna and Milford. Multi-million dollar properties frequently sell before auction in the wake of multiple offers and homes listed with a price or for "sale by negotiation" are selling within 24 and 48 hours of stepping into the market limelight.

Real estate agents confirm that all the signs were there a year or so ago, but the pace has become strong and sustained without the market wobbles that threatened to derail buyers. Twelve months ago they say there was much more property for sale. Homes that had hung around on the market for a while have long since changed hands. Now there are many waiting to buy whatever the price bracket, with properties down on the water's edge changing hands for $6 million and more. More new apartment blocks are offering buyer choice for those wanting to own property with spectacular 360-degree views or to lease out for both short and long-term financial gain. For premium lifestyle choice, a big part of the appeal is the range of fine restaurants in a seaside suburb literally at your doorstep.

Typical prices

First entry point is a $270,000 two-bedroom brick and tile unit, up from about $230,000 a year ago. It suits investors or elderly people downsizing but it's certainly not traditional first home-buyer's stock. The mid-range of the market is homes located well back from the water in the $400,000 to $800,000 price range. In keeping with market trends, houses worth $750,000 five years ago are now $1 million-plus. Homes in streets leading down to the beach go up in price dramatically the closer they are to the sea. In these streets, it's location rather than the quality of the house that dictates the $1 million prices being realised at the top of the street; $1.5 million half way down and $2 million-plus by the water. More affordable $500,000 property is much further back than the waterside/clifftop/lakeside locations most popularly requested from buyers moving from further up the North Shore and in from the western areas of the North Shore.

Prices for homes fronting Lake Pupuke range from $1.5 million to $3 million. Takapuna's wide choice of designer apartments continues to see most sold off the plans. These include the luxury apartments at Clifton Pt that have sold for between $2.5 million and $3 million each pre-construction; three-bedroom apartments at The Rocks that pre-sold for $1 million and the 18 apartments at Promenade Terraces which all pre-sold for between $600,000 and $850,000.

Average sale prices

	House	Flat	No. sales
2002	$558,344	$368,248	465
2003	$597,982	$340,491	391

Rental and investment

The rental market in Takapuna and Milford has softened since the heady days of America's Cup competition when syndicates would pay as much as $3000 a week for prestigious on-shore, off-duty luxury pads. Most homeowners who leased their homes moved their families back afterwards, but houses fetching those prices would now realistically fetch $1500 a week if offered back to the rental market. A house that

Local hero - Rangitoto Island

Rangitoto blew its top 800 years ago - and could go up again any time. It's Auckland's youngest volcano and its most stylish one, slumbering long and low in the Hauraki Gulf across from the North Shore.

All of the houses along the illustrious beachfront at Takapuna and Milford have a view of the island's classic long and low cone shape as a permanent sort of artwork beyond the window. In its turn, the island has a great walk to the summit that offers extensive views back to the North Shore.

previously returned $1250 a week would now yield its owner an $850 weekly return.

High-end rental figures such as this are a small part of the market. Most rental stock falls into the $450 to $600 a week range sought after by families wanting a three-bedroom house in an average street.

Top quality apartments are sought after for those on business transfer from outside Auckland and professionals preferring a lockup-and-go out kind of lifestyle. Such two or three-bedroom apartments return rentals of between $800 and $1200 at The Sands; $630 and $800 at the Promenade Terraces and $450 to $850 in the Mon Desir Apartment blocks, depending on size and location. The most exclusive penthouse apartments such as the two-level, three-bedroom apartments in Spencer on Byron cost about $1000 a week. In Hauraki a three-bedroom home costs $550 to rent; a four-bedroom home about $600 and a two-bedroom brick and tile unit about $300.

Best streets

Anything between Lake Rd and the beach in Takapuna, especially Minnehaha St, O'Neills

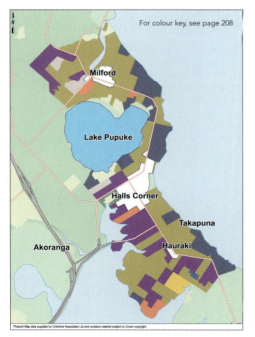

Ave and Brett Ave. Anything between Kitchener Rd and the beach in Milford, especially Tiri Rd, Cecil Rd, Holiday Rd and Clifton Rd, Hauraki.

AMENITIES

Schools ★★★★★

As the only co-educational high school in the immediate area, Takapuna Grammar School is a popular choice for teenagers. Westlake Girls' and Westlake Boys' High are zoned for most of Takapuna, Milford and Hauraki - check school zone maps for specifics. There is also Carmel College for girls in Milford and Rosmini College for boys in Takapuna. Intermediate education is offered by Takapuna Normal Intermediate and Belmont Intermediate. There are state primary schools in all of the suburbs, and some Catholic primary schools.

Shops ★★★★★

Takapuna has traditionally been the commercial heart of the North Shore. Other commercial and retail areas on the shore are now bigger but Takapuna holds its own, in part because of its bar and restaurant culture, and in part because it is a nice mix of mall and high street style.

Home to the North Shore City Council, Takapuna also has a popular Sunday morning market where you'll find an eclectic range of crafts, plants, food, vegetables and bargains.

Milford's suburban shopping strip and mall provide for the needs of the immediate locals. Those wanting more choice need only travel five minutes to Takapuna. At the southern end of Takapuna lies Hauraki Corner's shops, including a couple of good restaurants.

Leisure ★★★★★

Ah - the beaches! Takapuna and Milford beaches have boat ramps, toilet facilities and plenty of space for visitors as well as locals. You'll see lots of water toys, particularly at Takapuna Beach where jet-skis are common.

A cruising club and marina is based at Milford Beach. Milford has rock pools that children love to fossick around in. When they're weary of sand, there is a reserve and playground.

Sailing and windsurfing are popular sports at both beaches, as well as at Lake Pupuke.

No powered vessels are allowed on this freshwater lake, making it a favourite with canoeists and learner windsurfers. Sylvan Park, which edges the lake, is another popular spot. When beach activities pale, there is the 18-hole Takapuna Golf Course, with driving range, 10-pin bowling centre and Takapuna Aquatic Centre. The Bruce Mason Centre is popular for theatre, along with the converted Pumphouse. Arts are also catered for through centres such as the Lake House. Takapuna has the multi-screen Berkeley Cinema, said to be one of the most comfortable on the shore.

One of New Zealand's most famous writers, Frank Sargeson, lived in a modest fibrolite bach on Esmonde Rd for more than 50 years. His home became a refuge, place of inspiration and gathering point for Kiwi writers, including Janet Frame, who lived in an old army hut on the back of his property. The sturdy old bach is now preserved as a literary museum.

The bar and restaurant scene rocks at The Strand end of Hurstmere Rd, particularly at the weekend and during summer holidays. Whether a leisurely brunch, quick coffee before the beach, or a lively dinner or drinks after an afternoon swim, the crowds are there. Milford has fewer eating spots, but then Takapuna is just round the corner. The only real nightclub in the area is Poedium, over the motorway at the Poenamo Hotel on Northcote Rd.

Don't buy thinking you can cut down that pesky pohutakawa tree blocking your view of the sea. If there's one obscuring your outlook, you are required to notify the North Shore City Council, who will have an arborist examine the tree to decide how much - if any - of the tree can be trimmed.

Travel times

From Takapuna

CBD	off-peak 10 min
	peak 40 min
Motorway and Harbour Bridge	
	off-peak 5 min
	peak 15 min
Airport	off-peak 40-45 min
North Shore Hospital	5-10 min
Takapuna or Milford shops	5 min

Regular bus services into the city increase in frequency during peak times.

Beside the seaside

When Kiwis go on holiday they tend to head to the coastline, chasing beaches and sunshine. To live at the beach is considered the ultimate in home location. It's little wonder, therefore, that the most sought-after property in an area like Takapuna and Milford is the Golden Mile, which lies between Craig Rd and Clifton Rd.

The most prestigious of properties are the 42 homes that front up to the golden sands of beach. Most of these properties are palaces and playgrounds for the rich and wealthy, like entrepreneur Eric Watson. His home, which sold for around $6 million, is a state-of-the-art, architecturally designed mansion. Neighbouring homes boast landscaped gardens, sun-drenched terraces, large entertainment areas, pools, home theatres and other amenities the average Kiwi could only dream of owning. Helicopter pads are not uncommon

There are also a couple of rather modest houses, however, that would only be worth $300,000 to $400,000 if located in any other suburb of the North Shore. It is believed the land alone, which must be at least 600m^2, would sell for $2 million-plus - if it ever came up for sale.

Those that can't have beachfront properties chase homes with easy beach access and stunning views across the gulf. Some of Auckland's wealthiest residents live in streets such as Minehaha Ave, O'Neills Ave and Clifton Rd. In central Takapuna, off Blomfield Spa, a home in Gibbons St changed hands for $8.3 million about two years ago. Its new owner is a Kiwi living overseas who intends returning home to live sometime in the future. The best views from the most desirable street, Minehaha Ave, are on the left-hand side overlooking Thorne Bay. People can pay up to 30% more for homes on that side.

UPPER EAST COAST BAYS ★★★★☆

including Browns Bay, Waiake, Torbay, Pinehill, Long Bay, Northcross and Okura

"Lifestyle" sums up the northern East Coast Bays. Relaxed, quiet - philistines may even say downright slow! It's a haven for beachie and boatie types who love a contemplative beach stroll, want a relaxed outdoor lifestyle for their children and are patient about long drives into the city - if they go near the rat race, that is. As with other East Coast settlements, these bays have grown from sleepy holiday spots to permanent neighbourhoods. Being at the northern end of the winding, scenic Beach Rd makes them more affordable, although clifftop properties still fetch big prices. Many choose to live around the Browns Bay main street shopping centre - the retail hub for the bays. The centre has a friendly Kiwi small-town feel, with the beach only 100m away. The beach isn't all this area has to offer. Away from the coastline lies Okura, a favoured lifestyle block area edging around Long Bay Regional Park.

Who lives there?

Buyers stepping up to a little coastal living move here from Glenfield and the cheaper inland North Shore suburbs. Long-established families will move within a 3km radius to upgrade to a bigger home on a bigger section. Those concerned about good schooling will settle for any style of home that gets them into their desired zone. South African, Asian and English migrants like putting down roots here too. Browns Bay's apartments have given locals the chance to downsize from family homes to holiday-style living. Overseas buyers include one American couple who paid $665,000 for a holiday apartment that they say would be worth $6.5 million on the Californian coast. A few local buyers have also bought apartments for investment and they're typical of buyers settling here for long-term capital gain.

Typical dwellings

Sea views are the big focus for homes near the coast or along the ridges that make up the bays terrain. Plenty of 1970s, architecturally designed family homes give the area refreshing individuality. Big new homes in subtropical landscaped grounds add a Mediterranean flavour. Browns Bay is a lifestyle village and it has embraced the apartments that have brought 200 people into the heart of the area's thriving retail area. Both The Bacchus and new Bay Palms apartments feature a mix of local owner/occupiers and investors, and overseas-based owners. A six-unit apartment complex is shortly to be built along from the 23-unit Ocean Beach development by the water. Redevelopment in the retail area is likely to bring studio/apartments into the housing stock within the next year or two.

REAL ESTATE

Trends

Significant increases in house prices, more

movement at the upper end of the market and the resulting change in demographics are the biggest trends. Real estate agents selling across the board agree that changes parallel the expansion of Albany's hinterland as the commercial, retail and industrial centre of the North Shore.

The northernmost bay areas have traditionally been cheaper than those closer to Takapuna and well-informed buyers know that the area has been perceived to be under-valued. Now, with many workplaces just 10 minutes away in the developing light industrial area of Albany, this region is coming into its own. Just a step away from the beach, it also has huge lifestyle appeal. Local efforts are being stepped up to have a wharf built at Browns Bay for recreational use and a future ferry service from Gulf Harbour.

Prices

The scarcity of sections for new homes has helped pushed up prices, close to the 20% that was estimated a year ago. Top dollar is close to $4 million paid recently for a clifftop property in Sharon Rd, Waiake Beach. Most top end property is in the $1 million to $2 million bracket. Around $1 million will buy a do up on Torbay's clifftop, a family home back from the beach, a penthouse in The Bacchus or an entry level apartment in the new complex about to be built on Browns Bay beach.

Most family homes sell for $400,000 plus; entry level has increased from $180,000 and $220,000 a year ago to $260,000 and $290,000 for a basic home, usually on a half site.

The Bacchus two- and three-bedroom apartments, which sold from high $200,000s to $300,000s four years ago, now sell in the mid $300,000s to high $400,000s.

Average sale prices

	House	Flat	No. sales
2002	$314,031	$234,928	840
2003	$358,087	$254,607	1168

Rental and investment

An older three-bedroom home on the seaward side of Torbay rents for $375 a week, which is typical of the average $360 to $380 return for a basic three-bedroom home. A home selling for $500,000 to $600,000 returns between $400 and $650 a week. Interest comes from families for school zones and migrants.

Best streets

Surprise, surprise - all the coastal spots are considered tops. Sharon Rd in Browns Bay is where you'll find multi-million dollar properties. Churchill Rd in Rothesay Bay, and Cliff Rd and Gilberd Pl in Torbay.

AMENITIES

Schools ★★★★

Long Bay College in Torbay, the school that serves most of this area, is nationally recognised for its creative, performing arts and technology achievements. It is much smaller than neighbouring Rangitoto College - and that appeals to a lot of East Coast Bays parents. Some homes in the southern end of Browns Bay are in Rangitoto College zone. Check school zone maps for specifics.

Northcross Intermediate School is the main intermediate for the northern bays. There are seven primary schools, one of which is private.

Shops ★★★

The retail hub of the East Coast Bays area is the Browns Bay main street shopping centre. It has the friendly feel of small-town New Zealand, but with a beach only 100m away from the main street. Whitcoulls, Farmers, banks, supermarkets - you name it, Browns Bay has it, including the first nightclub on the coast! Youngsters can now do their thing without having to head out to Takapuna or downtown Auckland.

The East Coast Bays library, a medical centre and the North Shore City Council's area office are all based in Browns Bay, and there are weekly Sunday markets.

Torbay also has a small service centre, including a superette with postal facilities,

pharmacy, doctor, dentist, three restaurants and four takeaway bars. Nearest shops for Okura and Long Bay residents are Torbay, Albany and Northcross.

Leisure ★ ★ ★

All the beaches are lovely, but Waiake Beach in Torbay is particularly special. It is a 1ha beachfront reserve with an impressive block of phoenix palms and Norfolk Island pines.

Long Bay (Oneroa) Regional Park is the area's big asset. Aside from the ubiquitous pohutukawa hanging low over the long, safe, golden beach, there is bush, an estuary, rock

For colour key, see page 208

Pinpoint Map data supplied by Critchlow Associates Ltd and contains material subject to Crown copyright.

pools, sand dunes, coastal walks - and then those modern but useful amenities, a restaurant and playground. Oh, and a gun emplacement! The crowds that descend on the area during the summer holidays put locals off a bit, but then locals have access to the bay all year round.

No fishing or taking of seafood is permitted in this area because it includes Okura Marine Reserve, where an education and recreation centre is based.

Those wanting a break from the sun and sea will find plenty of comfort and good food at Long Bay Restaurant, nestled in the sand dunes above the beach.

The area has all the usual Kiwi sports grounds and clubs, plus East Coast Bays Leisure Centre, in Browns Bay.

Pupuke Golf Course is a couple of bays along in Campbells Bay.

Art Ducko at Waiake Beach is a favourite for those who don't mind a drive. Browns Bay has a good selection of drinking and dining spots - two favourites are Speakers Corner Ale House and Spaghetti. There is no going past Beach Rd Takeaways in Browns Bay for people wanting good old Kiwi fish and chips to munch on the beach or take home to scoff while admiring the view of Rangitoto Island.

Talking of food and beaches - Long Bay Restaurant is all about location. The restaurant at Long Bay beach looks straight over the sand dunes to the sea. Food is simple, good and cheap, but totally surpassed by the stunning setting.

Travel times

CBD	off-peak 20 min
	peak 40-45 min
Northern motorway	10 min
Airport	45 min
Milford mall	12 min
Albany Mega Centre	10-15 min
Massey University at Albany	10 min

Stagecoach Auckland provides bus services through the area to Takapuna and Auckland's CBD. One is along Beach Rd, another along East Coast Rd. During the weekends buses come through every half hour.

including Sunnynook, Forrest Hill and Crown Hill

Nice and handy is how most locals sum up the Sunnynook, Forrest Hill, Westlake and Crown Hill area. This may not sound terribly exciting but then, does every suburb have to be? For some, a quiet affordable suburb is bliss. Thirty years ago, Sunnynook was a new subdivision of cheap housing, one of the nappy valley areas of the shore. But times are a-changing. Many of those low-cost homes are getting a makeover as people decide to make the most of an affordable area in the middle of the North Shore and a short drive to the beaches.

Adjoining suburbs Forrest Hill and Crown Hill are more upmarket, the place to go if you can't afford an East Coast Bay location but want to be a step up from Sunnynook or closer to Milford. Many homes get great views of the city but even more appealing to many families are the popular Westlake Boys' and Westlake Girls' High schools.

Who lives there?

Young couples with children move into this area looking for affordable housing on the eastern side of the motorway. This area attracts people who can't afford, or don't want to pay, coastal real estate prices. Instead they buy a reasonably sized home here with access to good schools and within striking distance of east coast beaches and the shore's amenities. Asian families gravitate to Forrest Hill, looking for roomy new homes in the Westlake schools' zones.

Typical dwellings

A lot of Sunnynook dwellings are traditional solid Kiwi homes: concrete piles, fibroplank construction and aluminium joinery. Forrest Hill has more diverse housing, such as the clusters of older homes built when the area's farmland was first subdivided 40 years ago. There are also a lot of large 1970s homes - properties with basements, good garaging and plenty of bedrooms. Pools are sometimes a feature. Forrest Hill also has a number of new, modern homes.

There's not a lot of infill housing here because homes established 30 or 40 years ago were built on sites not able to be subdivided under current town planning regulations. The nature of Sunnynook's development is such that it is more likely to have sections large enough to divide and these are sought after by keen developers.

REAL ESTATE

Trends

Forrest Hill is a favourite stepping stone for buyers moving out of their first homes on their way to the dreams that North Shore people have of living nearer the water. Buyers move here from Glenfield and Sunnynook and other traditional first-home buyer areas. Investors are active here too. Homes built here in the 1970s were generous and sunny and, unlike villas, which need major structural changes to suit modern living, these homes are ripe for renovation and open-plan indoor/outdoor living.

In the past few years, real estate has shown steady increases in value with a standard house in Sunnynook increasing by $30,000 to $50,000 a year. The past year has seen this area priced out of the traditional first home-buying market except for single-level brick and tile units (traditionally bought by elderly people). Demand for these units is strong and those that sell quickest have either been done up or are sought by keen DIY home improvers. Location is as important here as elsewhere. Understandably, homes near the motorway are more affordable than those near the water. For those with limited money, you get more for your dollar here which makes it a good starting point, even if you aspire to head to the water in the future

Prices

In Sunnynook prices for an average three bedroom home on a full site have jumped from last year's $220,000 to $280,000 range to $300,000 and $350,000.

In Forrest Hill, prices for a family home range from $350,000 for an older three bedroom home to as much as $500,000 for a four bedroom home with double garaging. Homes in the popular Knightsbridge Dr, Ravenwood Dr area of Forrest Hill are selling in the high $300,000s to high $400,000 for those with nice views. One real estate agent believes that this mid level of the housing market has probably had a 15% to 20% increase in price over the past year or so.

Homes in Crown Hill are centred on a small block of local shops. They hold the same appeal as Forrest Hill's homes, although they're more closely related geographically to the northern parts of Milford. Two bedroom units that sold for $180,000 or $190,000 a year ago now start at $220,000 and more. And that probably won't even get you a garage or a

carport. A one bedroom unit is likely to fetch less than $200,000, but they're not a popular choice because of their limitations.

Average sale prices

	House	Flat	No. sales
2002	$296,536	$213,641	749
2004	$335,709	$225,512	768

Best streets

Sycamore Dr in Sunnynook; Knightsbridge Ave, Grenada Ave and Ravenswood Ave in Forrest Hill; Gordon Ave in Crown Hill.

Rental and investment

Some letting agents report a glut in rental property in the Westlake zone with rental prices easing compared with last year. A three bedroom home now costs in the mid-to-high $300s a week. Two bedroom brick and tile units cost up to $320 a week depending on the street, compared with $350 last year. Four bedroom homes can cost $450 a week.

AMENITIES

Schools ★★★★

High schools are a major attraction. Sunnynook and Forrest Hill teenagers are zoned for the reputable single-sex Westlake Girls' High and Westlake Boys' High. Note, though, that the northern boundary for Westlake Boys' High is a little different to that of Westlake Girls.

Local heroes - the high schools

Two of them actually - Westlake Boys High School and Westlake Girls High School. They began as one co-educational secondary school in February 1958 and split in 1962 when Westlake Boys High School was established up the road in Forrest Hill Rd. Westlake Girls is on the original site. Separate they may be, but in many school activities they are keen and enthusiastic partners including sports, social events, drama, orchestra and debating.

Don't be concerned about the fact that their street addresses are each listed as Takapuna. They're the heart of what Westlake is all about as a thriving family place to live, and when everyone talks about the "Westlake zone", they're not only talking about houses and real estate, but about a way of life that is centred around these popular, academically successful secondary schools.

If teens are wanting to rub shoulders on a regular basis with the opposite sex, their options are more limited. Sunnynook and Forrest Hill are not zoned for neighbouring co-educational Rangitoto College, the largest high school in New Zealand. However "Rangi" does have an out-of-zone enrolment scheme. Primary schools include Sunnynook Primary and Forrest Hill School. Wairau Intermediate in Forrest Hill is the local intermediate school. Wairau Valley Special School is nearby in Glenfield.

Shops ★★★

Sunnynook has a shopping centre with a Foodtown supermarket as well as essential shops, such as a bakery, video shop, stationery shop, chemist and bank.

When it comes to big mall shopping, locals are spoilt for choice. Wairau Park, Glenfield Mall, Milford Mall and Shore City are all just a short drive away. Forrest Hill doesn't have a shopping centre as such.

Leisure ★★

There are a couple of eating places in Sunnynook, including a large Chinese restaurant, but it is rare to see a Ponsonby-style cafe - although there are plenty down the road in Takapuna and Milford. Locals often head to the more intimate eateries dotting the East Coast Bays, such as those in Mairangi Bay.

There are several parks and sporting facilities,

including Becroft Park, where rugby and soccer are played and Greville Park, which has soccer grounds.

The beach is only a few minutes drive - just head across East Coast Bays Rd and down to the nearest bay.

LOOK OUT!

People are attracted to these suburbs for the high schools as well as beach access. It is important to check individual school zones carefully if you decide to buy on that basis. We have provided school zone maps at the back of this book but it pays to contact each school.

SMART BUY

Saved hard and ready to buy? On the sea side of the motorway and with good schools nearby, Westlake is a sensible option, and it's still relatively cheap in North Shore terms. If it's your first home, start modestly near the motorway and head towards the views when you can afford it.

Travel times

From Sunnynook

CBD	off-peak 10 min
	peak 40 min
Airport	45 min
Shopping malls	10-15 min

There is a regular and frequent bus service along East Coast Bays Rd that connects to Takapuna and the city.
A less frequent but regular service is also provided along Sunnynook Rd and Forrest Hill Rd.

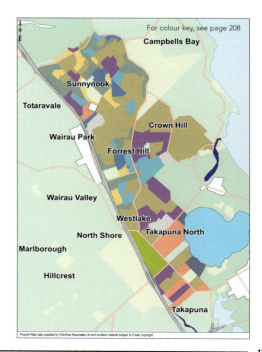

For colour key, see page 208

Campbells Bay · Sunnynook · Totaravale · Crown Hill · Wairau Park · Forrest Hill · Wairau Valley · Westlake · North Shore · Takapuna North · Marlborough · Hillcrest · Takapuna

Pinpoint Map data supplied by Critchlow Associates Ltd and contains material subject to Crown copyright.

WEST
West

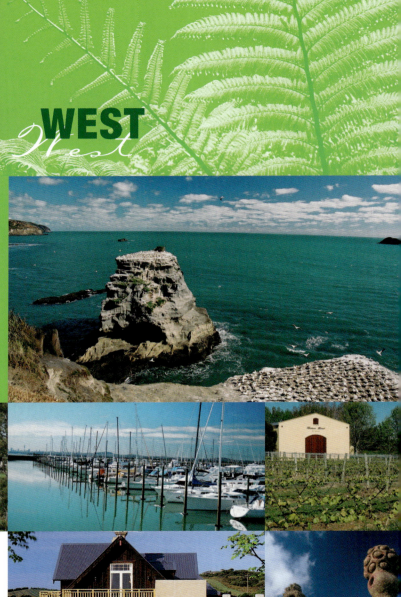

AUCKLAND

WEST

Dominated by the moody, bush-clad Waitakere Ranges and with the wild Tasman Sea running along its coast, west Auckland, or the "wild west" as it's often called, has a character quite unlike Auckland's other areas. This is Westie country, which means utes, big dogs, black jeans and tie-dyed velvet. But that's not all there is. It's a major centre of tourism, arts and culture, with everything from gentrified lifestyle blocks, fabulous native bush gardens and architecturally designed homes on bushy hillsides.

The last three census surveys show that Waitakere City is consistently becoming more ethnically diverse. The number of people identifying themselves as European continues to drop. Waitakere residents have become financially better off, too, which reflects Waitakere's high proportion of working people compared to other parts of Auckland.

The west is diverse in landscape as well as people. The urban area, shaped by rapid post-war expansion, consists of a series of town centres and surrounding suburban sprawl. Areas of industrial land add to the mix, and further out you find extensive orchards, market gardens, viticulture and rich farmland. West Auckland has always had a strong industrial base, beginning with timber and flax milling, and kauri gum digging, followed by brickworks and pottery industries. During the 1970s New Zealanders ate dinner or drank tea from the heavy cups and plates made at New Lynn's Crown Lynn factory. The factory has closed, but terrace houses and apartments on its land and collectible Crown Lynn china pieces endure as its legacy.

The houses are diverse, from original farmhouses, 1970s cedar homes in the bush and suburban bungalows to palatial mansions. Lifestyle quality is the impetus that is bringing semi-rural buyers out to Kumeu/Huapai and city-based professionals to Te Atatu Peninsula.

Come the weekend many Aucklanders head to west Auckland's open beaches or bush, for walks, picnics, scenic driving, fishing, boating or to experience the notorious west coast rips. Surfers come from all around Auckland to catch the wild waves. The fabulous 10,000ha Centennial Memorial Park includes a large chunk of the Waitakere Ranges, and some of the beaches.

Back in 1902 Assid Corban helped kick-start west Auckland's wine industry. Viticulture is becoming an ever-more significant industry in west Auckland these days with much of the area's winemaking activity now situated further west around Kumeu.

The city was the first in New Zealand to be declared nuclear free, thanks to the grinning, student-radical-turned mayor Tim Shadbolt. Today its green image is well-established. Its residents are unhappy at the prospect of an ongoing aerial spraying programme which is making significant progress in eliminating the painted apple moth. The moth, which could seriously harm our forestry, was first found in Glendene in May 1999.

rain-dripped
native bush

pounding
surf beaches

black jeans and
big dogs

green,

green,

green

HENDERSON ★★★☆☆

including Lincoln, Sunnyvale, Western Heights, Henderson Valley, Te Atatu Peninsula and Te Atatu South

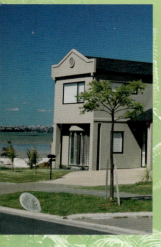

Go west young man, where the water turns into wine (via a grape or two) and the wild country begins - fern-clad, ponga-lined gateway to roaring ocean beaches, black sands, black jeans and salt of the earth.

At the heart of it all lies Henderson. This is where it's happening in west Auckland. What began over a bottle or two of homegrown wine, like so many good ideas, has developed into a buzzing town where you can live, work and shop till you drop without the need to travel into the city.

The area is still evolving. Te Atatu Peninsula, for example - now there's a change. Its old name "Te Atatu North" has gone and taken with it the lowly and dour association of the cheap group housing that burdened it in the 1950s and 1960s when compared to Te Atatu South. The peninsula is enjoying a revival, with enclaves of new homes, some with sea views, complete with leafy reserves and a village green by the shops.

Who lives there?

Everyone from first-home buyers, to second and third-home movers come to Henderson and surrounds. There are generations of families who have moved within the area as their families' housing needs have changed. They have also happily retired here close to local shops, public transport and Waitakere Hospital, which is about to be expanded from a maternity facility to full hospital status.

The new Waitakere Gardens retirement complex means the area's settled elderly no longer have to leave to find suitable retirement homes.

Te Atatu Peninsula is one of Auckland's fastest growing suburbs, popular with commuters,

families and affluent buyers who are upgrading from older, high-maintenance homes in established suburbs to executive homes in landscaped grounds complete with their own local reserves.

The influx of Asian buyers - jumping from 5% to 25% in the past five years - has continued to boost Henderson's cosmopolitan flavour. In addition to Asia, new residents are coming from Eastern Europe, South Africa and the African continent.

Typical dwellings

Mention Henderson and houses in the same breath and everyone will quote the "Dally Palaces" that the Dalmatian migrants built with pride. They're the big homes that were built for show in traditional red brick with a tiled roof, a basement garage and white wrought-iron balustrades defining the steps down to the front lawn, with its "must-have" roses along the front and fig trees up the side of the house.

These houses are now popular among young homeowners moving up from the first simple group housing Keith Hay-style homes that predominate in Lincoln, older areas of Henderson and in Sunnyvale, or from homes on subdivided sites.

Brick homes are the modern choice, whether it's single-level new homes in the Braeburn estate (built by Fletcher Homes) or the enclaves of executive homes in Te Atatu Peninsula or the Georgian-style mansions of Henderson Heights, complete with garaging for four vehicles. On grounds as large as 2000m² (half an acre), they boast prestigious addresses with such mouthwatering names as Chardonnay, Semillon, Cognac and Shiraz. Such is Henderson's expansion, there are plenty of sections in new subdivisions that are available in the form of house and land packages.

REAL ESTATE

Trends

Te Atatu Peninsula's appeal as a chic destination for city professionals is gaining pace. It's also increasingly popular for second-home buyers within the area and throughout Henderson. Buyers priced out of inner suburbs including Pt Chevalier are buying status, low maintenance and magnificent coastal views here too.

Homes in Te Atatu South, on the other side of the north-western motorway, are a sought-after step up for first time buyers within the wider area.

Henderson's affordable, diverse range of housing stock and good schooling continues to deliver housing options across all price ranges throughout the whole area.

Henderson has many pockets of quality homes with steadily increasing values and solid family appeal, including the golden triangle bound by Swanson Rd, Rathgar Rd,

Lincoln Rd and Universal Dr, which has six schools. Another quality area is around the Glendene, Te Atatu South border with Henderson.

Homes in the first entry, under $200,000, bracket are becoming increasingly scarce with both home owner and investor demand increasing. Most of the sections still available for new homes are house and land packages, including those in the new Lake Panorama development in Henderson Heights, an area that is popular among families.

Prices

Te Atatu Peninsula's older stock includes group houses for under $200,000 or a two-bedroom do-up without garaging for $235,000. Older homes with a garage and/or sleepout sell for around $320,000.

What little land is left along the peninsula coast looking towards the city comes at premium prices of $300,000 plus. A semi-detached three-bedroom home with double garaging in the newest Edgelea Estate sells in the $500,000s; a three-bedroom, two-bathroom terrace house is about $330,000.

In both Te Atatu South and Henderson, most homes sell in the $200,000 to $300,000 bracket, up from $130,000 to $200,000 two years ago. In Te Atatu South an established 1950s-style family home sells in the $300,000s and newer homes sell for around $500,000. A three-bedroom home and income property recently sold in the $700,000s.

In Henderson a small home on a 450 to 500m² site, worth $150,000 18 months ago, is now close to $200,000. Homes worth $180,000 then now cost around $250,000. Executive

Why I live there
Entertainer Pio Terei

Pio, his wife Debbie and their three children share their 1.6ha West Auckland property with calves, chooks and a few sheep, and they love it. Pio has lived here for 10 years and he says he'd never swap the lifestyle. "It's rural, it's ideal for bringing up children and it's close to wonderful shopping and restaurants. We've got cafés and vineyards and we're just over the hill from Piha." Based from his home, Pio can juggle appointments to avoid peak hour motorway traffic and get into the central city in 20 minutes when he needs to. "Lots of people come out here and they're quite amazed. It's this great place that's got everything here but it's still close to town."

homes cost $300,000 to $400,000, with the finest in Henderson Heights ranging from $500,000 to $1.5 million.

Average sale prices

	House	Flat	No. sales
2002	$215,171	$176,076	1370
2003	$235,767	$166,167	1543

Rental and investment

School zones have pushed up rental prices with demand from local families and British migrants in key areas. In Henderson Heights rentals for family homes range from $350 for a three-bedroom home to $450-plus for a four-bedroom home plus family room. Older homes in Henderson return rentals of $280 a week for a three-bedroom home to $420 for four bedrooms. Henderson Valley homes near the town centre rent out at $280 a week.

In Te Atatu larger homes in the coast developments return $500 a week; a terrace house about $360 a week.

Best streets

Burgundy Park Ave in Henderson Heights. Frank Evans Pl in Henderson. Spinnaker Dr in Te Atatu Peninsula.

AMENITIES

Schools ★★★★★

Abundant primary schools (up to 16) serve both new and established family areas, Summerland Primary School in Henderson Heights opened last year and it already has an enrolment zone. Intermediate schools number four and secondary schools include Waitakere College, Liston College, St Dominic's College and Henderson High School all in Henderson, and Rutherford College on the Te Atatu Peninsula. Unitec's Waitakere campus is in the heart of Henderson. The Bible College of New Zealand is near the motorway end of Lincoln Rd.

Shops ★★★★

The West City mall in the heart of Henderson's busy strip shopping has grown in size and sophistication to reflect the tastes of the wide west Auckland area it services. At the Corbans Estate Arts Centre, a Pacific cultural market

Once were wineries

Grapes and apples used to grow where many of today's Henderson residents live. West City shopping mall stands on the site of the former Nikau vineyards and Waitakere College is on the site of the Vitasovich family's former vineyard and part of the former Platts Orchards.

Henderson has many enduring links to the days when the influx of winemakers from Croatia  (formerly Dalmatia) made it famous for its wines. It's certainly obvious in the new Corban Estate Arts Centre in the refurbished 17-room Corban family homestead, on the site of the first vines that founder Assid Corban planted 100 years ago.

Alongside the centre, the new Corbans Estate courtyard villas epitomise some of Henderson's modern housing developments. They are an example of what the council wants to encourage in the heart of Henderson - the sort of apartment-style living that has revitalised Auckland's city centre.

Familiar faces on the Henderson scene include the descendents of those early wine-makers, such as Leza Corban, Assid's great granddaughter, who runs the town's Moka cafe and restaurant with her parents. She's proud to be called a Westie because of the down-to-earth nature of the self-made business people who, with their unassuming wealth, have retained strong business links with the area.

In Henderson Valley the Pleasant Valley winery remains the oldest winery still in business in west Auckland. Along Lincoln Rd, now one of the main motorway links, the vines of the Collard Brothers Winery rub shoulders with the evolving retail, commercial and light industrial centres.

is held on the first Saturday of every month. Lincoln Rd has several shopping centres.

Leisure ★★★

Opanuku Reserve at the city end of Henderson Valley Rd offers a restful playground area for weary parents; for those keen to stretch the legs there's the International Walkway of Trees alongside the Henderson Creek off Central Park.

The 7.2ha Kiwi Valley complex in Henderson Valley Rd includes farm tours, an equestrian centre, a stunt school that services the film industry and Old MacDonald's travelling farmyard.

On the Te Atatu Peninsula, 80ha of waterfront land looking across to Auckland City is about to be developed into a "people's park", a four-year project, and will eventually link up with the Te Atatu Peninsula walkway.

The village green includes the Jack Pringle skate park. In the heart of Te Atatu South there's the Lloyd Morgan Lions Park.

The Waitakere City Aquatic Centre is in the heart of Henderson. The Waitakere City Stadium is located off Central Park. The Taikata Sailing Club is based at the tip of the peninsula.

For eating out, try Moka on Great North Rd or any of the fine ethnic restaurants along the main shopping route. Or there's the Last Straw Café in the Kiwi Valley complex on Henderson Valley Rd. On the Te Atatu Peninsula the Peninsular Palms Cafe, the Compass Point Cafe and Connections family restaurant are popular.

Travel times

From Henderson

CBD	off-peak 10 min
	peak 25 min
West Coast beaches	20 min
Airport	30 min

A train line and good bus services run throughout Waitakere city. Henderson and its surrounding areas are well served with access routes to the north-western motorway via either Lincoln Rd or Te Atatu Rd. The train ride into the CBD takes about the same time as the drive via the motorway.

LOOK OUT!

If you're touchy about the negative connotations of the label Westie, then you either need to get over it or keep saving for that yuppie Ponsonby pad. The term Westie was once part of the surfie lingo, but Auckland's self-appointed yuppies use it liberally to refer to their cousins "out west", who they see as unsophisticated by comparison, with mullet haircuts, black jeans and a Holden ute as their steed. But as one proud west Auckland resident reminds us all, "there are Westies everywhere aren't there?"

SMART BUY

There are still many great bargains in this area. The smartest buy is probably Te Atatu Peninsula, where new homes close to the shoreline walkways, within walking distance of cafes and with views across the Waitemata Harbour to the city cost upwards of $500,000. As a starting point it's on the high side, but waterfront exclusivity is likely to command premium prices in the long-term.

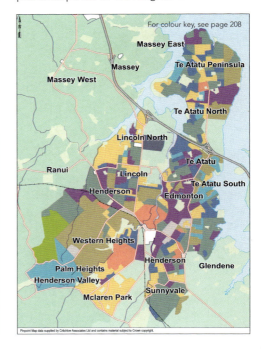

KUMEU/HUAPAI ★★★★☆

including Coatesville, Riverhead, Waimauku, Dairy Flat and Taupaki

Urban sprawl and the growing attraction of the semi-rural lifestyle have literally brought the little villages of Kumeu and Huapai together. Once quite separate, they're now known as Kumeu/Huapai, with a conjoined name that has become part of the branding of this popular haunt for city escapees, equestrian enthusiasts and expat Kiwis.

The past five years have seen burgeoning commercial development on the fringes of a retail area that's in the heart of some of the finest lifestyle countryside in the region. The centre services everything from the hobby farms to the horticulturalists who produce olives, grapes and persimmons. Ten years ago no-one looked twice at the chap who'd call into the dairy on his tractor for milk and bread. Now it's the four-wheel drive vehicles that queue up with the sort of style that's de rigueur in affluent city suburbs. Unlike the Ponsonby puddle-jumpers, here four-wheel drive vehicles are justified.

Who lives there?

Young middle-age professionals and an increasing number of city families are the significant buyers in this area. Often they will have established themselves in business so that by the time they can afford this kind of lifestyle, they'll be bringing with them a young, school-age family. They're keen on the land for the lifestyle rather than for any productive returns. As a result, many of the big farms have progressively been subdivided from big acreages down to 4ha and the most popular 1ha blocks that are ideal for keeping a few pets and a horse or two. Rural locals sling off at city trendies driving their four-wheel drive "shinies", but it's all in good humour. Newcomers love the lifestyle and they don't mind being seen embracing it.

Typical dwellings

Kumeu/Huapai's lifestyle blocks include new executive homes and city villas that have been removed to make way for townhouses and given new status in keeping with the "original farmhouse" style of living that suits rolling countryside. Some newer subdivisions here have their own sewerage systems that replace the must-have septic tanks on older properties. New residential sections are large by city standards and have been surveyed at 1500m² to accommodate a filtration system alongside the house to avoid the need for septic tanks.

Sprawling executive properties - with tennis courts, pools, outdoor fireplaces, stables and the like - are a feature of the Coatesville countryside. Tucked among a scattering of market gardens, they epitomise the affluent end of country living.

In Huapai the new 32-unit Parkview Retirement Village gives long-term residents some lifestyle choices when they are no longer able to cope with life in a big home or on the land.

REAL ESTATE

Trends

Lifestyle property is hot out here, from the lifestyle blocks close to Kumeu to the new, and pending, subdivision developments at Dairy Flat. Throughout Coatesville and Dairy Flat there is a shortage of land zoned for small holdings rather than rural development because, according to real estate agents, local authority planners haven't appreciated the pace of change.

In Kumeu, one large tract of land is selling in blocks of 4ha and more, able to be built on now but unable to be subdivided until the water and sewerage infrastructure is in place. Waimauku's 26-section Solan Estate has sprouted new homes and at least one property has been onsold for a respectable capital gain. There's steady demand for established homes and relocated villas on lifestyle blocks, but far fewer for sale than in recent years, because the owners have limited options for moving up in the area.

Demand for lifestyle properties is equally buoyant at Muriwai Beach, which locals consider part of their patch (see our West Coast Beaches chapter). Premium prices are being fetched for existing homes and sections. Rental demand regularly exceeds the supply because many prospective lifestylers prefer to "try before they buy". When they do buy here, they rarely regret the move and shift only within the area rather than back to the city.

Prices

Land for lifestyle blocks and future subdivision is fetching some of the highest prices here. Recent sales include 4ha near Kumeu for just over $1 million and a 7.2ha block for $2.2 million.

One 4ha Kumeu property with two dwellings sold for $450,000 three years ago and recently sold again for $700,000. The only "improvement" was the demolition of the older, larger dwelling. Prices can vary widely, with small blocks selling for as much as larger blocks depending on the quality of house.

In Kumeu/Huapai, 1500m^2 sections have increased from $180,000 to well over $200,000, with one premium 2200m^2 section selling for $250,000. There have been fewer $1 million plus house sales this year, with most house sales in the $400,000 to $500,000 range.

The recent sale of a new home at the Solan Estate for $400,000 is an indication of the capital gain off an initial purchase price of $130,000 for the 1000m^2 section a year or so ago. Then, that house would have been worth about $320,000. Other 1500m^2 sections have sold in the $165,000 to $185,000 range.

The first of Dairy Flat's subdivisions - the 63-section Goodlands Country Estate - saw 2000m^2 to 4000m^2 sections selling for between $300,000 and $450,000.

Dairy Flat also has its share of million dollar 2ha to 4ha lifestyle blocks with good homes.

Such properties are attracting affluent buyers from the North Shore, for whom space and privacy, rather than cost, are the issues.

Average sale prices

	House	Flat	No. sales
2002	$283,006	$271,800	139
2003	$340,880	$246,000	140

Best streets

Matua Rd in Kumeu, Merlot Heights in Huapai, Solan Estate in Waimauku.

Rental and investment

In Kumeu/Huapai the two-bedroom "minor dwellings" that feature on lifestyle blocks are the ideal chance to taste a rural lifestyle for $250 a week. A one-bedroom cottage at Waimauku rents for $150 a week but such properties are not commonly available. At Muriwai rental property is in high demand with a one-bedroom cottage costing $150 a week and an executive home on 4ha costing about $550 a week.

AMENITIES

Schools ★★

Everything that's great about rural schools is here, like "ag days" when kids show off their pets and produce. Four primary schools take children up to and including Year 8, which means children only have to travel outside the area at secondary school age. The choices include Westlake Boys and Westlake Girls schools on the North Shore and Massey High School and Waitakere College in the Henderson area. Private co-ed schooling is offered at Kristin School in Albany. Kumeu has a playcentre that is a parent-run cooperative for preschoolers.

Shops ★★★

There's energetic commercial and retail expansion going on in Kumeu. Both Kumeu and Huapai have shopping areas, with plenty of safe parking off the main road. The compact array of shops sells everything from envelopes to antiques. There's even a place to get your lawn mower fixed, a library at Huapai and Plunket rooms at Kumeu.

For more substantial shopping, the Westgate Shopping Centre is about 10 minutes' drive

Local hero – Kumeu Showgrounds

The 82nd annual Kumeu show is scheduled for March 2004. Each year this traditional agricultural and horticultural show gets bigger and busier. Entrants come from throughout the North Island with their animals, to compete in the competitions and enjoy the famous village camaraderie. Equestrian events include show jumping; there are 500 trade sites that showcase agricultural businesses and craft stalls. The volunteer Kumeu A&H Society owns the 34ha showgrounds, which are also used for annual events including a hot rod show, the Kumeu Wine and Food Festival and a folk festival.

away at the end of the north-western motorway link into the city, and there's shopping on the North Shore via Upper Harbour Dr.

Leisure ★★★★

Woodhill and the Riverhead forests offer the best terrain for the likes of motorcycling, orienteering and horse riding. Closer to Kumeu/Huapai there's the Huapai Domain.

In Kumeu/ Huapai sporting facilities include golf, squash and tennis courts, and a driving range. Muriwai Beach with its long stretch of sand is a short drive away (see West Coast Beaches).

The world-class wineries here include Soljans Estate Winery, Coopers Creek, Selaks, Nobilos, Kumeu River, Matua Valley and Westbrook.

For movie buffs, there's a cinema complex at Westgate Shopping Centre.

By its lifestyle nature, Kumeu/Huapai has several large restaurants tucked among the vineyards including River Mill, the Allely House Vineyard restaurant, Gracehill Vineyard Restaurant, Settlers Lodge and The Hunting Lodge at Waimauku, and the Soljans' new facility.

For top café fodder, tuck in at the award-winning Carriages restaurant created out of refurbished railway carriages, complete with platform and signage. There's also the new Friends Café in Kumeu that's run by ex-All Black Inga "the winger" Tuigamala, Blossoms at Kumeu, Misada at Huapai and Beesonline at Waimauku. Ethnic tastes are catered for with the Japanese/Korean style Long Meadow Restaurant in Kumeu and The Curry Leaf restaurant with its famously authentic Indian cuisine just before Kumeu township.

Map labels:
For colour key, see page 208
Puhoi
Tahekeroa
Orewa
Kanohi
Wainui
Kaukapakapa
Silverdale
Waitoki
Parakai
Dairy Flat
Helensville
Wharepapa
Coatesville
Albany
Rewiti
Riverhead
Huapai
Brighams Creek
Kumeu
Hobsonville
Muriwai
Royal Heights
Waitakere
West Auckland
Swanson

Pinpoint Map data supplied by Critchlow Associates Ltd and contains material subject to Crown copyright.

Travel times

From Kumeu

CBD	25 min
Westgate Shopping Centre	10 min
Airport	off-peak 40 min
	peak 80 min
Muriwai Beach	10 min

It's getting hard to pull out of side streets into the main road now and to the delight of locals, traffic lights are set to be erected at - fittingly - Access Rd. Ironically, city traffic has at last arrived at the place where everyone moves to get away from the traffic lights!

including Glendene, Kelston and Glen Eden

Solidly suburban, New Lynn is probably best known for its signature mall. New Lynn and Kelston are both in demand for infill potential and for schools, including Kelston Boys High School, current world secondary school rugby champions. Substantial water's edge properties add to Kelston's appeal. Suburb status is important here. People who live on the fringes will politely make sure you know exactly which suburb they're in.

Glen Eden has been seen as a bit of a backwater, but that's changing, with initiatives by the Glen Eden Community Protection Society. The refurbished Art Deco Playhouse Theatre has now reopened, and there's the restored railway station with its upmarket cafe. The new library is scheduled to open early next year, and a large medical centre is planned. Glen Eden is often confused with nearby Glendene, a newer, more upmarket area developed in the 1960s and 1970s.

Who lives there?

New Lynn is popular with Kiwi and migrant families and attracts huge developer interest for its large properties with subdivison potential.

Glen Eden continues to be a traditional first home buying area, although those who aspire to homes of status tend to step up to neighbouring Titirangi. Families who settle long-term do so for the popular primary and intermediate schools, the local shopping and the proximity to the rail link.

Glendene has young families with long family ties to west Auckland, attracted by its new houses. A high tenanted population in the older homes has attracted investors into the area. The streets developed in the 1960s include affordable three-bedroom homes keenly sought by buyers and investors. Manhattan Heights has families who've been there since the area was developed in the 1970s. Kelston is a family suburb sought after by buyers and renters for its schooling. It has homes in long-term family ownership, including some enviable water's edge homes largely unseen from the street.

Typical dwellings

Older homes on large sections are common to all these suburbs, built when weatherboard and corrugated iron were the materials of choice for affordable homes.

Such homes have been snapped up for their subdivision potential, so there's also a good choice of modern brick-and-tile houses on half sites.

Glen Eden and Kelston both have a wide range of house styles including a few original farmhouses, some Art Deco homes and post-war bungalows. Glen Eden also has some terraced housing and some group housing. In New Lynn the Waitakere City Council encourages residential development close to the transport centre. The Ambrico Pl development is New Lynn's only terrace house development, built on old Crown Lynn Potteries land. Crown Lynn Condominiums (also on potteries land) has just added a new block of 72 apartments to its 200 total.

REAL ESTATE

Trends

Once the poor relation of neighbouring suburbs, New Lynn is enjoying a revival as a destination suburb, partly due to its comparative affordability against pricey inner city suburbs. Older weatherboard houses are definitely back in favour. In New Lynn these homes, on large sections with a driveway, continue to be snapped up by developers with subdivision in mind.

Glen Eden's weatherboard homes are popular with families, who'll stretch their budget to get one on a full site for future subdivision.

New Lynn's apartments and terrace houses appeal to professionals. The Condominiums development is 80% owned by investors from throughout New Zealand and overseas.

Manhattan Heights' substantial 1970s homes have held their value well, depending on how they've been maintained. Glendene homes have traditionally held their value and continue to do so. In Kelston families stay put for years, and very little of this suburb's finest water's edge real estate ever comes on the market.

Prices

New Lynn's sale prices and volumes have increased dramatically in the past year or so. One real estate company quotes an average price of $248,000, up from $174,000 18 months ago. Entry point is $180,000 for a basic house on a half site. Top dollar in New Lynn is generally $350,000, with properties bordering Titirangi fetching even higher prices. One agent tells of a vendor who sold his house for $275,000, only to receive a backup offer of $295,000 four hours too late. Another house worth close to $190,000 last year has since sold for $270,000. A house in the area near Titirangi that locals like to call New Lynn Heights, sold for $450,000.

Ambrico's terrace houses, which sold in the $160,000s three years ago, now fetch $200,000 plus, with the most expensive selling for $270,000. A one-bedroom apartment costs $130,000 to $135,000; a two-bedroom one $330,000 to $360,000.

In Glen Eden prices range from $180,000 to the early $300,000s and capital gains have been as much as $100,000 over the past three years. Homes bought in the $160,000 to $200,000 bracket three years ago are now fetching $250,000 to $290,000. There aren't many under $200,000; most are $200,000 to $250,000. A tidy three-bedroom 1960s bungalow with a garage sells for around $230,000; a restored character weatherboard home on a good-sized section for closer to the top dollar $300,000 mark. Terrace houses at Pinnacle Ridge that initially sold for $178,000 are now selling around $205,000.

In Glendene, Manhattan Heights' well-designed substantial homes range from $350,000 to $550,000, depending on whether they've been kept up-to-date. The difference between a tired home and an up-to-date home here can mean $100,000.

Glendene's 1960s Hardiplank homes sell for around the $230,000 to $250,000 mark, as low as $180,000 to $210,000 around the light industrial area of Hepburn Rd.

Kelston prices are creeping up. A 1950s bungalow sells for $250,000, while waterfront properties are worth a fraction of what they would sell for on the inner harbour.

Average sale prices

	House	Flat	No. sales
2002	$188,748	$152,335	1066
2003	$206,077	$169,257	1253

Rental and investment

Rentals are standard throughout New Lynn, Glen Eden and Kelston for a standard weatherboard home. An average price is around $300 with rent ranging from $260 to $330 for a home with ensuite and double garaging. In Glen Eden a unit costs $275 a week. In Glendene a 1960s house costs $280.

Best streets

Ryehill Close in New Lynn. Konini Rd and Pleasant Rd in Glen Eden. Manhattan Heights in Glendene. Anything by the water in Kelston.

Why I live there
Waitakere City Mayor Bob Harvey

Glen Eden has been Bob Harvey's home for more than 30 years. To him, it epitomises the best of community living. "It's got garage sales and boot sales, markets and malls with little shops. It's everything good about being local, with so many groups that gather together just to hang out, and superb community facilities. It's all just 15 minutes from my favourite beaches, the bach at Karekare and the world's only subtropical rainforest next to a metropolis. I like it."

AMENITIES

Schools ★★★★

Kelston has primary and intermediate schools, the separate boys and girls' high schools and the Kelston Deaf Education Centre. Children from Glen Eden's primary intermediate schools and Glendene primary schools usually travel to Kelston for secondary schooling. Kelston Boys High are the current secondary school rugby champions.

Shops ★★★★

Each community has its own shopping mall, including the Kelston Shopping Centre, which is undergoing expansion, Glenmall in Glen Eden and the Glendene village shops. Glen Eden holds its market day on the first Saturday of every month. The Lynnmall Shopping Centre is the hub of the wider area with more than 120 shops, as a result of its re-development three years ago. Established in 1963, it is one of the country's earliest malls and it's popular for more than just shopping, drawing enthusiastic crowds to its weekly fitness "mall walks".

Leisure ★★★

Waitakere City's aim is to have a quality walk within 10 minutes' walk of every residence and the list of neighbourhood parks in this area is considerable. Glen Eden has Ceramco Park, the Clarence Reserve and Virgo Common. Kelston has Kelman Park as well as the Cobham Reserve and Archibald Park. New Lynn's pride is the 2ha

Travel times

CBD	off-peak 15 min
	peak 45 min
Airport	off-peak 20 min
	peak 40 min
New Lynn shops	off-peak 10 min
	peak 15 min

The New Lynn transport centre is next door to the New Lynn railway station and from there, Stagecoach runs bus services to both the CBD and west Auckland. Services also run from New Lynn on separate routes to Otahuhu, Panmure and Manukau City. Passenger rail services run through New Lynn from West Auckland to the CBD with connections onto the southern line to Papakura and Pukekohe and the south-eastern line through Orakei to Glen Innes.

Manawa wetland reserve. Using a series of interconnecting ponds to improve water quality, the Waitakere City Council has transformed the wetland reserve into a recreational amenity for both people and wildlife to enjoy.

The New Lynn Community Centre in Totara Ave is the first large new facility in Waitakere City to have artistic concepts intergrated into its design and construction. Lead artist Neil Miller worked with Architectus from concept to completion, which includes commissioned artworks with the award-winning building.

Glen Eden has its famous Glenora Rugby League Club, the swimming centre at Parrs Park and the Ceramco Park Functions Centre Both New Lynn and Glen Eden have a large selection of ethnic eateries that reflect their multi-cultural communities including Asian and Mediterranean. Kelston has the Arum café at Palmers Gardenworld. For fine dining, locals look to Titirangi and Henderson.

Definitely one to watch. In particular, look for well-priced homes on the water's edge, or on a big section with subdivision potential.

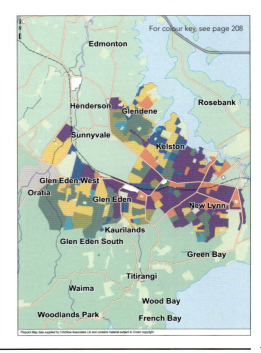

SWANSON ★★★★★

including Ranui, Waitakere and Massey

The Waitakere Ranges are to Swanson what the Sky Tower is to central Auckland. Those green hills define its arty semi-rural image. Swanson and Ranui are vastly different in flavour but, as one long-time Swanson resident says, "we're very happy neighbours". Swanson attracts progressive young professional families with loads of community spirit. Ranui, developed in the 1960s and 1970s, has a high Maori and Pacific Island population. Waitakere township's influx of young families is lifting its profile. Being at the end of the passenger rail line, many a backpacking tourist mistakes the "Waitakere" sign for the city destination and ends up pitching a tent on the large front lawns of hospitable local residents! Closer to suburban buzz, sprawling Massey has its own identity - Massey north locals have unofficially renamed their area Westgate. Massey east includes the more upmarket Royal Heights, looking out across the water to Te Atatu.

Who lives there?

Old hippies, youthful yuppies and everything in between live either out of sight in the ranges above Swanson or down in the communities. Swanson is attracting young families keen on the upmarket, semi-rural fringe alternative it offers to city life.

It's also an inspirational retreat for creatives, including potters, artists, writers and designers, and a popular choice for professionals who commute to city jobs. Swanson is proud of its multi-generational links to the area, and the Swanson Heritage Committee is gathering the life stories of some of its oldest residents.

Ranui's population includes a 50% mix of Maori and Pacific Islanders. The rural appeal of Waitakere township is a big drawcard for family living and large families with four or five children are common here.

Massey has a mix of renters, first-home buyers and long-term residents among the young families and established professionals who move here from throughout west Auckland.

Typical dwellings

Swanson and Ranui both have older homes that have retained their appeal to buyers. Each area also has new developments, including brick-and-tile houses in Swanson Oaks off Swanson

Why I live there
Fashion designer Karen Walker

The Swanson Art Deco home of fashion designer Karen Walker and her husband Mikhail Gherman is the ultimate contrast to her business life under the spotlights of the world's fashion capitals. For the past seven years, their 4.8ha property down a private, unsealed road in the bush has delivered her perfect privacy. "I've always been drawn to extremes in my life," she explains. "Our collections are always extremes - very masculine and feminine, very tailored, very street. We're never middle of the road. That bores me and I guess that's what we love about this house, in the remote bush, in a remote village, in a remote city, in a remote country. It's the complete opposite of what I'd be doing in the middle of Soho and where we lived before in Parnell." The monthly Swanson car boot market is Karen's favourite local activity. "There's a very strong sense of community on a Sunday and I love it ... I call it my Swansonby lifestyle."

Rd, and the enclave of brick cottages down Glen Ardern Way off Ranui's Universal Dr.

Locals talk about "Old Ranui" - the original character homes - and "new Ranui", the hundreds of affordable homes built around Universal Dr during the late 1960s and early 1970s by Universal Homes. The latest version of the "new" Ranui includes the two-level, two and three-bedroom brick and tile units in Pooks Rd and the single-level buildings of the Coroglen Gardens development off Swanson Rd. Swanson is also well-known for lifestyle blocks, while at nearby Waitakere township there is a far greater proportion of larger sections. The houses face the street, as in the suburbs, but the "backyard" can be up to several hectares. The township has relocated villas and cottages among its housing stock, and that's a big part of its attraction.

Massey North, or Westgate, has a mix of Fletcher homes (the Rush Creek development) and Universal Homes' Stonegate enclave, close to the Westgate shopping centre. Massey's finest homes include the exclusive Royal Heights area, with architecturally designed homes that have views of coastline looking east.

REAL ESTATE

Trends

Everyone loves new homes out here - and that hasn't changed. Families will quit their old house to live in a new one, even if they can only afford to rent it. Buyers will move from throughout west Auckland and even the North Shore. In a lot of cases they may have sold their first homes in the $180,000 to $200,000 bracket and will happily rent until they can afford the hefty financial step up into the $200,000s to get back into home ownership. Big capital gains have been posted for the new brick and tile townhouses in the Westgate and Stonegate developments of Massey North. These are still attracting investors and professionals who need to be close to the motorway access to the city.

Swanson's appeal continues to grow, largely for its semi-rural lifestyle, but also for its enclaves of low maintenance homes.

Prices

Swanson's 2ha and 4ha lifestyle blocks range from $200,000 to $600,000 and $700,000, with most properties with a nice home costing around $400,000. Homes in Swanson's new brick and tile housing subdivisions range from the high $200,000s to $400,000s.

In Ranui a two-bedroom brick and tile home on a small site, typical of those in Coroglen Gardens and Glen Arden Way developments sells for between $188,000 and $193,000, compared with $150,000 to $160,000 a year ago. The terrace houses in Pooks Rd close to the rail link have increased from around $200,000 to $250,000.

In Westgate, the Rush Creek development has seen typical price increases of between $80,000 and $100,000 on three-bedroom brick and tile homes now costing around $360,000. Many were bought by investors snapping up the $360 a week rental on their initial circa $260,000 investment. As one real estate agent put it: "Those investors were smart - but they didn't know they were smart when they bought them." Massey has good do up housing stock for less than $200,000. A tidy three-bedroom home with a garage costs $210,000. Good quality homes in the $230,000 to $240,000 range sold for around $170,000 two years ago. Top dollar in Massey will buy four bedrooms and two living areas for around $340,000.

Waitakere township prices range from $170,000 to $250,000 for a three-bedroom home on a 1000m^2 section. There's a mix of old and newer homes with plenty now worth $500,000 to $600,000 on lifestyle blocks.

Average sale prices

	House	Flat	No. sales
2002	$190,014	$164,130	612
2003	$206,048	$182,874	969

Rental and investment

In Massey, an older home costs $270 to $290 a week to rent. In Westgate, a new brick and tile home costs $350 a week. In Ranui a three-bedroom townhouse near the railway station costs $300 a week; an older home between $240 and $260 a week. Swanson has plenty of tenanted properties but comparatively little rental stock available. Expect to pay around $300 (compared with $250 a few years ago) for a three-bedroom home if you can get it.

Best streets

Christian Rd in Swanson. White Heron Dr and Petrel Pl in Royal Heights.

AMENITIES

Schools ★★★★

There's Swanson Primary School in Swanson, Ranui Primary School and Birdwood Primary in Ranui and Waitakere Primary in Waitakere township, which also takes children from nearby Bethells Beach.

Secondary school children travel from Swanson, Ranui and Waitakere township by train or bus to Waitakere College off Swanson Rd as well as high schools in Avondale, Henderson and Massey.

Shops ★★★

The Westgate Shopping Centre has become a huge focal point for Massey and surrounding suburbs. It includes cinemas, a supermarket, pharmacy, medical centre, gym, chain stores and boutique shops.

Ranui and Swanson have local shops and are also served by retail on Lincoln Rd. Swanson has a car boot sale and plant, produce and craft market. Royal Heights mall in Royal Rd includes the well-known Swiss Royal Heights Butchery. Waitakere township has its own dairy.

Leisure ★★★

The Waitakere Ranges, bordered by wild west coast beaches, are the area's obvious major asset. On the fringe of the ranges is the Redwood Park Country Club. The Swanson Station Park in front of the Station Cafe is the locals' pride and joy. Royal Heights has Moire Park, which extends to the water's edge. Ranui Park includes a camping ground.

The Massey Leisure Centre includes a library and indoor sports facility. It was built using the creative input of local artists - a great example of Waitakere City Council's artistic vision.

The Auckland Outdoor Health Club in Ranui is a private naturalists' (ie nudists) club set in parklike grounds, complete with a swimming pool.

The Signal Gallery in Swanson showcases the work of local artists and artisans. Golf courses include the Waitakere Golf Club, the Massey Golf Club and the Redwood Park Golf Club in Swanson. There are pony clubs in Massey and Waitakere township. Massey also has archery and athletics clubs.

There are plenty of foodie possibilities. Tastebud Tours creates customised cuisine, arts and wine trail tours throughout the area. Top stop in Swanson is the famed Swanson Station Cafe. Three great eateries in the Waitakere Ranges include the Waitakere Park Lodge, The Nikau Club and Devines, with its Tuscan/Provencal influence. At Crystal Mountain the Cafe on the Rocks serves lunches and brunches.

There are several cafes/restaurants and ethnic eat-outs in the Westgate Shopping Centre. And the best of the rest of west Auckland's fine food and wine is only 10 minutes away in Henderson.

SMART BUY

Want a pony or two and have a child or two, or three or four or more? If your big family needs room to move in the country, then head out to Waitakere township. It's as rural as you can get - and as close to town as you need to be. And you'll be in great company.

For colour key, see page 208

Taupaki
Massey North
Massey
Waitakere
Swanson   Ranui   Lincoln
Western Heights
Palm Heights
Mclaren Park
Oratia

Travel times
From Westgate

CBD	off-peak 20 min peak 40 min
North Shore via Upper Harbour Dr	20 min
Airport	45 min
Devonport	30 min

A well-patronised passenger train goes from Waitakere township to the CBD.
Ritchies Coachlines run from Massey and Ranui to the CBD. Stagecoach runs from Swanson to the CBD.

including Green Bay, Wood Bay, French Bay, Konini, Waiatarua, Oratia, Parau and Kaurilands

The wooded suburb of Titirangi is inextricably linked with certain enduring images: tree-huggers, potters in home-spun jumpers, old Rovers in British-racing green with Greenpeace stickers disappearing up bush-lined driveways. Trees are to Titirangi what coffee is to Ponsonby. Mention the place and most people have some idea of where and what you are referring to.

Sitting high above the city, Titirangi's best homes are tucked away from the road, nestled amongst the bush, with lush subtropical and native gardens dripping with rainwater. They might have impressive tree-framed glimpses of the cityscape or Manukau Harbour. Such places really convey the feeling you are far from the madding crowds.

There's a tendency for residents in the lower-lying border suburbs to fudge suburb boundaries, but the beginning of the bushline is Titirangi's natural and indisputable boundary.

Who lives there?

Traditionally, Titirangi has appealed to the artistically inclined and to bush-lovers. In the 1960s it was a thriving community of potters, weavers, writers and a variety of alternative lifestylers. These days Titirangi is still home to lots of artists and craftspeople as well as a large number of professionals who commute to the city or work from home. Titirangi has been described as the "elite of the west"; anecdotal evidence suggests many doctors, dentists, engineers, university staff and teachers can today be found living among its trees. As with other suburbs that offer a point of difference, Titirangi has of late become very popular with returning expats and wealthy immigrants (mostly English, American, European, and South African). Such buyers are looking for coastal access and bush views, and are prepared to commute to enjoy these added lifestyle aspects. Titirangi still attracts young up-and-coming artists, though steadily rising house prices mean they tend to be renters rather than buyers.

Typical dwellings

The Titirangi area saw a lot of growth in the 1960s and 1970s, so many houses have been built in the distinctive style of the era. Wood is a popular building material, used both outside, such as board and batten, and inside with cathedral-style beamed ceilings or tongue-and-groove paneling. The sloping terrain means pole houses are common, as are split-level floors. Houses dating from this period are "sympathetically modernised" rather than restyled altogether.

REAL ESTATE

Trends

Titirangi has benefited from renewed interest in weatherboard homes after the horror of the leaky building syndrome and its association with terrace houses. The traditional weatherboard cottage is a popular entry point for new buyers and established professionals buying homes are keen on slightly higher priced property. Areas beyond Titirangi village including Oratia, South Titirangi and Woodlands Park are particularly sought after by buyers from within the area, greater Auckland and overseas.

Oratia, with its larger open sections, north-facing aspect and harbour views, is increasingly popular with families. It's difficult to buy into because newcomers stay put for the excellent primary schooling and the lifestyle appeal.

In Green Bay there's keen competition for the most humble of homes in an area with price rises that are seeing active investor and second home buyer interest. First home buyers compete keenly at auction to buy a home here on a typically 650 to 800m^2 site. Chances are they'll stay put and move up within the area rather than into another suburb. There's a nucleus of three-bedroom homes in Green Bay that has historically reflected city-wide real estate trends and they've predictably increased steadily in value.

Prices

In Titirangi entry prices for a basic home are $250,000 to $300,000. Several offers saw one three-bedroom bach-style bungalow sell for $350,000; vendors selling one small three-bedroom home considered six offers before signing for $420,000. There's steady stock and steady demand for family homes in the $300,000 to $500,000 price range. Sales over $600,000 in wider Titirangi, Laingholm and Green Bay have more than doubled in the past two years. A recent $1.2 million Titirangi sale was a one-off, but several premium properties

have hit the $800,000 mark. In Green Bay ex-group houses that ranged from $180,000 to $200,000 a year or two ago now sell for between $230,000 and $260,000. In Oratia don't expect to buy anything for less than $300,000. A board and batten home worth $340,000 two years ago now sells for $440,000. A good quality home with views of both the Manukau and Waitemata harbours is worth $600,000 to $700,000; a substantial family home on a few hectares of land is likely to surpass $1 million.

Average sale prices

	House	Flat	No. sales
2002	$265,569	$192,136	584
2003	$288,143	$183,167	600

Rental and investment

Titirangi is predominantly owner/occupier territory but more recently there has been investor interest in slightly high priced property for long-term, rather than short-term, gain. Bigger homes cost $600-plus to rent. There's comparatively little rental stock at the cheaper, $300 a week end of the market, unlike Green Bay where a three-bedroom home returns $320 to $360. Here, a top quality property will command a premium rental but size, quality and whether or not there is garaging is a bigger determination of the return than location per se.

Best streets

South Titirangi Rd, Cliff View Rd, Rangiwai Rd, Park Rd and Westridge Rd in Titirangi; Carter Rd and Parker Rd in Oratia.

Why I live there
Fashion stylist Alice Rycroft

"Natural surroundings are important to me," says freelance fashion stylist Alice Rycroft. "I couldn't bear looking out the window onto another house." A Titirangi resident of 16 years, Alice has views across the bush to Puketutu Island in the Manukau Harbour. Neither Alice nor husband Mick Sinclair, an entertainment lawyer, work normal hours so rush-hour traffic isn't a concern and it takes only 20 minutes for them to drive into the city. "A great aspect of coming home to Titirangi is the feeling of leaving the city behind. Come the weekend, friends pop in, or there's always something interesting on at Lopdell House. There are lots of bush walks and it's quick to get to Karekare or Whatipu."

Local hero - Lopdell House Gallery

Lopdell House Gallery is the public art gallery for Waitakere City. Located at one end of the Titirangi village overlooking west Auckland, the 1930s building is a dynamic exhibition space showcasing established and emerging artistic talent from the region, New Zealand and elsewhere. It has approximately 30,000 visitors a year. The gallery hosts events such as The Portage Ceramic Awards. New Zealand films are also promoted, as well as the latest in music and performance and a range of talks and debates. The gallery runs tours to artists' studios, travelling exhibitions and sculpture gardening projects with local schools.

AMENITIES

Schools ★★★

There are seven primary schools, including a Rudolf Steiner school. Both Kauriland's Primary and Konini Primary are sought after by parents who move to be within zone of these schools. Glendene Intermediate is the closest intermediate and the closest secondary school is Green Bay High, with Kelston Boys and Kelston Girls High schools also nearby.

Shops ★★

The Titirangi shopping centre is a quaint strip with alfresco dining, stone walls and cobbling contributing to a real village feel. There are about half a dozen restaurants and cafes, including a German/Italian bakery in Lopdell House, and Toby's Kitchen, one of the oldest drinking holes in west Auckland. The village car park and the ASB offer some of the best views in Auckland. The Titirangi Village Market is held on the last Sunday of every month, featuring live music and more than 100 stalls of art, craft and collectables. Locals complain the market is so popular that parking is hell.

Leisure ★★★★

Bordering the Waitakere Ranges Regional Park, the area is also well served with small neighborhood green areas, including Ceramco Park, Crum Park, Bishop Park Scenic Reserve and Laingholm Domain. As well as bush, there's the coast with its many attractive bays and beaches.

Titirangi has numerous groups catering for the arts and crafts (see Lopdell House Gallery above) plus a number of sporting facilities and clubs for badminton, tennis, squash and yoga and so forth. There is at least one fitness centre and a spinal exercise clinic. The Titirangi Golf Club is located past Green Bay. There is a local theatre and drama company at Lopdell House. A selection of restaurants and cafes draw locals as well as diners from nearby suburbs like Blockhouse Bay. The Hardware Café, Long Drop Café and Toby's wine bar are particular favourites.

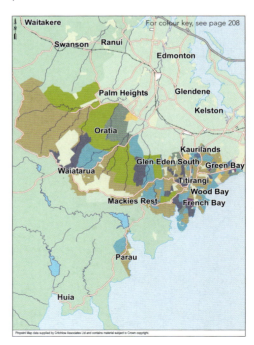

LOOK OUT!

If you hanker after wide-open spaces and plenty of sun, Titirangi is probably not for you. For tree-huggers the heavy bush is the ultimate haven; for others it is potentially sunless, mozzie-laden and claustrophobic.

South-facing areas like Wood Bay and French Bay are reasonably priced, have fantastic harbour views and are wonderful summer places, but may require a strong constitution during winter.

SMART BUY

Bordering Titirangi's bush verge is the little suburb of Green Bay where an average three-bedroom bungalow can be bought for $250,000, while $400,000 buys newer properties. The suburb has a mix of residents and its shops are well frequented by locals. Green Bay still has many full-sized sections and many solid 1960s weatherboard houses. Local attractions include fishing, the Rahui Kahika Reserve, a skating area and Green Bay beach. Another plus is having a kindy, primary, intermediate and secondary school all on Godley Rd, though Green Bay High School doesn't enjoy the greatest reputation and in the past there has been white flight to Avondale and Lynfield.

The coastal Cliff View Dr is the neighborhood's swanky street. New demand has come from people pushing out from the city after realizing the suburb is good value for money compared with slightly more central places like Blockhouse Bay and Hillsborough. Prices have gone up during the past six months but opinion says the suburb is still undervalued and therefore a good buy.

Travel times
From Titirangi village

CBD	off-peak 30 min
	peak 1 hour plus
North-western motorway	10 min
Airport	30 min
Lynnmall shopping centre	5 min

The nearest train line runs through Glen Eden but Stagecoach buses serve most of the main streets of Titirangi.

Saving the bush

The thorny issue of bush clearance in properties throughout Waitakere City is covered in a number of zones designed to protect the unique green network that weaves its way through the city. Every property in Waitakere city has two zones - one that is listed under the heading "Human Environment Rules", which covers building issues including site coverage, and the second one under the heading "Natural Area Rules" which covers activities on the land including tree pruning and removal. The rules that determine how much bush you can clear off your coastal section to turn that old bach into a big flash family home depend entirely on which combination of zones your property is defined by. The different "human" zones that relate to residential living include ordinary residential living, to "bush living", "foothills", "countryside", "rural village" and "coastal village". The "natural" zones cover protected areas and coastal areas as well as the most common "general" and "managed" zones. As you can see, it's a complex issue affected by a number of factors. So before you consider removing anything more than any trees 3m out from the eaves (that's allowable to reduce the fire risk) contact the Waitakere City Council's planning officers for advice.

including Muriwai, Bethells Beach, Anawhata, Piha, Karekare, Huia, Cornwallis and Laingholm

Wild and rugged, the beauty of the West Coast beaches brings out special qualities in the people who live in these scattered and remote communities. They're arty and creative with a keen spiritual connection to the land. Locals talk about the special energy of the west that comes from the wind, the surf and the brooding dark sands.

Each coastal community has its own flavour. Piha and Muriwai Beach are the most accessible - and therefore the most expensive. There are the smaller communities at Anawhata, Bethells Beach with its open farmland, and Karekare with its 4ha blocks and picturesque beach - which served as the backdrop to the 1993 movie The Piano.

The little villages of Huia and Little Huia are tucked inside the entrance to the Manukau Harbour on its northern edge and are reached by road beyond Titirangi, Laingholm and Cornwallis. Whatipu Beach is further along this road.

Who lives there?

World-class creatives, local artists, architects, and writers hide away in their leafy retreats. Many locals commute to work in Auckland city while others are happily home-based in these inspirational surroundings. Where else can you wander down to the store barefoot and without wearing a shred of pretence? Holidaymakers are part of the scene, although many baches are now home to permanent residents.

Sadly, Piha is losing its aged population as long-time residents move closer to town, to medical services and the amenities that were never part of Piha's style but an essential part of its appeal. Muriwai Beach has a mix of residents of all ages that includes young surfies, families and commuters.

Laingholm has attracted interest from both Asian and European migrants. Down at Parau near Laingholm, there is a retreat set up by a group of Korean monks.

Typical dwellings

Houses of all shapes and sizes are tucked into the bush and anchored to the cliffs. The ubiquitous Kiwi bach is still a reassuring sight in Piha, in an era when baches are making way for palatial holiday homes. In one panorama you can take in contemporary minimalist, 1930s Art Deco, 1970s board-and batten rustic, and an old post-war bach with peeling paint. Properties can only be cleared of sufficient trees to allow space for the dwelling. "It's strict but fair," says one long-time resident whose solid plaster house is coloured with a slurry made from the red clay of Piha Rd. "It'd be an insult to build a big fence out here."

Piha has some 700 titles compared with neighbouring Anawhata which has little more than 30 houses in two blocks, many of which are built of wood. Those nearest the road access have electricity; those on the seaward

side rely on solar and wind power generation yet they're the most sought-after for their spectacular sea views.

Karekare has its 4ha blocks but comparatively few properties with sea views. At the other end of the coast, Muriwai Beach has a huge diversity of housing from old baches to clifftop mansions.

Laingholm, Cornwallis and Huia were once full of old baches but these are slowly making way for more suburban-style housing and some substantial homes.

REAL ESTATE

Trends

One local real estate agent's word picture of Piha is also an indication of growing overseas interest in this coastal settlement. In her words: "Piha is to Auckland what Malibu is to Los Angeles." It's the overseas buyers rather than Kiwis who are nudging along interest in Piha's highest priced homes. Since Piha's first $1 million-plus sale a year ago, a few other properties have fetched similar prices. Other similarly priced homes continue to invite steady local and international interest, but be warned against talking up the market down here by the beach. Agents confirm there is "no rush" of buyers making the big purchases,

probably because Kiwis are sceptical of such big prices. They make serious inquiries, but tend to hold back from purchasing until they hear overseas buyers heaping acclaim on the untouched rugged charm of the area. When they do sign up, Kiwis tend to invest in a second home rather than making the huge leap of faith that a permanent shift from built-up suburbia to beachside isolation represents. Muriwai also shares Piha's million dollar status and a population of die-hard surfies, which is part of the reason that property in these two beachside communities is so hard to secure. Muriwai's geography is such that its top streets include the priciest homes with views at one end and the cheapest without much of an outlook down the other end.

Muriwai people traditionally stay in the area, buying to upgrade then moving up to more expensive, better quality properties. There's very little property left to subdivide in Muriwai. In Piha, which is protected against intensive subdivision and high rise developments, there are a few sections left.

In Laingholm and Huia recent huge demand for limited stock is seeing property selling, often within days of listing, amid stiff auction bidding.

Prices

The biggest demand for Piha property is in the $400,000 to $600,000 range, which will buy you a 20 year old house up the hill by the beach, possibly with a view. Karekare's popular 4 to 5ha blocks range in price from about $500,000 to $600,000 and higher, depending on the quality of the dwelling. Properties at Anawhata sell for $300,000 plus, if they ever come onto the market. Prices at Bethells Beach have also been caught up in the increasing values. A bach fetching $200,000 a year ago is now likely to carry a price tag closer to $300,000.

At Muriwai the price of a knock-down bach in the bush has increased from $150,000 to the $200,000. A quality do-up costs around $300,000. Homes at the upper end of the market bring valuations ranging from $600,000 to well over the $1 million mark into the buying frenzy if they come onto the market.

In Laingholm, the recent days of a little cottage selling for around $160,000 have been

Why I live there
Artist Dean Buchanan

After 10 years living in Karekare, artist Dean Buchanan is still hugely inspired by the maturity of the rejuvenating native bush, the sunsets and the raging energy of the West Coast beaches. "It's dynamic," he enthuses. "It drives me. It's a healing place. I'm tuning into it even more than before. I cycle a lot and I can jump off my bike along the Piha Rd and walk into the bush and really feel a part of it, whether it's the weathered bark of a tree or a nikau palm."

surpasssed by first entry prices of $220,000 and more. The $600,000 to $700,000 top-end price bracket is unchanged but many more homes are selling in this range.

In Huia a one-bedroom home with views costs $265,000; a home-and-income property about $420,000.

Average sale prices

	House	Flat	No. sales
2002	$267,028	$ n/a	147
2003	$292,176	$ n/a	122

Rental and investment

Rental property is eagerly sought after throughout these local communities. A one-bedroom bach can return an investor $200 plus a week with larger homes in Piha returning between $300 to $450 depending on size, location and condition.

Muriwai is seeing an increasing demand for rental property from ex-city families keen to try a lifestyle change without burning all their bridges. A two-bedroom home will cost $260 to $280 a week; a three-bedroom home $350 a week. In Laingholm the two-bedroom cottage that cost $250 a year ago, is likely to cost a tenant $300 a week now. A simple three-bedroom weatherboard home costs about $320 a week. Larger family homes cost up to $600 depending on size and location.

Best streets

Oaia Rd and Ngatira Rd, Muriwai; Marine Pde and Garden Rd, Piha.

AMENITIES

Schools ★

Local schools are a bus ride away from the West Coast beach communities. Children in Huia can take buses to Laingholm, Woodlands Park or Titirangi to primary schools and further afield to Glen Eden Intermediate School. From Muriwai, children head by bus to Waimauku; from Piha buses ferry children to primary, intermediate and secondary schools on the fringes of Henderson. The Lone Kauri Community School at Karekare is officially part of Oratia Primary School.

Shops ★

General stores are the mainstay of these communities, selling household wares, food stuffs, freshly baked cakes (at Piha's store), and displaying notices about local services and where to start looking for the best bed and breakfast overnighter.

Supermarkets are at the nearest major town - for residents in Muriwai Beach its Kumeu, for Piha residents it's Henderson and from Huia, it's Titirangi.

Leisure ★★★★

The beaches, the bush and the sky - you can't beat the West Coast beaches for open spaces. Tucked out of site are little scenic reserves and bush walks with hidden waterfalls and swimming holes. There are even tramper's huts for those keen to do an overnighter. The fit can walk from Piha to

Anawhata in about an hour and to Bethells Beach in about three hours.

Muriwai Beach's horse riding facilities reflect its popularity among equestrian enthusiasts. The famous gannet colony is a popular tourist destination.

Piha has a private saltwater lagoon - the locals might tell you how to get there. And before Bethells Beach, freshwater lakes can be reached via a walk over the sand dunes.

The upgraded fishing club at Cornwallis is popular. There's a tennis court and petanque pitch at Parau but generally leisure time here means lazing at the beaches and good fishing. There are surf clubs at both beaches and the golf clubs near Bethells and Muriwai. Among Muriwai Beach's numerous facilities, there's a motorcycle course and tennis courts. Posh nosh means a trip into some of the Waitakere Ranges restaurants that include The Nikau Club and the Waitakere Park Lodge.

Both the Piha RSA and the Piha Surf Club put on good meals throughout the year and there are deli foods and German-style pastries available at the Piha Store and good take-aways and take-home meals at the Muriwai Lodge Store. WUZ's cafe at Muriwai Beach is well-known for its seaside breakfasts.

In the summer Bethells Beach hosts its own Ponsonby-style sand dune mobile cafe.

Coffee and takeaways are all you get from Laingholm onwards but Titirangi is close by.

LOOK OUT!

Watch out for rogue waves. Auckland's West Coast beaches are notorious for rips and local children are well-schooled by the Piha Surf Lifesaving Club's nipper programme in how to respect the sea. When you're down at Piha beach, do as the locals do - never turn your back on the sea.

SMART BUY

A bach - whatever the condition - anywhere on the West Coast beaches is the chance to grab a piece of Kiwiana that is fast disappearing. For the price of a simple box in the suburbs, you can own a slice of beach or bush lifestyle that will only increase in value as such picturesque seaside locations become harder to source but easier to reach.

For colour key, see page 208

Pinpoint Map data supplied by Critchlow Associates Ltd and contains material subject to Crown copyright.

Travel times
From Piha

CBD	off-peak 45 min peak 1 hour
North-western motorway	20 min
Airport	off-peak 45 min peak 1 hour
Henderson centre	20 min
From Muriwai	
CBD	off-peak 30 min
From Laingholm	
CBD	off-peak 40 min

Public transport is non-existent at most of the beaches out this way, so you'll need to rely on either your own car or a neighbour's, or the pushbike (if you're fit). Then again, this is the sort of place where locals will happily stop and offer you a lift. From Muriwai Beach, there's a limited bus service into Auckland city.

including Hobsonville, Whenuapai and Herald Island

Twenty years ago the suburb of West Harbour was little more than a name on the map, a couple of dozen homes and acres of fertile rural land. The airforce villages of Hobsonville and Whenuapai lay to the north and west, with Royal Heights at the end of the north-western motorway. Tiny Herald Island, reached by a causeway beyond Whenuapai, has always had a distinct personality and been home to a few alternative lifestylers and hippies.

These days West Harbour, with its centrepiece marina, abounds with prestigious homes looking out across the Waitemata Harbour to the North Shore and Auckland City. It's appropriate that the homes here and those in the developments taking shape near the marina are predominantly brick. A key part of the area's history was the Clark pottery and brickworks at Limeburners Bay, which eventually moved to New Lynn as the iconic Crown Lynn works.

Who lives there?

A mix of airforce personnel, young professional families with boating interests and people who have retired from large farms makes up the picture of the people who've chosen to settle "north-west" as they describe it.

Locals like the airforce presence because the properties are well maintained by the Ministry of Defence and the high security is a bonus for those in private dwellings.

Moves to secure the Whenuapai Air Base as a second regional commercial airport are being watched with interest by the wider community. The local economy reportedly stands to lose more than 1500 jobs and $230 million a year if the Air Force quits its Whenuapai base within five years and nothing is in place to fill the gap. Expat Kiwis are giving West Harbour and the surrounding water's edge properties close attention as they seek to invest back home. West Harbour is also attractive to Asian buyers for the style of its executive homes and the value for money that it offers.

Among those people retiring to West Harbour are former rural landowners opting for a fine home with a harbour outlook, rather than the culture shock of moving into the inner city. The Hobsonville Villas retirement village is another choice for older people.

Typical dwellings

The state house-style duplex dwellings and the signs on the wire fences tell you you're close to airforce lands. Yet a corner or two away from the Hobsonville base, down Scott Rd, pukekos live among some of Auckland's finest homes. Scott Rd is an unusual blend of rural 4ha to 7ha sites bordered by residential land, with water views to the city.

Whenuapai has million-dollar homes on Pohutukawa Rd, with magnificent views across the upper reaches of the Waitemata Harbour. They're substantial houses on residential-sized sites, largely hidden from view - unless you happen to sail past - and they rarely come on the market because of their idyllic setting. Nearby Totara Rd has million-dollar homes on lifestyle blocks. Herald Island's mix of old and newer homes includes some cottages.

In West Harbour the most palatial homes are in enclaves that hug the coastline. The frontages are pristine - graffiti doesn't happen here - and the gardens are as refined as the stylish interiors. So contemporary is the atmosphere that the few older homes, such as the restored villa known as The Baker's Cottage on Wiseley Rd, stand out from the crowd.

Down at the marina, developments include The Cove, a 49-unit mix of terraced and stand-

Local hero - Westpark Marina

For a spot of "ooh" and "aah" on a sunny day, wander down to the Westpark Marina at West Harbour, accessed via Clearwater Cove, and gaze at the array of yachts and launches. The 600 berths make this marina one of the largest in Auckland. Established in 1985, the marina facility supports a large number of marine-related businesses including chandlery, sailmaking, boat haulage and brokerage. There's even a marina dentist and hairdresser so you can look smart for lunch at the Plain Sailing Cafe.

alone houses. Most of the first stage has been sold; a second stage is on the drawing board.

REAL ESTATE

Trends

West Harbour has traditionally reacted to real estate market changes a little later than its inner-city suburban cousins and the current buoyant market has now caught up with this popular water's edge area.

The upper end of the market with its $1 million plus sales in top streets has been vigorous with both local and overseas interest. However there haven't been any more of the standout sales that put Scott Rd in the limelight with the $2.9 million sale of a 5.2ha property there last year.

Quality property to buy is in short supply because buyers here settle for the appeal of waterfront/city views and lifestyle rather than making money by "doing up" and "moving on". To the delight of the local community, air force personnel at the nearby Hobsonville and Whenuapai bases are showing their loyalty to the area by investing in their own homes here.

Most of West Harbour's stylish homes that fall into the $300,000 to $400,000 price bracket are enjoying earnest attention from a vigorous market. At the lower end of the market, well-priced properties in good condition are selling within days. The unique community of Herald Island continues to hold its value well, with interest in its waterfront properties coming from local rather than overseas buyers.

Prices

Recent sales of $1.2 million for a waterfront property in Hobsonville and $1.125 million for a house close to the water in Courtneys, West Harbour, are indicative of prices here. Expect to pay another $300,000 or $400,000 for a house on the water in West Harbour's top streets. Equally appealing for vendors is the sort of quick sale that saw one weatherboard home in Hobsonville Rd marketed for $270,000 and sold for $255,000 within two days.

Average sale prices

	House	Flat	No. sales
2002	$318,096	$197,700	413
2003	$330,231	$229,917	459

Rental and investment

Homes for rent are also snapped up within days, ranging from $300 a week cottages on Herald Island, to $400 plus homes in Hobsonville. A three-bedroom house will cost between $350 to $550 depending on location.

Best streets

Mansion Court and Courtneys in West Harbour. Scott Rd in Hobsonville. Pohutukawa Rd in Whenuapai.

AMENITIES

Schools ★★★

The area is well served by preschools, reflecting the large number of young families here. Hobsonville Primary School, Whenuapai Primary School and Mariner View Primary School serve the wider area.

Local children travel by bus to secondary schools including Westlake boys' and girls' high schools on the shore, Rutherford High School in Te Atatu, Waitakere College, Henderson High and the private Kristin School in Albany. The area is to get its own secondary school on the corner of Hobsonville Rd and Buckley Ave in Hobsonville. The Ministry of Education has recently confirmed purchase of surplus airforce land for the school, which is due to open in 2006.

Shops ★★★

Hobsonville and West Harbour have plenty of shops, whether you need beauty therapy, computer equipment, reading glasses, tickets for a holiday or a bunch of flowers. Services include vets at West Harbour and Hobsonville, a cattery at West Harbour and a local police constable for the area. Down at the marina, the shops include a bakery, a superette and cafes. At the top of the north-western motorway, Westgate is a retail centre with all the usual outlets as well as a cinema complex.

Travel times

From West Harbour

CBD	off-peak 20 min
	peak 40 min
North-western motorway	5 min
Takapuna shops	25 min
Glenfield mall	15 min

Commuters have a choice of two routes to Auckland City - via Upper Harbour Dr and through the North Shore, or down the north-western motorway.

Ritchies Coachlines runs bus services from Whenuapai, Herald Island and West Harbour to Auckland City. Buses from New Lynn to Takapuna travel through West Harbour. There are also services through Hobsonville.

The proposed new motorway linking Albany to Westgate is seen as a positive solution to traffic pressure on Hobsonville Rd, which is the only access to Whenuapai and Herald Island. Known as the Upper Harbour Expressway, it is expected to add impetus to residential development of rural land west of Hobsonville Rd. Work has started on a new bridge across the upper harbour and widening of the Greenhithe bridge causeway.

Leisure ★★★★

Apart from the ever-present water views and boat-watching, playgrounds are dotted throughout West Harbour. The Luckens Reserve meanders down to the water opposite the Mariner View School. There's a coastal walkway from the marina.

Monterey Park at the Hobsonville end of the Upper Harbour Dr has a vintage car display at the Monterey Park Motor Museum. Sports facilities include the Hobsonville Bowling Club and the Belvedere Tennis Club.

Local Hobsonville eateries include Indian Summer and the Wings Restaurant in Hobsonville Rd, and Whenuapai has the Surreal Cafe. At West Harbour, the Clearwater Cove brasserie and the Plain Sailing Cafe are popular for weekend brunches. There is also a restaurant that's part of the Monterey Park museum complex.

LOOK OUT!

The outcome of current negotiations over the future of the Air Force's Whenuapai base will shape the future of this area. But the rewards could be sizeable for clever investors.

For colour key, see page 208

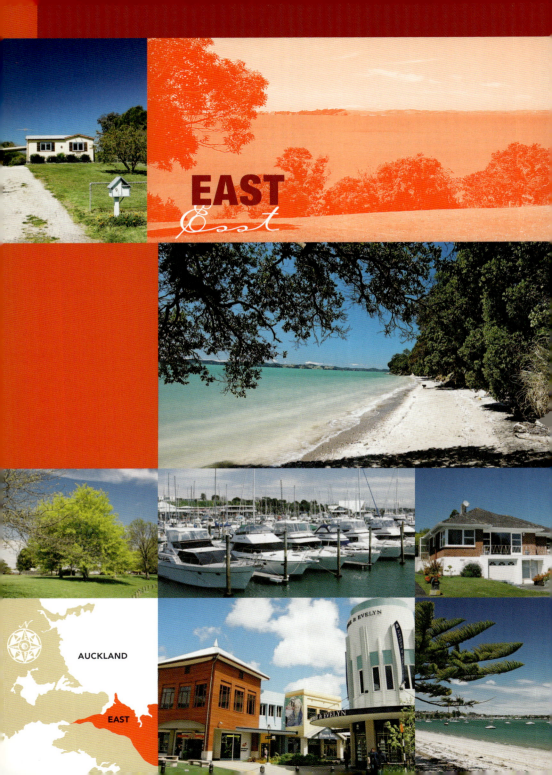

EAST

East

AUCKLAND

EAST

East Auckland has long epitomised suburbia to the rest of Auckland. Places like Pakuranga, Howick and now Botany Downs reinforce this part of Auckland as a great place to bring up the kids, a place where you can have a quarter-acre slice of paradise and like-minded neighbours.

It has long been a fairly insular place, priding itself on knowing what makes a good beach and a good community. Seeing itself as a cut above its neighbour, south Auckland, eastern residents are facing an enforced merger. They've always been officially part of Manukau City, but now the farm land which once divided east and south is being sold to developers; the developers are building houses, and the houses are filling with people. And each new development reduces the gap between south and east.

The proposal for a six-lane eastern corridor expressway to Auckland City will gladden the hearts of locals who work in the CBD - unless the chosen route goes past their back door. It should also help to eventually raise property prices.

A major attraction of east Auckland is its beautiful beaches - from the secluded and pohutakawa-fringed Maraetai beach to the mansion-studded Bucklands Beach. East Auckland is a haven for people who love to mess about in boats; there is a multitude of yacht clubs and fishing clubs, and two excellent marinas.

The new housing developments near Howick and Botany Downs are startling to many New Zealanders, who have never encountered such high-density housing. But to many new immigrants from Asia it is absolute luxury to have a stand-alone house at all. If you exclude Whitford and Maraetai, the eastern suburbs have a 22.71% Asian population compared with 14.34% for the whole of Auckland.

The Pakuranga Country Club might now be well and truly fenced in by suburbia, but further east towards Whitford and beyond, rural scenes are still the norm. And, given local body determination to constrain the growth of Auckland within a firmly fastened green belt, they should remain this way for many years.

East Auckland is also loved by the horsey set (the tiny settlement of Brookby has a world-class indoor equestrian centre, and Auckland polo has its spiritual home at Clevedon), and by those who want to be closer to the countryside than the city, but without forsaking all manner of facilities.

The housing styles are generally new, from large family friendly 1970s houses with rumpus rooms and lots of decks to brand new plaster-clad porticoed houses dominating their easy-care sections. Howick and some of the previous farming areas have some old colonial houses, but they are fairly rare.

In terms of value, houses in east Auckland have increased by approximately 15% over the past year, along with the rest of Auckland. And yet surges in median sales prices have been pulled up by stronger price increases at the market's top end. Proximity to those beautiful eastern beaches, attractive views and reputable schools certainly count!

safe and **secure**

settled suburbia

a boatie's **dream**

new, new, **new**

BEACHLANDS/MARAETAI ★★★★★

Beachlands and Maraetai are a pair of seaside hamlets - a little bit staid, a little bit isolated and a little bit behind the times, and that's just the way the locals like it. People want to live here when they're after the sort of lifestyle Howick offered 30 years ago. Kids can have the kind of freedom that's rare in modern city life. You'll see youngsters cycling and playing outside in a carefree nostalgic-New Zealand sort of way. These suburbs are a real mix; modern mansions sit next to Kiwi baches, but the next few years could easily see an upmarket

makeover, with the slightly sleepy feel disappearing completely. Beachlands is a "destination suburb" (because there's nothing else on that road); you might pass through Maraetai en route to or from Clevedon, Kawakawa or Orere Pt (very scenic, but not a short cut). According to the locals, you're either a Beachlands type or a Maraetai type, and it's pretty rare for a local to up sticks and move from one to the other. You collect your own water here, and this adds to the holiday ambience. Not needing to dial 0800 WATER TANKER in the middle of summer is a matter of serious pride for locals.

Who lives there?

It's a family-oriented community, popular with lifestylers who want access to the city without having to crowd their dearly beloved onto a puny section. People come here for the space plus the community atmosphere, according to real estate agents. Those who are fed up with the new high-density city norm don't have to swallow it here! They can have the family home on the quarter-acre (or near enough), and be near the sea!

Beachlands and Maraetai are naturally popular choices for fishing and boating people, and for anyone wanting to live somewhere with a village feel, where you know your neighbours. Many of those currently buying are making their escape from the eastern suburbs; there's demand, too, from expat Kiwis returning home (and driving up house prices with their US dollars and UK pounds). There's not a lot of work here, so Beachlands and Maraetai are commuter suburbs.

Typical dwellings

Development - on a very small scale - first began in the area in the 1920s, as a holiday spot served more by sea than by road. More permanent homes have been gradually added

since, so there's virtually every type of home represented.

REAL ESTATE

Trends

Demand rises and rises. Seekers of the old-fashioned family life on a site anywhere from 800 or 900m² to the quarter acre can still afford it here, although maybe not for long!

There's the ubiquitous subdivision happening here also, starting with Spinnaker Bay in March 2003. Sections anywhere between 900 and 1400m² (with great views) were sold in a bit of a bun-fight, and prices rose by the hour accordingly. Prices ranged between $180,000 and $260,000. One piece of land selling for $190,000 was re-sold half a year later for $250,000. More subdivisions are scheduled in the future.

Prices

Recently real estate prices have been rising by about $5000 a month. An increased local ferry service has boosted the area's popularity, say real estate agents. Across the board, it's been a dramatic time in the price stakes. Clever you, if you bought a section out here a year ago! In the best streets, i.e. waterfront, don't expect anything for under $800,000, no matter how "bachy".

However, in places with limited outlook it's possible to get a lot of house and ground for your money, relative to central Auckland.

Entry level to Beachlands is now nudging $300,000. And that could mean just two bedrooms. Indeed, many Beachlands sections are selling for upwards of $250,000, although it's still possible to get a fairly uninspiring one for less.

For a four-bedroom home in Beachlands with good sea views, expect to pay the best part of $600,000. Without such a hot view, the same cash will buy a newish four or five-bedroom "luxury" home on a generous 1500m² site. You could also, given a substantial wallet, buy yourself a prime Beachlands pad with just three bedrooms for upwards of $1 million! External forces are obviously at work. As with other waterfront and panoramic view-endowed properties in New Zealand, values reflect who wants them, and what they're prepared to pay, more than any other factor.

In Maraetai, the same applies. With a view, expect to shell out around $400,000. Or for similar money buy yourself the true family home with five bedrooms, double garage and a generous section, but no views.

Average sale prices

	House	Flat	No. sales
2002	$308,078	$367,083	166
2003	$328,282	$448,800	133

Best streets

In the well-known, coveted "best streets", phenomenal recent value increases have put smiles on some faces. A year ago we documented the minimum price for Pohutukawa Rd in Beachlands as over $500,000. Now there's nothing under $765,000. That sum would pay for a "cottage", and not in the romantic sense of the word.

In Maraetai, Omana Esplanade is great for its beach access and its substantial homes. Think around the $900,000 to $1 million mark.

Carlton Cres is also a great address. Views from this elevation are stunning, and not just in real-estate-speak!

Rental and investment

For a single-bedroom unit, you'll pay $200 a week. If it's two bedrooms you're after, prices range between $230 to $300 weekly. For three, and sometimes even four bedrooms, you'll be charged in the region of $350 to $400, and after that it all depends on views and position.

AMENITIES

Schools ★★

Beachlands and Maraetai each have a combined primary/intermediate school, which provides middle-school continuity. Interestingly, these schools are not strong on zoning, so you can choose between them.

For secondary schooling, a free school bus takes half an hour to transport teenagers to Howick College.

Shops ★★

Most residents who are mobile enough to have a choice do the bulk of their buying out of the area, but the local shops do cover many of life's essentials, including liquor, hot bread, videos, hardware and butchery.

Local hero - Shelly Bay

A short walk down a bush track takes you to this classic little east coast Auckland beach. At either end, rocky outcrops make for calm seas. As a backdrop, pohutukawa-riddled cliffs make for a suntrap. Best of all, it's rarely crowded - probably because there are so many other beaches nearby where you don't have to walk more than a minute from your car. And you feel a million miles from anywhere, because you can't see or hear any cars, and there are only the slightest glimpses of houses.

Leisure ★★★

As well as being surrounded by farmland and beaches, Beachlands and Maraetai also have generous reserves. There's a leisurely holiday ambience here, which is the region's soul. Between the two hamlets is Omana Regional Park, with beach, bush and farm (and the kids can get up close to some of the animals).

For colour key, see page 208

There are paths for mountain biking, walking and horse riding in nearby Whitford Forest.

Despite the area's popularity, it's not growing rapidly and - thanks to constraints including district plans, the Resource Management Act, the limitations of the sewerage scheme and the fact that there's not much room for expansion - the existing wide green belt looks safe for the medium-term.

The Formosa Auckland Country Club has a golf course designed by Kiwi golfing legend Bob Charles, luxury accommodation, a gym and swimming pool. Next door is Pine Harbour Marina.

There are sports fields at Te Puru Park, again, between Maraetai and Beachlands.

Club culture runs fairly strong, along with community spirit. Boaties can choose between the Beachlands boating club and the Maraetai Beach boating club. Beachlands has a "chartered club" which is another name for a friendly cosmopolitan club (members range in age from their 20s to 80s); and the past year has seen the formation of a Pohutukawa Coast cricket club which uses Te Puru Park, and caters to several age groups. And of course there's a Beachlands-Maraetai pony club and adult riding group for the horsey set.

As far as eateries go there isn't a huge selection, although if you're into golf or boating you may find club restaurant meals a bonus. Takeaways are always an option, or you can get yourself onto the Pine Harbour ferry to the CBD and be spoiled for choice!

Travel times

From Beachlands

CBD	off-peak 35 min
	peak 1 hour
Southern motorway	20 min
Airport	30 min
Manukau City shopping centre	20 min
Botany Town Centre	15 min

Beachlands and Maraetai are both served by Howick & Eastern Buses, but it's a commuter service only.

An increasing ferry service from Pine Harbour to both central Auckland and Waiheke Island is making life easier for many locals. The earliest weekday departure at 6.30am will have you into town by 7.05am. The latest weekday sailing home again leaves Auckland at 6.30pm.

During weekends you can depart from Pine Harbour at 9am, with the last sailing home leaving Auckland at 5.10pm.

More demand for ferries may result in extra sailings during summer months.

Check out any schedule changes on: www.pineharbour.co.nz, or phone 536-5157.

including Northpark, Somerville, Pt View Park, Dannemora, Cumbria Downs and Burswood

To a visitor, the sheer newness is the most striking feature of Botany Downs and its surrounding mini-suburbs. If you last drove through a couple of years ago, the change is bewildering in its entirety. Gone are farms and fields; well and truly ensconced are roads, houses and shops. The best viewing point for grasping the enormity of it all is up Whitford Rd where the housing meets the remaining farmland, and where you look down over a sea of roofs. Each new subdivision is christened by its developers - some of the names make it to the Auckland street hall of fame (aka an official map), while others are doomed to be nothing more than a set of brass letters on a rock wall at their designated suburb.

Dannemora, though, has done the opposite of disappear – it's grown and grown. Originally it was strictly between Chapel Rd and Point View Dr, but now it's creeping ever west.

Who lives there?

The new houses are proving extremely popular with people from established parts of the eastern suburbs who are looking for low-maintenance homes with such modern necessities as internal-access double garaging, ensuites, walk-in wardrobes, indoor/outdoor flow and good insulation. Many people have moved here from Howick, Bucklands Beach and Pakuranga.

There is an eclectic mix of immigrants from a range of countries, such as South Africa, China, Hong Kong, Taiwan, Korea, England, Singapore and Australia. Yes, Australians are on to the value of Botany Downs and Northpark real estate. Many of the immigrant buyers have been renting or have decided to upgrade their home and position, and buy into the area.

An interesting feature is the number of apparently ordinary homes with signs advertising the occupants' skills as beauty therapists, hairdressers and nail technicians.

Typical dwellings

New, new, new. The streets are new and short; the gardens are new and small and immaculate. The houses are new and loom large on their tiny sections. The houses are predominantly brick or pastel-coloured plaster, or a combination of both. Double-height porticos supported by soaring classical-style columns are favoured as entrance ways (and variations on porticos have also been noted framing windows). Although to many Kiwis the houses seem too large for their sections, many of the buyers are immigrants from countries and cities where your own stand-alone house is a dream come true, no matter how small the land surrounding it.

REAL ESTATE

Trends

The more elevated sections are usually the more desirable - especially if you're in a north-facing home, such as those along Pt View Dr, looking out to the foothills. Newer properties, built during the past six to eight years, are

most popular. Most buyers are looking for larger homes - four-bedroom single-level with two living areas, ensuites and double internal-access garaging.

Until recently the new houses were very similar prices to the older homes without walk-in wardrobes, so you could get the mod-cons without a bigger mortgage. Recently, though, demand for new properties has seen prices rise – so some people who moved from established eastern parts are now selling their new houses and moving back. They lose their internal-access double garaging but make a profit of $100,000.

Within the perimeter of the new town centre, house prices have inflated considerably more than other local properties. The attraction is new housing close to the shopping centre, and the southern motorway via Te Irirangi Dr. The construction of a brand new secondary college opposite the shopping centre has also helped property prices rise.

The new subdivisions of Somerville and Northpark tend to have smaller sections, around 400m² to 450m².

Prices

As with everything around here, things are on the move. Prices have risen by at least 15% in the past year. Sales of the ubiquitous three-bedroom, two-bathroom townhouse on its own site of around 400m² will set you back in the range of $390,000 to $420,000. Of course you can spend a huge amount more for a larger property.

Average sale prices

	House	Flat	No. sales
2002	$354,154	$274,463	356
2003	$407,522	$305,191	1278

Best streets

Anything that's new and elevated enough to get views is much in demand - the streets closer to Point View Dr (which runs along a ridge) are more sought after than those closer to Chapel Rd.

Fairfield Lane is highly regarded, although it's not elevated, because it has a good number of masonry homes which give a sense of solidity and respectability to the place.

Rental and investment

This is good investor country, because reasonably high rents attract families with substantial incomes who tend to look after their abodes. Rents hover around $400 a week for a three-bedroom townhouse, and between $450 and $500 for something glossy and new with four or more bedrooms.

AMENITIES

Schools ★★★★

Botany Downs Primary, Willowbank School and Point View School are the local primaries, and Elim Christian College (formerly Cascade Christian College) takes pupils from Year 1 to 13. The big local news is happening on the secondary school front. Botany Downs Secondary College, a co-ed state school, opens its doors in January 2004, and will follow a "whanau house" concept, after the highly regarded Macleans College model. Tight zoning is planned for this school, as "population density seems to be increasing every ten minutes". A new Sancta Maria Catholic College in the same locale is opening around the same time.

Shops ★★★★★

This is the land of consummate consumer culture. Shopping is the raison d'etre of Botany Downs. Spend a while walking around this "village" of over 150 stores, cafes and restaurants and you too will be able to say, like Jennifer Aniston of her fitness circuit along Rodeo Dr: "I don't go to the gym. I shop."

Rather than being one huge mall, Botany Town Centre is intended to mimic a traditional town centre. Oh, that it could be thoroughly pedestrianised and as such, a peaceful retail experience - but no - this is Auckland. However, the centre has a certain charm. Streets, lanes and piazzas have been thoughtfully designed and include characterful, picturesque features. There are enough fashion and homewares stores to make your head spin and your wallet tingle.

This town centre seems like a social experiment to the extent that it's intended as the hub of the community - the venue for community gatherings. A sound shell is planned for the Town Square as a place for school and local bands to perform.

Holiday-weary parents are encouraged to take their charges to Whitcoulls for children's activities like storytelling, while they enjoy uninterrupted cafe time.

Other boons to the community opening during 2004 are the Botany Town Centre library and an eight-cinema movie complex.

Leisure ★★★★

If you're into shopping, eating out, ice-skating or bowling, these are your suburbs. Ice-skating and bowling centres are over the road from Botany Town Centre. If you love walking through trees and in wide open spaces, drive on. You're not too far from countryside. (Although reserves are being developed, such as that at the Dannemora subdivision which runs from Chapel Rd through to Point View Dr.) For sports clubs and sailing, nearby Howick has them all. Lloyd Elsmore Park in Pakuranga has fantastic recreational facilities, including a recently upgraded pool complex. No doubt clubs of all kinds are sprouting as you read.

LOOK OUT!

All that newness might seem alluring but many Kiwis eventually find it claustrophobic. Any new suburb needs to have the ingredients that will allow it to slide gracefully into an established look - quality, well-built houses, planted gardens, green spaces, trees on the street - rather than the sort of ingredients that will make it look shabby quickly or keep it eternally sterile.

Travel times

From Botany Downs

CBD	off-peak 30 min peak 50-60 min
Southern motorway	10 min
Airport	25 min
Botany Town Centre	5 min

Buses go in every direction and with the new Ti Irirangi Dr expressway, car traffic is improved to all points south, particularly to the southern motorway and central Manukau.

A new Britomart bus service, from November 2003, will travel between central Auckland and the Botany Town Centre every half hour.

Bus services from Half Moon Bay's Marina to the Botany Town Centre are also being beefed up. So expect easier access to public commuting, along with more tourist traffic out here for the macro-retail experience.

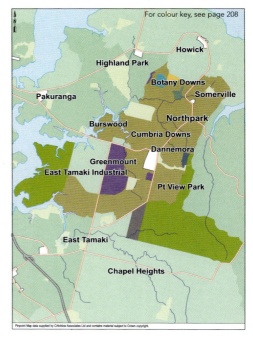

For colour key, see page 208

Pinpoint Map data supplied by Critchlow Associates Ltd and contains material subject to Crown copyright.

BUCKLANDS BEACH ★★★★★

including Eastern Beach

Bucklands Beach and Eastern Beach occupy a stunning part of Auckland's geography - but if you don't live there, it's hard to tell without looking at a map. These comfortable, desirable waterside suburbs north of Pakuranga are located on a pointy finger of a peninsula, the end of which reaches as far north as St Heliers. People who buy here tend to stay put - that's how pleasant it is around here! Sadly, you can't see either coast of the peninsula from the road, so as you're driving through it feels pretty much like any other part of eastern suburbia - until you get right down to the beach, or the reserve at the end of the peninsula.

When you finally do see the sea, the outlook is truly stunning and almost surreal, with the azure waters of the Tamaki Strait, and the islands of Rangitoto, Motuihe and Waiheke filling up a 180-degree panoramic view.

Who lives there?

These suburbs are deservedly popular with beachgoers, lovers of watersports and anyone who just loves staring at the sea. With many upmarket residences, as well as smaller properties available, people from all walks of life are enticed to live here. Many professionals have also opted to make their homes in this area, which is isolated enough to make you feel like you're in the leisure zone, yet close enough to Auckland's CBD to ensure that commuting to work is still relatively painless.

Typical dwellings

Most of the housing in this area is large and often multi-storey with large, well-landscaped sections. At water's edge there are elegant, luxurious houses with big, big windows to take in the amazing views. Back from the water, units and townhouses can also be found.

REAL ESTATE

Trends

Once people buy here, they're a tad reluctant to sell. A good proportion of homes around here tend to be roomy, which is a great bonus to families. Another bonus is to be situated in the in-demand Macleans College zone, and prices seem to be zoned accordingly.

Buyers are now also paying a premium for any land with a water view. They're increasingly prepared to ignore the bricks and mortar already there, in favour of shifting a less desirable house off a desirable building site and starting afresh. Basically anything with sea views and in the Macleans zone is seen as a great investment.

Prices

Across the board, prices are on the move - up. Even for houses in the areas of land-locked suburbia dubbed "Nappy Valley", with cheaper building materials into the bargain, values have moved up in the past year.

For an older, three-bedroom home in Bucklands Beach, expect to pay between $350,000 and $400,000.

Most other housing is more expensive, though; in the bracket of $600,000 to $700,000-and-the-rest.

At the top of the spectrum, and often on the top of available Bucklands Beach hillsides, are palatial homes which sell for upwards of $1 million. These have commanding sea views. For a brand new home with four or

Local hero - Musick Pt

Musick Pt, on the end of the peninsula, is home to a wonderful Art Deco building constructed in 1939 as a base for marine radio communications. It's now leased by a group of amateur radio enthusiasts, and it's well worth the slow pot-holed drive through the course of the Howick Golf Club to get there. The fabulous sea views include Browns Island (Motukorea), which is just off the point, surprisingly close to the mainland.

more bedrooms and a study, plus a wonderful water view, you could easily be shelling out as much as $2 million.

Average sale prices

	House	Flat	No. sales
2002	$407,273	$351,092	365
2003	$420,602	$391,562	314

Best streets

People want a "moving view" if possible; not the sort which moves you to tears, but one including the interest of aquatic traffic as well as distant sea and sky. Streets with these are obviously the peninsula roads: Clovelly Rd, and The Parade.

Rental and investment

Rentals here are a step up from Pakuranga prices. Bucklands Beach rental demands are in roughly the same league as those for Howick and Half Moon Bay.

You can pick up a single-bedroom basement flat in Bucklands Beach for $250 a week; a two-bedroom unit for between $270 and $350; a three-bedroom house for between $330 and $420; and a four or five-bedroom home for between $350 and $500 per week.

AMENITIES

Schools ★★★★

There are several good primary schools in Bucklands Beach, including Bucklands Beach Primary and Macleans Primary. Waimokia School, also a primary, caters to children with special needs.

Buckland's Beach Intermediate school occupies a central position in Bucklands Beach Road, and the local secondary schools are the well-regarded Macleans College and Pakuranga College.

Shops ★★★

There are small clusters of shops along the peninsula, but if you want selection, venture a little further afield and take your pick from Highland Park, Howick Village, or the 70-shop Pakuranga Mall. Shopping meccas for serious retail splurges include The (recently expanded) Hub, and the Botany Downs complex, which also boasts a plethora of eateries.

Leisure ★★★★

Million dollar views place many of the leisure pursuits of Bucklands Beach locals fairly high on the desirability scale.

For instance, if you love playing golf and you don't mind the odd ball risking its life in the ocean, the Howick Golf Course on Musick Pt is for you. It's already a favourite haunt to around 1000 club members, and the club allows for casual green-fee players.

Then there's the Bucklands Beach Yacht Club, cheek by jowl to Half Moon Bay's Marina. The yacht club's membership list pushes up toward the 1,400 mark, and the club caters also to owners of powerboats. Both golf and yacht clubs have facilities for social functions.

Public boat ramps for occasional boaties exist at both Bucklands Beach and Eastern Beach. The latter boasts a ski lane, picnic area, and children's playground. Note that there's a rahui, or traditional ban, on the taking of

shellfish from Eastern Beach.

Around the corner from Bucklands Beach, Half Moon Bay Marina is home to hundreds of pleasure craft. There are two tennis clubs and nearby Lloyd Elsmore Park in Pakuranga is Manukau City's largest recreational park.

For those seeking dining out experiences, there's The Beach House and Barracuda restaurants, plus Eastern Beach's Esplanade restaurant, Oasis on the Beach.

Cafes in Bucklands Beach itself are not thick on the ground, and if you're dying for a decent caffeine hit, it might pay to keep driving! Close by, Pakuranga and Highland Park have a number of restaurants offering international cuisine, including Indian, Korean, Chinese, Italian and Irish. Howick Village also has a variety of sidewalk cafes and eateries.

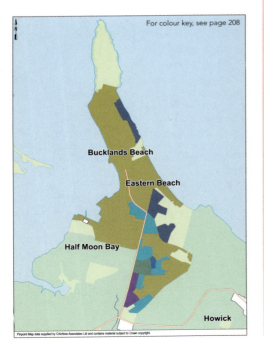

For colour key, see page 208

Bucklands Beach

Eastern Beach

Half Moon Bay

Howick

Pinpoint Map data supplied by Critchlow Associates Ltd and contains material subject to Crown copyright.

Travel times

From Bucklands Beach

CBD	off-peak	20 min
	peak	40 min
Southern motorway		10 min
Airport		20 min
Manukau City shopping centre		15 min
Botany Town Centre		10 min

Commuting to Auckland's CBD is relatively easy with regular Howick and Eastern Buses services. These have been beefed up for 2004, with an increased number of trips on both the Bucklands Beach and Howick corridors. A bus service runs through to Manukau City also. Rideline can be contacted for details. Another non-motoring option is to catch a ferry from Half Moon Bay - to either central Auckland and back or to Waiheke Island. (See other East Auckland chapters for more detail on this ferry service.)

The south-eastern highway links the peninsula to the airport and Onehunga.

including Farm Cove and Sunnyhills

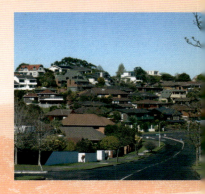

Northwest of Pakuranga, the highly sought-after areas of Sunnyhills and Farm Cove guard a fantastic outlook to Tamaki River and Panmure. Further north is the plush coastal suburb of Half Moon Bay, with outstanding views of the Hauraki Gulf and Rangitoto Island. Half Moon Bay was developed in the early 1970s; Farm Cove and Sunnyhills are newer neighbours. Sunnyhills has gently curving roads, with reserves winding along the water's edge. Farm Cove, formerly dairy farming land, is more established, with large trees.

Life is comfortable here; the self-contained communities are supported by a wealth of amenities - beaches, boat ramps, a marina, a large park and several great shopping centres.

Although these suburbs are beautiful they are not bland, with glimpses of eccentric character showing through - one residence, for example, has been built to resemble a medieval castle.

Who lives there?

These waterside suburbs close to Pakuranga are popular with boaties and beachgoers. With both upmarket residences and affordable smaller properties available, people from all walks of life are enticed to live here. Many young families have also opted to make their homes in this area.

Typical dwellings

Multi-storey modern housing is dominant, with large, well-landscaped sections. At the waterfront, there are many Mediterranean-style larger houses. Back from the water, units and townhouses can also be found. Newer areas like Sunnyhills offer an upmarket lifestyle, while some of Farm Cove's older homes present an opportunity to soak up some 1970s retro cool.

REAL ESTATE

Trends

Until a year ago not much development was going on in the settled suburbs of Half Moon Bay and Farm Cove. Now there's at least one major change afoot. The wonderfully positioned pie-slice of coastal land bordering Ara Tai and Pigeon Mountain Rds is to be the upmarket Compass Point subdivision of 64 new sections, ranging from approximately 500 to 1089 m². The suburb of Sunnyhills is still experiencing growth. Two factors influence this: proximity to St Kentigern College, plus the sea views afforded by many Sunnyhills homes. Consequently, this is where you'll find the area's domestic opulence.

Prices

At the top end of the market in the best water-view pockets of Farm Cove and Sunnyhills, prices have rocketed away in the past couple of years. In the good streets a cheaper option can still be a weighty $800,000, whereas other homes are up around $1.5 million. Back from

the water and without a view, house prices have also pulled away - you'll still be paying at least $260,000. An average family home on a typical 700m² site will set you back between $550,000 and $600,000 in these settled, sea-loving suburbs.

Average sale prices

	House	Flat	No. sales
2002	$368,623	$247,950	326
2003	$415,574	$298,982	338

Best streets

Takutai Ave overlooks Half Moon Bay and delivers a breathtaking view of the Hauraki

Gulf and Rangitoto Island. Classy Farm Cove and Sunnyhills addresses include Sanctuary Pt, Bramley Dr and Fisher Pde.

Rental and investment

Rentals in these suburbs are closely allied with those in Howick and Mellons Bay. For an under-house one-bedroom unit you'll pay $180 a week; for a two-bedroom unit or apartment $270-350; $280-300 for a two-bedroom house; $290-400 for a three-bedroom house; and $330-$600 for a four-bedroom house.

AMENITIES

Schools ★★★★

Local primary schools are excellent, namely Wakaaranga Primary in Farm Cove, Pigeon Mountain Primary in Half Moon Bay, and Sunnyhills Primary. Intermediates include Pakuranga Intermediate and Farm Cove Intermediate, and local high schools are Pakuranga College and St Kentigern College. The latter is a private school, no longer just for boys.

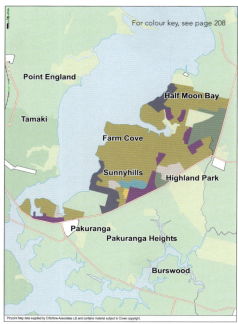

Local hero - Half Moon Bay Marina

The reputation of Half Moon Bay's Marina as a boatie's paradise reaches way beyond Auckland's borders. It's a beautiful spot - a fully subscribed 500-berth marina with support businesses attached. For instance, not only can you bolt down a caffeine hit on-site, you can also visit the doctor or hairdresser, pick up a prescription or buy sea-worthy accessories. While around 90% of the pleasure craft here are owned by Aucklanders, the rest hail from further afield and are owned by predominantly summer boaties. This is one busy maritime site, operating to capacity and with constant demand for berths.
The marina is the essence of Half Moon Bay; it would be unimaginable without!

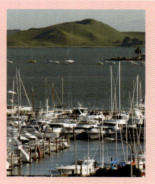

Shops ★★★

The area is served by local dairies and small, centralised pockets of shops like the Farm Cove Shopping Centre. The nearby Pakuranga Town Centre, recently renamed Westfield Shoppingtown Pakuranga, has more than 70 shops. Other shopping centres in the greater area include The Hub and the utopian Botany Town Centre.

Leisure ★★★★

Residents of these suburbs have many reserves and parks, as well as the vast expanse of ocean to stare at. Just head down to the water and breathe in some sea air! There are public boat ramps at the Bramley Dr Reserve in Farm Cove and at the Ara Tai Reserve in Half Moon Bay.

Sunnyhills has a great tennis club at Oleander Pl and there's also the Pakuranga Tennis Club on Pigeon Mountain Rd. Half Moon Bay Marina is a leisure focus point with an excellent boat haul-out area, and includes a host of boat-related and unrelated businesses and services. Nearby Lloyd Elsmore Park is Manukau City's largest active recreational park.

Close by, Pakuranga, Highland Park and Howick have a number of eateries offering international cuisine.

Travel times

From Farm Cove

CBD	off-peak 20 min
	peak 35 min
Southern motorway	10 min
Airport	20 min
Manukau City shopping centre	15 min
Botany Town Centre	7 min

The brilliant thing about living in or near Half Moon Bay is your easy access by boat to either the CBD, which takes about 35 minutes, or to Waiheke Island. Waiheke trips are set to become more frequent, with another boat in commission for 2004. Passenger trips into the CBD cater for commuters, and more city workers are opting to go by water and jettison parking hassles. Commuter ferries depart from a base at the Half Moon Bay Marina. Trips to and from the CBD run every half-hour at peak weekday times, and approximately two-hourly at non-peak times, starting from 6am. Weeknight return trips from central Auckland to Half Moon Bay include sailings at 5.15pm, 5.45pm, 6.30pm and 8pm, along with a couple of later sailings on Friday evenings to accommodate nights on the town.

Commuting by bus to the CBD is also easy, with regular bus services run by Howick and Eastern Buses from the corner of Prince Regent and Pigeon Mountain Rds. Buses leave for the CBD as early as 5.40am, returning until 12.30am. Services are half-hourly at peak times and hourly at others.

HOWICK ★★★★ ☆

including Mellons Bay, Cockle Bay and Shelly Park

Howick is an up-market, newer Pakuranga. It's the modern, slightly more swept up suburban dream. And yet, paradoxically, it's notable in Auckland for its history. Many of the area's older residents hold fond memories of Howick's more rural past. Mellons Bay, Cockle Bay and Shelly Park are havens for those looking for a smallish community next to the sea, with ever-present opportunities for fishing, boating and swimming.

Originally a holiday area, it began to develop in the 1950s and 1960s. There is a lot of loyalty and when kids grow up, they often look to buy back into their childhood area.

Many English and Dutch immigrants settled here in the 1950s and 1960s bringing a unique flavour through delicatessens and specialty shops.

Nowadays there are new waves of immigrants, particularly Asian and South African, who are adding their own local colour. These areas appear less harsh on the eye than new developments, such as Dannemora and Chapel Downs.

Mellons Bay is the least developed part of this area and unfortunately the beach is somewhat marred by a large outlet pipe.

Who lives there?

Howick is one of Manukau City's wealthiest suburbs. (It was a stand-alone borough until the big local government re-organisation of 1990, when it became a ward within Manukau City.) Two-parent families are the norm, and the majority of workers are professionals or in white-collar jobs.

Locals appreciate living with like-minded people in a safe community in easy reach of amenities, including eastern beaches. There is a reasonably sized community of people who, having retired, have chosen to downsize but stay in the area.

Families upgrade into these suburbs, keen on the community feel and Macleans College zoning. While not quite the magnet that Auckland Grammar School is to Epsom or Rangitoto College to the East Coast Bays, Macleans College is still a huge drawcard.

Multiculturalism is alive and well. While a number of Indian, Middle Eastern and South African families are buying into the area, the largest immigrant groups are Asian, particularly mainland Chinese, Hong Kong Chinese and Korean. They choose the area because of its middle-class environment and reputable schools. New homes are also a plus.

A decade or so ago, when Howick's largely European population saw a sudden influx of Asian business immigrants, the multicultural picture was less rosy and more tense. There were politically incorrect mutterings about the place being renamed Chowick. Today, relations seem peaceful - presumably anyone who was disgruntled either got used to it or moved elsewhere.

Typical dwellings

There is a range, from old homes with established gardens to new homes surrounded by raw landscapes. The older homes tend to be brick and tile or weatherboard, while the new homes are usually plaster exterior or a mix of brick and weatherboard. Porticos and other impressive entranceways are common on new properties, a feature which Asian buyers apparently prefer. Many older 1950s houses in streets such as Marine Pde are being substantially renovated and extended, or replaced by new designer homes.

A heritage zoning means sections on the seaward side of Bleakhouse Rd can't be smaller than 1400m². However, other areas don't have this restriction and many larger sections in streets, especially within the Macleans zone, now have infill housing.

REAL ESTATE

Trends

As in most parts of Auckland, prices have been on the rise, sometimes steeply. A year ago we said that on average, homes in the Eastern Beach suburbs were selling 14% above capital valuation. In some cases sale prices have leapfrogged way beyond that! With these boom times of course comes increasing development and infill housing.

Howick is another area which has been developed to the hilt in recent years. Whether or not home buyers would like more land, mostly they have no choice. The majority of subdivisible sites have been carved up. In the non-heritage zone, many sections are between 400 to 500m².

Some older couples are selling their 1950s homes on large sites and buying into townhouses or retirement villages. Other families are leaving the suburb because of its comparatively crowded, contemporary feel. Until a few years ago, you drove through country fields to get here, and that was the attraction.

However, Howick also has plenty of established homes and sections, and many would rather reside here than in the starkly new subdivisions further south.

Why I live there
Alan la Roche

Alan la Roche grew up on a five-acre block in Howick, and his grandparents, who lived in Devonport, used to catch the ferry over to their rural Howick holiday home. His father was Mayor of Howick, and former dentist Alan is on the local community board, as well as being founding director of the Howick Historical Village. He now lives in Cockle Bay. "I love having the beach nearby - I swim almost every day during summer - and I love the strength of community spirit in the area. We've got beautiful mature trees planted by residents many years ago, and here at the Historical Village we have 150 volunteers."

Local hero - All Saints Church

The All Saints Anglican Church on the corner of Selwyn Rd and Cook St, Howick, is the oldest building in Manukau City.

Built in 1847 under Bishop Selwyn, it was designed by Frederick Thatcher ready for the arrival of the first European settlers in November of that year. The church, prefabricated in Auckland and brought to Howick by sea, is the second oldest wooden church in New Zealand.

Prices

Around Howick, the biggest price increases in recent months have been for mid-range houses, that is homes in the $300,000 to $550,000 bracket. Yet the bottom end of the market isn't looking too shabby either. West of the town centre, some houses which suffered sale prices below $300,000 have "firmed up" somewhat over the past year.

Logically, house prices are highest for property near water or with sea views, and lowest near busy roads. Bargain basement buying is around the $170,000 to $180,000 mark, which should score you a basic two-bedroom unit on a three-unit site. A slightly down-at-heel three-bedroom house might be a possibility at between $250,000 and $350,000, but smarter three-bedroom townhouses on half sites are usually commanding $350,000 to $400,000. And that's in the older part of Howick. In Mellons and Cockle Bay, prices have pulled away. On a par with each other, three-bedroom homes in these bays are more likely to be around $450,000, while larger homes will be in the region of $500,000 or $600,000.

Average sale prices

	House	Flat	No. sales
2002	$357,104	$273,665	720
2003	$389,195	$286,375	561

Best streets

There are, of course, several. In Cockle Bay, Cockle Bay Rd, Churchill Rd, and Litton Rd are fairly hot contenders. Tainui Rd, Pah Rd and Stevenson Way are pretty good too.

For Mellons Bay the sought-after addresses include Marine Pde, Mellons Bay Rd, Page Pt, Burford Pl, Seymour Rd and Pleasant Pl.

In Howick itself, Bleakhouse Rd and Sale St are the business.

Rental and investment

Renting a one-bedder in Howick may cost you anything between $200 and $300 weekly, depending on quality. A two-bedroom unit is typically between $250 and $350 a week, whereas the average cost of renting a three-bedroom home is $380. For four or more bedrooms, expect to pay around $450 weekly.

AMENITIES

Schools ★★★

The big drawcard on the local educational scene is Macleans College, in Bucklands Beach, but only some Mellons Bay/northern Howick streets are in its coveted zone. Other Howick secondary schools include Howick College and Elim Christian College (the latter located in the neighbouring suburb of Botany Downs).

For middle years education there are Howick Intermediate and Somerville Intermediate.

Primary schools in Howick and surrounding bays are numerous, and include Mellons Bay Primary, Cockle Bay, Star of the Sea, Howick

Primary, Owairoa Primary, and Shelly Park.

Shops ★★★

Howick Village prides itself on being a good old-fashioned community shopping area, quaint in a sort of sub-Parnell way. Its more than 100 owner-operated stores have pretty much everything you could need with a bit of local colour and character thrown in.

Soccer Locker Ltd is a treat if you're keen on sports memorabilia, or for authentic South African treats visit Beef on the Beach, in Highland Park.

Leisure ★★★★

Howick and neighbouring bays have everything going for all sorts of leisure pursuits. You name it, Howick seems to cater to it. The best reserves here are, naturally, by the beaches, and the beaches themselves. They get crowded in summer, but locals know all the off-the-beaten-track paths to the water. A great new attraction for walkers is the Mangemangeroa Reserve walkway, which stretches from 108 Somerville Rd to the Shelly Park Yacht Club.

There's the Howick Sailing Club at Howick Beach, and boat ramps there and at Cockle Bay Reserve. Other Howick sports clubs include those for cricket, netball, rugby league, squash and tennis, and there's a petanque pitch at Cockle Bay.

For the arty, Howick boasts a Little Theatre, and has an Operatic Society of its own. The Uxbridge Arts Centre is worth checking out too, for its range of exhibitions and classes.

The Howick Historical Village continues to attract large numbers of visitors to its well-worn doors. Comprising 30 buildings constructed between 1840 and 1880, the village has experienced at least a 10% upsurge in visitor numbers over the past year. Village volunteers have begun and plan to continue hosting "Live Days" on the third Sunday of each month, when costumes are worn and fires are lit, while entrance fees remain standard.

The Howick restaurant and cafe scene is vibrant and healthy. One destination restaurant is the fully licensed Windross at Cockle Bay, with its homestead ambience, ocean views and Italian fare. This old kauri building formerly housed the Howick Borough Council.

Travel times

From Howick

CBD	off-peak 30 min
	peak write off an hour
Southern motorway	15 min
Airport	30 min
Botany Town Centre	10 min

There is a regular bus service for the area. For the latest bus route and time information, phone Rideline on 366 6400, or check out www.rideline.co.nz

If you don't relish rush-hour commuting stress but want to live out here, why not catch ferries from the Half Moon Bay Marina? See Travel Times under Half Moon Bay for more details.

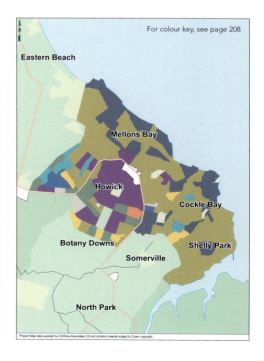

For colour key, see page 208

Road blocks and hazard lights ahead

Clogged motorways are part of life in any large urban centre - but in Auckland they're a relatively recent phenomenon, which is why our politicians are still getting their minds round what to do about them. In Auckland's case, there's a strong argument that the city's traffic jams are constipating the entire country's business productivity. The proposed eastern corridor motorway is probably the most controversial of a raft of new initiatives aimed at cutting commuting times into the city in half and improving the region's traffic flow.

Critics of the new eastern motorway have been sounding alarm bells on environmental and aesthetic grounds - with minimal impact on decision makers. Ditto for other critics who've cited international findings that more highways merely encourage more traffic and

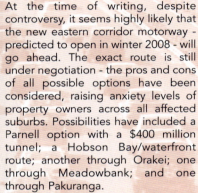

therefore even more clogging further down the track.

At the time of writing, despite controversy, it seems highly likely that the new eastern corridor motorway - predicted to open in winter 2008 - will go ahead. The exact route is still under negotiation - the pros and cons of all possible options have been considered, raising anxiety levels of property owners across all affected suburbs. Possibilities have included a Parnell option with a $400 million tunnel; a Hobson Bay/waterfront route; another through Orakei; one through Meadowbank; and one through Pakuranga.

A preferred-route decision is scheduled to be made by 2004, with design work to be finalised by August 2005. Construction of the motorway is optimistically planned to begin in mid-2005 also. Equally likely, of course, are unforeseeable hold-ups and Murphy's law factors which could delay everything.

While route uncertainty continues, there's a huge number of possibly-affected residents and home-owners waiting in limbo.

Having initially estimated the motorway would cost millions, the council is now talking billions of dollars for this project. Inevitably, houses, clubs and places of beauty will be destroyed. Huge planning difficulties and resource consent hurdles are looming. Excavation work and new roading is bound to impact on protected coastal environments, on recently refurbished public spaces and facilities; maybe even on culturally sensitive or tapu land. And, of course, on many individual homes.

Keep an eye on the council's plans - that's the obvious advice. The Auckland City website at www.aucklandcity.govt.nz will keep you posted on any progress - or lack of it. Here's hoping the outcome's positive for you and your property.

including Highland Park and Edgewater

Immortalised on countless television ads, Pakuranga is the original Vim Valley, full of "Pakuranga housewives" - truly, this is "Madge, you're soaking in it!" country. Pakuranga has been high profile ever since it was developed as a family lifestyle suburb in the 1960s. It is easy to see why it is still so popular. There's access to beaches, boating and good schools. Pakuranga is both a great place for young families and a haven for the retired. The focus shifted when the upmarket areas of Sunnyhills and Farm Cove were built, but Pakuranga's reputation as a place to live the suburban dream has endured.

To the north is Highland Park, where properties at the high points of Bradbury Rd, up on the ridge, have fantastic views to Auckland City and the Sky Tower. Edgewater lives up to its name, bordering on the Tamaki River, south of the highway. Inlets and reserves offer water views, and sections here are tidy and more affordable.

Who lives there?

People from all walks of life, young and old, call Pakuranga home. However, the suburb's population has a slightly older skew, with 15% of its residents beyond age 60, compared with the city average of 11%. Because Pakuranga was established in the mid-1960s, many families have grown up here and new generations with young families have returned to stay.

Pakuranga and the surrounding suburbs are popular with boaties and beachgoers. Many locals say they don't often need to leave - they've got it all here! Cultural diversity is on the increase, too. During the past decade many highly skilled immigrants from a variety of countries have moved to Pakuranga, making it a vibrant and exciting place to live. So while about 73% of Pakuranga's population are of European descent, 16% are relatively recent immigrants from Asia.

Typical dwellings

Much of Pakuranga is a time capsule straight out of the suburban 1960s. Maybe because of this, it is a cheaper residential option than neighbouring Highland Park, Sunnyhills and Farm Cove. Typical homes are solidly built weatherboard and brick, with three or four bedrooms, on generous, often landscaped sections with plenty of internal-access garaging. There's more modest - read cheaper - housing, still mainly weatherboard and brick, to be found in Edgewater.

REAL ESTATE

Trends

When people move to Pakuranga, they tend to settle and stay. By the 1980s Pakuranga had pretty much ceased to grow, as few sites were left for development. However, a recent trend towards infill housing has led to a steady population growth during the past 10 years. Extensive subdivision is underway in the Highland Park and newer Golflands areas, with more residential sites continuing to be developed. Development also continues in Edgewater.

Prices

Pakuranga Rd, the main highway, divides the area into the seaward side and the older, more established Pakuranga and Pakuranga Heights. Prices have moved significantly, even in the past year. You can still, by the skin of your teeth, acquire a run-down three-bedroom family home

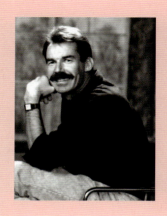

Why I live there
Athlete Dick Quax

Former Olympic and Commonwealth Games athlete Dick Quax has lived in Pakuranga for a dozen years, and he loves it. "Almost everything is very close by, including gyms, doctors, dentists, great shops and excellent schools. We're close to the southern motorway for when we do want to go further afield, and we can catch the ferry into Queen St from Half Moon Bay."

And he says Pakuranga has excellent running tracks, including one that winds for many kilometres along the edge of the Tamaki Estuary with "spectacular and ever-changing tidal views" from St Kentigern College to Half Moon Bay and beyond. He runs at least part of that trail four or five times a week.

in Pakuranga for under $300,000. Mostly, though, prices have crept up to the $320,000 to $340,000 mark for a reasonable family house. First-time buyers who used to be able to notch up a family home for less than $250,000 can now afford only a two-bedroom unit. At the upper end, some Pakuranga houses command prices of more than $1 million.

Average sale prices

	House	Flat	No. sales
2002	$273,141	$223,977	752
2003	$307,731	$241,693	799

Best street

There's not a lot of agreement on this. Some say Riverlea Ave, others say Bradbury Rd in Highland Park, and yet others say Kentigern Close or Millen Ave.

Rental and investment

A one-bedroom unit will rent for about $200 a week. A two-bedroom house will cost you about $280 and a three-bedroom house goes for $320 - $350.

AMENITIES

Schools ★★★★

Pakuranga has plenty of good primary schools. The list includes Elm Park, Anchorage Park, Pakuranga Heights, Riverhills and Riverina School. There are two intermediate schools, Pakuranga Intermediate and Farm Cove Intermediate. For secondary students there is Edgewater College and Pakuranga College. The decile ratings (often correlated with academic results) can vary markedly from school to school, so check them out. The highly regarded private school St Kentigern College, which has recently turned co-ed, is also located in Pakuranga.

Shops ★★★★

There's retail therapy aplenty in Pakuranga. The Pakuranga Town Centre, originally built in 1965, recently had a complete makeover after being bought by the Westfield retail group. Renamed Westfield Shoppingtown Pakuranga, it has more than 70 shops. Plans are also underway for an extensive upgrade, with a proposal for about 170 shops plus cinemas.

Just a few minutes down Ti Rakau Dr are more shopping meccas. At 451 Ti Rakau Dr there's The Hub, extended during the past year with the opening of several new shops including a supermarket. Opposite is the famous Botany Town Centre. North of Pakuranga town centre, on the Pakuranga Highway, Highland Park's shopping centre has almost 30 shops and cafes.

Leisure ★★★★

Pakuranga is well catered for when it comes to open spaces - spoiled for choice, in fact. Lloyd Elsmore Park hosts a huge range of leisure activities - facilities include tennis courts, three golf courses, a driving range, horse riding, croquet, badminton, swimming, sailing, and bowls. A new extension to the Lloyd Elsmore Pool & Leisure Complex includes a six-lane lap pool, in addition to a five-laner incorporating a kiddies' splash pool with fountains. Extensions have also been made to the creche, café and gymnasium, spa pool, sauna and steam room.

Pakuranga offers no excuses to would-be couch potatoes, as it has a couple of gyms, plus a big skate park. Elsewhere, trees and reserves are abundant. There is also the beautiful Pakuranga Country Club Golf Course on Cascades Rd. A boat ramp at Tiraumea Dr reserve allows access to the Tamaki Estuary.

A community, cultural and arts centre called Te Tuhi (the mark) is in Reeves Rd, Pakuranga, opposite the Pakuranga Library.

International food fans will find plenty to tempt their tastebuds, including Metro Bar & Brasserie, Ajadz Indian Cuisine, Ye Won Korean BBQ Restaurant, Steamboat Delight Chinese Restaurant, Pavia Italian Restaurant and O'Hagans Irish Pub & Grill.

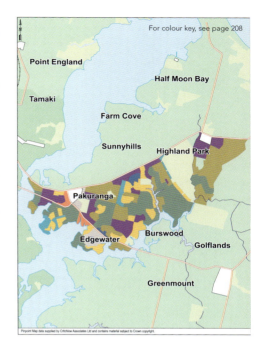

For colour key, see page 208

Pinpoint Map data supplied by Critchlow Associates Ltd and contains material subject to Crown copyright.

Travel times

From Pakuranga

CBD	off-peak 20 min
	peak 40 min
Southern motorway	10 min
Airport	20 min
Manukau City shopping centre	15 min

Howick & Eastern Buses provides a regular service. A regular bus service also runs between Pakuranga and Manukau. The south-eastern highway links Pakuranga to the airport and Onehunga.

Ferries run from Half Moon Bay to Waiheke Island and Auckland's CBD. Ferry services run from Half Moon Bay to Waiheke Island and Auckland's CBD. Ferries into the city are happily becoming more frequent, and take around 35 minutes of relatively low-stress commuting. They currently run every half-hour at peak weekday times, and approximately two-hourly at non-peak times, starting from 6am. Weeknight trips from the CBD to Half Moon Bay include sailings at 5.15pm, 5.45pm, 6.30pm and 8pm, with a couple of later sailings on Friday evenings accommodating nights on the town. Another passenger boat for the Half Moon Bay to Waiheke commute will be in commission before 2004.

The Britomart train service handiest to Pakuranga runs half-hourly or hourly, depending on the time of day, from Panmure into the CBD, starting from 5.50am on weekday mornings. The last evening train departs the CBD at 8.40pm. Note, however, that these eastern train services are currently limited to non-public-holiday weekdays.

Many of the city bus stops serving the Pakuranga area have recently been moved within the new Britomart Bus Precinct. For the latest bus route numbers and stops, phone Rideline on 366 6400, or check out www.rideline.co.nz

WHITFORD ★★★★★

including Brookby and Clevedon

This rural greater-Auckland paradise is where we'd all live, given half a chance. It's the bucolic dream - the carefree existence, the rolling countryside, the abundance of space. A relative lack of urban conveniences is its only downside. Clevedon Ward, which in city council terms includes Whitford, Clevedon, Beachlands, Maraetai, Kawakawa Bay and Orere Point, makes up more than two thirds of the land area of Manukau City, yet its population accounts for only 4% of the residents. There's a horsey, sporty feel to the place and plenty of money on hand, although people out here are pretty tasteful and discreet. As with many country communities, there's a fierce pride and spirit about getting involved with local events. If you hold a public meeting, locals will actually turn up!

Brookby, just south of Whitford, is definitely country - it's a pretty little place; green, undulating, and dotted with oldish farm houses. Clevedon, slightly south again, is also picturesque and even more horsey, hinting at English countryside with its willows and oaks. A sense of community is evident, in the many signs at roundabouts and intersections, detailing forthcoming events.

Who lives there?

Well-heeled families love this area because of its sense of community, its generously proportioned homes and estates, its proximity to beaches and pony paddocks - and its relatively easy access to shops, work and community facilities in the eastern and central parts of Auckland.

A smaller percentage live here because they have farmed locally and have moved to smaller holdings. Interestingly, the population in the Cleveland ward is predominantly (over 80%) European. Some are new to New Zealand, and are taking advantage of a wonderful style of life very difficult (read prohibitively expensive) to replicate in other countries.

This is a good place to be if you're keen on horses. People out here breed them, ride them, race them, house them, bet on them and talk about them.

Typical dwellings

Most of the houses are set back from the road amidst tasteful clumps of mature trees; ornate gates are often the only clue to the casual passerby that there's a spectacular residence down the driveway and around the corner. Because the area has developed slowly and over a long time, the style of houses is pretty eclectic - what doesn't vary much is the quality. Most of the houses are of excellent pedigree, spacious and set in generous grounds.

In Brookby there's an enclave of 1970s homes on Ara-Kotinga Rd, because that's when the farm there was developed into lifestyle blocks. Apart from that cluster, you'll find a smattering of homes from every period from the 1890s to the 1990s.

In the rolling hills of Clevedon there are stately villas and quaint little cottages dating back to the turn of the (previous) century. Most of the houses built more recently are fairly luxurious - or were in their time.

REAL ESTATE

Trends

This is a very popular lifestyle-block part of greater Auckland, and sales of landed homes have been going strong. Typically during winter months, demand for lifestyle blocks tends to ease, but not in the past year! Prices have continued to rise out here also.

With Dannemora's high density housing just over the vale, Whitford's green roominess is becoming even more cherished. Agents say there's a steady turnover of properties and a steady increase in prices.

In Brookby there's not much for sale at any one time - partly because people tend to stay put, but also because there are so few properties there. Both areas have the obvious dilemma of wanting to be lively, sustainable communities with decent numbers of people - but without falling prey to a virulent version of the subdivision disease. Properties are being subdivided here, and development is happening, even though the majority of locals would prefer a non-existent or at least slow rate of change. Resource consents for developments are hotly contested, by locals and by the ARC, which wants to contain Auckland's growth.

Prices

Think big. This is the home of big air, big land holdings and houses not short of a metre or two. Most of what's on the market gives very little change from $700,000 or $800,000. That's not to say you can't buy a small Whitford property. It's just not the norm. If you're looking at around a hectare of land with a big house and great water views, anything below $1.5 million is probably a bargain. If money's no object, there'll be plenty to choose from, incorporating water views, stabling, tennis courts, pools, and of course heaps of land.

These sorts of properties are increasingly being marketed on the internet, so don't be surprised to see a downloaded price-tag stating: "Asking $US1.8 million", and the like. For this sort of cash you're looking at "resort-style living", and can expect all the extras: bars, a sauna, games room, fitness room, spa pools, six-car garaging.

If your living standards are somewhat more modest, i.e. a three-bedroom house on 0.4ha or less, you may still need around $500,000. The starting price is about the same for Brookby, with prices here ranging up to around $3 million.

In Clevedon, $800,000 will buy you a lovely old original villa with four bedrooms and two bathrooms, a large barn, great views and fences, on two hectares. It would also buy around 5ha of land with an older style house and barn, plus a pond and building site.

Average sale prices

	House	Flat	No. sales
2002	$293,211	$ n/a	38
2003	$236,085	$ n/a	41

NB These prices may not be representative as so few properties in this area change hands.

Best streets

Rather than best streets, Whitford has two very desirable peninsulas: Broomfields and Clifton, with the former perhaps being slightly more desirable because of the fact that it's marginally closer to Howick.

Neither Brookby nor Clevedon have enough streets for any of them to be the best!

Rental and investment

There's not a huge rental market out here, and prices will be as much associated with position and views as the number of bedrooms.

You can pay as little as $300 weekly for a two-bedroom place in Whitford, and for a three-bedroom property with expansive land and views you might pay $1000 or more! Often though, you can find a decent-sized four-bedroom family home to rent for between $550 and $650 a week.

AMENITIES

Schools ★★

Whitford primary aged children have to head elsewhere for schooling. Many go to Point View School in Howick. Brookby has its own little school (including intermediate students). Clevedon School is also a full primary (years 1-8). Quite a few secondary students around here go private - there's a bus service which helps those bound for Pakuranga's St Kentigern College (now co-ed). It's possible there'll be more (relatively local) choice for students once the two new colleges in Botany Downs and the new Alfriston College open their doors in 2004.

Shops ★★

Whitford village covers the basics, with cafes, superette, gas station and liquor store - but for anything more extensive, you need to head closer to suburban civilisation. Brookby-ites have to travel to shop, and will often avoid the hustle and bustle of city and suburb by heading to nearby Clevedon for their shopping. Here you'll find all the shops you'd expect at any small shopping centre - plus a touristy handcrafts shop, an engineering workshop, an excellent little antiques and collectables shop, a farm supplies yard, and even an organic food shop.

Leisure ★★★★

This is the place to be when your preferred leisure activities happen in the great outdoors! Reserves and public spaces include the Turanga Creek reserve, the Whitford War Memorial Domain, and the Whitford forest, with paths for walkers, mountain-bikers and horse-riders. The Clevedon Show Grounds off Monument Rd have in the past few months doubled in size, thanks to a recent council addition of approximately 20ha. Increased ground capacity was the aim, and it's good news for all users, including local cricket and soccer teams as well as equestrian eventers.

If you're hankering for golf, you're blessed with the Whitford Park Country Club, which will doubtless also bestow valuable networking opportunities! Whitford Park encourages new members, and has a good additional nine-hole section. Its 56ha of native trees would rival any in greater Auckland.

For the younger Whitford horsey set, there's the pony club. And on that topic, the Tipapa indoor

equestrian and special events centre in Brookby also has a top reputation.

In Clevedon, sporting clubs include bowling, a thriving lawn tennis club (which includes spring and summer coaching for children), and for launch owners, a cruising club. However the latter's so fully subscribed you may be put on a waiting list!

The New Zealand Polo Open is held at Clevedon each February, with club games from November to March. Polo is huge here.

Duders Regional Park is an historic and absolutely beautiful farm by the sea, with numerous tracks for walking, riding and bird-watching. There's great swimming at adjacent Duders Beach - because it's a bit further from civilisation than other east coast beaches, it's less crowded on summer weekends.

There are two cafes and a restaurant at Whitford, and cafes and restaurants at Formosa Country Club and at Pine Harbour Marina. Clevedon has several eating spots.

There are at least five vineyards in the area, including Arahura, Twilight, Inverness and Puriri Hills.

SMART BUY

Established in a leafy, green, refined and luxurious way, places like Whitford and surrounding areas will never go out of style. Also, the more crowded the eastern suburbs get, the better this area looks.

For colour key, see page 208

Waiheke Island
Ponui Island
Beachlands
Pakihi Island
Wade Island
Whitford
Orere Point
Orere
Brookby Clevedon
Ness Valley
Ardmore
Wairoa Reservoir
Drury
Ararimu
Ramarama
Paparata Valley
Bombay

Pinpoint Map data supplied by Critchlow Associates Ltd and contains material subject to Crown copyright.

Travel times

CBD	off-peak 25-30 min
	peak 45 min
Southern motorway	12 min
Airport	20 min
Botany Town Centre	10 min

The area is not well served by buses, but if you can afford to live here then public transport probably isn't at the top of your list of priorities.

An increasing Pine Harbour Ferry service (from 6.30am weekdays) serves locals well, getting them to the CBD just 35 minutes after departure. For a timetable check out www.pineharbour.co.nz After all, who needs the stress of traffic and city car parking?

It's a lifestyle choice

Pulling on gumboots at the end of a day's work may not be everyone's idea of utopia - but it is for those Aucklanders choosing to live on lifestyle blocks in areas such as Whitford, Clevedon and Brookby! Don't get us wrong, not all lifestyle block owners have to wear gumboots to get in and out of their properties, but the choice is one of many on offer if you own one of these blocks of land.

"It's a lifestyle choice. We are close enough to enjoy the city but we have the luxury of space in beautiful surroundings and all the associated advantages of living in a country community," says Cathie Sherning, who moved to Brookby with husband Doug about 13 years ago, and hasn't

regretted it for an instant. Doug was brought up on a Hawkes Bay farm and likes nothing better than pulling on his gumboots and getting out into the paddocks for some action after a day's work in the city. Cathie, who works as an editor from home, tackles the gardens rather than the paddocks, while their two boys just enjoy having the space to run about, ride their bikes and tend the calves and lambs that are a compulsory item at the local Brookby School's annual agricultural day.

The family has just moved into a new property - right next door to their previous one. "It is on a slightly larger block and has glorious views but with greater privacy from the road than we previously enjoyed. The property was developed 40 years ago and we've inherited a well-developed garden with mature trees, including gums and macrocarpa," explains Cathie. They've been busy renovating, adding two more bedrooms to the original three-bedroom low sprawling ranch house. The property has a pool, and a tennis court and barn are part of the long-term renovation plan - something for everyone!

Across the way in Whitford, Jenny and Tim Alcock, who immigrated from England with their two children Harry and Georgina (8 and 6) almost two years ago, say their 1.8ha property is more than living up to expectations. They came looking for a lifestyle block with the intention of replicating the rural village life they led in Gloucestershire.

"We're really enjoying it here. It is excellent for riding and walking the dogs and is such a good location. Although there isn't much in Whitford itself, we're not far from great schools, the pony club, golf courses, the sea, good shopping, the motorway and the airport. So we have everything we want," says Jenny.

The eight-year-old house is two-storey with five bedrooms surrounded by decking, and a spa and tennis court. It was built to look out over the estuary to Cockle Bay. They've recently built stables for their two horses, as well as adding a self-contained flat for visitors. They've found Whitford to be such a great place for child-rearing that they're having a third, this time a "Kiwi". Lifestyle blocks are following the national trend of strong sales, according to Real Estate Institute of NZ figures. These days lifestyle blocks can range from less than a hectare to 15 or more, with most being 2-5ha.

What attracts people to the land? Some are looking to blow away cobwebs and a certain city-dwellers' malaise. Others are keen to develop gardens, experiment with grapes, or other horticulture. All see the properties as great places to bring up children, being close to schools and city amenities while offering space, space and more space.

It is true that some city families find the reality of mowing acres of lawn, weeding huge gardens and tending to animals loses its appeal after a few months. For the most part, lifestyle owners are a pretty satisfied lot. Think about it! Wide open spaces with room to add a tennis court, swimming pool, spa pool - without having to worry about what the neighbours might think. The opportunity for the children (and parents) to have lambs, dogs, calves, horses... For lifestyle block owners there is simply no comparison at all!

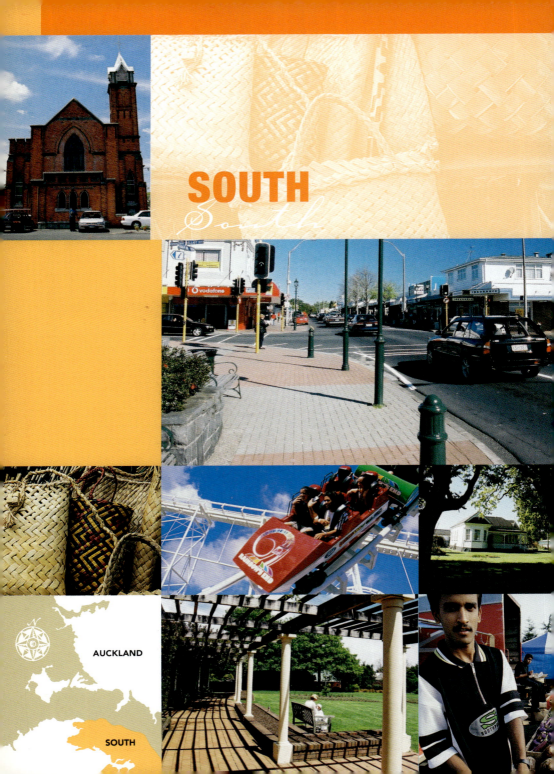

SOUTH
South

AUCKLAND

SOUTH

SOUTH

If you don't live in south Auckland and you're not going to the airport or Rainbow's End theme park, you never go there, right? South Auckland is probably one of the best-known and least-understood parts of New Zealand. Its problems (poverty, ill-health and crime, for example) make the news frequently. But there's much, much more to the place than that. There are tranquil areas of bush, picturesque harbour strolls, lively markets and main-street shopping, and lush rolling green fields.

This southern territory starts at the narrowest point of the Auckland isthmus, Otahuhu, which, unlike the rest of south Auckland, is part of Auckland City, rather than Manukau City. From Otahuhu, south Auckland fans out to the west and down along the shores of the Manukau Harbour - and the southern motorway.

South Auckland does deserve some of the stereotypes with which it's been burdened. There are indeed streets in Mangere and Otara where snotty-nosed young kids on the street are supervised only by slightly older snotty-nosed kids; there are scary-looking dogs with their ribs sticking out. But those are the exceptions. Far from being a wasteland of state housing, south Auckland has plenty of good facilities, and an incredibly diverse range of housing and people.

South Auckland is generally a young city - about a third of its population is aged less than 15 years, compared with one-fifth for the wider Auckland region. True to stereotype, it has large Pacific Island and Maori communities. More than 22,000 students attend Manukau Institute of Technology for its huge range of degrees, diplomas and certificates. Its main campus is in Otara.

South Auckland is a place of contrasts. Take, for example, King's College (one of the most exclusive private schools in the country) sitting back-to-back with Otahuhu College (an institution which represents its staunchly working-class neighbourhood). Or the glamorous function centre on Puketutu Island, right next to the Mangere sewage treatment plant. Areas such as Flat Bush, which border the rural south, are expected to become major suburbs within only a few years. Pockets of 1960s cool such as Hill Park are yet to blossom, as is the older suburb of Otahuhu. Areas of opulent living exist in The Gardens and Mahia Park. Further away, Papakura and Drury have affluent lifestyle blocks.

South Auckland is home to the Auckland Regional Botanic Gardens which hosts the hugely popular Ellerslie Flower Show. Manukau has more than 600 individual reserves totalling more than 2000ha, and esplanade reserves along more than 150km of the city's coastline and along major streams.

Years ago there was an ad campaign which tried to embarrass New Zealanders into travelling around their own country before they hopped on a plane to more exotic destinations. Maybe residents of Auckland City, North Shore and Waitakere could be similarly persuaded to explore the delights of South Auckland?

multicultural and **exciting**

colourful, character-filled

diverse

easy-going

including Mangere Bridge and Favona

The word Mangere has the power to strike fear into the hearts of many people - especially those who've never been there. Certainly, there are pockets of poverty. There are streets where shabby houses, unkempt gardens, graffiti-adorned fences and roaming dogs are the norm. But there are also gracious old villas, beachfront homes with spectacular harbour views, and some of the city's best reserves.

For many years, it also boasted some of the city's strongest smells, thanks to the sewage treatment ponds, which did rather ruin the scenic delights of the area between the foreshore and pretty Puketutu Island. The treatment plant, however, has been upgraded and updated. The new treatment process smells less and 13km of shoreline is being restored, including the creation of beaches and bird-roosting islets, purification of coastal water, restoration of a tidal inlet, and creation of a freshwater wetland.

Who lives there?

For the past few decades Favona and Mangere have been popular with immigrants - perhaps for their closeness to the airport, but certainly for the low house prices. They make it a colourful place. On Favona Rd, for example, just before the mangroves, a former state house has been converted into a Vietnamese Buddhist temple, complete with a gold statue of Buddha in the front yard; directly across the road is the huge Free Wesleyan Church of Tonga, built like an inflated traditional Pacific Island building, amidst a veritable sea of lawn. There are still a few market gardens scattered around Mangere and the odd dry stone wall harks back to the area's long history of farming.

Off-shore, Puketutu Island is privately owned and home to Kelliher, an upmarket function centre.

Typical dwellings

Weatherboard state-style houses are the stereotypical residences in Mangere and Favona, built in the 1940s, 1950s and 1960s. But Mangere, because of its proximity to the harbour, was one of the first parts of Auckland to be settled by Europeans, and there are also a few large villas associated with old farms or market gardens.

There's very little state housing in Mangere Bridge. There are a lot of 1950s and 1960s bungalows - especially two-storeyed with a brick top and a concrete block base.

REAL ESTATE

Trends

Mangere was formerly a big market garden and glasshouse area, and this land is gradually becoming available for development.

Although there's nothing on the scale of eastern suburbs' development, Mangere does boast a few new upmarket subdivisions, including Peninsular Park and Puriri Grove, which are lifting the average house price of the area.

There has been an increase in the popularity of Mangere Bridge since the sewage plant upgrade. Restoration of the shore has increased the suburb's appeal and drawn attention to its village atmosphere.

Prices

In Mangere and Favona you can get a three-bedroom house on a decent section for $190,000 to $240,000. A promising Mangere do-up will cost around $210,000. For a mortgagee sale in a less desirable part of town you might pay as little as $105,000. Large pieces of land are valuable for their subdivision potential: say up to $400,000.

Houses in new subdivisions are selling for between $220,000 and $300,000 (the latter boasting five bedrooms, three bathrooms).

In Mangere Bridge good waterfront homes on large sites now start at around $400,000, while substantial mountain-side homes with views sell for $350,000.

Average sale prices

	House	Flat	No. sales
2002	$189,668	$165,198	593
2003	$198,661	$161,662	756

Rental and investment

Rent for a three-bedroom house in Mangere Bridge is anywhere between $280 and $360 a week. In Mangere East and Favona a three or four bedroom house rents for $350.

Best street

Mangere Bridge's Kiwi Esplanade.

AMENITIES

Schools ★★★

Numerous primary schools (up to 16) service the area including several with religious affiliations and four institutions that cover all ages. For post primary, there are two intermediates, and three public high schools - Kingsford High School, De La Salle College and Mangere College.

Shops ★

Mangere Bridge has an old established shopping area, and being slightly off the beaten track is more self-contained and village-like. It's also more genteel than Favona and Mangere central, but shops like Waka Nathan's Pork Bone Shop confirm that this isn't Remuera.

Mangere town centre has the essentials but isn't first shopping-as-entertainment choice for most who can go further afield. In Favona, local shops are mostly dairies and liquor outlets.

Leisure ★★★

Mangere Mountain has sports fields, excellent walking, curious cows and spectacular views. It was once the site of one of the largest fortified Maori pa in the region. Enormous kumara pits carved into the crater edge are still obvious.

Ambury Farm Park is a large harbourside working farm where visitors are welcome to pat and talk to the animals; the coastal reefs and inlets on the park's Manukau foreshore are home to more than 86 species of birds.

The Otuataua Stonefields Historic Reserve is a new 100ha reserve just before the tiny settlement of Ihumatao. It has a prime location by the sea and fascinating remains of Maori and European occupation. Armed with a brochure from Manukau City Council, you can wander around and identify the remnants of garden mounds, cooking areas, storage pits and a pa site made of rock.

There's a narrow reserve meandering along Mangere Bridge's pretty foreshore; the old bridge is a popular spot for fishing and escaping from the office at lunch time.

Moana-Nui-a-Kiwa Leisure Centre has a full range of gym and swimming facilities, while Mangere Community Arts Outreach Service has regular exhibitions.

The many takeaway outlets are augmented by lunch bars and casual ethnic cafés.

Travel times

From Mangere	
CBD	off-peak 20 min
	peak 35 min
Southern motorway	10 min
Airport	5 min
Manukau City shopping centre	15 min

Mangere is well served by buses running to all points of Auckland.

For colour key, see page 208

including Totara Heights, Flat Bush, East Tamaki Heights, Goodwood Heights, Chapel Downs, Wiri and Puhinui

Much of this area has developed recently and quickly. Chapel Downs looks like a more modest sister to Botany Downs. Just around the corner the cows march across Ormiston Rd twice daily, between field and milking shed. At the northern end, East Tamaki has new light industry and manufacturing companies. Totara Heights is more established, and these hillside properties feel surprisingly affluent, making this an attractive lifestyle choice. At the rural edge there's Flat Bush with the best of urban and country living, depending on which window you're looking out of.

Across the motorway, the Manukau/Wiri/Puhinui area is dominated by the huge Manukau shopping centre, and by the surrounding wholesale outlets and office blocks. Wiri and Manukau are largely commercial. Puhinui still has some rural areas towards the airport.

Who lives there?

These areas reflect the rich diversity of cultures that make up Auckland in the 21st century. Newer areas like Chapel Downs are attracting both young families and the semi-retired. Driving through areas like Totara Heights, it's evident that there are a lot of young and outgoing families living here. Manukau is largely blue collar, although east of the shopping centre there are more executive-type homes. Many new Asian migrants are moving into the area, initially as renters and then as buyers.

Typical dwellings

Chapel Downs features modern houses built of plaster and/or brick. Clover Park and Flat Bush are set on a large, level area and have pitched their aesthetic much lower, the predominant construction material being weatherboard. Due to these areas being relatively new, the sections are often lacking greenery, with front lawns appearing quite naked. In sharp contrast, Manukau Heights and Totara Heights have many multi-storey houses, often with internal-access garaging and surrounded by native bush.

Manukau and Wiri have some streets of pastel-painted fibrolite weatherboard state houses with untended front gardens, and some streets of solid brick and tile 1970s (and beyond) houses with more mature landscaping.

REAL ESTATE

Trends

Newer areas, such as Chapel Downs in particular, are experiencing steady growth, with sections and housing in the newly formed subdivisions being snapped up by eager buyers.

There are plans to develop the semi-rural Flat Bush into New Zealand's first new town since the 1960s. It's expected that 40,000 people will live in Flat Bush town by the year 2020. The planned Barry Curtis Park will be the prime outdoor recreation and open space area for the township and is being designed and developed by Manukau City Council.

There are some new properties under development at Manukau Heights, but less movement in the hills of Totara Heights, where things are more established.

The Manukau/Wiri/Puhinui area is popular with renters, investors and first-home buyers, especially those who've grown up in the area and want to start out somewhere they're familiar with.

Being in zone for Papatoetoe High School or Manurewa High School can put a premium of about $20,000 on your house price. A house in an elevated position might sell for 40-50% more than a similar place lower down the same hill.

Prices

Modest homes in the Clover Park and Flat Bush areas can be as low as $160,000 for a three-bedroom weatherboard house. New homes in Chapel Downs sell for $240,000 to $300,000. In Totara Heights and Manukau Heights, comfortable housing is between $300,000 and $450,000. At the top end of this range you can find four- to five-bedroom multi-storey houses with internal-access garaging and tree-filled sections.

A three-bedroom home in Puhinui could cost between $180,000 and $250,000 if it's close to Papatoetoe, or $160,000 to $200,000 if it's further away from Papatoetoe.

You could buy a three-bedroom Manukau home on a full section for around $200,000, but head for the more elevated parts (anything with "Heights" at the end of its name) and you could be paying closer to $400,000. For less than $150,000 you could have a one-bedroom Manukau apartment, including a furniture package and carpark.

Average sale prices

	House	Flat	No. sales
2002	$223,479	$198,555	463
2003	$247,404	$175,017	717

Best streets

The gentle curves and altitude of Goodwood Dr in Goodwood Heights, on the western side of Totara Park, which has views of the city.

In Manukau and Wiri the elevation of your site, and proximity to the shopping centre and/or to Papatoetoe High School, are desirable, rather than any particular street.

Rental and investment

Affordable properties and a good pool of potential tenants make this area popular with renters and investors. Approximate rental in Puhinui for a one-bedroom place is $160 a week, for two bedrooms it's $220, and three bedrooms is $265.

In Manukau a two-bedroom rental will typically cost around $270 a week, and a three-bedroom between $275 and $500 depending on the age, location and condition of the property.

Renting a three-bedroom house in Clover Park you can expect to pay between $270 and $350 a week; up to $250 for two bedrooms.

If lifestyle is what you're after, a large family home with barn included on 2ha can be rented for around $850.

AMENITIES

Schools ★★

There is a good range of primary schools in the area. Papatoetoe High School, for which much of the Manukau/Wiri/Puhinui area is in zone, is very highly regarded, and drives up property prices. From Clover Park, Totara Heights, Flat Bush etc, high school aged kids head out to Otara, Manurewa or Papatoetoe.

Shops ★★★★

Westfield Shoppingtown Manukau has a Farmers store and a Foodtown supermarket, and more than 120 specialty stores. It's a bustling, sprawling, friendly place. You can shop 'til you drop, pick yourself up, and shop some more.

The main shopping centre is surrounded by a vast ocean of retail and wholesale outlets, especially big bargain-style operations. They're large, so the area is very spread out, and it's definitely oriented towards people travelling

Local hero - Rainbow's End

Opened in 1982, Rainbow's End was an immediate hit and is New Zealand's largest theme park. Opposite the Manukau shopping centre, it has something for every level of adventure and daring from the more mild mini-golf, dodgems, bumper boats and karts to the stomach-lurging roller coaster that takes you 30m off the ground and the dreaded (or eagerly anticipated) Fear Fall. There's also a pirate ship, interactive games, a log flume and dream castle.

by car. There's a shopping centre at Chapel Downs, and it's a short drive to shopping centres at The Hub and Botany Downs.

Leisure ★★★★

These suburbs have good (car) access to recreational spots. Totara Park has large tracts of native bush and rolling farmland, with pleasant woodland walks, picnic areas and playgrounds, and one of Auckland's most picturesquely sited swimming pools. Mountain biking is permitted in some parts of the reserve.

Next to Totara Park is Auckland's popular regional botanic gardens where there's a fabulous range of plants and flowers on display all year round.

Murphy's Bush Scenic Reserve is another local treasure; a beautiful patch of mature native bush which has survived generations of development in the area.

Hayman Park, opposite the mall, is an oasis of mature trees, with a creek and a duck pond, and satisfyingly expansive areas of grass. It also has a concrete in-ground skate park.

Rainbow's End Theme Park is a favourite with families. The Manukau Sports Bowl facilities in Clover Park include a tennis centre, cycling velodrome and a greyhound-racing stadium.

Manukau's newest landmark, the Millennium Sculpture, stands 10m tall at the intersection of Great South and Wiri Station Rds, Manukau City Centre.

For eating out, there's an extensive food court at the mall, and various large-scale pubs and eateries in the wholesale/retail areas, including a Denny's. There's also the Headin' Home Bar & Grill on Ti Rakau Dr. Aside from these, it's a matter of takeaways.

Travel times

CBD	off-peak 20 min
	peak 40 min
Southern motorway	5 min
Airport	10 min
Manukau City shopping centre	5 min
Botany Town Centre	10 min
Britomart CBD by train	30 min

This entire area is well served by buses. Access to the southern motorway is quick from even the most rural of these parts, and there's a train station at Puhinui (on the southern line).

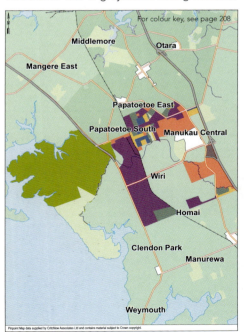

including Weymouth, Clendon Park, Homai, Hill Park, Manurewa East, Randwick Park, Wattle Downs and Conifer Grove

Manurewa is an extremely varied area, and it's growing fast. This collection of small suburbs has a lot of coastline, thanks to three peninsulas which jut into the Manukau Harbour. And the seaside areas aren't all occupied by the smartest suburbs. It has a varied mix of houses and people, from some upmarket suburbs to some quite scruffy streets. The area is also well-endowed with reserves, including patches of bush and waterfront parks. On the eastern side of the southern motorway, it's home to the Auckland Regional Botanic Gardens which includes a renowned rose garden and hosts the high-profile Ellerslie Flower Show.

All in all, Manurewa and its surrounding suburbs probably offer some of the cheapest Auckland real estate, while being some of the closest to bush and sea.

Who lives there?

Cheap buying and renting in parts of Manurewa makes the area attractive to those on restricted incomes, including some refugees. There's also a growing Indian community, with a Sikh temple on Great South Rd.

Some of the area's biggest recent sales have been to former residents of the North Shore and the eastern suburbs. It's believed that visitors to the Manurewa-based Ellerslie Flower Show were so taken with the relaxed lifestyle, greenness and native birdlife that they came back, buying lifestyle blocks in the area or homes backing on to the botanic gardens.

Typical dwellings

Most Manurewa homes were built in the 1960s or later. They are a modest size, typically family homes on full sections. There are few old-style villas or bungalows, and a few home units. There are also some new developments with impressive brick and plaster homes.

REAL ESTATE

Trends

The most popular area at the moment is The Gardens. A recent development, The Gardens is flanked by Totara Park and the Auckland Regional Botanic Gardens, and that no doubt contributes to its popularity. But it's also popular because the new local primary school is highly regarded and includes the intermediate years. Hill Park is slowly gaining ground, with houses that radiate 1960s chic.

Prices

Properties in Clendon Park - which follows the coastline to the west, and has a reserve all the way along - sell for $130,000 to $160,000. Weymouth, at the end of the same peninsula, is more expensive and desirable. Prices in Hill Park, between Great South Rd and the southern motorway, average $260,000 to $300,000, and east of the motorway in Manurewa East (around the botanic gardens) prices range from $350,000 to $600,000. South of the gardens, houses in Randwick Park fetch $160,000 to $260,000 (the higher price is for brick and tile). There are also lifestyle blocks around the borders of this area.

Average sale prices

	House	Flat	No. sales
2002	$203,462	$157,715	1062
2003	$223,060	$145,893	1803

Rental and investment

Manurewa has such a wide range of socio-economic strata that average prices are

Local hero - Auckland Regional Botanic Gardens

It has impressive numbers - its 65ha are home to 10,000 different plants - but mostly it's just a nice place to be. The Auckland Regional Botanic Gardens joins the bush of Totara Park on one side, has gentle grassy slopes where kids love to run about and roll around, and is laid out in an informal but informative way. The gardens are just off the southern motorway and are open every day from 8am to 6pm, and to 8pm during daylight saving.

difficult to gauge - an overall average of around $260 a week for three bedrooms is reasonable. In Clendon you might rent a three-bedroom house for as low as $200 a week although $240 is more common (and more pleasant to occupy). In The Gardens you could easily pay around $400 a week for a three or four-bedroom house.

AMENITIES

Schools ★★★

Manurewa and surrounding suburbs have many schools, including 19 primaries, three intermediates and three secondaries. Alfriston College's new zone touches on the area. Homai National School for the Blind is based here.

Shops ★★

Shopping in Manurewa is a combination of main street (along Great South Rd) and mall (Southmall). The mall is looking rather tired and old-fashioned. There are numerous bargain-style shops in the main street and the mall; also notable are the number of Indian shops. If you like Indian sweets and meals, this is your shopping centre! On the whole, though, most people go straight to Manukau.

Leisure ★★★

There are numerous parks and reserves throughout the area, many of them along the coastline. Wattle Downs, for instance, has the extensive Kauri Point Reserve, Wattle Farm Reserve, Wattle Farm Wetlands Reserve, and a golf and country club. The Auckland Regional Botanic Gardens are a key feature.

Nathan Homestead on Hill Rd was built in 1925 and has more than 3.5ha of well-maintained lawn and gardens. It is now an arts, community and function centre. Manurewa Leisure Centre offers full gymnasium facilities and a swimming pool. Manurewa is a bit of a desert when it comes to eateries but it does have all the usual takeaway outlets.

SMART BUY

With the same money you could spend on one decent property in Epsom or Parnell, you could buy up and bulldoze half a dozen waterfront houses here and build your way to a very fine seaside residence.

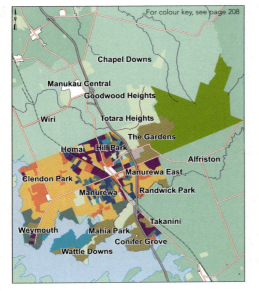

For colour key, see page 208

Chapel Downs
Manukau Central
Goodwood Heights
Wiri
Totara Heights
The Gardens
Homai   Hill Park
Alfriston
Clendon Park
Manurewa East
Manurewa   Randwick Park
Takanini
Weymouth   Mahia Park
Conifer Grove
Wattle Downs

Travel times

From Manurewa	
CBD	off-peak 20 min
	peak 40 min
Southern motorway	2 min
Airport	15 min
Manukau City shopping centre	5 min
Botany Town Centre	15 min
Britomart CBD by train	35 min

Manurewa is served by both bus and trains on the southern line.

including Middlemore and Papatoetoe

From Otahuhu College - a low-decile school that looks like an English public school - to tranquil estuary-side properties and a myriad of races, this is a diverse and fascinating area. Otahuhu is on the narrowest part (1.3km across) of the Auckland isthmus. It was settled early by Europeans because of the water access, and even earlier by Maori. Middlemore, south of Otahuhu, has two major and starkly contrasting institutions: King's College, an elite private school; and sprawling Middlemore Hospital, which serves some of the poorest families in New Zealand.

South again is Papatoetoe, a comparatively gracious area where the names of the "old" families are still proudly spoken, and the carving up of their once-extensive estates is lamented. It is made up of two parts - old Papatoetoe and Hunter's Corner, the latter appealing to a younger, funkier crowd.

Who lives there?

Otahuhu and Middlemore are staunchly blue collar. Their affordability - and, no doubt, proximity to the Mangere Immigration Hostel - makes them popular with less-affluent immigrant families. The main street of Otahuhu is teeming with people from the Pacific Islands and throughout Asia, especially India (Otahuhu has a Sikh temple). Papatoetoe High School is considered "the grammar school of the south", enticing families who would prefer a private school, but don't have the money.

Typical dwellings

Otahuhu and Middlemore are dotted with older character villas and bungalows, but many are badly neglected. There are many rather shabby low-rise blocks of flats. A large new subdivision behind the hospital has good brick-and-tile homes at affordable prices.

The homes in Papatoetoe have fared better although many are now being subdivided or crossleased, where protected trees allow. Papatoetoe also has street after street of 1960s and 1970s brick-and-tile homes, most with a camellia bush in the front garden.

REAL ESTATE

Trends

This is a renter's market more than a buyer's market. There's high demand among investors for big sections which can be subdivided, and land currently used for glasshouses is being seized upon for its residential potential. First home buyers have started to spot the old railway cottages and Californian bungalows that dot the area and there's talk of Otahuhu becoming the "next Onehunga". Despite the

Why I live there
League player Odell Manuel

Odell Manuel gave up his place with the Canberra Raiders because he was homesick for his family and his hometown of Otahuhu. The former Warriors player loves his suburb for the friendly people. "I know everybody here. When I first got into the Warriors in 1999, everybody was proud of me, even people I hadn't met before."

cultural breadth and historic value of this suburb, it's still considered downmarket, so is still relatively affordable.

Prices

In Otahuhu and Middlemore, a first home buyer might buy a tidy two-bedroom unit in a block of 10 for around $100,000. For $160,000 you could get a four-bedroom home which needs a lot of work. For about $300,000 you could have a solid renovated bungalow right by the water in Princes St East.

In Papatoetoe's most desirable area houses built between 1940 and 1970 cost $240,000 to $260,000 (most are two-bedroom plus sunroom). More substantial homes on the best street cost up to $450,000. In Papatoetoe Heights, a 20-year-old three-bedroom home on a half site will cost $150,000 to $200,000.

Average sale prices

	House	Flat	No. sales
2002	$197,399	$171,294	710
2003	$208,419	$195,335	830

Rental and investment

In Otahuhu and Middlemore investment properties are popular: for $426,000 you could own a block of five two-bedroom units.

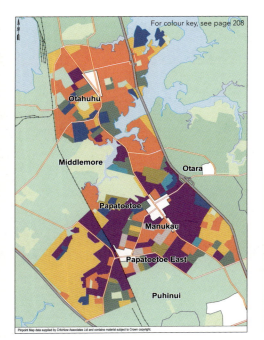

For colour key, see page 208

Pinpoint Map data supplied by Critchlow Associates Ltd and contains material subject to Crown copyright.

Rents are between $140 and $160 a week for a one-bedroom unit, an average of $300 a week for a three-bedrom house and $420 a week for four bedrooms.

Best streets

In Otahuhu/Middlemore, Princes St East. In Papatoetoe, Omana Rd.

AMENITIES

Schools ★★

There are two state primaries in Otahuhu and three private. There are intermediate schools in Otahuhu and Papatoetoe. Otahuhu College and King's College, a study in socio-economic contrast, are physically separated by just a fence.

Shops ★★★

Otahuhu has made a great success of its main street revival - it's lively, friendly, busy and interesting. It's been deserted by many of the larger chains, but if you want cheap shoes, Indian sweets or fabric leis, this is your spot. Papatoetoe has good shopping, if a little less lively. Hunter's Corner has a shopping mall.

Leisure ★★★

The Auckland Golf Club and the Grange Golf Club sit back to back, divided by the Tamaki River. Of course, rugby, league, kilikiti and netball are more likely to be sports of choice with the locals. There are numerous little reserves, many of them by the Tamaki River.

Papatoetoe and Otahuhu have recreation and fitness centres, plus the usual rugby and bowls. Papatoetoe has the Centennial Pools and a skating rink; Otahuhu has rowing and bad-minton. Otahuhu is great for eating out - if you like good cheap, authentic Asian food, and you don't mind fluorescent lights and Formica tables.

Travel times	
From Otahuhu	
CBD	off-peak 20 min
	peak 40 min
Britomart CBD by train	20 min
Southern motorway	5 min
Airport	10 min
Manukau City shopping centre	10 min

The area is well catered for by buses and the train stops at Middlemore and Papatoetoe.

including East Tamaki

Otara has a bit of an image problem, but as is often the case, the reality is more complicated and rather better than the stereotype. Alongside the characterless state housing and pretty dire poverty, Otara has many things going for it. It's home to the bustling Manukau Institute of Technology, vibrant churches of all persuasions and a market that's worth forsaking your Saturday morning sleep-in for. Otara is also the home stomping ground of some truly funky New Zealand musicians.

Otara was largely rural and the residents were largely Pakeha until the 1950s when a state housing project was initiated, with the aim of building 4500 houses for 20,000 low-income residents. This coincided with a pro-immigration campaign, and the area attracted large numbers of Pacific Island residents new to New Zealand, and Maori who moved from more rural areas looking for work in the surrounding industrial areas.

Who lives there?

From the faces at the Saturday market, you get the impression there's a large Asian population in Otara and East Tamaki, but most of these people apparently come in from other areas far and near, especially for the market. The Maori and Pacific Island businesses which dominate the Otara town centre are a much more accurate guide to the area's ethnic make-up.

Typical dwellings

State houses dominate, and they come in all flavours of the past few decades, especially weatherboard and fibrolite. There are also stand-alone houses, duplexes and multiple unit townhouses.

REAL ESTATE

Trends

This area is dominated by renters and investors, rather than owner-occupiers. Properties are in demand from both sectors. The streets surrounding the Manukau Institute of Technology are in most demand: there is no accommodation specifically for students. There's also strong demand from extended families who choose to stay in the area they've always lived in, so they can be close to family

(especially if the grandparents are looking after children whose parents are working) and their church. "They support their church as loyally as someone in Ponsonby might support their favourite cafe," says one real estate agent.

Prices

Three years ago you could pick up a three-bedroom house at a mortgagee sale for between $90,000 and $110,000. Once common, mortgagee sales are fortunately now more rare. Now demand means you won't get a three-bedroom house for less than $120,000 - unless it's in an appalling condition. For Otara, prices between $125,000 and $145,000 are usual. In East Tamaki, a three-bedroom house sells for around $165,000.

Average sale prices

	House	Flat	No. sales
2002	$129,639	$132,333	86
2003	$126,577	$104,000	96

Best streets

Piako St, Bairds Ave and anywhere near MIT.

Rental and investment

There's strong demand from both renters and investors in this area. Rents seem surprisingly high. You'd be hard pushed to find anything under $200 a week, and you can expect to pay $240-$270 a week for a three-bedroom house. But real estate agents say it's a high-risk business in this area. Many tenants don't have a culture of home ownership, there's a high turn-over, and people don't always pay the rent before they go.

Schools ★★★

The Manukau Institute of Technology is a focus for the area, offering a huge range of full-time and part-time courses for 22,000-plus students, from academic degrees to trade certificates. It covers an area of more than 12ha, with two large campuses in Manukau and a smaller one in central Auckland.

Bairds Mainfreight Primary gained national profile as the first school to win business sponsorship. There are six other primary schools. Sir Edmund Hillary Collegiate has separate junior, intermediate and senior schools. Ferguson Intermediate and Tangaroa College are the post-primary institutions.

Shops ★★

Otara town centre has the basics, including fabric flower necklaces, CDs of Pacific Island music, huge buckets of corned beef and tapa cloth by the kilometre. The nearest big mall is at Manukau.

Leisure ★★

There's an extensive reserve including a walkway along the foreshore of the Otara Creek, which is being rejuvenated under the Manukau City Council's maintenance programme. Other reserves in the area include the popular basketball courts at the O Tamariki Reserve.

The Otara Music Arts Centre, Takutai-a-kiwa, is a community centre with a difference - it has a recording studio, which is used by local amateur and professional musicians.

There's a free swimming pool by the Otara town centre.

This is takeaway city. The most interesting option is probably the ethnic food at the Saturday morning flea market.

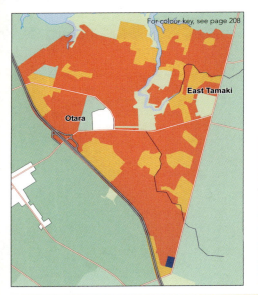

For colour key, see page 208

East Tamaki

Otara

Travel times	
From Otara	
CBD	off-peak 20 min
	peak 40 min
Southern motorway	3 min
Airport	12 min
Manukau City shopping centre	10 min
The area is served by numerous bus routes.	

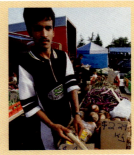

Local hero - Otara Flea Market

One of Auckland's weekly landmark events, Otara Flea Market is held in the carpark between the Otara town centre and the Manukau Institute of Technology. Get there early on a Saturday morning and enjoy the sights, sounds and smells. Sample ethnic delicacies like barbecued pork buns, rewena bread and poke (a Cook Island pudding which manages to be simultaneously gelatinous and doughy) while you wander around. Take home great armfuls of Asian and Pacific fruits, vegetables and herbs. It gets very crowded, and it's probably a good idea to keep your hand on your wallet. But it's definitely worth a visit.

including Takanini, Red Hill, Ardmore, Rosehill, Drury, Hingaia and Pahurehure

Papakura is a country town on the edge of Auckland's sprawling suburbs - and it's still surrounded by enough farmland for it to feel like a rural and individual place. The orderly and well-maintained cemetery is very close to the centre of town, and signs advertising the next Calf Day look authentic rather than a community struggling for some identity. It's often used as the service town for the wealthier lifestyle block areas of Whitford, Clevedon and Brookby. Papakura is large enough to have its own suburbs: Red Hill and Pahurehure. In the next decade there's expected to be more development to the west of Pahurehure, into the Hingaia Peninsula and north at Takanini.

There are newer subdivisions just south of the town and in Red Hill, which is five minutes from the centre of town. Papakura has its own local authority.

Who lives there?

In the past couple of decades Papakura has lost a lot of industry and government-funded operations (including an army base, teachers' college and Kingseat psychiatric hospital) which brought a lot of people - and their spending power - to the area. It's a fairly conservative place, says one local, with a population that included 25% Maori at the last census.

"Papakura is quite a traditional New Zealand town," he says, "and we haven't yet got the same mixture of people that has developed in other areas." True to its country-town feel, Papakura is a close-knit community, a great place to raise kids, and there are many families who have been in the area for several generations. The town serves the surrounding rural community. There's also a move for Papakura townies to retire to lifestyle blocks outside of town, and for retired farmers to move closer to town.

Typical dwellings

The central area of Papakura was mostly built in the 1950s, 1960s and 1970s: good solid standard Kiwi homes. Newer homes predominate around Red Hill and Pahurehure, although there are also substantial older farmhouses up on Red Hill, with rural views and glimpses of the Manukau Harbour. Pahurehure is the most desirable area, with real estate demand outstripping supply, particularly for new homes.

REAL ESTATE

Trends

Papakura prices are gradually increasing as the rural ambience of this affordable country

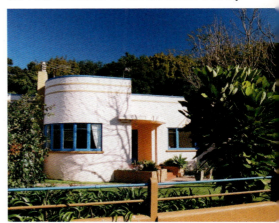

town and the surrounding countryside becomes more appreciated.

Prices

Property is still reasonably affordable in Papakura, with an average three-bedroom home on a full section going for about $150,000. There's plenty of choice in the $200,000 - $300,000 range and you may even get four bedrooms for $250,000. Lifestyle properties more than 0.4ha in size start at about $350,000.

Average sale prices

	House	Flat	No. sales
2002	$205,644	$166,545	628
2003	$223,892	$163,475	862

Best street

Red Hill Rd has great rural views, bush reserves and beautiful homes.

Rental and investment

A one-bedroom unit will rent for about $150 a week, a two-bedroom house for $180-230 and a three-bedroom house will be $280.

AMENITIES

Schools ★★★

The areas is well-served with five primary schools. Rosehill and Papakura are the names of the two intermediate schools and the two high schools. Rosehill has a good reputation.

Shops ★★★

There's an air of self-sufficiency to the main street of Papakura. You can find most of what you need here (albeit with more bargain-oriented stores than upmarket boutiques) so constant trips to big malls aren't necessary. The shopping area isn't trendy by any stretch of the imagination, but has a good, solid neighbourhood feel to it.

Leisure ★★★★

There are numerous parks, reserves and recreation areas, and a golf course. Papakura is also virtually surrounded by rural land. Within minutes you can be heading to the pleasant rolling countryside of Whitford, Clevedon and Brookby and can access some nice beaches to the east.

The township boasts a museum and an art gallery (as well as a large courthouse, if you have a macabre voyeuristic streak).

Papakura is well-served by exotic eateries (mostly casual), including Korean, Indian, Thai, Turkish and Japanese.

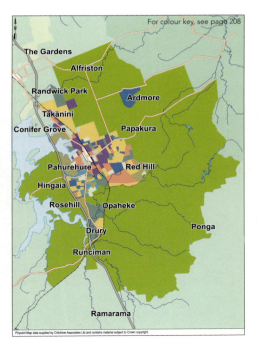

For colour key, see page 208

Travel times

From Papakura

CBD	off-peak 35 min
	peak 1 hour
Southern motorway	5 min
Airport	25 min
Manukau City shopping centre	12 min
Britomart CBD by train	45 min

The Papakura region is served by buses and trains. Papakura train station is a 45-minute trip from Auckland central station; the bus takes 1 hour 20 minutes for a similar result. At the southern end of Auckland's suburbia, Papakura is close to all points south.

where to live in
AUCKLAND

FACTS & FIGURES

POPULATION PROFILES

Each neighbourhood in this book features a map colour-coded according to eleven population groups. This neighbourhood classification system, known as MOSAIC® is created by Pinpoint Target Marketing, a division of PMP Limited.

MOSAIC® combines information on consumer demographics, households, lifestyles and attitudes so you can see who might live next door if you choose to buy in an area. The detailed descriptions on the following pages highlight characteristics such as what sports and activities people enjoy, typical occupations and even what they eat for dinner.

Information is gathered from the following sources:
- Property attribute data provided by Quotable Value NZ
- New Zealand Census data from Statistics NZ
- Motor vehicle data from Cadmus
- Market research data sourced from Roy Morgan Research

For more information on MOSAIC® and other segmentation and mapping solutions, contact Pinpoint Target Marketing on 0800 938 555.

GROUP A

Elite Professionals

Elite Professionals are upper class mature families, located in affluent urban areas, though also increasingly on rural lifestyle blocks. They are typically between 45 and 54 years of age. Elite Professionals are successful, degree-qualified and work long hours in occupations that provide them with the highest median household incomes of all MOSAIC Groups, at over $78,000 per annum. The majority are employed as white-collar professionals and managers. Their houses are of the highest value, and consist mainly of large separate houses and apartments, with many of these being owned outright. These neighbourhoods revel in social interaction and their residents can often be seen sailing around the harbour, enjoying a game of tennis or golf, or at the beach. Keeping up with the cutting edge of fashion and technology at exclusive stores is considered a must. Fine dining at exclusive restaurants and cafes or hosting dinner parties is enjoyed regularly, especially over a premium bottle of wine. Elite Professionals like attending cultural activities such as ballet, opera and live theatre. Their occupations demand that they keep abreast of current affairs and the latest trends, so they are avid readers of newspapers and business, motoring and home lifestyle magazines.

GROUP B

Comfortable & Secure

Comfortable & Secure are typically middle-aged families with teenage children, or empty nesters. They are reasonably well qualified, and work as mid-level managers, professionals and technicians. Their household incomes are high, at over $60,000 the second highest of all MOSAIC Groups. They predominantly live in separate houses that they own outright. Busy with work and family commitments, these people generally don't have much time to spend cooking. When they do have a chance to relax, they like to spend it keeping up-to-date with ways to improve their homes. Given that home ownership is high this is not surprising, and many even admit to being more interested in their house than their career. Popular pastimes include jogging and going to the gym, as well as water sports such as sailing and power boating. Surfing the internet, shopping, frequenting cafes and weekends at the beach are other common ways to relax. Motor vehicle ownership is high across the group, with cars often purchased on looks - particularly by the teenaged members of the household. They keep up to date with current affairs through newspapers, television and the internet, and read major women's, home and lifestyle and business magazines.

Stylish Singles

Stylish Singles represent a mix of young professionals and students, and are typically aged between 20 and 34. The majority live in inner-suburban flats or close to tertiary campuses. Success-driven and with high qualification levels, most work in professional and technical occupations where they earn well above average household incomes - over $48,000 per annum. Stylish Singles live for the moment and will try anything once. They are extroverted and sociable, often letting their hair down at bars and clubs. Cars, clothes and

accessories are seen as an extension of themselves. They wear stylish clothing with the right labels, and express themselves through conspicuous purchases. They were born to shop, and aren't afraid to use credit to buy the things they want. These people are technologically savvy - "early adopters" - and are into computers, DVD players and associated technical gadgets. They are heavy internet users and also cultured, generally appreciating art and fine food, but are just as comfortable with takeaways and a movie. Keeping fit is important, and exercise is often slotted into their busy schedules. Stylish Singles enjoy sporting activities such as aerobics, rugby, surfing and jet-skiing. On winter weekends, they can often be seen on the slopes of the nation's skifields.

GROUP C

Family Balance

Family Balance are usually middle-aged families with young school-aged children, located in the outer suburbs. A high proportion have two or more children. They predominantly live in separate houses in average condition, with slightly below average property values due to their location. Home ownership rates are high, and Family Balance take pride in their homes. Balancing family and career, they work hard to support their families in a variety of occupations, from trades to professional and technical occupations. Household incomes average just under $46,000. Shopping is completed after work or on weekends. Value for money is a key factor in the purchase decision process and Family Balance make a conscious effort to buy New Zealand-made products. Family Balance are not technically minded

or particularly concerned with fashion. They prefer the familiar and simple things in life, such as motor sport, hunting and fishing. While not overly concerned with image, some are increasingly concerned with health issues, such as cholesterol. Increasing numbers are taking up physical activities such as walking, jogging, and working out at the gym.

GROUP D

Kiwiana

This group of classic Kiwis contains a mixture of ages and family groups - from young families to older retirees. Kiwiana live in a mixture of localities, including big city suburbs. Their houses are valued close to the national median, if not slightly below, and are in average condition. These tend to be rented privately, or owned with a mortgage. Occupations are more manual in nature or in trades, which bring home slightly below average household incomes of $38,000. Having to make their earnings stretch, Kiwiana look for bargains and are the most attracted to discounts, promotions and special offers. Although

influenced by price, Kiwiana still only buy products they know and trust, including brands they have grown up with. This reluctance to try new things is highlighted by the fact they are likely to buy the same food from week to week. When it comes to fashion these people prefer function over style, and are somewhat hesitant when it comes to technology and the internet. Traditional Kiwi sports such as rugby, rugby league and cricket are popular with younger people, with pursuits such as darts popular with older people. Magazine readership is high within the Kiwiana types.

GROUP E

Local Pride

Local Pride contains a mixture of young families, and older 50-somethings, with a relatively high incidence of households containing more than one family. These people are proud of their close-knit local communities. Houses are generally separate dwellings, of average quality and below average capital value. However, their homes are built on above average sized sections, typically the classic quarter acre section. Homes are generally mortgaged. Education levels are among the lowest, and consequently some struggle to find employment. The most common jobs include trades, manual occupations and work in the primary sector, such as in agriculture and fishing. Household income levels of $37,000 are below average, but this doesn't necessarily mean they struggle, as the cost of living is significantly lower in their neighbourhoods. Local Pride live conservatively and are more likely to watch television at home than hold dinner parties or attend cultural events. They do not spend extravagantly and rarely eat at expensive restaurants. They can occasionally be found buying takeaways such as fish and chips. Local Prides don't welcome change, and are not particularly interested in technology.

Blue Collar Owners

Blue Collar Owners consist of families, generally aged between 20 and 34. These households contain a mixture of married and defacto couples, along with the occasional solo parent family. Home values are low and there is a mixture of government owned, privately rented and mortgaged houses. Tertiary qualifications are not common, and the average household income, at $35,000, is below average. Common occupations include agriculture and fisheries, trades and manual jobs. Unemployment is high. Blue Collar Owners are not interested in fashion, nor exercise such as aerobics and running. However, tough team sports such as rugby and rugby league are popular. Blue Collar Owners enjoy entering competitions and using coupons. One luxury is beer, particularly New Zealand beers, which are often consumed with mates. Wine is less popular than with other consumers. These people also enjoy fast food. Blue Collar Owners are sceptical about issues such as globalisation, believing they have yet to see any benefits from the so-called "global community". They are particularly wary of genetically modified food. New technology is not found particularly interesting or important, and internet usage is below average.

Grey Power

Grey Power are the oldest MOSAIC Group, with most aged over 55. Housing types consist of separate houses, flats and retirement homes. These properties have a capital value slightly below average and conditions vary from good to poor. Average household incomes are approximately $29,000. These people are proud of their country and try to buy the New Zealand-made products that they have grown up with, wherever possible. Set in their ways, they are not interested in trying new products often, even when discounted or on special. Grey Power rarely eat out. Instead they enjoy cooking and traditional meals at home. They don't often eat new, or foreign foods. Grey Power are indifferent to new technology, particularly the internet, and usage rates are some of the lowest of all New Zealanders. They enjoy reading magazines, however, and are particularly fond of women's lifestyle and home lifestyle magazines. When it comes to activities, slower games such as lawn bowls and darts are preferred, though they do enjoy watching active sports such as rugby and cricket on TV. They also watch horse racing which they occasionally flutter on. They spend more time watching TV than other consumer groups, though pay television subscriptions are low.

Cultural Diversity

These neighbourhoods are the most culturally diverse, with strong representations of Maori, Pacific Islanders and Asians. Households range from large young families to one-person retirees. Single parents are more commonly found in these neighbourhoods, making use of lower cost services and accommodation. Housing is low cost and below average quality, with the average home value being $139,000. A significant proportion of these people live in government-owned rental accommodation. Education levels are lower, and unemployment is higher, than all other MOSAIC Groups. Workers are usually employed in manual or service occupations, earning an average household income of just under $30,000 per annum. Bargain basement emporiums, factory outlets and traditional stores are favoured, with more expensive items frequently bought on credit. Takeaways and pre-prepared meals are regularly purchased to eat at home. They believe environmentally friendly products are overpriced. Betting on sport and racing is a popular pastime, albeit with minimal disposable income. Cultural Diversity also enjoy watching TV, recording the heaviest television viewing levels of all MOSAIC Groups. Tough sporting activities such as rugby and league appeal to this group.

GROUP I

Rural Lifestyle

Rural Lifestyle are located in country farming areas and rural service towns. This group includes school children with middle-aged parents, with grandparents, ranging in age from 25 to 64. Employment is generally on the farm, however there are lifestyle types within this group, such as Suits & Gumboots, who work in the city while living on lifestyle blocks or "toy farms". Rural Lifestyle types spend a disproportionate amount of time tending the land, and as most live at work, they find it difficult to switch off from their jobs. Average household income is approximately $48,000. Rural Lifestyle like to have traditional meals at home, often eating meat, and rarely buy frozen or ready prepared meals. New Zealand beer is popular, and preferred over wine. Self sufficient, they consider themselves as do-it-yourself kind of people, and are surprisingly adept at using computers and other technology. They are light internet users, however, as the technology is often not practical in remote areas. Rural Lifestyle don't trust the government, feeling the agricultural sector is increasingly neglected in favour of more "fashionable" industries. They enjoy a beer after a hard day and rarely eat at restaurants.

GROUP J

Brand New Houses

Brand New Houses are predominantly found in new subdivisions on the outskirts of the city. Many of these new subdivisions are being built on what was farmland. Some new houses are also found within established areas, where in-fill and higher density housing is occurring as vacant land runs out. These are typically homes built by executive families, but also include some lower cost first homes and retirement homes. Brand New Houses contain a cross section of age groups, and are mainly family households occupying larger than average sized homes. Although these homes are larger than average, mean prices are lower due to lower land prices further away from the central city. There are more Asian and fewer Maori and Pacific Islander new homeowners than elsewhere, and quite a few new homeowners are recent immigrants. Occupations are often managerial, technical or trades oriented. Brand New Houses are slightly more educated than the rest of the population, which results in an above average median household income of approximately $45,500. Internet access is high in these neighbourhoods. Motor vehicle ownership is high, with many households having three or more vehicles, and very few have only one car.

GROUP K

WHO LIVES WHERE?

Suburb	Population in 2001	% Change since 1996	% Aged Under 15 years	% Aged Over 65 Years	% European	% Maori	% Pacific Peoples	% Asian
CENTRAL								
Auckland City	11,193	47.09	4.02	4.10	58.21	6.26	3.92	35.35
Parnell / Newmarket	7,593	7.27	10.27	8.06	88.06	4.61	1.96	9.55
Remuera	18,660	2.68	20.00	12.28	85.39	2.25	1.60	13.25
The Eastern Bays	24,801	3.24	17.54	14.47	86.66	4.86	2.11	9.55
Glen Innes / Pt England	16,125	3.98	26.98	11.81	50.40	16.69	34.29	9.58
Panmure / Mt Wellington	26,046	5.26	23.62	8.81	47.98	17.07	26.02	20.17
Meadowbank	24,348	3.82	17.52	10.95	74.77	5.12	4.54	19.37
One Tree Hill	11,271	5.22	19.11	12.83	73.21	4.18	3.19	23.80
Onehunga	25,890	6.40	20.03	10.76	64.68	9.37	18.38	15.57
Mt Roskill	21,936	6.56	20.91	13.09	52.66	5.67	14.22	31.31
Blockhouse Bay	26,280	5.75	22.45	12.24	52.61	6.20	15.31	30.32
Avondale	25,206	10.40	22.79	10.08	48.68	11.79	26.51	22.68
Grey Lynn	23,778	2.78	18.09	9.85	76.42	8.97	15.51	8.51
Ponsonby	14,415	0.37	14.19	7.62	86.37	6.98	8.53	5.02
Kingsland	5,421	9.57	13.56	3.98	72.67	9.28	16.71	11.12
Mt Albert	28,668	4.58	19.56	9.11	63.29	7.32	12.69	22.18
Mt Eden	26,001	2.25	19.42	7.65	73.90	6.88	7.55	17.17
Epsom	9,846	2.77	20.29	9.57	64.16	2.68	1.91	33.83
Hauraki Gulf Islands	7,242	10.94	20.05	13.84	92.69	11.99	3.39	2.18
NORTH SHORE								
Devonport	7,374	-5.41	21.20	10.74	95.36	5.69	2.01	2.09
Beachhaven / Birkdale	18,603	0.89	24.35	7.76	77.10	14.64	9.57	8.75
Belmont / Bayswater	9,018	-4.26	21.76	13.94	89.77	9.64	2.64	5.15
Takapuna	12,819	2.81	14.86	19.07	86.48	4.19	1.36	10.86
Westlake	20,631	3.74	18.44	14.70	76.62	4.68	2.07	19.39
Lower East Coast Bays	18,456	0.91	19.64	11.64	89.31	2.63	0.77	9.78
Upper East Coast Bays	28,629	12.92	21.21	10.67	88.79	4.52	1.42	9.07
Hibiscus Coast	31,488	14.52	21.34	19.83	94.54	6.97	1.51	2.60
Albany	11,634	37.73	24.32	5.62	86.63	7.36	1.94	8.64
Glenfield	30,099	9.52	22.34	6.74	72.34	8.35	4.77	18.71
Northcote	27,558	3.70	18.79	12.02	76.02	6.21	4.12	17.37

Who lives where? • FACTS & FIGURES

WEST								
New Lynn	42,216	8.02	23.95	9.77	62.45	13.24	19.93	15.72
Titirangi	24,123	2.75	24.06	8.67	91.53	7.56	4.12	4.34
Henderson	50,013	10.75	23.72	10.95	68.16	15.81	15.27	12.26
Swanson	31,485	7.86	27.59	6.04	69.16	16.51	19.35	7.86
West Harbour	16,062	6.97	25.36	5.94	76.83	10.16	8.31	13.13
Kumeu / Huapai	14,745	11.96	24.13	8.16	94.51	7.18	1.84	2.71
West Coast Beaches	6,894	6.14	24.76	5.87	95.38	9.57	2.80	1.77
EAST								
Pakuranga	23,451	2.83	20.23	13.05	68.11	7.15	4.49	25.07
Half Moon Bay	9,153	-0.79	20.78	10.65	73.76	4.46	2.03	22.36
Bucklands Beach	10,875	4.41	21.63	9.57	73.96	2.62	1.35	24.01
Howick	18,888	4.81	20.90	12.74	89.00	3.82	1.44	9.41
Botany Downs	26,064	39.74	22.43	7.39	64.57	3.48	1.60	32.73
Whitford	5,121	6.03	23.73	9.26	94.35	7.43	1.17	1.78
Beachlands / Maeratai	4,422	7.80	25.10	10.38	96.00	8.15	2.11	1.82
SOUTH								
Mangere	53,304	5.45	31.61	6.61	25.94	20.24	57.32	9.67
Otahuhu	39,006	4.58	25.78	10.41	43.12	18.08	29.50	21.34
Otara	16,371	-1.37	35.53	5.24	11.36	22.77	76.57	2.34
Manukau / Clover Park	31,632	13.97	29.46	5.73	37.53	18.74	38.91	17.38
Manurewa	61,434	11.01	28.84	7.04	56.08	28.80	21.33	8.79
Papakura	36,135	3.19	25.58	9.95	73.55	25.69	8.23	5.50
Total	1,092,417	7.73	22.85	9.88	67.35	11.48	14.72	14.37

Source: Statistics New Zealand Census Data 1996 and 2001

FACTS & FIGURES • Who lives where?

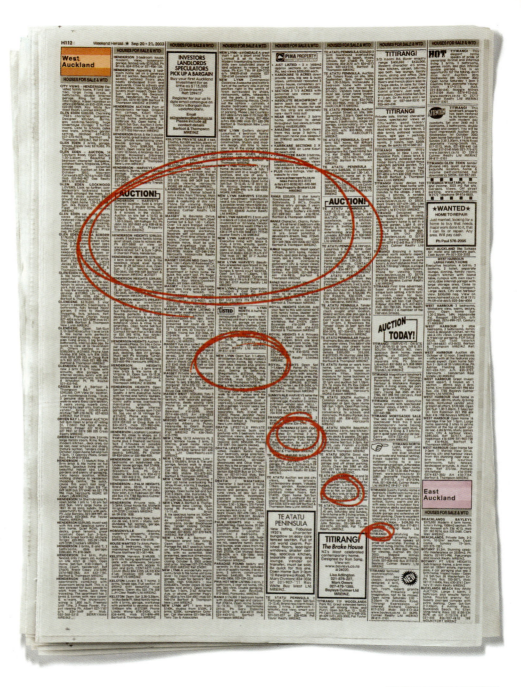

Thinking of buying?

The New Zealand Herald

THERE'S A LOT MORE TO IT

nzherald.co.nz

Tycoons, captains of industry

Remuera
Epsom
Takapuna / Milford
Parnell / Newmarket

Arty, media, intellectual types

Ponsonby
Parnell / Newmarket
Grey Lynn
Kingsland
West Coast Beaches
Devonport
Titirangi

International flavour

Howick (Asian)
Sandringham (Indian)
North Shore (South African and Korean)
West (Croatian and Dutch)
Otara (Pacific Island)
Auckland City (young Asian)
Mt Albert (Somalian)
Botany Downs (Asian)
Epsom (Asian)
Blockhouse Bay (Asian)
Manukau / Clover Park (Pacific Island)
Mangere (Pacific Island)
Mt Roskill (Asian)

Families

Mt Albert
Howick
Pakuranga
Mt Eden
The North Shore
Henderson
New Lynn
Otara
Manukau / Clover Park
Mangere
Mt Roskill / Hillsborough
Epsom
Westlake

First-time buyers and renters

Otahuhu
Otara
Mangere
Manurewa
Glen Innes / Pt England
New Lynn
Papakura

Expensive

Remuera
Epsom
Meadowbank
Ponsonby
Takapuna / Milford
Devonport
Parnell / Newmarket
Eastern Bays
One Tree Hill (Greenlane)

Heritage lovers

Devonport
Ponsonby
Onehunga

Bargain basement

Glen Innes
South Auckland

Young professionals

Auckland City
Ponsonby
Grey Lynn
Meadowbank
Parnell / Newmarket
Onehunga

Seniors

Eastern Bays
Remuera
Mt Roskill
Blockhouse Bay
Hauraki Gulf Islands
Belmont / Bayswater
Pakuranga
Whangaparaoa

Boaties and beach bums

Lower East Coast Bays
Upper East Coast Bays
Eastern Bays
Beachlands / Maraetai
Bucklands Beach
Half Moon Bay
West Harbour
Belmont / Bayswater
West Coast Beaches
Hauraki Gulf Islands
Devonport
Takapuna / Milford
Whangaparaoa

Greenies

Titirangi
Grey Lynn
Swanson
West Coast Beaches
Hauraki Gulf Islands

Country set

Whitford
Kumeu / Huapai
Swanson

Information about New Zealand house prices in one place.

Wondering how the market has affected the value of your house, or the one you're interested in? Or, have you ever asked yourself these questions:

I like that house – I wonder what its value is?

They did a lot of work on that house – I wonder what it sold for?

This area seems really popular – I wonder what type of neighbourhood it is?

Then visit **www.quotable.co.nz**

Simply register so you can access information on nearly any property in New Zealand. Registration is simple, and for Casual Users, free.

Once registered, why not try an e-valuer report. At a cost of only $29.95 (less for Subscribers), the e-valuer report will provide:

• A current estimate of the property's worth

• Up to 10 comparable sales, including the Sale Price and Rating Valuation information

• The property's Rating Valuation and Land Use information.

NB: Due to lack of comparable sales, in some instances e-valuer will not be available.

So, before you consider buying or selling a property, why not increase your knowledge, simply by visiting **www.quotable.co.nz**

HOUSE SALE STATISTICS

What are house prices doing?

A history of house sales is always a good yardstick on which to base your house-buying decisions. None of us wants to pay over the odds for a house but knowing what is reasonable, especially in a buoyant market, can be difficult to assess. While the information on the following pages is based on averages and is therefore broadbrush, it gives some useful guidelines, using three key measurements :

1. Average house prices 2003. Check out the most expensive suburbs, and the cheapest. As with any figures based on averages, these can be skewed by particularly high or low sales prices in the area. They are likely to be more representative where the number of property sales are highest (see Number of Sales figures in each neighbourhood). If, for example, a large terraced housing development was launched and sold at very affordable rates during the year but located in an expensive suburb, it will bring the averages down.

2. House price changes from 2002 to 2003. This shows the percentage increase in each suburb for the year ending July 2003 compared with July 2002. Again, certain sectors of the market, may appear to buck the trend in each area.

3. Average 2003 house prices compared to capital values. Depending on when capital valuations for an area were last made, this can be a particularly good guide to market values. You can determine what premium property is attracting, say, 10% above capital valuation. This may then influence any offer you might make for a property in that area.

N.B.

Average Sale Price : The average net sale price of the properties sold (excludes chattels).

Average Capital Value: The average capital value of the properties sold at the date of latest Rating Valuation.

Source: Quotable Value New Zealand www.quotable.co.nz

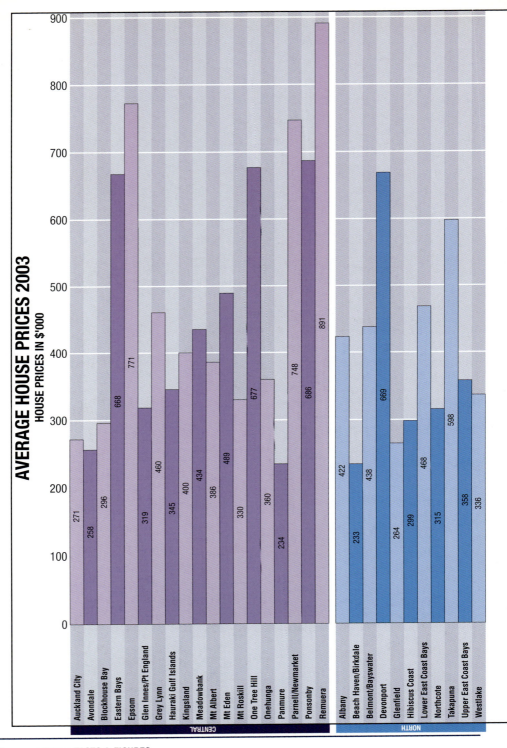

AVERAGE HOUSE PRICES 2003
HOUSE PRICES IN $'000

CENTRAL

Area	Price
Auckland City	271
Avondale	258
Blockhouse Bay	296
Eastern Bays	668
Epsom	771
Glen Innes/Pt England	319
Grey Lynn	460
Hauraki Gulf Islands	345
Kingsland	400
Meadowbank	434
Mt Albert	386
Mt Eden	489
Mt Roskill	330
One Tree Hill	677
Onehunga	360
Panmure	234
Parnell/Newmarket	748
Ponsonby	686
Remuera	891

NORTH

Albany	422
Beach Haven/Birkdale	233
Belmont/Bayswater	438
Devonport	669
Glenfield	264
Hibiscus Coast	299
Lower East Coast Bays	468
Northcote	315
Takapuna	598
Upper East Coast Bays	358
Westlake	336

Average prices • FACTS & FIGURES

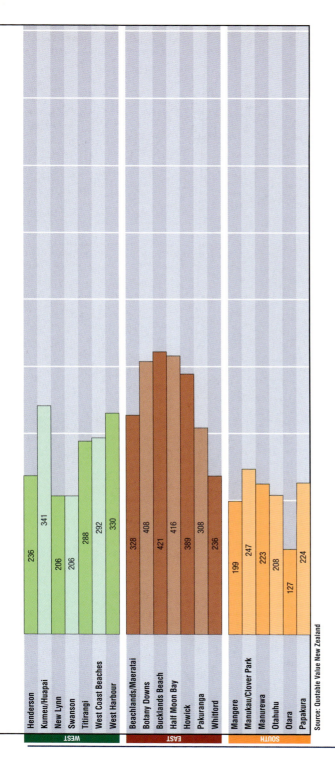

Region	Location	Value
WEST	Henderson	236
WEST	Kumeu/Huapai	341
WEST	New Lynn	206
WEST	Swanson	206
WEST	Titirangi	288
WEST	West Coast Beaches	292
WEST	West Harbour	330
EAST	Beachlands/Maeratai	328
EAST	Botany Downs	408
EAST	Bucklands Beach	421
EAST	Half Moon Bay	416
EAST	Howick	389
EAST	Pakuranga	308
EAST	Whitford	236
SOUTH	Mangere	199
SOUTH	Manukau/Clover Park	247
SOUTH	Manurewa	223
SOUTH	Otahuhu	208
SOUTH	Otara	127
SOUTH	Papakura	224

Source: Quotable Value New Zealand

FACTS & FIGURES • Average prices

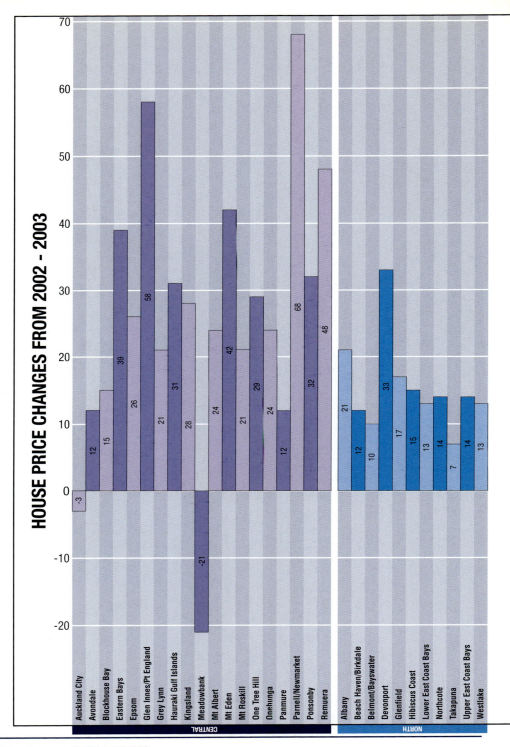

HOUSE PRICE CHANGES FROM 2002 - 2003

CENTRAL

Auckland City	-3
Avondale	12
Blockhouse Bay	15
Eastern Bays	39
Epsom	26
Glen Innes/Pt England	58
Grey Lynn	21
Hauraki Gulf Islands	31
Kingsland	28
Meadowbank	-21
Mt Albert	24
Mt Eden	42
Mt Roskill	21
One Tree Hill	29
Onehunga	24
Panmure	12
Parnell/Newmarket	68
Ponsonby	32
Remuera	48

NORTH

Albany	21
Beach Haven/Birkdale	12
Belmont/Bayswater	10
Devonport	33
Glenfield	17
Hibiscus Coast	15
Lower East Coast Bays	13
Northcote	14
Takapuna	7
Upper East Coast Bays	14
Westlake	13

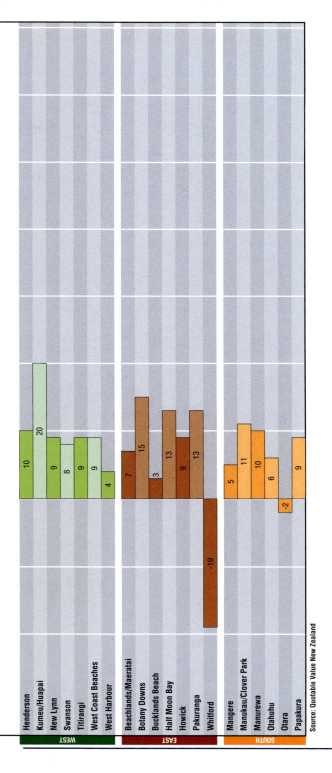

Region	Area	Price change
WEST	Henderson	10
	Kumeu/Huapai	20
	New Lynn	9
	Swanson	8
	Titirangi	9
	West Coast Beaches	9
	West Harbour	4
EAST	Beachlands/Maeraitai	7
	Botany Downs	15
	Bucklands Beach	3
	Half Moon Bay	13
	Howick	9
	Pakuranga	13
	Whitford	-19
SOUTH	Mangere	5
	Manukau/Clover Park	11
	Manurewa	10
	Otahuhu	6
	Otara	-2
	Papakura	9

Source: Quotable Value New Zealand

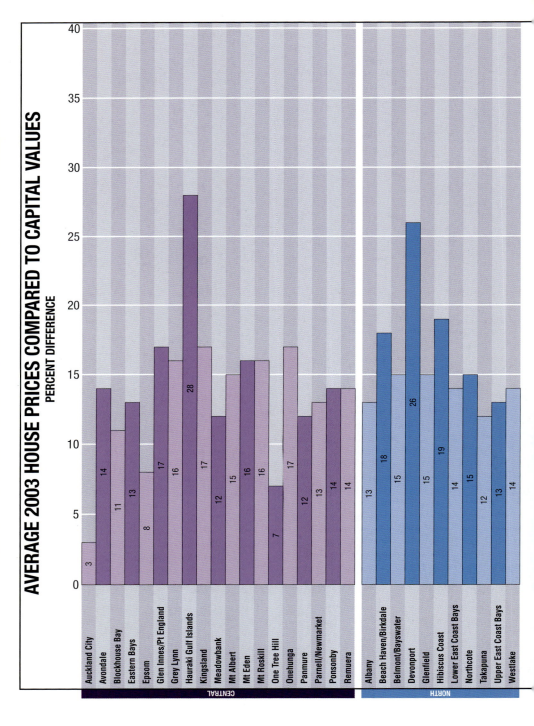

AVERAGE 2003 HOUSE PRICES COMPARED TO CAPITAL VALUES
PERCENT DIFFERENCE

CENTRAL

Area	Percent Difference
Auckland City	3
Avondale	14
Blockhouse Bay	11
Eastern Bays	13
Epsom	8
Glen Innes/Pt England	17
Grey Lynn	16
Hauraki Gulf Islands	28
Kingsland	17
Meadowbank	12
Mt Albert	15
Mt Eden	16
Mt Roskill	16
One Tree Hill	7
Onehunga	17
Panmure	12
Parnell/Newmarket	13
Ponsonby	14
Remuera	14

NORTH

Area	Percent Difference
Albany	13
Beach Haven/Birkdale	18
Belmont/Bayswater	15
Devonport	26
Glenfield	15
Hibiscus Coast	19
Lower East Coast Bays	14
Northcote	15
Takapuna	12
Upper East Coast Bays	13
Westlake	14

Capital values • FACTS & FIGURES

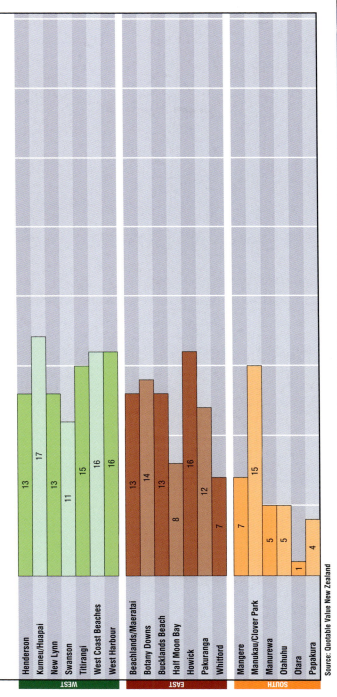

WEST	
Henderson	13
Kumeu/Huapai	17
New Lynn	13
Swanson	11
Titirangi	15
West Coast Beaches	16
West Harbour	16
EAST	
Beachlands/Maeratai	13
Botany Downs	14
Bucklands Beach	13
Half Moon Bay	8
Howick	16
Pakuranga	12
Whitford	7
SOUTH	
Mangere	7
Manukau/Clover Park	15
Manurewa	5
Otahuhu	5
Otara	1
Papakura	4

Source: Quotable Value New Zealand

AUCKLAND'S SCHOOLS

If you have school-age children, good schools are pretty high on the list of lifestyle factors to take into account when you're choosing where to buy a home. Auckland has many excellent schools, but as the city's school-age population has mushroomed, access to good schools - or more specifically, the school of your choice - can't be taken for granted these days. And this has had a huge impact on the real estate market, in particular in the suburbs around prestigious state schools like Auckland Grammar and Epsom Girls' Grammar.

In the past decade, student numbers at many of the city's most popular schools have rocketed, reflecting both a school's outstanding reputation and the increased numbers of families living locally. To limit school size and prevent overcrowding, the Ministry of Education has introduced a system of enrolment schemes - which means oversubscribed schools can have a home zone with clearly defined boundaries. If you live within the home zone, the school legally has to accept your child as a student.

If you don't live in a particular school's zone, but would still like your child to attend that school, most schools have a few out-of-zone places available by ballot - applications close in September for the following year. Currently around 25% of Auckland schools (including primary, intermediate and secondary) have enrolment schemes - but the best known and most popular ones certainly do.

The result of all this is that parents keen to send their children to prestigious state schools are clamouring to buy a family home in the right zone. They may not be paying private school fees, but they will certainly pay a premium for living in-zone. Real estate agents estimate, for example, that you will generally pay up to $100,000 more for a property in the Auckland Grammar School zone. The consolation is that these houses are seen as an investment. Once the kids are past school age, the house can be on-sold, with a heftier price tag - as long as the zone hasn't changed, that is.

Some families opt out of the zoning problem by sending their children to private schools - the premium they would pay for an in-zone home goes a fair way towards private school fees, buying a larger property in a non-zone area, better lifestyle opportunities, etc. See our guide to private schools later in this section.

There are a number of factors to take into account when assessing local schools. Most schools now have their own websites with up-to-date zoning details and enrolment information. Another source of information is the Education Review Office, which regularly reports on individual schools, and publishes its findings at www.ero.govt.nz.

The Ministry of Education publishes schools' academic results - these are worth looking at for purposes of comparison (see our charts later in this section). However, bear in mind that currently the national assessment system is in transition, with the phasing in of the new NCEA over 2003-2005 (see below).

Another official measurement you'll come across with schools is the decile rating. A school's decile rating is based on census information and reflects the socio-economic level of the population from which the school draws its students - not academic results. Schools are rated from 1 to 10 - low decile means a higher proportion of students come from low socio-economic groups. Factors determining decile ratings are household income, occupation, crowding levels, tertiary educational qualifications, income support levels and ethnicity.

A school's decile rating may change, reflecting the area's changing population.

Lower decile schools get more government funding than higher decile schools. (This means higher decile schools need to do more parent-driven fundraising and will also charge higher school fees or "donations" - which aren't legally compulsory, but are important to a school's budget.)

What is the NCEA?

The NCEA is the New Zealand high school system's rather controversial new assessment regime. It is currently being phased into schools - Level 1 (for Year 11) was introduced in 2002, Level 2 (Year 12) in 2003 and Level 3 (Year 13) is on schedule for 2004.

NCEA stands for National Certificate of Educational Achievement, and it is intended to completely replace the old system of exams and certificates with standards-based assessment (or SBA), which evaluates students against a standard, rather than in competition with each other. Students are given grades of Excellence, Merit, Credit or Incomplete, rather than marks or percentage ratings. It involves a combination of end-of-year exams run by the NZ Qualifications Authority, internal tests and assignments.

Some school principals are very much opposed to the NCEA, arguing that it will result in lowering standards and a loss of competitive edge. Some schools (including Auckland Grammar, King's College and Macleans College in Howick) have opted to offer the English-based Cambridge International Examinations instead of the NCEA, or alongside it. However the Cambridge exams are geared to the British school system, and there are concerns that while this overseas qualification is internationally recognised, it doesn't have any New Zealand content.

The private co-ed St Kentigern College, which has opted to work with the NCEA, says on its website, "we have determined that following a New Zealand curriculum is the key element in obtaining a high quality New Zealand education".

Other educationalists, including Pakuranga College principal Bali Haque, have gone on record to support the NCEA, saying the old system did not recognise many students' achievements, and the new system will be a much better way to meet the needs of a wider range than just the academic elite. (The old system was designed when many New Zealand students left school at 16 (Year 11) to enter the workforce, but these days a much larger proportion are remaining at school to Year 13 and hoping to go on to tertiary education.)

Adding to the controversy, teachers have been very concerned that the NCEA will greatly increase the amount of paperwork they need to do and will sap their energy for actually teaching students.

The NCEA is here to stay, but it's currently very much in a settling-in stage, and it seems likely that there will be some fine-tuning over the next few years.

Until the dust settles, judging a school's success based on NCEA results will be tricky. Auckland Grammar comments on its website that "it is very difficult to meaningfully analyse these results. The results thrown up show very little correlation between externally and internally assessed achievement standards."

The academically very successful Rangitoto College, on the other hand, says the NCEA is giving students a chance to gain credit "for skills that were not previously assessed. It also provides them with a challenge - ie taking greater responsibility for their assessment."

The school zone maps on the following pages are designed to enable you to see which public secondary schools your children may be eligible for. We strongly recommend, however, that you contact the school to confirm the zone status of any particular street - or check the school's website. The star on each map shows the location of the school.

If a public high school is not on these pages, that means it doesn't have a defined zone, so its roll is open to all-comers. Please contact your local school for more details. See our NCEA, University Entrance etc charts later in this section for a list of Auckland schools. They're grouped by region so you can compare schools in your area.

If you're considering a private school, we've compiled a list of Auckland's main private schools, including fees and other details.

We have also chosen a few of Auckland's most talked-about secondary schools to profile on these pages - the top public schools, a top private school, two of the new breed of private schools, the biggest public college and one that's been hitting the news.

ALFRISTON COLLEGE
7 Hill Rd, Manurewa
Tel: 64 9 266 8982
www.alfristoncollege.school.nz

Zone boundary: Starting at the Gt South Rd, Hill Rd intersection the zone travels northeast up the centre of Hill Rd until the motorway bridge is reached. From there the zone travels north, following the boundaries of the botanical gardens and Totara Park (the zone does not include the suburbs of Totara Heights or Goodwood Heights). The northern boundary of the zone is the intersection of Totara Park, Redoubt Rd and Hilltop Rd. From this point the zone moves east, encompassing both sides of Redoubt Rd (and its side streets) and travels northeast (excluding Bownhill Rd) and intersects Whitford Park Rd at the bridge. The northeast direction is followed until the end of Ara Kotinga is reached and then travels southeast until it reaches the Clevedon Scenic Reserve. From the Clevedon Scenic Reserve the zone travels southwest, intersecting Twilight Rd at the Quarry, and West Rd at their highest point, then continuing southwest along the Watershed until the intersection of Alfriston-Ardmore Rd with Clevedon-Takanini Rd. From here the zone travels south down the centre of Alfriston-Ardmore Rd until Airfield Rd. From there down the centre of Airfield Rd until Takanini School Rd and then down the centre of Taka St. From the Gt South Rd/Taka St intersection the zone moves northwards through the centre of Gt South Rd until Hill Rd is reached.

AUCKLAND GRAMMAR SCHOOL
Mountain Rd, Newmarket
Tel: 64 9 623 5400
www.ags.school.nz

Zone boundary: Northern boundary is the south side of Victoria St East from the Queen St intersection; Bowen St (south side), Waterloo Quadrant (south side) and Alten Rd (south side). Left into Stanley St (east side) and the Strand (south side), and north to Mechanics Bay. Western boundary is the east side of Queen St, Upper Queen St, Exmouth St, New North Rd to Dominion Rd. The east side of Dominion Rd to Grange Rd. Both sides of Grange Rd. South into Henley Rd (both sides) to Balmoral Rd. The north side of Balmoral Rd to Mt Eden Rd. The east side of Mt Eden Rd to Landscape Rd. Southern boundary is Landscape Rd (both sides), Selwyn Rd (both sides), Glenferrie Pl (both sides) and Rostrevor Ave (both sides) to Pah Rd. Both sides of Pah Rd and Manukau Rd to Golf Rd (both sides) and Fern Rd (both sides). The western boundary of Cornwall Park to Claude Rd, and thereafter in a direct line from the Cornwall Park end of Claude Rd to the intersection of Greenlane West and Pohutakawa Dr. The north side of Greenlane West to the intersection of Wheturangi Rd. Greenlane West (north side) from Wheturangi Rd to Great South Rd, and then Greenlane East (north side) to the intersection with Remuera Rd. Remuera Rd (north side) to Upland Rd. Eastern boundary is Upland Rd (west side) to the northern intersection with Orakei Rd to Hobson Bay, and the western foreshore of Hobson Bay to Judges Bay and Mechanics Bay.

Pinpoint Map data supplied by Critchlow Associates Ltd and contains material subject to Crown copyright

Auckland Grammar is Auckland's highest-profile school in more ways than one. It's a state school with lots of status - it carries all the born-to-win authority of the best private school (and then some). The "grammar zone" takes in some of Auckland's top suburbs - and the school's reputation is responsible for adding a substantial price premium to properties in those already desirable areas. Plenty of parents keen to make sure their sons get top education and sporting opportunities in a traditional all-male school think the investment is worth it. Auckland Grammar occupies a prominent chunk of real estate on the slopes of Mt Eden, with a historic Mission-style main building overlooking the motorway. (The school also boasts an outdoor education centre in Ohakune.) The school is mega-high-profile in educational achievement - its students top the exam tables year after year. In 2002 it grabbed 21% of the university scholarships awarded for the whole country. Grammar's principal, John Morris, has been one of the strongest critics of the NCEA system and the school is offering the Cambridge International examinations, to ensure its students' qualifications are internationally recognised.

Former students are a veritable Auckland old-boys' network of business leaders, doctors, lawyers, judges, rugby and cricket stars, including famed All Black captain Wilson Whineray, actor and Auckland Festival director Simon Prast, and Maori leader Professor Sir Hugh Kawharu of Ngati Whatua - and the school also lays claim to the most famous living New Zealander, Sir Edmund Hillary, the man who conquered Mt Everest.

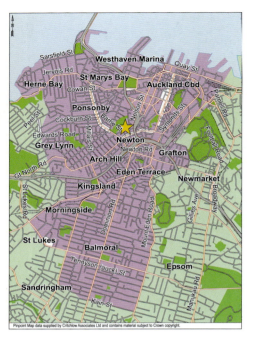

AUCKLAND GIRLS' GRAMMAR SCHOOL
Howe St, Newton
Tel: 64 9 307 4180
www.aggs.school.nz

Zone boundary: From Waitemata Harbour via the Strand, Stanley St, Grafton Rd, Nugent St to Mt Eden Rd taking in Park Rd and Boston Rd and the streets in between. Along Mt Eden Rd to Landscape Rd, along Landscape Rd to Lambeth Rd to Sandringham Rd. Along Sandringham Rd to St Lukes Rd. Along St Lukes Rd to New North Rd. Along New North Rd to Kingsland Ave. Along Kingsland Ave to the north-western motorway. From the corner of Great North Rd and Surrey Cres up Selbourne St including Dryden St, Cockburn St, Jessel and Farrar St. From Farrar St along Richmond Rd to Cox's Creek (Bayfield Park side) to Marine Pde along Marine Pde to the harbour. Both sides of all streets on the boundaries are included.

AVONDALE COLLEGE
Victor St, Avondale
Tel: 64 9 828 7024
www.avcol.school.nz

Zone boundary: From Oakley Creek to the junction of Great North Rd and Carrington Rd; the western side of Carrington Rd to the railway, along the railway to Woodward Rd. Both sides of Richardson Rd to the corner of Maioro St, across New Windsor Rd and Whitney St to both sides of Holbrook St. Across Blockhouse Bay Rd to both sides of Miranda St; across to the Whau Creek and Great North Rd; the rest of Rosebank Peninsula.

BOTANY DOWNS SECONDARY COLLEGE
575 Chapel Rd, Botany Downs
Tel: 64 9 273 2310
www.bdsc.school.nz

Zone boundary: Millhouse Dr - even numbers only from 130-182, Botany Rd - from the Millhouse Dr intersection south to Te Irirangi Dr. Starting from the Mangemangeroa Bridge, the boundary follows Whitford Rd (both sides included) westward until Chapel Rd. From there southward down the centre of Chapel Rd to the intersection with Kilimanjaro Dr. From there westwards along Kilimanjaro Dr (including Matterhorn Cres and streets off it) to the intersection with Milhouse Dr. From there southwards along the centre of Milhouse Dr to the intersection with Botany Rd. From there westwards along the southern margin of the Pakuranga Country Club Golf Course to the bank of the Pakuranga Creek. From there southwards along the eastern bank of the creek and stream to intersect with Ti Rakau Dr and Huntington Dr. From there southward across country until the intersection of Smales Rd and Sir William Ave. (Inclusive of Huntington Dr, Guys Rd and all the streets directly feeding off them.) The boundary then follows, but excludes Sir William Ave, Lady Ruby Dr and Accent Dr until it intersects with Ti Irirangi Dr. From there eastwards across country until the intersection of Chapel Rd and Baverstock Rd. Along Baverstock Rd (both sides) and across country to Inchinamm Rd (both sides) until the intersection with Gracechurch Dr. From there eastward across country until the intersection of Sandstone Rd and Whitford Rd. South-eastward along Whitford Rd (both sides, including Brownhill Rd) until Polo Lane (included). From there follow the Whitford-Maraetai Rd (both sides included) eastward until the intersection with Henson Rd. From there head north to the coast and follow the coast westward until the Mangemangeroa Bridge.

EDGEWATER COLLEGE
Edgewater Dr, Pakuranga
Tel: 64 9 576 9039
www.edgewater.school.nz

Zone boundary: Left hand-side of the Pakuranga Highway. Gossamer Dr to Pakuranga Creek then Harris Rd. Crook Rd to Highbrook Dr. Tamaki River to the Panmure Bridge.

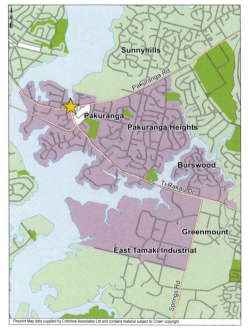

Map data supplied by Critchlow Associates Ltd and contains material subject to Crown copyright

EPSOM GIRLS' GRAMMAR SCHOOL
Silver Rd, Epsom
Tel: 64 9 630 5963
www.eggs.school.nz

Zone boundary: The area bounded by Upland Rd (from the harbour), Remuera Rd, Greenlane East, Greenlane West, around One Tree Hill as far south as Golf Rd, to Manukau Rd, to Pah Rd to Selwyn Rd via St Andrews Rd to Landscape Rd, to Mt Eden Rd to Balmoral Rd. Balmoral Rd to Dominion Rd, to Valley Rd to Horoeka Ave, to View Rd to Mt Eden Rd to Normanby Rd, Boston Rd to Khyber Pass to Park Rd to Carlton Gore Rd, George St and along the eastern side of the Auckland Domain, to Parnell Rd, The Strand to the harbour at Mechanics Bay. (Note: houses on both sides of the road on the boundaries plus any cul-de-sacs off an included road are in the zone.)

Epsom Girls' Grammar is the girls' equivalent to Auckland Grammar - perhaps not as high-profile, but every bit as popular and also very successful in educational terms. It is one of New Zealand's premier girls' schools, and also one of the largest, with around 1900 students.

Like Auckland Grammar, the EGGS home zone takes in some of the city's most desirable suburbs. (Warning: both schools may have their zones cut in a few years' time, to allow for a proposed new co-ed high school adjacent to Cornwall Park scheduled to open in 2006.) Epsom Girls' is on a pleasant 7.2 hectare campus between Gillies Ave and the Newmarket end of Manukau Rd - the site is actually a bit of a squeeze for the current size of the school.

EGGS has long been respected for the high quality state education it delivers to young women, aiming for an ideal mix of traditional and modern. Its success is reflected in its exam results, and in the performance of its students in tertiary education. The school reports that 98% of its Year 13 students go on to university or other tertiary study. It has a great reputation for teaching languages - all Year 9 students study a second language. Arts and music are also strong, with an award-winning school orchestra, instrumental groups, choirs and jazz band. Epsom Girls' students regularly work together with Auckland Grammar boys to present stage shows and drama productions.

A couple of Epsom Girls' Grammar's more famous ex-students are Prime Minister Helen Clark (a boarder at the school's on-site hostel, Epsom House) and Green Party co-leader Jeanette Fitzsimons.

GLENDOWIE COLLEGE

Crossfield Rd, Glendowie
Tel: 64 9 575 9128
www.glendowie-college.school.nz

Zone boundary: In Glendowie and St Heliers, the area bounded by West Tamaki Rd, Grampian Rd, Allum St from Grampian Rd, Melanesia Rd from Allum St to Sage Rd, Sage Rd and the coastline from Sage Rd to West Tamaki Rd. Both sides of the boundary road are included.
In St Johns Park, the area bounded by St Johns Rd, Remuera Rd, Koraha St, Abbotts Way and College Rd (these boundary roads are excluded and therefore not considered to be within the zone).

HOWICK COLLEGE

Sandspit Rd, Howick
Tel: 64 9 534 4492
www.howickcollege.school.nz

Zone boundary: *Year 9 (2004)*
From Howick Beach via Uxbridge Rd (included), Picton St and Ridge Rd (both excluded). From Howick Intermediate School to Golflands Dr along Botany Rd (excluded). Golflands Dr and all side streets (included) and continuing south down Botany Rd (included). From the end of Botany Rd, east along Ti Rakau Dr until Chapel Rd. North along Chapel Rd until Whitford Rd (Kingsgate included), east along Whitford Rd (including The Mews) until Mangemangeroa Bridge. From there down Whitford Rd (including all roads leading off it) and down Whitford Park Rd as far as Ara-Kotinga (including Ara-Kotinga, Brownhill Rd and Polo Lane), and beyond within walking distance of the Ara-Kotinga bus stop. From Whitford Rd, along Whitford-Maraetai Rd until the end of Maretai Dr (including all roads leading off it).

Zone boundary: *Year 10 -13 (2004)*
From Howick Beach via Uxbridge Rd (included), Picton St and Ridge Rd (both excluded). From Howick Intermediate School to Golflands Dr along Botany Rd (excluded). Golflands Dr and all side streets (included) and continuing south down Botany Rd (included). Then to the intersection of Chapel Rd and Kilkenny Dr (included) continuing to Middlefield Dr (included) and on to the intersection with Point View Dr and including all of the Point View Dr and side roads. From Point View Dr, down Whitford Rd (including all streets leading off it) and down Whitford Park Rd as far as Ara-Kotinga (including Ara-Kotinga, Brownhill Rd and Polo Lane) and beyond within walking distance of the Ara-Kotinga school bus stop. From Whitford Rd, along Whitford-Maraetai Rd until the end of Maretai Dr (including all roads leading off it).

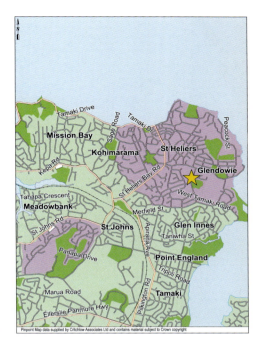

LYNFIELD COLLEGE

White Swan Rd, Mt Roskill
Tel: 64 9 627 0600
www.lynfield.school.nz

Zone boundary: Along Dominion Rd Extension, through Richardson Rd, May Rd (not included), Stoddard Rd (not included), Mairoro St (not included) through Trevola St, across Holbrook St (not included), Miranda St (not included), Wolverton St (not included) and down Taylor St (not included). For a full list of street names within the zone boundary please visit the Lynfield College website.

MACLEANS COLLEGE

Macleans Rd, Bucklands Beach
Tel: 64 9 535 2620
www.macleans.school.nz

Zone boundary: A line from Howick Beach via Uxbridge Rd (both sides excluded), Picton St, Ridge Rd (1-47, 6-60 included) and Bleakhouse Rd (both sides included) to Gills Rd, then via Gills Rd (both sides excluded and with Udall Pl and other no exit streets off Gills Rd similarly excluded) to the junction of Pigeon Mountain Rd. Via Pigeon Mountain Rd (1-69, 2-60 included) and to the end of Ara Tai Pl (both sides included).

MANUREWA HIGH SCHOOL
67 Browns Rd, Manurewa
Tel: 64 9 268 3888
www.manurewa.school.nz

Zone boundary: Northern boundary: Redoubt Rd, Wiri Station Rd to Roscommon Rd. Western boundary: cnr Wiri Station Rd along Roscommon Rd to Browns Rd. Manukau Harbour coastline from Browns Rd to Burundi Ave. Southern boundary: Burundi Ave, Wordsworth Ave to Swallow Dr. Russell Rd to Weymouth Rd east along Weymouth Rd. Alfriston Rd to Brookby/Alfriston. Eastern boundary: Brookby Alfriston.

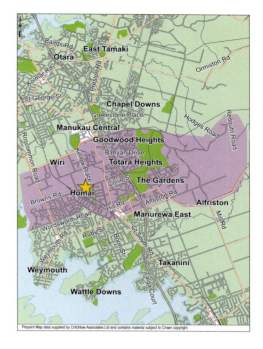

MASSEY HIGH SCHOOL
274 Don Buck Rd, Massey
Tel: 64 9 831 0500
www.masseyhigh.school.nz

Zone boundary: Northern boundary is Muriwai Beach, Muriwai Rd and side roads to Waimauku. Matua Rd, Deacon Rd, Cobblers Lane to Wake Rd. Eastern boundary is Waitemata Harbour. Southern boundary is the bottom of Don Buck Rd, Chamberlain Rd, Crows Rd, Kay Rd, Waitakere Rd, ANZAC Valley Rd and side roads, Te Henga Rd and side roads, Bethells Rd to Bethells Beach.

Pinpoint Map data supplied by Critchlow Associates Ltd and contains material subject to Crown copyright

MT ROSKILL GRAMMAR
Frost Rd, Mt Roskill
Tel: 64 9 621 0050
www.mrgs.school.nz

Zone boundary: From the Manukau Harbour via Waikowhai Rd and Hillsborough Rd (both excluded) to Dominion Rd Extension; via Dominion Rd Extension (excluded) to Richardson Rd; thence via Richardson Rd (excluded), May Rd and Stoddard Rd (both included) to Sandringham Rd; via Sandringham Rd (excluded) to Mt Albert Rd; via Mt Albert Rd (included), Renfrew Ave (excluded), Invermay Ave (included), Landscape Rd (excluded); via St Andrews Rd (excluded) to Mt Albert Rd (included); then via Hillsborough Rd (excluded) to Hillsborough Cemetery/Richardson Rd corner and Manukau Harbour.

In the past decade or so, **Mt Roskill Grammar** has grown from a relatively low-profile suburban co-ed to a school with a city-wide and even national reputation. In 2002 Mt Roskill Grammar was named Goodman Fielder Secondary School of the Year, reflecting the school's successes across the curriculum. It's now one of the most sought-after high schools on the Auckland isthmus - family homes in the Mt Roskill zone are in huge demand.

Mt Roskill is one of Auckland's bigger co-ed schools, with around 2500 students on the Frost Rd campus, alongside separate primary and intermediate schools. The school offers a top-quality array of facilities, cultural and sporting activities to match its size, including 16 new science labs, six new computer rooms, a fully equipped music suite, floodlit artificial turf, fitness centre and two gyms.

Students reflect the rainbow cultural mix of the surrounding suburbs - 30% Pakeha, 19% Chinese, 18% Indian, 4% Maori, 8% Samoan, and 5% Tongan, among others. Academic standards are high, with the school producing the nation's top scholar in 2002. Mt Roskill Grammar aims to meet the needs of students with a wide range of abilities and interests.

Mt Roskill Grammar was established in the 1950s to cater for the post-war baby boom in the then-new surrounding suburbs. In 1993 it celebrated its 50th Jubilee.

Mt Roskill Grammar's most famous former student just has to be Academy Award-winning actor Russell Crowe - a couple of other notables are Auckland City Councillor and yachtswoman Penny Whiting and former All Black coach John Hart.

MT ALBERT GRAMMAR SCHOOL
Alberton Ave, Mt Albert
Tel: 64 9 846 2044
www.mags.school.nz

Zone boundary: The northern boundary is the north-western motorway. Then all areas north of the junction of the north-western motorway and Carrington Rd, via Carrington Rd, to New North Rd, to Richardson Rd, to Stoddard Rd, to Sandringham Rd extension, to Mount Albert Rd, to Renfrew Rd, to Invermay Ave, to Landscape Rd, to Mount Eden Rd, to Symonds St, to the motorway. All no exit roads off the boundaries are included in the zone.

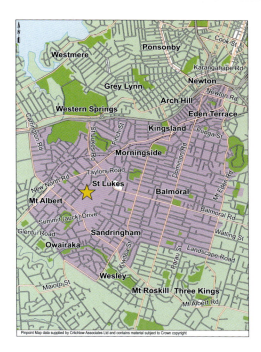

NORTHCOTE COLLEGE
Kauri Glen Rd, Northcote
Tel: 64 9 481 0141
www.northcote.school.nz

Zone boundary: Home zone is from Balmain Rd, Mokoia Rd, Roseberry Ave, Parkhill Rd, Glenfield Rd. Coronation Rd, Archers Rd, Sunnybrae Rd, Northcote Rd, the motorway to the Harbour Bridge and the harbour to Kauri Pt Domain and Balmain Rd.

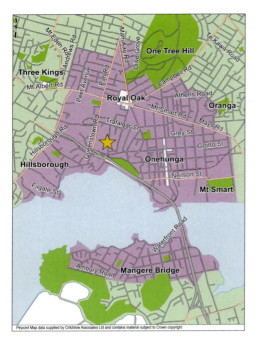

Pinpoint Map data supplied by Critchlow Associates Ltd and contains material subject to Crown copyright

ONEHUNGA HIGH SCHOOL

Pleasant St, Onehunga
Tel: 64 9 636 6006
www.ohs.school.nz

Zone boundary: On the northern side of the Manukau Harbour the boundary runs from Hillsborough Cemetery via Hillsborough Rd (including both sides), St Andrews Rd to Selwyn Rd, Pah Rd and Ngaroma Rd (included in each case) to One Tree Hill Domain; from the domain across Campbell Rd at its intersection with Moana Ave - then via Moana Rd, Namata Rd, Curzon St, Mays Rd and Captain Springs Rd (included in each case) to the Manukau Harbour. South of the Manukau Harbour the boundary follows a line south of Ambury Rd, Taylor Rd, Domain Rd and Hastie Ave so that both sides of these streets, and the no exit streets leading off them, are included.

Pinpoint Map data supplied by Critchlow Associates Ltd and contains material subject to Crown copyright

OTAHUHU COLLEGE

Mangere Rd, Otahuhu
Tel: 64 9 270 1170
www.otahuhucollege.school.nz

Zone boundary: The northern boundary line goes from Anns Creek at Westfield, along the railway line through Sylvia Park on a direct line to the Tamaki River. The other boundary line begins at the Favona Bridge over Harania Creek to the junction of Massey Rd (up to and including 240 and 249) and Gray Ave, along Gray Ave (both sides included in the Otahuhu College zone up to and including 102 and 115A) to the railway line, along the railway line and across Swaffield Rd (62 and 41 and over) and the Grange Gold Course (so that Middlemore Cres is included), then to the motorway (Motatau Rd is excluded and Bairds Rd east until the motorway is included) and along the motorway to the Tamaki River.

PAKURANGA COLLEGE

Pigeon Mountain Rd, Bucklands Beach
Tel: 64 9 534 7159
www.pakuranga.school.nz

Zone boundary: Western boundary is from the Tamaki River around the eastern boundary of St Kentigern College to the Pakuranga Main Highway so that Grammar School Rd is included, then along Pakuranga Rd to the Pakuranga Creek, with the northern side of the main highway included; along the line of the creek using Pakuranga Creek and its tributaries as the southern boundary as far as it can be taken, then taking a straight line to the intersection of Ti Rakau Dr with Botany Rd, including those streets coming west from Botany Rd and excluding Ti Rakau Dr and any streets coming from it. Northern boundary commences at Half Moon Bay then via Ara Tai and Pigeon Mountain Rds (both excluded) to the junction of Gills Rd, then via Gills Rd to Bleakhouse Rd, along Bleakhouse Rd (excluded) to Ridge Rd and along Ridge and Botany Rds (both included).

PAPATOETOE HIGH SCHOOL

Nicholson Ave, Papatoetoe
Tel: 64 9 278 4086
www.papatoetoehigh.school.nz

Zone boundary: To the east, the zone is defined by the southern motorway. To the south, by Wiri Station Rd. To the west, by Roscommon Rd, Wyllie Rd (including Fenton St, Romford St and 296 Puhinui Rd) and then the railway line (excluding Station Rd). To the north, by a line following the Tamaki inlet from 27 Swaffield Rd to 753 Great South Rd, Otahuhu (including Grange Rd, Laureston Ave and adjoining streets) and then in a straight line from Motatau Rd to the southern motorway.

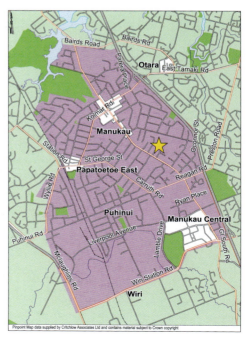

Pinpoint Map data supplied by Critchlow Associates Ltd and contains material subject to Crown copyright

RANGITOTO COLLEGE

564 East Coast Rd, Browns Bay
Tel: 64 9 477 0150
www.rangitoto.school.nz

Zone boundary: From Browns Bay via Anzac Rd (excluded) and Glencoe Rd (included) to the bridge over the Taiatoa Creek and then via John Downs Dr to East Coast Rd so that John Downs Dr and all no-exit streets off it are excluded from the enrolment area. Then via Andersons Rd (excluded), the southern boundary of the sports fields to the junction of Masons Rd and Oteha Valley Rd, then via Oteha Valley Rd (excluded) to the motorway and south via the motorway to Sunset Rd (excluded to the junction of Juniper Rd), to East Coast Rd and then via East Coast Rd (included) to the southern boundary of Pupuke Golf Course, along the southern boundary of the golf course, excluding Aberdeen Rd and Rae Rd, to Beach Rd at the intersection of Red Bluff Rise (included) to the sea.

On a ridge overlooking the prosperous suburb of Mairangi Bay on Auckland's North Shore, *Rangitoto College* is not just the biggest school in Auckland, with a whopping 3000 plus students - it's the biggest secondary school in the country. It's the most popular state school on the shore - a high-performing co-ed that's in big demand among shore families, longstanding residents and new migrants alike.

High-profile principal Allan Peachey leads a hugely successful staff team with a good reputation for meeting the needs of students with a wide range of learning abilities. Rangitoto has a strong tradition of academic excellence, with outstanding results in national examinations. The school's size means it has superb international-class facilities (including a new auditorium and an Olympic-standard hockey turf) and can offer a wide range of study options, both traditional and modern. Despite the large number of students, the school aims to be warm, personal and friendly, and manages to make sure each student is catered for as an individual.

Rangitoto's student body provides a snapshot of the local community demographics - 70% Pakeha, 8% South African, 8% Korean, 8% Chinese and Taiwanese.

Sports activities are high-profile here - last year, Rangitoto students boasted no fewer than 20 national sporting titles. The school offers a Sports Talent Development Programme, which aims to support talented and committed students to achieve success in sports without sacrificing academic achievement.

ROSEHILL COLLEGE
Edinburgh Ave, Papakura
Tel: 64 9 295 0661
www.rosehill-college.co.nz

Zone boundary: Western rural boundary Waiau Beach, Manukau Harbour, Pahurehure Inlet. Southern rural boundary (west of motorway): North bank of Taihiki River to Glenbrook Rd. Both sides of Glenbrook Rd. All areas between Glenbrook and Karaka Rds and Manukau Harbour, Gellert Rd, Sim Rd, Bycroft Rd, Woodlyn Rd, Snelgars Rd, Burtt Rd to intersection with Needham Rd (from 155 Burtt Rd onwards), Needham Rd, Solataire Rd, Cheriton Lane, Runciman Rd to the intersection with Coulston (from 377 Runciman Rd onwards, not 368 Runciman Rd). Tuhimata Rd to the first stream from the Runciman/Tuhimata intersection (includes 479 Tuhimata Rd), Ingram Rd. Southern rural boundary (east of motorway): Ararimu Rd to intersection with Dunn Rd includes Dale, Maxted, Fausett, Turner Rd, Steel Rd, Ponga Rd to intersection with McEntee Rd (includes all roads off Ponga Rd up to and including McEntee Rd, from the Opaheke Rd end). Urban boundary Manurewa/ Takanini motorway inter-change, Manukau Harbour, Pahurehure Inlet, east of motorway, main trunk railway line.

RUTHERFORD COLLEGE
Kotuku St, Te Atatu Peninsula
Tel: 64 9 834 9790
www.rutherford.school.nz

Zone boundary: The proposed Rutherford College home zone starts at Lincoln Bridge (Triangle Rd), following a line down the centre of Lincoln Rd South until the railway line. Along the railway line south until View Rd. Along the centre of View Rd turning south into Great North Rd. Along the centre of Great North Rd turning east into Hepburn Rd. Along the centre of Hepburn Rd until the Whau River. Along the coast of the peninsula until reaching the Lincoln Bridge.

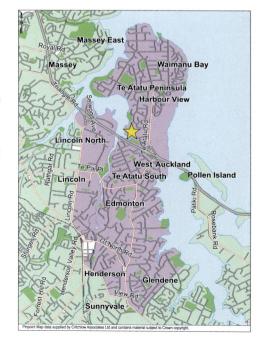

TAKAPUNA GRAMMAR SCHOOL
210 Lake Rd, Takapuna
Tel: 64 9 489 4167
www.takapuna.school.nz

Zone boundary: The Devonport peninsula from King Edward Pde and Jubilee Ave north to a boundary defined by and including Northcote Rd and its intersection with the northern motorway, Shea Tce and the southern shores of Lake Pupuke including Hurstmere Rd, Kitchener Rd and all side roads up to and including Fenwick Ave, Otakau Rd, Omana Rd and Craig Rd.

WAITAKERE COLLEGE
42 Rathgar Rd, Henderdon
Tel: 64 9 836 7890
www.waitakere.college.net.nz

Zone boundary: The Waitakere College home zone boundary starts to the north of Bethells Beach. Starting at Te Waharoa Pt the boundary is a north eastern line until it meets the Makoroa Stream, then eastwards to the Wairere Stream. From the Wairere Stream the boundary joins Gregory Rd then to Wairere Rd (including Arrowsmith Rd). From Wairere Rd along Bethells Rd into Waitakere Township. The boundary crosses Waitakere Rd and the railway, it includes Township Rd and McEntee Rd. Then Sunnyvale Rd to Crows Rd. Where Crows Rd meets Birdwood Rd the boundary crosses directly to the Momutu Stream that runs through Te Rangi Hiroa Park. Momutu Stream joins the Swanson Stream and crosses Don Buck Rd at the point where Don Buck Rd meets the Huruhuru Creek. The Huruhuru Creek and Henderson Creek are the northeastern and eastern boundaries. Henderson Creek into the Opanuku Stream. The Opanuku Stream forms the southern boundary until a line from the headwaters of the Opanuku Stream crosses Scenic Dr and travels west to the coast at Wigmore Bay to the south of Bethells Beach.

WESTLAKE BOYS' HIGH SCHOOL

Forrest Hill Rd, Takapuna
Tel: 64 9 410 8667
www.westlakebhs.school.nz

Zone boundary: From the sea along Earnock (included), across Hurstmere Rd and along the edge of Lake Pupuke, excluding Killarney St and Manurere Ave to Taharoto Rd, but including Kowhai St and Pupuke Rd. It crosses Taharoto Rd at Killarney St and continues south of Dominion Rd (included) to Onewa Domain. Through the domain it crosses Northcote Rd and goes up by the golf course, excluding all streets to the west, to Benders Ave (included). Along Coronation Rd (included, also including Nicholson Pl) until Beatrice Ave (excluded). South of Archers Rd to Chivalry Rd, then north along Chivalry Rd (included, and including Edgeworth Rd) to Diana Dr. Along Diana Dr to Weldene Ave (excluded). North to Hogans Rd (excluded, Ngatoa Pl and Normanton Rd are also excluded). South of Hogans Rd and across Wairau Rd at Kathleen Pl, which is included. North of Ellice Rd (excluded), across Target Rd and south of Sunnynook Rd to the northern motorway. The northern boundary leaves the motorway at Sunset Rd and runs east along Sunset Rd (included) to East Coast Rd, along East Coast Rd (included) to Kowhai Rd (included). Along Kowhai Rd and across Beach Rd to the sea. Whitby Cres is included.

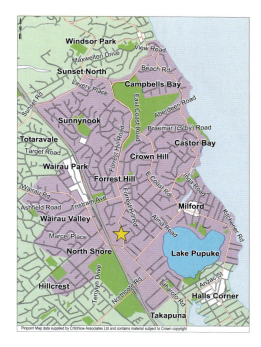

WESTLAKE GIRLS' HIGH SCHOOL

2 Wairau Rd, Takapuna
Tel: 64 9 489 4169
www.westlakegirls.school.nz

Zone boundary: Southern boundary is from Hauraki Rd, across Lake Rd and Jutland Rd, including all streets to the north, around Shoal Bay and to the western boundary of the Esmonde Rd interchange, along Akoranga Dr, crossing Northcote Rd, along Sunnybrae Rd to Coronation Rd, which is included, as is Nicholson Pl, until it reaches Beatrice Ave, which is excluded. It runs south of Archers Rd to the junction with Chartwell Ave, then up Chartwell Ave (included) to the junction with Diana Dr (included) and along Diana Dr until Weldene Ave (excluded). Ngatoa Pl and Normanton St are also excluded. The zone runs south of Hogans Rd and crosses Wairua Rd at Kathleen Pl, which is included. North to Ellice Rd (excluded), across Target Rd and south of Sunnynook Rd to the northern motorway. From the northern motorway down Constellation Dr to the junction at East Coast Rd, along East Coast Rd to Maxwelton Dr and done Maxwelton Dr to Ramsgate Tce and Sidmouth St to the sea.

PRIVATE SCHOOLS

If you're considering sending your child to private school, this information will provide an at-a-glance guide to what you'll pay and what you'll get for your money.

Different private schools have different fee structures for the four-term academic year and some of the fees quoted may include a discount for prompt payment. In most cases, the fees quoted don't include essential extras such as school trips, sports fees, uniforms, laptop computers etc. Boarding fees are in addition to tuition fees. Some schools (*) quote a per term rate which we have converted to an annual fee for easy comparison.

DIOCESAN SCHOOL (*)
Epsom; girls only; Years 1-13; 1500 students including 35 boarders; Anglican; founded 1903. Fees: Years 1-6 $9748; Years 7-13 $11,216.

KING'S COLLEGE
Otahuhu; 915 students; Years 9-13; boys only up to Year 11; accepts girls in Year 12 and 13. Boarders and day students. Established 1896; Christian (Anglican) ethos. Special features: "World class education"; Cambridge International examinations. Fees: middle school $8776; senior school $9416.

King's College is where you'd send your son to get a guaranteed blue-ribbon education. It's one of the top private schools in New Zealand, accepting both boarders and "day boys". It's the closest thing Auckland has to the traditional public schools of Great Britain - in fact it was established in 1896 on the public school model, with the rigorous values of "discipline, patriotism, military training and corporate spirit", aiming to "mould boys into men".

These days Kings is a lot more modern and cosmopolitan, without throwing out the tradition completely. There's now top-quality teaching and cutting edge information technology - and King's also takes girls as day students in the senior school (Years 12 and 13).

King's is invariably near the top of the national exam results tables and along with Auckland Grammar is now offering the Cambridge International examinations to its senior students. The school also takes other areas of education very seriously - senior students are involved in a series of leadership seminars; the school has a rich tradition of music, drama, oratory and debate, and sport is compulsory to Year 11 level. King's is sited on a spacious campus in Otahuhu, South Auckland, and there's also a junior school - known as "Little King's" in Remuera.

As you might expect, old boys include people with connections to the power networks of New Zealand, such as prominent businessmen Hugh Fletcher (husband of Attorney-general Sian Elias) and Jim Fletcher (married to politician Christine Fletcher) and famous artist Don Binney.

KING'S SCHOOL (PRIMARY)
Remuera; boys only; 645 students years 1-8; established 1922; Christian (Anglican). Fees: $8132.

KRISTIN (*)
Albany, North Shore. Co-ed; 1400 students from kindergarten to Year 13; established 1972; non-denominational Christian ethos; second language teaching; International Baccalaureat syllabus and exams. Fees: Years 0-6 $8040; Years 7-8 $9640; Years 9-10 $9960; Years 11-13 $10,160.

Kristin School is a popular, well-respected private co-educational school providing education for 1400 students from kindergarten level to Year 13 on Auckland's North Shore. The school has a beautiful park-like campus on 20 hectares of land at Albany in north Auckland, the fastest growing region of New Zealand. Kristin is one of the "newer" private schools in Auckland - established a mere 30 years ago by a group of parents who wanted a high quality independent school for the North Shore. Since then, the school has gone from strength to strength.

Kristin has a traditional (but non-denominational) Christian ethic, emphasising student welfare, values-based education and pastoral care. It has a strong international focus, aiming to prepare students to be "responsible world citizens". Kristin aims to provide all-round education that's "vibrant, innovative, yet rigorous". Academic standards are high, and it offers the International Baccalaureate diploma examinations to senior students, who have gone on to study at some of the world's top universities. Since 1991 the International Baccalaureat programme has been available in the junior school. Kristin encourages strong arts and culture involvement. Foreign languages are a feature - there's an innovative programme in the junior school from kindergarten to Year 6, where students study Mandarin Chinese language and culture. The school also has great sports facilities, with water polo, equestrian sports, yachting and climbing on offer - plus a school of snow sports.

Kristin's former students maintain strong links to the school community, with regular reunions, including one in London in 2003.

JUNIOR COLLEGE

Parnell (alongside the domain). Co-ed; 360 students; Years 9-10; established 1998. Special features: junior high school; high-interest academic programme. Fees: $9500.

SENIOR COLLEGE

Central Auckland. Co-ed; 440 students, Years 11-13; established 1995. Special features: Senior students only; "challenging schooling for students to reach their potential" in a pre-university environment; specialist teaching; Cambridge International Examinations. Fees $11,500.

Senior College is a co-ed private school with a big point of difference - it's not a complete high school, but a specialist school for Year 11, 12 and 13 students. It aims to be a "specialist pre-university centre", meeting the special needs of senior secondary students.

The school's stated intention is "educating young men and women who will make a difference", and there's a focus on giving students the freedom to make choices and take responsibility for their learning.

The school was founded in 1995 and is part of the Academic Colleges Group, which is the largest provider of private education in New Zealand, and also includes the Junior College (established in 1998) and the new Strathallan College in South Auckland (2001). Senior College has been very successful and has grown steadily, with 440 students in 2003. Its campus is in central Auckland, near the public library.

The school unashamedly aims for academic excellence - sport isn't much of a focus here, unlike at most other New Zealand high schools. The highly qualified and experienced staff are all specialists in their own areas of teaching, critical and creative thinking skills are highly valued, and the college offers the International Cambridge examinations from Year 11. Students' exam results are often outstanding.

As well as the usual subjects (maths, English, science, languages etc) Senior College also offers courses in psychology and sociology, and in 2004 is planning to introduce law as a course of study.

ST CUTHBERT'S COLLEGE (*)

Epsom; Years 1-13; girls only; 1360 students, including 130 boarders. Established 1915; Presbyterian; very strong academically - in 2002 top school in country for scholarships, second for A bursary, top for School Certificate. Fees: Year 1-6 $9360; Years 7-8 $10,780; Years 9-11 $10,880; Years 12-13 $11,100.

ST KENTIGERN COLLEGE

Pakuranga; Years 7-13; fully co-ed (since 2003); 1065 students; established 1953; Presbyterian; "broad, sound, innovative education"; strong in academics, IT and extra-curricular activities; sports academy (aimed at overseas students). Fees: $10,500.

ST KENTIGERN SCHOOL (PRIMARY)

Remuera; Years 1-8; boys only; 500 students; Established 1959; Presbyterian. Fees: Years 1-3 $8535; Years 4-6 $9315; Years 7-8 $10,650.

STRATHALLAN COLLEGE

Hingaia Peninsula, South Auckland; Years 1-13, plus kindergarten; co-ed; 1000 students; established 2001; part of AGC private education group (which also includes Junior and Senior Colleges); Cambridge International exams; one of largest independent school complexes in New Zealand; offers complete pathway from kindergarten to Year 13. Fees: Years 1-6 $8500; Years 7-11 $10,000.

CATHOLIC SCHOOLS

Some of Auckland's most prominent secondary schools are part of the Catholic education system. Unlike the schools listed above, they aren't strictly independent. They are called "integrated" which means they get government funding but can also provide a "special interest" Catholic education within the New Zealand school curriculum. They also charge fees but these won't be as high as those for independent schools. Generally you have to be a practising Catholic to attend, although they do accept a few non-Catholic students.

Catholic primary schools are smaller and are found in most areas throughout the city.

Here are a few of Auckland's best-known Catholic high schools:

BARADENE COLLEGE

Remuera; Years 7-13; girls only; 930 students; established 1910; Catholic.

CARMEL COLLEGE

Milford, North Shore; Years 7-13; girls only; 850 students; established 1957; Catholic.

SACRED HEART COLLEGE

East Tamaki; Years 7-13; boys only; 970 students including boarders; established 1903; Marist Catholic education.

ST PETER'S COLLEGE

Epsom (across the motorway from Auckland Grammar); Years 7-13; boys only; 900 students; established 1939; Catholic.

2002 SCHOOL CERTIFICATE AND NCEA RESULTS

School	Total	Average Credits for all Standards	Achievement Standards % Achieved	% Merit	%Excellence	NCEA Level 1 Qualification No. Eligible	% Achieved
ACG Junior College	31	29	31.8	49.9	12	0	0
ACG NZ International College	29	11.3	28	25.8	8.3	0	0
ACG Senior College	89	27.7	37.5	27.6	16.6	0	0
Auckland Girls' Grammar School	508	67.4	39.9	23.5	8.8	283	74.2
Auckland Grammar School	566	70.6	41.6	28	7.6	309	60.8
Avondale College	927	54.4	39	23.8	9	510	64.5
Baradene College of the Sacred Heart	165	83.1	40.2	30.9	12.2	113	89.4
Corran School	81	86	37.4	31.1	17.7	51	96.1
Dilworth School	129	46.4	43.9	26.3	9.8	55	81.8
Diocesan School for Girls	284	103.9	31	36.3	24.6	196	98
Epsom Girls' Grammar School	765	68.2	35.1	32.1	17.2	354	88.1
Glendowie College	367	61.2	41.8	27	8.5	186	74.2
Hebron Christian College	24	77.2	32.6	31.3	20.8	16	81.3
Immanuel Christian School	2	137	3.8	29.1	67.1	2	100
Kadimah College	9	67.2	38.6	34.8	11.9	4	75
King's College	250	82.6	38.8	31.3	15.7	168	89.3
Lynfield College	493	53.5	40	18.8	6.1	257	49.4
Marcellin College	214	44.2	40.9	19.7	4.6	93	45.2
Marist College	124	73	40.6	28.3	12.2	72	87.5
Michael Park School	59	26.1	42.8	18.6	14.7	6	33.3
Mt Albert Grammar School	784	46.2	35.9	18.5	6.8	326	49.7
Mt Roskill Grammar	781	55.8	38.5	25.7	8.7	343	63.3
Onehunga High School	378	47	36.6	15.1	4.8	199	43.2
Penrose High School	399	47.5	41.6	16.4	4.4	120	47.5
Sacred Heart College (Auckland)	238	71.7	43.4	25	9.7	141	89.4
Selwyn College	380	43.3	34.3	18	5.9	165	45.5
St Cuthbert's College	182	122.8	25.1	36.9	33.4	149	98
St Mary's College	136	52.3	39.1	23.9	8.4	69	63.8
St Paul's College	78	24.6	25.4	9.7	1.9	36	16.7
St Peters College	254	58.2	42.6	19.2	5.1	150	63.3
Tamaki College	171	35.7	29.8	10.3	1.7	98	15.3
Waiheke High School	97	54.6	43.8	20.7	5.1	50	64
Western Springs College	196	59.9	44.3	20.9	6.5	103	66
Birkenhead College	249	55.1	42.7	23.2	8.2	115	69.6
Carmel College	277	66.7	37.2	35.5	16.2	131	94.7
Glenfield College	409	57.3	40.1	24.1	7.5	209	63.6
Hato Petera College	46	65.7	43.8	16.2	6.5	33	69.7
Kingsway School	41	68.5	37.4	32.9	13.3	26	88.5
Kristin School	317	56.7	39	33.3	15.7	109	95.4
Long Bay College	475	54.7	40.8	18.4	5.9	220	56.8

Northcote College	440	62.1	41	26.1	10.4	219	72.1
Orewa College	459	62.6	40.8	23.1	8.2	241	71.8
Pinehurst School	89	19.4	37.7	24.8	7.1	0	0
Rangitoto College	686	94.7	37.3	31.6	12.7	601	78
Rosmini College	223	65.9	38.8	25.2	11.1	134	73.1
Takapuna Grammar School	489	76.7	40.5	24.4	9.5	303	76.9
Westlake Boys' High School	601	76.7	42.4	26	9.1	383	82.5
Westlake Girls' High School	478	81.2	39.1	25.3	10.4	286	76.9
Green Bay High School	265	47	39.5	14.8	4.3	109	47.7
Henderson High School	126	47.8	40.9	20.2	9.4	58	58.6
Kelston Boys' High School	355	46.1	41	15.7	4.4	164	47
Kelston Girls' High School	344	49.6	36.4	14.7	4.7	182	37.9
Liston College	126	67	42.6	17.4	5.2	103	52.4
Massey High School	616	42.5	43.2	21.1	6.7	229	59
Nga Kakano o Te Kaihanga Reo E Rua Kura	1	12	0	0	100	0	0
Rutherford College	419	48.2	43.1	21.9	6.9	157	65
St Dominic's College	208	54.8	40.6	24.6	9.2	75	72
Te Kura O Hoani Waititi Marae	21	43.8	37.3	13.5	4.4	11	45.5
Waitakere College	456	49.4	38.4	13.9	3.3	245	35.9
Edgewater College	462	39.4	40.6	21.9	5.7	171	43.9
Elim Christian College	49	61.3	41.3	27.8	7.9	26	80.8
Howick College	837	61.7	40	24.4	8.2	472	66.5
Macleans College	575	88.1	39.8	31.3	12.9	445	85.2
Pakuranga College	641	62.7	39.7	23	7.7	380	67.4
St Kentigern College	247	91.1	38	30.4	14.2	192	83.9
Al-Madinah School	47	52.4	50.2	16.5	3.3	18	55.6
Aorere College	319	33.1	26.5	8.4	2.9	176	18.2
Auckland Seventh-Day Adventist School	117	65.4	46.5	14.2	4.6	96	52.1
Bridgemount School	22	84	39	28.9	9.6	20	75
Clover Park Middle School	11	17.5	38	8	2	0	0
De La Salle College	331	38.6	38.4	14.8	3.5	154	42.9
James Cook High School	347	52.1	34	12.4	4.7	228	42.1
Mangere College	281	43.7	36.2	13.2	3.2	158	21.5
McAuley High School	300	53.6	43.7	16.1	4.4	173	47.4
Otahuhu College	552	45.9	34.4	9.1	2.9	143	55.9
Papakura High School	332	39.4	39	16.9	4	138	37
Papatoetoe High School	722	48.3	38.8	17	4.7	395	45.1
Rosehill College	891	50.5	45.1	24.6	7.6	335	75.8
Sir Edmund Hillary Collegiate Senior Sch	168	35.1	33.3	10.6	2.5	35	22.9
Southern Cross Senior School	260	29.4	29.2	9.5	2.3	104	11.5
St Andrew's Christian College	3	66.3	46.1	31.6	2.6	2	50
Tangaroa College	289	45.2	32.1	6.7	1.4	118	38.1
Te Kura Kaupapa Maori a Rohe o Mangere	8	45.8	27.1	9.7	1.4	7	0
The Manurewa High School	670	49.5	38	19	5.5	336	44.3
Tyndale Park Christian School	8	93.8	45	22.2	9.1	8	87.5

2002 SCHOLARSHIPS, UNIVERSITY ENTRANCE AND BURSARIES

School	Total	Total Scholarships	% University Entrance	% A Bursary	% B Bursary
ACG NZ International College	1,912	94	98	64.4	29.7
ACG Senior College	817	81	99.3	71.2	24.7
Auckland Girls' Grammar School	745	20	81.7	38.3	26.1
Auckland Grammar School	1,993	211	96.1	58.8	28.9
Avondale College	1,617	90	87.4	40.6	34.7
Baradene College of the Sacred Heart	501	13	88.8	25.8	44.9
Corran School	124	2	85.7	9.5	57.1
Dilworth School	192	4	74.3	28.6	20
Diocesan School for Girls	724	62	97.8	57.8	35.6
Epsom Girls' Grammar School	1,393	103	94	54.1	33.9
Glendowie College	617	19	86.9	38.4	37.4
Hebron Christian College	1	0	0	0	0
King's College	894	87	97.5	60.4	27
Lynfield College	888	35	84.4	28.9	40.6
Marcellin College	150	3	60	15	25
Marist College	272	5	92.3	41	46.2
Mt Albert Grammar School	704	18	76.2	37.6	28.7
Mt Roskill Grammar	1,166	82	94	48.3	33.3
Onehunga High School	579	3	67.9	16.7	26.2
Penrose High School	256	7	82.8	41.4	20.7
Sacred Heart College	403	11	88.9	23.8	52.4
Selwyn College	487	10	81.5	18.5	46.3
St Cuthbert's College	631	77	100	76.1	20.4
St Mary's College	204	9	96.7	23.3	46.7
St Paul's College	127	1	55.6	11.1	22.2
St Peters College	314	10	92.7	26.8	56.1
Tamaki College	70	0	33.3	0	0
Waiheke High School	115	2	66.7	26.7	6.7
Western Springs College	327	7	82.9	26.8	36.6
Birkenhead College	372	12	85.7	37.5	35.7
Carmel College	478	25	98.7	55.1	32.1
Glenfield College	590	9	85.1	31	34.5
Hato Petera College	7	0	0	0	0
Kristin School	299	8	97.6	43.9	43.9
Long Bay College	503	5	90.6	37.7	35.8
Northcote College	565	17	85.3	40	37.3
Orewa College	575	12	72	21.3	49.3

School					
Rangitoto College	1,681	85	94	46.8	38.5
Rosmini College	489	24	83.5	44.3	29.1
Takapuna Grammar School	862	40	92	45.3	35.8
Westlake Boys' High School	1,234	43	97.3	46.3	37.2
Westlake Girls' High School	1,060	36	96.6	45.3	43.2
Green Bay High School	324	4	71.4	14.3	31.4
Henderson High School	123	1	42.9	21.4	21.4
Kelston Boys' High School	515	7	74.5	37.3	29.4
Kelston Girls' High School	433	6	64.6	18.8	29.2
Liston College	236	6	69.2	23.1	30.8
Massey High School	842	19	81.9	33.6	34.5
Nga Kakano o Te Kaihanga Reo E Rua Kura	1	0	0	0	0
Rutherford College	437	10	90.7	20.4	44.4
St Dominic's College	295	4	74.5	13.7	37.3
Te Kura O Hoani Waititi Marae	22	1	0	0	0
Waitakere College	451	12	75.4	23.1	30.8
Edgewater College	420	15	84.3	27.5	39.2
Elim Christian College	101	5	100	50	16.7
Howick College	1,011	26	85	27.5	40.7
Macleans College	1,208	86	93.8	49.3	33.9
Pakuranga College	1,016	50	88.5	48.1	23.7
St Kentigern College	626	48	93.1	46.1	33.3
Al-Madinah School	6	0	17.2	0	10.3
Aorere College	197	0	100	0	33.3
Auckland Seventh-Day Adventist School	75	0	56.7	3.3	36.7
De La Salle College	155	1	52.6	5.3	21.1
James Cook High School	156	0	40	0	20
Mangere College	70	0	50	0	27.8
McAuley High School	135	0	52.4	0	14.3
Otahuhu College	282	0	72.7	0	50
Papakura High School	195	1	78.8	4.5	43.9
Papatoetoe High School	446	3	85.2	13.6	38
Rosehill College	708	21		30.6	0
Sir Edmund Hillary Collegiate Senior Sch	19	0		0	0
Southern Cross Senior School	74	0	14.3	0	
Tangaroa College	60	0	50	0	16.7
The Manurewa High School	586	18	88	37.3	37.3

Note: Entrance and A and B Bursary percentages are now calculated from candidates taking five or more subjects. Previously these percentages were calculated from candidates taking three or more subjects

Source: New Zealand Qualifications Authority

Auckland City

Civic Centre - Main Council Office
1 Greys Ave
Auckland Central

Private Bag 92516
Wellesley St
Auckland

Tel: 64 9 379 2021
Tel: (24 Hours) 64 9 379 2020

Email: enquiry@aucklandcity.govt.nz
Website: www.aucklandcity.govt.nz

North Shore

North Shore City Council
1 The Strand
Takapuna

Private Bag 93500
Takapuna

Tel: 64 9 486 8600
Fax: 64 9 486 8500

Actionline: 64 9 486 8600

Email: actionline@northshorecity.govt.nz
Website: www.northshorecity.govt.nz

Waitakere

Waitakere City Council
6 Waipareira Ave
Lincoln
Waitakere City

Private Bag 93109
Henderson
Waitakere City

Tel: 64 9 839 0400
Fax: 64 9 836 8001

Email: info@waitakere.govt.nz
Website: www.waitakere.govt.nz

Manukau

Main Council Office
Manukau City Council
31 Wiri Station Rd
Manukau City

Private Bag 76917
Manukau City

Tel: 64 9 263 7100
Fax: 64 9 262 5151

Email: contactus@manukau.govt.nz
Website: www.manukau.govt.nz

Rodney District

Rodney District Council
50 Centreway Rd
Orewa

Private Bag 500
Orewa

Tel: 64 9 426 5169
Fax: 64 9 426 7280

Email: info@rodney.govt.nz
Website: www.rodney.govt.nz

Papakura District

Papakura District Council
35 Coles Cres
Papakura

Private Bag 7
Papakura

Tel: 64 9 977 8900
Fax: 64 9 298 1906

Email: customerservices@papakura.govt.nz
Website: www.pdc.govt.nz

Real Estate Institute of New Zealand

PO Box 9284
Auckland

DX Mail CX 10095
Auckland Mail Centre
Auckland

Tel: 64 9 356 1755
Fax: 64 9 379 8471

Email: reinz@reinz.co.nz
Website: www.reinz.co.nz

Quotable Value New Zealand

Auckland Office
Level 2, 70 Shortland St

PO Box 3698
Auckland

Tel: 64 9 375 3828
Fax: 64 9 375 3820

Website: www.quotable.co.nz

Ministry of Education

39-45 College Hill
Auckland

Private Bag 47911
Ponsonby
Auckland

Tel: 64 9 374 5400
Fax: 64 9 374 5401 or 64 9 374 5402

E-mail: enquiries.auckland@minedu.govt.nz
Website: www.minedu.govt.nz
School Listing: www.tki.org.nz

Ministry of Housing

Takapuna
Level 1, 9 Anzac St
PO Box 331431

Fax: 64 9 486 0929

Auckland
Level 11, 67 Customs St
Cnr Customs & Gore St
PO Box 90 172

Fax: 64 9 302 0253

Henderson
Lincoln Manor,
295 Lincoln Rd
PO Box 104081

Fax: 64 9 838 9850

Manukau
Level 1, CST Management Centre
22 Amersham Way
PO Box 76469

Fax: 64 9 263 6013

Email: info@minhousing.govt.nz
Website: www.minhousing.govt.nz

Auckland MPs	Electorate	Party	Contact phone number
Tizard, Hon. Judith	Auckland Central	Labour	64 9 360 2782
Clark, Rt Hon. Helen	Mt Albert	Labour	64 4 471 9998
Worth, Richard, OBE	Epsom	National	64 9 471 9893
Tamihere, John	Tamaki Makaurau	Labour	64 9 820 3276
Goff, Hon. Phil	Mt Roskill	Labour	64 9 624 2278
Gosche, Hon. Mark	Maungakiekie	Labour	64 9 276 4050
Mapp, Dr. Wayne	North Shore	National	64 9 486 0005
McCully, Hon. Murray	East Coast Bays	National	64 9 478 0207
Hartley, Ann	Northcote	Labour	64 9 419 9644
Smith, Dr the Hon. Lockwood	Rodney	National	64 9 425 8603
Cunliffe, David	New Lynn	Labour	64 9 827 3062
Carter, Chris	Te Atatu	Labour	64 9 835 0915
Pillay, Lynne	Waitakere	Labour	64 4 470 6968
Williamson, Hon. Maurice	Pakuranga	National	64 9 471 9999
Collins, Judith	Clevedon	National	64 9 299 7426
Field, Taito Philip Hans	Mangere	Labour	64 9 276 4799
Robertson, Ross	Manukau East	Labour	64 9 278 9972
Hawkins, Hon. George, JP	Manurewa	Labour	64 9 267 0934

Feel at home in Auckland.

With over 25 Mobile Mortgage Managers and 50 branches (some open extended hours and weekends), we're here to help Auckland home buyers. Call us on **0800 47 87 25** or visit any branch.

The National Bank
The thoroughbred among banks

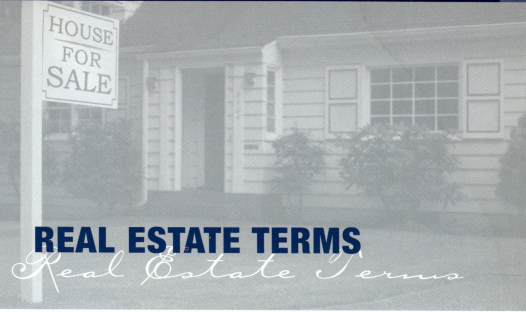

REAL ESTATE TERMS

Agreement: The written contract for the sale and purchase of a property between the vendor (seller) and purchaser (home-buyer). See Conditional Agreement and Unconditional Agreement for more details.

Asking price: The price the vendor initially asks for the property, which is often higher than the final price negotiated between the vendor and purchaser.

Auction: A method of selling property in which potential buyers bid against one another at a special meeting.

Bungalow: Houses dating from the 1930s and 1940s. Usually of timber construction, they are typified by curved or square bays, casement windows, simple leadlights, shingle decoration and beamed ceilings.

By negotiation: A method of selling property where the vendor usually states an asking price, potential buyers make offers and negotiations are entered into.

Capital valuation: The value placed on a particular property by the local authority and reassessed every few years (this used to be called government valuation). It comprises two ingredients - land value and improvements (ie, value of buildings etc).

Cash offer: An offer made to buy a property which is free of any conditions.

Chattels: Items, which might be fixed or not fixed, that are included in the sale of the property. Examples include the stove, television aerial, fixed floor coverings, blinds and curtains and light fittings. These must be specified in the agreement.

Commission: A flat fee or percentage of the sale price paid by the vendor to the real estate agent responsible for the sale.

Conditional agreement: When an agreement is made subject to a certain condition or conditions being satisfied by a set date, usually by the purchaser (eg, arranging finance, seeking a builder's report or selling an existing home). Conditions can also be included by the purchaser requiring the vendor to do something by a specified date, eg, that maintenance be completed on the house.

Conveyancing: The process by which the legal ownership of a property changes hands.

Crosslease: An increasingly outdated form of subdividing land where each party owns their piece of property but "rents" common areas like shared driveways.

Deposit: A percentage (usually up to 10%) of the purchase price paid by the home-buyer when the agreement is signed. This is normally paid to the real estate agent and held in trust until the contract becomes unconditional.

Equity: The amount of cash (including the deposit) the purchaser puts into the property, ie, the purchase price less the amount borrowed.

Expats: An abbreviation of expatriots, being people who live away from their native lands.

Freehold: Also known as fee-simple estate, this means you own the land on which your house sits, as opposed to leasehold where you pay ground rent for the land rather than own it.

Home-buyer: The person who buys a residential property: the purchaser.

Home loan: The funds the home-buyer has to borrow (from a bank or other financial institution) to buy the property, generally secured by a registered mortgage to the bank over the property being purchased.

Infill housing: Where a piece of land under one title is legally split into two or more and houses built on each piece.

Installments: The amount of the principal and/or interest repayments that you make on your home loan.

Interest: The amount the bank charges for the money lent to you to purchase your property.

Leasehold: This is when the land on which your house sits is owned by someone else and you pay ground rent in exchange for the right to occupy the land. Any improvements on the land, ie, building of a house or additions, legally belong to the occupant. Leases are usually long term, say 99 years, and with a right to renew.

LIM: An abbreviation of Land Information Memorandum, a report supplied by the local authority for a fee showing any legal changes to a property.

Mortgage: The security the home-buyer gives the lender to be registered against the title to the property being purchased. This secures the home-buyer's debt to the lender. (Note: The mortgage charges the title in favour of the lender so that the property cannot be sold without the loan to the lender being repaid and the mortgage discharged. Legal ownership of the property remains with the owner, but in the event of the owner failing to comply with the requirements of the loan, the lender can, after giving notice and following the procedures set down by law, take steps to sell the mortgaged property to recover the debt.)

Mortgagee sale: When a homeowner defaults on loan payments to the bank or lender,

sometimes the bank is forced to sell the assets held as security (usually the property) in order to recoup its money. Any money left over after the bank's loans and costs are met are paid to the homeowner.

Principal: The total amount of money you borrow to buy a house.

Rates: A charge made by the local authority to property owners in exchange for services (eg, rubbish collection) and amenities.

Reserve: The figure set at auction by the vendor, at which level the property will sell once bidding has reached that minimum point.

Security: Assets offered to the bank or lender (usually the property) to guarantee that the loan will be repaid.

Settlement date: When the property is paid for in full and the keys change hands.

Strata title: A less common term for unit title (see below).

Subdivision: Where a property with one title is legally split into two or more parts.

Tender: A method of selling property in which potential buyers make an offer in writing and all offers are considered by the vendor at a set time.

Term: The period of time over which a loan is to be repaid.

Terrace houses: Where usually smaller houses are built joined together, normally sharing their side walls.

Title: The Certificate of Title is the document giving legal ownership to the property. The lender usually holds one copy until the loan is repaid, and the duplicate is held at the Land Transfer Office in the appropriate area.

Transitional villas: Villas built around the 1920s which display some bungalow-style characteristics such as casement windows and square bays.

Unconditional agreement: Following a cash offer, this is the legal contract between the purchaser and the vendor to sell at an agreed price on a set date. It is either not subject to any conditions or those conditions have already been satisfied. An unconditional agreement commits you in all respects to purchasing the property.

Unit title: A form of ownership of apartments, flats and home units (also known as strata title) where each owner has full freehold ownership of his or her particular dwelling and any ancillary units attached to it (such as garage or parking space) as defined by the unit plan. Each unit owner usually becomes a member of a body corporate which administers the unit plan.

Vendor: The person or entity legally authorised to sell a property.

Villa: A usually timber (kauri) house typically built during the late 1800s and first two decades of the 1900s. Characteristics are sash-hung windows, faceted bay windows, wooden lace and finial decoration, verandas and a layout opening off a central hall.

Water rates: A charge made by the local authority for both the use of water and the disposal of waste water. In some areas, this is charged separately and in others it is part of the total rates bill.

Zones: When referring to schools, this is an area defined by the school from which students are automatically entitled to enrol. When referring to land, it is a category put in place by the local authority specifying what type of activity and/or building can occupy the land.

Your move.

When you're planning to move into your first home, we have a comprehensive Home Buyer's Pack to guide you on your way. It's full of useful information – from doing your sums to things to look for when buying your home. To find out how you can get your Home Buyer's Pack, call us on **0800 47 87 25** or visit any branch.

The National Bank
The thoroughbred among banks

INDEX